SINATRA

SINATRA

---

by Earl Wilson

W. H. ALLEN · LONDON
A Howard & Wyndham Company
1976

First British edition, 1976

Printed in Great Britain by Fletcher & Son Ltd, Norwich
for the Publishers, W. H. Allen & Co. Ltd,
44 Hill Street, London W1X 8LB
Bound by Richard Clay (The Chaucer Press) Ltd., Bungay, Suffolk

ISBN 0 491 01967 X

TO MY WIFE, 'THE B.W.'
who was first to say
'He's another Bing Crosby'

ACKNOWLEDGMENTS

The author would like to give special thanks to Arnold Shaw, George T. Simon, Robin Douglas-Home, E. J. Kahn, Jr., Alec Wilder, Thomas Thompson, and Bruce Blivens.

CONTENTS

PREFACE

I bear Frank Sinatra no malice.

I feel it necessary to say this because it's known in the entertainment world that for more than a quarter of a century I was his friend, booster and most consistent defender among the columnists.

Then, suddenly, he excluded me from one of his opening-night performances. He said he would not do a show if I was permitted in the room. A publicist explained vaguely that I was barred by Sinatra because I'd written something he didn't like. Without being specific, the publicist charged me with inaccurate reporting. Never convinced that the decision was his, I attributed his action to another's misunderstanding or misinterpretation.

Such clashes between the stars and the press usually lead to vendettas. But as a follower of Sinatra's changing hates and loves, I believed there might be an apology or a reconciliation. I never attempted to retaliate in print; I simply quit being the Sinatra fan I had been since the 1940s and desisted from writing about him.

I did not quit observing him, although now I saw him as an outsider rather than an insider. It was considerably different. Strangely, from the new viewpoint, I saw much to admire that I hadn't seen before. I learned much about his generosity and kindness, and of the opinion of some critics that he is a genius.

Five years passed without us speaking to each other. Then a publisher asked me to write a Sinatra biography.

I took a long, long time answering. Over those years I had come to understand Frank Sinatra's complexities, and I believed I understood his anger at me. I still felt no malice. Even this long afterwards, I still thought we would at some time become friends again. But I still hesitated.

An editor pointed out, 'But you know Sinatra from both sides: as the friend, as one cast aside. You probably know him better than anybody in your field.'

But there must not be any character assassination, this could not be a hatchet job, I insisted. That was agreed.

Then I undertook the job of writing the biography of the most fascinating Show Business figure of our time. I learned hundreds and hundreds of fascinating facts about the two Frank Sinatras. For there are two Sinatras, always at war with each other.

'Write about his *guts*!' Irving Berlin urged me. 'He may have been wrong many times, but he had the guts to stand up for his position, whether it was the government, or a country, or whoever the hell it was!'

'They keep saying he's a friend of the Mafia,' said a Broadway realist. 'He worked in nightclubs and everybody knows that "the boys", the Mafia, ran the nightclubs. The Archbishop never ran any nightclubs!'

A witness to an interesting event told me that one sleety night in Manhattan, a black prostitute stood shivering under a nightclub canopy about 4.00 a.m. The police prostitution patrol was gathering girls in its van. A policeman ordered her into the van with the others.

'I'm waiting for my boyfriend,' she said.

'Come along,' the policeman said.

At that moment, Frank Sinatra stepped from a cab, overheard the conversation, and quickly said, as though he knew her, 'I'm sorry I kept you waiting.'

Leading her into the club, he bought her a drink at the bar, told her, 'I don't want you to work any more tonight,' handed her a $100 bill, and ordered her to go to wherever her home was.

Oh, he has been known to hit a woman, too—with provocation. That's the other Sinatra.

As I write this, Sinatra has had reversals, but appears now to have re-ascended the heights.

Towards the end of writing this book, I happened upon some facts about his booming concert tours, which I printed in my syndicated column as straight news, unadorned by any fan club-type exclamations. Sinatra was appreciative. He thanked me by letter and suggested we get together at one of his shows. We did meet briefly, shook hands, and he poured a drink. By this time the book was so close to completion that its contents have not been affected by the 'reconciliation'.

Illustrative of the widespread belief that there are two people in one Sinatra skin is the experience of a rather shy but attractive photographer, Alpha Blair, who's also an actress.

Going with her camera to cover a Friars Club dinner for Jack Benny and George Burns in New York in May 1972, she was warned by publicist Bernie Kamber to take very few shots of Sinatra so as not to antagonize him. She heard Sinatra say to the photographers, 'C'mon, let's get this shit over with.' After about a minute, Kamber hustled the photographers away from Sinatra.

Miss Blair discreetly shot some nonflash pictures later. Suddenly Sinatra turned on her. She expected a blast.

'It's okay,' he said with a charming smile. 'Go ahead and shoot all you want. Use up all your film.'

She did. Of course she was a *girl* photographer!

I have striven to write an honest book, without being influenced by the seven-year silence between us. From the standpoint of a biographer, perhaps I am lucky to have been both out of Sinatra's favour and in his favour, for I have known both Sinatras. The book is eminently fair to him, I hope, but in painting the portrait, I have not left out the warts.

EARL WILSON

PROLOGUE

The life story of Frank Sinatra! What an assignment!

How could this giant of a talent be explained in one book?

Francis Albert Sinatra began his career as a singing waiter, singing headwaiter and singing master of ceremonies—he had all three titles, but the salary was fifteen dollars a week—in a New Jersey roadhouse. And gradually he became recognized as one of the most remarkable men of our time, as he probably would have been in any time. Not just because of his celebrated singing, but because he has been one of the most magnetic, most charming, most loved—and, in a few areas, one of the most disliked—and most charismatic personalities of the last quarter of a century.

He is Mr. Magnetism; he is the possessor of the Sinatra magic; he actually rules some segments of Show Business and is truly feared. Some of the dislike is a resentment of his dictatorship, some is a protest against his outrageous outspokenness.

However remote from Show Business, nearly everybody has an opinion of Sinatra, and for many it is that 'he got too big for himself'.

'Ol' Blue Eyes' has found himself one of the most discussed—and discussable—persons in the world.

The gossip, the spread of the Sinatra mythology and the Sinatra mystique about his lush lifestyle and his ungovernable habits, make him a more fascinating subject for study than most of the world's real leaders. And that is Sinatra's own doing. Another of his talents is the artful projection of the Sinatra personality, often delightful, but also often irritating.

He displays a certain arrogance that came with his success. This infuriates many, but endears him to others who evidently like a little arrogance—if practised by Sinatra. His attitude, 'To hell with you, I'll do it my way,' turns many away. Some are jealous that he can live by his own rules, entertaining a tough guy one week, being entertained at cocktails by Princess Margaret another week.

The Sinatra mythology grows and grows, and the problem of a biographer is to cut through it and find the truth.

I have read in books horrendous tales about his alleged misconduct, which I believe are deliberate lies. A few newspaper persons have behaved towards him with a shameless lack of ethics. He has not been able to escape from the fiction that he was a striving kid growing up in the ghetto. Actually, he came from a comfortable family.

His loyalties—to Spiro T. Agnew, for example—demonstrate that he is a man with his own set of principles.

As a superstar, superstud and super-money-maker, Sinatra has held on to his position, fighting every step of the war, actually strengthening his grasp.

At sixty, he has a youthful swing, swagger and smile, and a cheerful cockiness. He can arouse more comment in the country with an uncomplimentary ten words about a female columnist than the President of the United States can stir up from the White House in an hour's address. There is ample reason for him to feel that he has power.

Today we may be seeing him at his very best. 'Ol' Blue Eyes' has just accomplished the seeming unaccomplishable: a million-dollar 'gate' at the Uris Theatre in New York. He has been in high spirits, ostensibly happy, performing brilliantly and with far fewer cracks in his voice than one expects from a sixty-year-old.

His sex appeal hasn't lessened. His ex-wife Ava Gardner recently saw a full-length, life-size picture of him in a nightclub. In the picture, he wore a raincoat and a hat, and was waving. Ava Gardner embraced the Sinatra in the photograph and kissed him full on the lips. Turning to the club's maître d', she said, 'Take care of him, John—he belongs to me.'

Sinatra, of course, would disagree with that and say that he belongs to himself and is his own man. But that is His Way.

Jerry Lewis painted a picture of Sinatra as a public benefactor, a 'supergent' and 'a real beautiful pussycat' when Sinatra made three appearances on his Muscular Dystrophy telethon. Sinatra, his shoulders shaking, his blue eyes glistening, belted songs at 10.00 a.m. when, Jerry said, 'most singers can't even whisper'. Sinatra paid for his own orchestra of thirty musicians and donated $25.000 besides. He was modest and co-operative all the way.

When he invited Sinatra to sing on the telethon, Lewis said, Sinatra replied 'You got it!' and said he regretted he hadn't been available previous years.

Against this portrait of a doer of good are the remembered words of a former sheriff in Las Vegas, Ralph Lamb. After one of Sinatra's brawls there, Lamb said, 'His actions have been despicable. I'm tired of his intimidating waiters and waitresses, starting fires and throwing pies. He's through picking on the little people of this town. Why the owners put up with this is what I plan to find out.'

He found that Sinatra is only rarely like that and he usually projects charm. Besides, his unfailing, indefinable magic brings such crowds of high-rollers thundering into the Nevada casinos that local businessmen forgive him and almost apologize to him. The town needs Sinatra.

What will happen to Sinatra now? Where does he go from here? What will he be doing with the rest of his life?

My opinion is that Frank Sinatra will practise extreme self control and attempt to gain total public esteem, to make everybody love Frank Sinatra. His magic has never been able to achieve that—up till now.

ALL HAIL THE KING!

Near the entrance, which, on the inside, was hung with red plush velvet, there was a great stirring and cheering, and then a surge of hundreds of people towards that doorway.

'It's Robert Redford . . . it's Robert Redford!' somebody yelled.

'Oh, it's Robert Redford,' a woman said, in disappointment.

Suddenly the crowd burst into a roar that built and built from the orchestra's first downbeat. The glaring lights lowered, and a single spot hit the red curtains.

Frank Sinatra had entered Madison Square Garden.

Convoyed by promoter Jerry Weintraub, radio disc jockey William B. Williams, Jilly Rizzo and others, the 'King' was hustled through the clutching, grasping crowd and deposited safely and securely onstage as the roar grew louder.

With a smile and a look of self-satisfaction, Sinatra nodded to the applause, but he did not appear surprised; he had had these extraordinary receptions many times before.

Presidents Kennedy, Johnson and Nixon have been received with less enthusiasm than Sinatra was getting. There was Jack Dempsey in the celebrity crowd . . . former Mayor John V. Lindsay . . . Carol Channing. Sinatra began singing, and the crowd cheered with the first line of each song. The stage was in the round, and Sinatra the master turned to face another direction, bringing a fresh outburst of applause from each darkened area.

It was 13 October 1974.

Scores of little cameras were flashing. Maybe it was the lights from those cameras that made him look grey—and lumpy.

He was showing his age.

He sounded hoarse.

The acoustics didn't please him, and he called out to the sound department, 'Can we watch that feedback, please?'

But in spite of his less than perfect performance the standing ovations began at once. With 'I've Got You Under My Skin' and 'I Get a Kick Out of You', they leaped and cheered.

Sinatra said, 'This is the perfect time of year and the perfect song—"Autumn in New York".' And they stood up again.

'Ssssh,' Sinatra kidded them. 'We've only got an hour.'

For a few minutes it seemed the crowd was out of control. Children and people of middle age, too, dashed down the aisles to the edge of the stage to get flash pictures, and the police ran right after them, chasing them to their seats.

One woman refused to go back. Police wrestled her back, but she struggled and yelled to Sinatra. Sinatra told them to let her get one picture. She returned to her seat smiling, and the people smiled. Sinatra grinned.

Frank walked around and around with the mike, singing and smiling, and from somewhere up in the rafters, a thin voice quavered, 'Frankieeee . . .' and then two girls were dancing wildly in the aisles.

'Ladies and gentlemen,' Sinatra spoke out. 'I have never felt so much love in one room in my life.'

The dancing in the aisles and the squealing took him back in memory to his beginnings here, he said. He was glad to be back in New York.

'I've had some of my best fights here.' The crowd loved that.

He drank something. 'It's Geritol,' he told them. 'It's tea with a little honey, and if you believe that I've got 400,000 acres of swampland in New Jersey I'll sell you.'

He told how he first came to New York: 'I actually got here on a four-cent ferry ride across the Hudson from Hoboken. I was a featherweight then. People would say "Let's go see 'Bones' at the Paramount".'

He recalled that they also called him 'Hoe-Handle' and 'No-Hips.' 'Now they call me "Ol' Blue Eyes", but in Australia they call me "Ol Big Mouth".'

'This next song is quite personal to me, and it should be because it's about this big imperfect country. My father wasn't born here, but he made sure I was. . . .' And he sang 'The House I Live In', which had won him an Oscar.

During previous concerts, he had often interrupted his singing to blast some members of the press and TV. But this time it was being televised, and the TV producers had him do his criticism during commercial breaks so the worldwide audience would not hear him attacking columnist-TV commentator Rona Barrett, his target of the moment.

'Congress should give a medal to her husband for waking up every Sunday morning and looking at her,' he said from the stage.

'I've had a lot of other names,' he said. 'There's one I got recently—"Ol' Granddad". . . .'

'I happen to be,' he said, 'the last of the saloon swingers, besides Tony Bennett and "Drunky" Dean Martin, and I'm going to sing one of Matt Dennis' that we can never leave out. . . .' It was 'Angel Eyes'—with its familiar close—"Scuse me while I disappear.'

'Now,' Sinatra said, 'I am going to give you a little reward—I'm so proud of what's happening here tonight. . . . We'll now do my national anthem—but you needn't rise. . . .'

Whereupon he sang 'My Way' and started a new controversy because some critics said it wasn't the national anthem, and he personally couldn't have a national anthem, and that it wasn't really very funny. And besides, it was disrespectful.

But now it was 10.00 p.m., Eastern Daylight Time, and the wondrous hour was over. As the words 'I did it my-y-y-y way-y-y-y-y' rose loud, high and distinct from the throat of the evening's hero, it appeared that every one of the

20,000 spectators was screaming his or her approval of this miraculous night.

Two hemispheres, from Halifax to Rio de Janeiro, comprising the biggest television audience in history, so they say, watched transfixed as the 'King' climaxed the evening by strolling happily around the stage, smiling and waving to the audience.

He bent down from the stage, he shook hands, he allowed an occasional woman to kiss him, he relished a delicious few minutes of his life.

As the adulation mounted, he looked nervously towards Jilly Rizzo, who had come onstage and was collecting candy and flowers, which the Sinatra fanatics brought as their myrrh and incense.

'Yeah, honey, thanks, honey,' said Jilly as the gifts rose above his head, but then a woman in an orange dress went beyond what Jilly considers good taste. She had taken Sinatra's arm. Jilly simply took the lady's arm off Sinatra and returned it to her in good condition.

Then a convoy of Sinatra security officers received Jilly's signal that it was time to get the Man out of this mess.

But what was that object some lady seemed to believe she should give to Frank Sinatra as a memento of her worship? Well, if it wasn't a black garter belt!

'Move it!' commanded Jilly. He grabbed the garter belt, and his group broke through the popping flashbulbs and the eager faces and swept down the ramp to the 'King's' limousine, where Sinatra stepped in, hardly having been touched except by those he wanted to have near.

'Hi, baby,' he said into the lips of a lady.

The love that millions of people feel for Frank Sinatra is one of the marvels of the cynical, hate-filled twentieth century.

Men, women and children love him for the friendly warmth of his baritone voice, for his independent spirit that enables him to spit in the eye of the authorities, and for his contempt for the press and the critics with whom he constantly battles.

Yet Sinatra, the man of many comebacks, was subtly engaged in still another comeback when, around Christmas

1975, he became purportedly the world's sexiest sixty-year-old, or sexagenarian.

'Ol' Blue Eyes', the 'King of Show Business', toured the USA, Canada and Europe trying to woo back some of the cult he'd lost for talking too much about 'the two-dollar hookers and pimps' of the press. In London, there were 350,000 orders for 15,000 available seats, and speculators got £100 (about $180) for one ticket. But the Toronto *Globe and Mail* said he was 'a vocal has-been, ripping off those who care about his music rather than his personality', and that he should know when to quit. The Toronto *Star* said his bodyguards punched a freelance photographer. He snapped back that newspapers were only good 'to cover the bottom of my parrot's cage and to house-break my dog on', and offered $1 million if they could prove him responsible for the photographer's beating.

In his private jet, with his girlfriend Barbara Marx, his lawyer, key musicians and bodyguards, he moved fast, not knowing how long his famous vocal chords would last. The New York *Times* advised him to quit making records and claimed he brought shame to the 1975 Academy Awards show, which he served as master of ceremonies 'looking and behaving more and more like a nightclub bouncer from Hoboken'.

One-time admirers scolded him for his conduct. Actress Shirley MacLaine, who had been a friend, told him candidly in Palm Springs, where he was a superking, 'In this town you're a closet dictator,' meaning he was a man who didn't come out in the open.

'Yeah, you're right!' Frank laughed.

'But why did you have to come out of the closet? Why did you have to support Ronald Reagan and Richard Nixon?' Shirley was full of the subject, having written in a book* that 'Sinatra has always loved gangsters in a romantic, theatrical way, as though he wanted to be one. Now he was up there with the best of them,' she said, 'but I still liked him. At least he had the good grace to drop his smile and look away in an embarrassed shame.'

Frank's political opinions have always been considered by

* *You Can't Get There From Here* (New York: Norton, 1975).

him to be his own business, and he and Shirley clashed over them again and again.

Critics asked why Frank and Sammy Davis, Jr., were on the 1975 Oscar show, since neither was at that time a big movie star. Why were Frank and Sammy Davis, Jr., shoving each other around onstage? Why couldn't they have kept it private? Frank had offended Sammy by saying, in what was intended as a joke, that Sammy in a high hat 'looked like a headwaiter in a rib joint'. Sammy, whom Frank affectionately calls 'Smokey the Bear', was 'in shock'.

The millions who loved Sinatra so wholeheartedly weren't impressed by these criticisms. The point was that Sinatra, trying to get out of a controversy, got into a fresh one. 'Who does he think he is—God?' somebody asked, and the answer came back, 'No—the Godfather.'

The allusions to Sinatra as the 'King', the 'Man', the 'Boss', led to remarks that Sinatra, having passed sixty, must eventually go on to the Great Beyond like all his subjects.

'Sinatra's going to give God a hard time for letting him be bald and make him wear all those toupees and hair transplants,' Marlon Brando said.

This was after a report that when Brando was offered the part of God in a picture, Sinatra had said, 'Marlon wanted to play something bigger.' A comedian's reply was ' "Mumbles" wanted to play Sinatra or nothing.'

All these remarks about Frank Sinatra being bigger than life, and having his own blind worshippers, have their origin in the fact that he is truly the greatest king that Show Business has ever had. Financially, Sinatra has dwarfed Al Jolson, his predecessor, with a reported $50-million fortune compared to Jolson's mere $6 million.

They could joke about him being king, but the sight of such a great entertainer as Sammy Davis, Jr., trembling before him is a little frightening. 'King Frank the First,' completely conscious of his power, could get half a million dollars for a TV special and $250,000 for a week in Las Vegas. Like one of the legendary shahs of Persia he reigned in Palm Springs over a compound with numerous guest houses, which realtors have appraised at $1.7 million. To be invited there was to be admitted to the 'King's' court.

Only the famous, very influential or extremely friendly have made it: vice-presidents, secretaries of state, ambassadors, golf and tennis champions, and celebrated comedians such as Milton Berle, who was court jester.

The King had a queen who was always a little shaky on the throne. She never knew just how long she was going to sit there. For it was well known that the King has had the most beautiful women in the world and is as faithful as Bluebeard.

As a battler he has no equal in Show Business, and his adversaries fear him, because he has been known to say of somebody who has offended him only slightly, 'I could have him put in a hospital, you know.' (Jokingly, I hope!) Yet his warmth and charm when he is friendly can cast happiness over any gathering that he graces.

One who could see both sides of him would have to say in all honesty that 'Ol' Blue Eyes' is a truly remarkable man with a conflicting dual personality—one good and one just a little bit bad—that makes him a house divided against itself. Looking away from the brawling, one finds an incredible doer of good. He has given away a fortune in secret assistance to people in trouble and another fortune in public charities, always requesting that no publicity be given his individual contributions.

He is so swift in arranging to pay hospital bills of sick and needy acquaintances that there is a joke to the effect that he must be getting tips on illnesses from doctors or ambulance drivers. His phone call frequently gets to the hospital before the patient. That is part of a tenderness and helpfulness and sympathy in the Sinatra personality that he tries to hide as though it were a weakness.

Sinatra cannot be completely happy because, though he is one of the most liked, admired and envied men, he is also widely resented. He has been favoured by fortune beyond most men. He had phenomenal success as a young singer, then suffered a nosedive, becoming a has-been in his thirties, then he had a comeback, retirement, unretirement, a second comeback and now he has trouble again.

Through a series of feuds with the press and television, mostly of his own making, he has accumulated an impressive list of enemies who think that he has become far too power-hungry.

When columnist Rex Reed wrote in October 1974, 'Somebody should do something about Frank Sinatra,' many of the people whom Frank counted as his friends privately agreed. A couple of years earlier those words would have been rejected by his own circle, but his constant harping about the 'two-dollar hookers' of the press while touring Australia and the US seemed to his intimates to be excessive.

'His public image is uglier than a first-degree burn, his appearance is sloppier than Porky Pig, his manners are more appalling than a subway sandhog's and his ego is bigger than the Sahara (the desert, not the hotel in Las Vegas, although either comparison applies),' wrote Rex Reed.

'All of which might be tolerable if he could still sing,' continued Reed. 'But the grim truth is that Frank Sinatra has had it. His voice has been manhandled beyond recognition, bringing with its parched croak only a painful memory of burned-out yesterdays. Frank Sinatra has become a bore.'

Their feud went back several years. Reviewing a film, Reed had written that Nancy Sinatra, Jr., dressed like a pizza waitress. But then, a few weeks before Reed's article appeared, Sinatra had, characteristically, made some extremely personal remarks about Reed from the stage during his concert tour:

'I was going to sing "God Save the Queen" tonight, but I won't out of deference to Rex Reed.'

To call Sinatra a bore was possibly over-strong. His big ABC-TV 'live' telecast from Madison Square Garden, 13 October 1974, was a major event. It demonstrated that the now almost chubby tycoon, who sometimes insisted upon being called 'Mr. Sinatra', could, after thirty years in a rough, tough business, still steam up the public and, with the celebrated Sinatra magic, make thousands upon thousands leap to their feet yelling.

On the sidewalk and stone steps outside Madison Square Garden that night, Sinatra T-shirts, with 'Frankie' on the front and decorated by a picture of a considerably younger Frank, were selling for three dollars.

Having obtained the Garden for this historic event, ABC Television and the promoter, Jerry Weintraub, built it up like a world heavyweight championship fight. Sports announcer Howard Cosell and the cameramen and the ushers wore black jackets with the words 'Sinatra, The Main Event' on the back.

Pat Henry, his favourite warm-up comedian, strolled out at 8.20 and announced, 'Welcome to the preliminaries, before the main event.'

At about 8.50, Henry bounded out again in his hockey shirt and with hands raised to get attention, said, 'You're a beautiful bunch—and I think you're ready for the king.'

They stomped and yelled. Henry appealed to them to give Sinatra a bigger ovation than he'd received in any other city.

'You gotta do it for me,' pleaded Henry. 'If he retires again, I'm back in the movies.'

Sinatra made a tremendous amount of money from the telecast and the two concerts—reportedly $500,000 from TV and $250,000 from paid admissions. In addition, he demonstrated a personal magnetism and excitement that unquestionably established him as the world's greatest entertainer.

Irving Felt, the head of Madison Square Garden, had invited the famous lawyer, seventy-three-year-old former Federal Judge Simon H. Rifkind, to the telecast.

'He didn't want to come,' Felt said.

But he went and was soon caught up in the near-delirium. Judge Rifkind exclaimed to Felt, 'Look at me, my foot is going with the beat! I can't believe this!'

Two nights later, a middle-aged man in a Broadway bar mentioned to the bartender that he had gone to the Sinatra spectacle at the Garden.

'Do you like Sinatra?' asked the other.

'No, I've hated him since World War Two. I had to leave my family for a couple of years, and he stayed home. I went to the Garden because I happen to be in that line of work. And I hate to say it, but I loved his show.'

'It was that good?'

'It was the tension and the build-up and the excitement of all those other celebrities—and of Sinatra himself. I'd consider it one of the great nights I've had.'

'You know that he bombed?' asked the bartender.

He opened up a newspaper. 'Here it is,

SINATRA CLOBBERED.

His rating wasn't as bad as his last special but he was way behind the competition.'

The man who'd gone to the Garden said, 'Even though I don't like him, that was a hell of a show. I wonder, what do they want?'

'I guess they don't want Sinatra,' the bartender said.

Sinatra himself shrugged off the ratings, happy only that the stories did say his New York City ratings had been good, better than those across the country. He had packed the Garden Saturday night, too, and he was again the man the whole country was talking about. He was still a national phenomenon just as he was in 1944, thirty years before.

What would he do next to keep them yelling?

He could be sure that wherever he went, things would happen, there would be explosions of excitement, simply because his presence made things happen. The private jet, the helicopters, the bodyguards, the beautiful girls, the celebrity parties, the $100 bills he tossed away as tips were a part of his life, which was a motion picture in itself. Not just one motion picture, but a series of movies or maybe a television series with Sinatra as the hero getting into a scrape or a brawl or a conflict every week and trying to get out of it.

There is little wonder that he should be a super-egotist as well as a superstar. When Sinatra wasn't yet thirty, the late Jo Davidson had sculpted a bust of him. Davidson thought that Sinatra, who then had a thin face and chin, looked like a young Abraham Lincoln.

Now with all his business enterprises, corporations and investments supervised by his Beverly Hills lawyer Milton

(Mickey) Rudin, who seems to be almost always with him, Sinatra will surely continue spending—and giving. He will continue to manoeuvre in politics, making occasional unpopular decisions as he did in Las Vegas when he backed a loser for district attorney.

Sinatra cannot comprehend his own fame.

Songwriter Sammy Cahn recalls that one night at Ruby's Dunes in Palm Springs, Sinatra was spooning some soup when he saw a man staring at him open-mouthed from across the room.

'What's that creep staring at me about?' Frank asked.

Sammy Cahn's eyes followed his gaze. The man was definitely staring. 'He's staring at you because you're Frank Sinatra,' Sammy tried to explain. 'You're Frank Sinatra. Remember?'

Frank returned to the soup but the next time he looked up, he said, 'That creep is still staring! What is he staring at me about?' Frank put down the spoon and got up. He strode over to the man's table, sat down, grabbed him by the lapels and demanded, 'What is it? What the hell is it? Why are you staring at me?'

The man looked at him worshipfully. 'I love you,' he almost cried. 'I love you. You are the greatest singer in the world, the greatest man ever!'

Frank got up. He called to a waiter. 'Give him a drink,' he commanded. 'On my tab.'

Sinatra returned to the table with Cahn and resumed spooning his soup. Then he looked across the room again. 'The creep is still staring,' he said. 'Why?'

'Because you're Frank Sinatra. Why can't you remember that you're Frank Sinatra?'

Sinatra knows he is a Dr. Jekyll and Mr. Hyde; a charmer one moment, an insulter the next; lovable now, hateful later; sweetly patient, then furiously hot-tempered; a paradox; a contradiction within himself.

'The private man, the private Sinatra,' declares the gifted composer Alec Wilder, an intimate for many years, 'would not be recognized by those who know the public Sinatra. The private man is a very gentle, dear, loving person. He is not brash and he is not cocky, but he is understanding and he says "Don't let anybody take advantage of you." '

Explaining his hatred of the press, Sinatra told Wilder that once, as he was getting off a plane, he saw a man leaning against a wooden stanchion and heard him cursing him outrageously. Sinatra remembers that he was about to advance on the man and beat him for his remarks when, in the distance, he saw a photographer. When Sinatra looked again at the man who had been cursing him he noticed that he was a cripple. Sinatra truly believes that the photographer had tried to trap him into a picture in which he would be shown beating up a cripple.

In the days when he was singing on the radio for carfare, Sinatra knew that he was going to be an American success story. Working towards it and attaining it in an incredibly short time, he then became a legend without even trying, by just being his own controversial self, with the bad temper and all. Frank Sinatra has always seemed to know that he was History.

The press criticism of Sinatra is given scant attention by millions of his fans who disregard anything uncomplimentary about him. Middle-aged women, now turning into old women, sigh softly, 'He is a very dear man.' Young wives in their thirties and girls in their twenties thrill to his sex appeal even though he's as old as their fathers.

Every fan finds his own enchantment in Sinatra. For some it may be his singing 'Strangers in the Night' with its unorthodox 'Dooby-dooby-do' closing. For others it's his voice lifted so defiantly in 'My Way'. For Noël Coward, it was Sinatra's 'impeccable taste'.

Arrayed against the Sinatra enemies and critics are many celebrities who adore him. They include actors and showmen who respect his work. For example, Tony Curtis, whom Frank warmly welcomed to Hollywood when Tony was still frightened; Broadway producer Max Gordon, now in his eighties, who recognized Frank's acting talent thirty years ago; producer Mike Frankovich, who has found Frank's generosity incredible; producer Mervyn LeRoy, whose devotion to Sinatra goes back to *The House I Live In*; director Otto Preminger, who praised Sinatra for making

The Man With the Golden Arm, an Oscar nominee and a great contribution to the cinema; producer Howard Koch, who received a lesson in vocabulary from Sinatra that he's never forgotten; plus, of course, Rosalind Russell, Claudette Colbert, Gene Kelly, Rex Harrison, Katharine Hepburn, Deborah Kerr, Jack Warner, Lena Horne, Bing Crosby, Princess Grace of Monaco and others who would be character witnesses for him any day. They have all felt the Sinatra touch.

There *is* a Sinatra magic. When he arrives at any public event, banquet, charity show, tournament, baseball game or what have you, there's an explosion of excitement as the words 'Sinatra's here!' crackle through the room. He generates more electricity than any other personality in Show Business.

Artistically, Sinatra should be judged with a respect he doesn't always receive. He is one of the creative geniuses of his field. Sinatra, resolutely following the 'I Did It My Way' theme of his life, can work conscientiously on a recording for hours and hours or knock one off in thirty minutes, never even getting up a sweat.

The unpredictability of Sinatra due to the paradox of his personality has made him one of today's antiheroes. He invites the most stinging criticism with his independence. Sometimes it appears that he's deliberately masochistic. His animalistic sex appeal has added to the Sinatra mystery and mystique. He is a romantic troubadour who loves them and leaves them with a grateful smile on their faces. In Hollywood, they said Errol Flynn and George Raft were always very cocksure of themselves. They pay Sinatra the same compliment.

Revelling in the role of a superstud, he laughed at comedian Alan King's remark at a banquet, 'Frank couldn't make it tonight. He made it twice this afternoon and he's tired.'

He has flailed himself into enormous energy to be the Number 1 star. He is constantly driving and plunging ahead. He has always been like a wild base-runner stealing second, then third, then home.

Every day Sinatra propels himself into the battle, cool,

calm and confident. He overcame a rough boyhood that had almost no prospect of success. He went on to become a millionaire and a power. He lacks the education of his critics and of those who attack him. But he looks with disdain on their opinions because by his standards he's more important than they can ever be.

'I'm so much better than all you other cats, any comparison would be very unfortunate for you—it would be pitiful,' he is thinking behind his smile. That's what powers Sinatra; that's what makes him tick.

'YOU'RE MEANT TO BE SOMEBODY'

The high drama that was to follow Frank Sinatra all his life began the moment he was born.

'I don't think he'll live so we'll try to save the mother,' Dr. Peterson said that Sunday morning, 12 December 1915, in the chilly two-family house at 415 Monroe Street in what was then downtown Hoboken, New Jersey. The docks, the soot, the tenements were only a few blocks away.

The doctor worked furiously over Mrs. Natalie Sinatra. She was then a nonentity, a housewife of twenty, a practical nurse and, occasionally, like her mother, a midwife. The trouble was, the new baby was *huge*. He weighed an incredible 13½ pounds. Dr. Peterson, working with antiquated forceps, in cramped quarters, with women shouting advice, accidentally lacerated part of the baby's head and almost severed an earlobe, leaving scars on the left cheek.

In the near-panic, there was one person who didn't accept that the boy was stillborn. That was the mother of the woman who had just given birth to the enormous baby. She was Mrs. Rosa Garaventi, who ran an Italian grocery. She knew midwifery, too. She had nine children.

Mrs. Garaventi held her grandchild under the cold-water tap. The baby coughed, and squalled, and breathed, and lived.

The baby began life with a torn ear and scars on the upper part of his cheek. From the first, he was fighting mad at the world that had tried to deny him entrance.

The 'little monster', Francis Albert Sinatra, heard it said

hundreds of times in his childhood that he 'was given up for dead', that he 'was an instrument baby; that's why he's got all those marks on him'.

'God loved you, he saved you for something,' his aunts and uncles told him. 'You're meant to be somebody', they predicted.

That set him apart at first, and years later he seems to have believed those words, and they sparked ambition in him. Frank was a rarity in an Italian family—an only child. He was soon spoiled rotten by the relatives. Although fat, he was a joy to all of them. He wasn't beautiful, he was just chubby, and he had glistening blue eyes. They were real 'baby blues'. Both his parents also had blue eyes.

As he grew old enough to understand what they were saying, he was disturbed by people saying that his mother had wanted a girl. She had assembled a pink outfit for the daughter she preferred—and she soon had him wearing it! But Grandmother Garaventi took over and dressed him in Little Lord Fauntleroy outfits. Still, he wondered: Had his mother not wanted him?

Growing from Francis Albert to little Frankie, advancing from toddler into school age, he heard so many references to his survival after being close to death that he wondered if it truly had meaning. Several psychiatrists have said that this accident at birth shaped his character and his life, that it explains how his charm changes to hostility. When he feels thankful for being alive, he is unexpectedly generous and kind; when it occurs to him that somebody doesn't want him, he is resentful. Then he remembers 'You're going to be somebody special!' and he feels superior—almost arrogant.

The scars on his face were physical and he never tried to hide them or remove them with plastic surgery, but there were mental scars, too.

A famous analyst, who wishes not to be named, says, 'Every day as he looks at himself in the mirror and sees the scars, he is motivated to sing and be heard and to prove that God was right in saving him. If he had patched over the scars, he might have lost the motivation, so he was right in not covering them.

'You will notice,' says this analyst, 'that he has been reported in the press as saying, "We who have God-given talent . . ." '

It's easy to see how Frankie became so complex and so ambitious.

Nevertheless, he was a happy little neighbourhood kid as he advanced without any noticeable scholastic excellence through the lower grades into David E. Rue Junior High. He was an annoyance to his teachers; he was popular; he was a show-off; he wore some flamboyant get-ups considering that he was often down by the railroad yards of the Erie and Lackawanna. Once he delighted classmates by producing a picture of himself in a riding habit complete with jodhpurs. In the eyes of his teachers, he was disruptive.

Many years later, his publicists, to gain sympathy, claimed he had suffered an unhappy childhood. Actually he had spent much of his childhood in ecstasy. How could he be unhappy when his family moved into a house, when he was about fourteen, with a bathtub and central heating? He 'manoeuvred'; he always had spending money, which he got from his parents or the relatives; even as a kid he was a big spender, a giver of gifts.

His mother, Dolly, an immigrant from Genoa, was a beautiful strawberry blonde, a jolly extrovert, fond of laughing, who became prominent as a Democratic district leader. Her father, John Garaventi, had been a stone-grinder for a lithographer.

Brainy, acquisitive and a go-getter, Dolly knew the hard facts of life and wasn't shocked by men's rough language. She was also direct. Once when she was trying to goad Frank on through school, she discovered a picture of Bing Crosby in his room and learned that he was thinking about a singing career: she threw a shoe at him.

The neighbourhood Democrats looked up to Dolly as being 'a fixture as well as a fixer' who could go down to City Hall and get a favour.

Dolly bossed around Frank's father, Anthony Martin Sinatra, shamelessly though he was a scrappy former bantamweight fighter who had used the name of Marty

O'Brien—the Irish names being more favoured in those days with ring fans.

Dolly's husband acquiesced as she ran the family. He was slight of build and somewhat asthmatic. After his ring days, he became a boilermaker. After he lost that job, Dolly borrowed money from her mother and opened a tavern for him. She often worked there as a barmaid.

Dolly got Marty appointed a city fireman and he worked himself up on merit alone to the rank of captain. He became known in the town as the 'Captain'.

While politicking Dolly tried to keep the family solvent, her husband Marty attempted to get Frankie to take time from his teenage social activities to hear about the glories of his native Catania.

'It's the beauty spot of the world,' Marty told his son, who grunted impatiently, 'Yeah, sure, yeah.'

Catania? Where the hell was Catania? Down by the toe of the Italian boot. Down by Taormina, by Siracusa, across the island from Palermo.

Despite all the competition, Marty Sinatra got across his message: 'Be proud of your Italian lineage.' Squaring off with him, he told his son he must always be ready to use his fists.

'I got my hot Sicilian temper and temperament from my dad,' Frank often said later.

Frankie tried deliberately to be a tough little bastard. Growing up in that rough waterfront city, he wanted to be as hard as the sons of stevedores, railroaders, bootleggers and hoodlums with whom he associated and fought. His father impressed upon him that Sicilians were proud and unbeatable fighters who were also unforgiving. They remembered. They held a grudge.

Frankie brought home many a bloodied nose or puffed eye.

'A big kid called me a wop,' he reported. 'But a Jew kid and me creamed him.'

Since Dolly was usually planning a Democratic boat ride or a Saturday night dance, he would repair his bloody nose with the help of Grandmother Garaventi, the woman who had held him under the cold-water tap.

Frequently he stayed with his grandmother when his mother, who'd become known as 'Lady Bountiful' in the community, was out ward-heeling. Sometimes he went to the home of an elderly Jewish woman, a Mrs. Goldberg and there he developed a friendship for Jewish people. In later years he wore around his neck a religious symbol that included a Star of David. It was a gift from Mrs. Goldberg.

Washing up after the street fights was important to Frankie Sinatra. He was fastidious; neatness was an obsession. He often smelled of soap. He was slender now, having long lost his plumpness, and wanted to be dapper like the movie stars. He wanted to be a snappy dresser.

Even in Hoboken, Show Business could get under somebody's skin, and that was happening to Frankie.

The 'talkies' were coming into their own as he was growing up. They were giving new importance to singers. On Broadway, Maurice Chevalier was appearing in an evening of French songs assisted by Eleanor Powell, the dancer, and Duke Ellington's orchestra. The celebrated Scottish comedian, Harry Lauder, was touring America. But it was Al Jolson and Rudy Vallee who captivated Frankie.

Rudy Vallee had come down from Yale with a saxophone and a megaphone, and he was mesmerizing his women followers at a nightclub, the Versailles, which later changed its name to the Villa Vallee. Mounted police charged up on the sidewalk to control his crowds at Keith's Albee Theatre. He called 'Heigh-ho, everybody,' on his radio programme, 'The Fleischmann Hour', and the women left their senses.

That's what 'Bones' Sinatra wanted. He was going to be somebody. Maybe he was going to be a star.

The Sinatras lived in well-kept, better-than-average apartments and houses on Madison Street and Hudson Street, and Frankie didn't need to be ashamed of where he lived or of his parents. He was also proud of his uncle Lawrence Garaventi, his mother's brother, who fought as a welterweight under the name of Babe Sieger.

Urged on by his father and his Uncle Babe, young Frankie boxed and was fast with his hands. He was a good little athlete for his size, an excellent swimmer, and he tried to play basketball. He was a capable forward before the giants took over basketball.

Frank was a member of the Park Athletic Club and the Tommy Carey Association, the latter named for the star shortstop of the Saint Louis Browns who'd come from Hoboken.

But he had singing on his mind and was working out, swimming at Palisades Park or running at nearby tracks, to improve his breathing—an idea that seemed to have been all his own. When singing, he used a small megaphone, imitating Rudy Vallee's popular style, twanging the ukelele, serenading the girls at Long Branch or other New Jersey resorts where the family took him.

He was usually the flashiest boy at the dances, and he didn't let them forget he was the son of Marty Sinatra, the fire captain, and Dolly Sinatra, the political leader.

'We were all trying to sing and there were many guys who could sing better than Frank, but he had a style—already he had a style,' Bob Anthony told me recently between introducing strip acts at the Follies Burlesk. Bob was one of Frank's Hoboken chums, who also aspired to be a singer and did become one. Now he manages some burlesque theatres in Times Square.

Frank was a scrawny, underfed-looking youngster who could hardly be left at home alone, so Dolly and Marty Sinatra took the boy along to gatherings of the neighbourhood Hoboken Sicilian Cultural League. He was often allowed to sing there and eventually even got paid as much as fifteen dollars a week to perform.

Frank's mother was a commanding personality whereas his father, despite having been a pugilist, was retiring.

'Have respect,' his parents lectured him. 'Respect your parents, but other people, too.' Growing up, Frank made *respect* a major word in his vocabulary. For his mother Frank developed such love and respect that nearly every important woman in his life had to be sized up and appraised eventually by her at an Italian dinner that she cooked. The lesson from his father that a Sicilian never forgets a wrong was to motivate Frank through life. He was forever chopping down those who'd crossed him.

(Frank was to become one of the most dutiful sons, constantly trying to gather his parents closer to him as they grew older. After his father died, Frank built a clinic in Palm Springs in the name of the man who had encouraged the fighting instinct in his personality when he was a small boy. As Frank got older and heavier, he looked remarkably like his father. His mother Dolly reasserted her independence by disagreeing with him at times in a loud voice that made Frank laugh.)

The dapper look that young Frankie acquired coincided with his ambition to get away from the drab Hoboken port atmosphere. Only a street fight or gangland shooting changed the dull neighbourhood. The violence he saw made an impression on Frank that he always remembered.

Frank decided at fifteen, while in his sophomore year at Demarest High School in Hoboken, to become a drop-out. There is no evidence that he was missed at school. He said twenty years later that he had been in gangs that were working themselves up from stealing candy to stealing bicycles. His father was disturbed by Frank's fondness for 'snappy clothes', and he thought the whole thing about Frank becoming a singer was idiotic. He wished to God he'd become a boxer. But Frank had to stay in school till he was sixteen, so he went to a business school for a few months.

Dolly Sinatra thought it was absurd that her son wanted to be a singer; she wanted him to go into business or engineering. His father kept saying 'Get something steady.'

Like millions of other boys, Frank decided to do just what his parents said he shouldn't do. He began singing secretly.

He wheedled a second-hand car out of his parents, who were now in better circumstances. He raced around town looking dapper but out of work. He drove the jalopy around New Jersey looking for roadhouses where he could sing. Years later he said that the police had beaten him bloody questioning him about how he had gotten some new clothes. He claimed that he had an eleven-dollar-a-week job on a newspaper delivery truck. He had bought the clothes. He said he has hated cops ever after.

As he tried to sing in various roadhouses, he had nothing to offer but guts. He had no reputation, no training, and the owners usually said no. He was so young and of such slight build, they couldn't envisage him entertaining their customers.

Frank could be so humble and charming and persuasive when he wished: he could charm the birds out of the trees—and the girls into bed.

He made friends with some little-known orchestra leaders and he persuaded them to let him accompany them on jobs. He carried a musical instrument case to give the impression that he was a member of the orchestra. Once inside, he would watch for an opportunity to sing during a break. In bigger clubs he'd never have been permitted to do this, but these were small New Jersey roadhouses. The orchestra leaders considered that the kid wasn't doing anybody any harm, and besides, he wasn't bad.

'Frank was always very big with the chicks, even as a kid,' they say around Hoboken, 'and he was a flirty little wolf when he worked on the delivery trucks of the Jersey *Observer*. He was something of a Romeo on that truck route with that spit curl down over his narrow brow.'

Nancy Barbato, a plasterer's daughter, was the 'chick' he was most devoted to then. He wasn't really in love with her, but he thought he was—so he said later. Meeting Frank at one of the Italian family gatherings, Nancy fell in love with him immediately. She liked his animal spirit and his jokes. When they met again at some beach parties, Nancy found him a romantic even then, and he was very aware of his appeal.

His father Marty had meanwhile acquired a tavern, and his mother was getting important in the neighbourhood. But his gregarious, back-slapping mother didn't approve of the match. Dolly was possessive of her only child and decided that no girl was good enough for her son.

Nancy Barbato trotted along with Frank as he hustled around Newark, Jersey City, and New York's Times Square, trying to capture somebody's ear besides Nancy's. She had a secretarial job, and the bleeding heart sob sisters of the press invariably recounted in later years that she gave of her tiny income to buy him sandwiches and coffee.

Frank escorted Nancy to a Jersey City theatre in 1933 to hear Bing Crosby sing in person. Bing had groaned through twenty straight weeks at the Paramount in New York. Frank had been plucking the uke dreaming of being another Bing.

Upon hearing Bing in Jersey City, the entranced Frank and his Nancy agreed that Frank was going to be the next Crosby. That made two of them. It would be sweet to record that Bing greeted them in his dressing room after the show and said to Frank, 'You're going to be another me,' but nothing so spectacular happened. Frank didn't meet Bing until several years later when he *was* another Crosby.

Frank had his eye on the Big Apple—New York and Broadway—and took the Hoboken or Weehawken ferry there almost every day. Standing on the heights of Hamilton Park, Weehawken, where Aaron Burr killed Alexander Hamilton in a duel in 1804, Frank could look across the Hudson and straight down Forty-second Street. It was an inspiring sight on a beautiful, sunny day.

He had the youthful confidence that enabled him to picture himself capturing the city. But he was just a singer, not even a handsome one, not even tall and muscular. He did have a disarming politeness, seeming sincerity, and a way of singing a song as though he meant it.

Frank saw an opportunity for himself in the talent contests where an amateur could instantly turn pro if he won. Frank and three other Hoboken boys went to a Major Bowes Amateur Hour audition as The Hoboken Four, with Frank as the lead singer. They got the most enthusiastic response from the listeners. They got a job as part of a Major Bowes touring unit, with board and fifty dollars per week. Frank was nearing twenty, and he decided that touring wasn't any way to get famous. For one thing, it kept him away from New York. After a few weeks, he left the unit.

Coming back to New Jersey, he began again riding the ferry over to New York. He hung around the radio stations hoping that somebody would let him sing for nothing. He was humble, grateful, persistent and courteous, and all he wanted was to get a chance to prove that he could sing.

Nancy thought he was the most charming boy she'd ever met, and he was also the most sanitary male of her acquaintance. He was always scrubbing his hands and worrying about looking well-groomed. He was adept at pressing his trousers with sharp creases before he went out.

Frank made Fifty-second Street his music school.

Fifty-second Street was New Year's Eve nearly every night, and he haunted the radio stations and the night spots, sopping up the atmosphere and the sound and the beat. He was often a visitor to the Onyx Club, where trumpeter Ed Farley and trombonist Mike Riley clowned 'The Music Goes 'Round and 'Round' into a national hit.

Jimmy Ryan's, the Famous Door, and Leon & Eddie's were hangouts, and the Hickory House had jam sessions starting at noon on Sundays. Frank used to sit around there waiting to get a chance to go on and sing—for nothing.

Frank was learning from all of them. Mabel Mercer, he said later, taught him to handle a lyric. She sang sitting on a stool at Tony's Place, a former speakeasy. He learned from Billie Holliday and Sarah Vaughan and Fats Waller and developed an admiration that continues today for Count Basie, who in those years was a hit with the college crowd at the Famous Door.

One of the 'upholstered sewers' where Sinatra studied not only music but also comedy was the celebrated Club 18, where Jack White, Jackie Gleason, Pat Harrington, Sr., and Frankie Hyers insulted the customers. When any woman went to the ladies' room, one of the comics would shout, 'Just mention my name and get a good seat.' A woman wearing almost any kind of a hat would be asked in a loud voice, 'How can we get laughs with you wearin' that?'

Jack White and his crew at Club 18 were long ahead of Don Rickles with the insult technique. White was the only entertainer who spat at customers. He expectorated freely at the patrons, and many were the minks and silver foxes he splashed.

It was the practice and exposure that Frank wanted. He also longed for a job with a band that had what they called in those days a 'wire'—a radio outlet.

He found it—or his mother found it—at the Rustic Cabin, a roadhouse near Englewood, New Jersey. The pay was fifteen dollars a week. Frank wasn't hired there so much to sing as to be the emcee introducing three comedians.

'I sang a little, but not enough to louse the place up,' Frank said later.

Nancy Barbato, whom he married at Our Lady of Sorrows Church in Jersey City on 4 February 1939, finally saw her would-be Crosby happy, with a radio wire open to him and his voice five nights a week.

The marriage wasn't entirely unnoticed by the music world. Frankie already had a following of sorts. They were the Broadway song pluggers who wanted him to sing their songs on WNEW 'Dance Parade'. Several pluggers chipped in two dollars each for a wedding present. Frank remembered them for many years.

The bride Nancy and her mother-in-law Dolly didn't often see each other. Frank's moodiness was showing. He was often cool and distant to his parents. Marty Sinatra, a gentle little man, didn't press his son to be closer, and Dolly was frequently busy with her own life.

Frank was acting like a loner. He was lonely despite his companionship with many people. He was always running, always pushing. He had a rare gift, and he knew it. He wanted to reach beyond the New Jersey horizons and become somebody great.

Frank thought he might make some money some day. The nights he had spent on Fifty-second Street had taught him a lot about music that he could never have learned in a conservatory. Frank believed that at twenty-three he was really ready to sing. If he could just get some breaks. . . .

'DISCOVERED' BY HIMSELF AND HARRY JAMES

The first to give Frank a break was star trumpet player Harry James, who himself had been discovered by bandleader Benny Goodman, the 'King of Swing'.

With money lent him by Goodman, James formed a brassy outfit called Harry James and the Music Makers. They were struggling to survive, playing at the Paramount Theatre, the great temple of entertainment at forty-fourth and Broadway. For personal appearances, the New York Paramount was paramount. It had a capacity of 3,645, which could be stretched to 4,800 or even 5,000. 'It was a bastion of elegance on tawdry Times Square,' one of the New York papers said.

In the great lobby one saw romantic statuary, oil paintings, all in a Hall of Nations where stones from all over the world were exhibited. In the *salle de musique*, a grand piano was played for patrons waiting in the lobby.

One night in 1939, James was in bed listening to remote broadcasts on WNEW's 'Dance Parade'. He heard a voice that sounded good, warm and different. James didn't catch the singer's name, but he did make out that he was at the Rustic Cabin. James phoned the club for the singer's name.

'We don't have a singer,' somebody said. 'We have an emcee that sings a little.'

James visited the club the next night, and his presence caused a buzz. Frank Sinatra heard it and didn't believe James was there.

'Harry James wouldn't be caught in this joint,' he said.

'I could use another singer,' Harry James told him, 'but I don't have much money—seventy-five dollars a week.'

James and Sinatra were about the same age, but James, tall and angular, and more experienced, seemed older. Frank thought this could be the break he wanted. He took the job.

Sinatra went to the Paramount the next day and looked down on the big crowd from the stage for the first time. He loved it!

James saw things he liked about Frank. Sinatra was shy and nervous, but there was a niceness and tenderness about him. Facing a big audience for the first time did not scare him. James also saw that young Sinatra actually loved to sing. The James musicians sensed that the boy had a sound that was distinctly new.

James had a peculiarity. He liked to change people's names. A singer arrived from Georgia with the name of Marie Antoinette Yvonne Jamais. James hired her, but changed her name to Connie Haines.

'I think you should change your name,' James said to Frank.

'Change it? You kiddin'? I'm gonna be famous,' Sinatra retorted.

Frank hungered for publicity and in the beginning couldn't get it. While the James band was playing at the 1939 New York World's Fair, Broadway press agent Ade Kahn tried to get mentions of the band in the newspapers. Most news of the midway seemed to concern the Aquacade show produced by Billy Rose, and starring Eleanor Holm. Kahn asked the musicians and three vocalists if they had any news, or had done anything fascinating. 'Do you have any famous relatives?' he finally asked.

Speaking right up, the slender vocalist said, 'I have a famous relative.'

'Who is it?' Kahn asked hopefully.

'Ray Sinatra!' Frankie bristled at the non-recognition. 'YES, RAY SINATRA! Ray Sinatra is very famous. Ray Sinatra leads the whole band at "Star and Garter", the

Mike Todd show that has Gypsy Rose Lee in it. Ray Sinatra is very famous, and he's my cousin.'

'Oh,' said the press agent sadly. It was one of very few Sinatra items that didn't get in the papers.

'The boy', as they called Frank, just had to have publicity. He asked Harry James' manager Jerry Barrett how to get it. When pop music critic George T. Simon went to review the James band, he was taken aside by Barrett.

'This boy,' Barrett said, 'wants a good write-up more than anybody I've ever seen. He's good, and we want to keep him happy and with the band. A good write-up is the only thing that will keep him happy.'

Frank got the good write-up—and he not only thanked Simon, but asked Simon the next time he saw him to get his picture on the cover of a music publication.

'They're not using pictures on the cover any more,' Simon said, but he smiled at Frank's cocky assurance and determination to push himself ahead.

A reporter for *Downbeat* magazine asked James the name of the new singer.

'Not so loud!' James answered. 'The kid's name is Sinatra. He considers himself the greatest vocalist in the business. Nobody ever heard of him, he's never had a hit record, he looks like a wet mop. But he says he's the greatest. If he hears you compliment him, he'll demand a raise tonight.'

Frank was feisty and scrappy—he was also good. Without any particular promotion or press agenting—because he couldn't afford it—Frank became a spectacular addition to the James band. The bobby-sox movement was just beginning.

'The first theatre we played on the road with James was the Hippodrome in Baltimore,' Connie Haines says. 'Already the kids were hanging around the stage door, screaming for Frank. People said those kids were "plants". Plants! That's ridiculous. Who could afford to pay plants? Harry James couldn't afford to pay plants, either. The band was having trouble financially, and we all hoped it wouldn't break up.'

Frank saw a chance for a break for himself when the

band moved on to Hollywood but the loud sound of James' music wasn't popular at Victor Hugo's, where they were driving away customers nightly. Frank was getting some nibbles for unimportant movie appearances. Nobody had much money. Nancy invited the musicians to an apartment they'd taken and fed them spaghetti. The Sinatras were broke, but comparatively happy.

The end was coming for the Harry James orchestra. Victor Hugo's wouldn't or couldn't pay them and blamed the 'noise from Harry James' trumpet' for the band's cancellation. Sinatra had seen the band's demise coming and was figuring out his own next step.

The break-up of the band was tragic. 'Most of them had to hitch-hike home,' Connie Haines remembers.

The Sinatras were in better shape. Nancy, who in the beginning had slipped money to Frank from her own small earnings as a secretary, was back in Newark, very pregnant, and swearing to Frank that she would always love him no matter what troubles they had. Frank hardly needed to tell her that he was inordinately ambitious and going on to far places. It was with sadness that he said good-bye to the musicians and to Harry James, with whom he'd become so close. James gave him his blessings.

Harry James happened to hold on to a contract from Frank, which had several weeks to go at seventy-five dollars a week. To this day, James—a Sinatra fan still—reminds him of that contract, and Frank good-humouredly responds, 'Any time you want me, Boss.'

It was about a year later—during his Tommy Dorsey era—that I, while covering Dorsey, first met the rising young singer Frankie Sinatra.

There was a bit of the buccaneer in Dorsey. With the James band in collapse, Dorsey moved in to grab Sinatra at a bargain. His singer, Jack Leonard, had become temperamental and was leaving him to go on his own. Tommy wanted to develop somebody to overshadow Leonard.

Tipped off to call Dorsey, Sinatra met him in Chicago at the Palmer House. 'T.D.' was restrained in his enthusiasm. He leaked word that the job was going to another singer, a manoeuvre to get Frank cheaper. Sinatra ached to join Dorsey's so-called singer's band, which presented vocalists importantly. After another meeting, he took on Sinatra at $100 a week. Connie Haines also joined the Dorsey band, along with Frank.

Thus, in the early part of 1940, after six months with Harry James, Sinatra broke in with Dorsey in Chicago, then went on to Rockford, Illinois, then on to Indianapolis.

It wasn't a smashing beginning. Frank and Dorsey were both troubled that the crowds still wanted to hear Jack Leonard sing 'Marie'.

Frank sang that, too and he had help on 'Marie' from the group called the Pied Pipers. Jo Stafford, one of the group, said in retrospect that she wasn't impressed by the new vocalist's appearance but 'Wow! What a sound!'

But there were also disappointments: *Billboard* magazine said he was a good ballad singer 'but nil on showmanship'; Frank was Number 22 in the *Billboard* Collegiate Choice of Male Vocalists, while Jack Leonard was up there in the Number 2 spot. It upset Dorsey that Ray Eberle of the Glenn Miller band was Number 1, and Bob Eberle of his brother Jimmy's band was Number 3.

Sitting around the Astor Roof and Lindy's those nights in 1940, Frank knew he was in the right spot—for the time being—even if he wasn't at the top in the listings. He had learned the value of work, and he was constantly trying to improve his phrasing. He was now twenty-four, going to be twenty-five in December. He had hoped he would be somebody important by his twenty-fifth birthday, but the prospects weren't bright. His tough boss didn't appreciate him. Frank, with that drive that would never stop, kept stubbornly at the phrasing and practising, just like a Horatio Alger hero. He was helpful and co-operative on the one-nighter trips by bus, always sanitary, well scrubbed, shoes shined and pants pressed.

Little Nancy Sandra Sinatra—'Nancy with the Laughing Face'—was born in Jersey City, 8 June 1940. Frank was at the Hotel Astor in New York, having worked that night. The Astor Roof was a popular entertainment spot where people went to get cool before air conditioning became common. Frank celebrated becoming a parent with some of his band clique. It is not unusual for the father to be absent when a child is born to the wife of a singer. If the father is present, it probably means he isn't working.

He was a man with a family now. He had to work harder.

'I gotta have a record,' he kept saying.

He got one, in a strange way.

'Tommy Dorsey ran a contest for new songs,' Connie Haines recalls. 'He would introduce the winning songs from the Astor Roof.

'Tommy couldn't be bothered going through all that mail, so he made Frank and me do it. Frank didn't want to do it either, so I did most of it. It was like a grab bag. You couldn't look at all of it. Besides, neither Frank nor I could read music. A woman mailed in a certain song, and we picked it out of the box. . . .'

A young woman named Ruth Lowe had been playing piano in a Toronto music shop that sold sheet music, trying to be a songwriter. Then her husband died suddenly during an operation. In her grief, she wrote a song titled 'I'll Never Smile Again'. The lyrics were 'I'll never smile again/Until I smile at you/I'll never laugh again/What good would it do?' The song about the woman's sorrow was recorded by the Dorsey orchestra, Dorsey's Pied Pipers and Connie Haines and Frank Sinatra. It became an instant hit. It helped make Sinatra famous.

Ruth Lowe's story of the song is different from Connie Haines' grab-bag version. Mrs. Lowe said she had given a recording of the song to Tommy Dorsey's guitarist when the Dorsey band played at the Canadian National Exhibition, he gave the record to Dorsey, and Dorsey wired for publishing rights.

'I got ten dollars for recording it,' Connie says. 'Frank got twenty-five dollars.'

Brothers Tommy and Jimmy Dorsey were having fist-fights after breaking up into separate bands, and it seemed to be a good story. Tommy was playing at Meadowbrook Ballroom, Meadowbrook, New Jersey, and I went there to interview him. By chance, I got an early glimpse of the youth who would become the 'King'.

My wife and I were driven to Meadowbrook by Tommy's road manager, George H. ('Bullets') Durgom, later a well-known agent and manager. When we arrived, something extraordinary was happening around Dorsey's bandstand. Dorsey was famous for his dance music, but the young couples who came there to dance quit dancing when the boy singer sang. They clustered around the bandstand, hand in hand or arms around each other, and I looked up at him as he sang. He was something I hadn't seen before. My wife, who was only a few years older than Sinatra and had already heard him sing, was rolling her eyes and saying things like 'Woo, woo!' I asked 'Bullets' if we could meet him.

There was a sharp light in Frank's blue eyes as he sat down and talked. He spoke of his dreams and ambitions, and he said he was going to write a book about counterpoint. He was going to be the biggest singer in the country. 'You'll see,' he said.

He returned to our table several times between sets, and his self-confidence impressed us. He was convinced that *he* was going to be the greatest. In fact, he was *already* the greatest, he said.

Physically, he was less impressive. The Sinatra frame was not only slender, but fragile-looking. The cheeks were hollow. He wore a bow tie, a thin wool sweater, a dark suit —he seemed still a boy, and that added charm to his cockiness. He had a lot of hair that straggled down the upper part of his right cheek, about to the bottom of his ear. He also had a spit curl. His hair, when he came offstage, was tousled-looking. 'Sexy,' the girls said later.

When we were returning to New York, my wife said, 'There's another Bing Crosby.' That was approximately what Frankie had told us.

'Sure,' I replied in a somewhat sceptical tone.

At twenty, my wife had been a Bing Crosby fan who stayed home to listen to him on the radio. Now she was electrified by this new voice. Reacting to the sex appeal in his crooning, she was a better appraiser than a man could be. She asked Durgom more about him.

'This boy's going to be very big,' Durgom said, 'if Tommy doesn't kill him first. Tommy doesn't like Frank stealing the show—and he doesn't like people who are temperamental—like himself.'

'He's very meek and mild,' my wife said.

'Ho, ho!' laughed Durgom. 'He's smart. He's human. He's a sweetheart, but he's also got a temper.'

My wife said he was 'cute'. She asked Durgom about the book on counterpoint Frank said he was going to write. Was he that informed?

'First time I heard that one,' smiled Durgom. 'He's got delusions and such ambition, you wouldn't believe! But he'll be very big—you watch.'

I didn't hear the name Frank Sinatra for a while. Then in late 1942, when I was Amusement Editor of the New York *Post*, I sat up sharply when a stageshow critic, Ted O'Gorman, turned in a review about Frank Sinatra giving the girls swooning spells when he sang with Tommy Dorsey's orchestra at the Paramount Theatre. 'He's chasing Bing Crosby in the popularity polls,' Ted O'Gorman said.

That was what the boy had said he was going to do.

Now I began covering the activities of the Dorsey band, not because of Tommy's off-the-bandstand exploits, but because its vocalist was even more interesting. The breaks Frank had begged for were coming. Frank looked forward to the band's opening at the Hollywood Palladium in the autumn. 'I'll Never Smile Again' was the big song, and Frank's fame was increasing.

Travelling with Tommy was a wildly happy experience for Frank. He developed a close comradeship with the musicians. Tommy was frequently late for rehearsal, and Frank would take over. When he finally showed up, looking weary, Dorsey never went to the trouble of apologizing for being late.

'I do what I ——ing want to,' Tommy said. 'Nobody tells me how to live my life.' Frank admired that.

Frank was perfecting his own breath control, learning to hold a phrase until it seemed that he had to burst his lungs; he got the idea from watching Tommy do the same with his trombone.

But he was thinking, 'I gotta get out on my own.'

Sinatra had several young crooners as competition. He especially feared Bob Eberle. Drummer Buddy Rich knew that and he once used it to take Sinatra down a peg or two.

Sinatra's popularity with the girls irritated Rich, who occasionally thumped so enthusiastically that Frank's singing was all but drowned out. Sinatra threw a tray of glasses at Buddy backstage. (He missed.) Buddy coached a girl into asking Frank for his autograph and then saying, 'Thanks, and if I can get three more of these, I'll be able to trade them all in for one of Bob Eberle.'

The popularity of 'I'll Never Smile Again' was building. Dorsey decided to re-record it with a greater emphasis on Sinatra. That pushed the record to Number 1 on the Hit Parade. Jo Stafford complimented Frank on working well with the Pied Pipers, blending his voice with theirs.

Even though it wasn't specifically his record, 'I'll Never Smile Again' gave him confidence. Friends noticed him getting cockier, and he began to be seen with women who were not Nancy Sinatra. He was grumbling about not making enough money. 'I could do better on my own,' he thought.

He was working hard—and successfully, he thought—cutting records with the Pied Pipers. The country heard him singing 'The One I Love Belongs to Somebody Else' and 'Whispering'. The kids who followed Frank with James knew a lot about him, but it was a struggle to sell records. Sinatra got a B-plus rating from *Metronome* magazine for 'The Night We Called It a Day' and 'Night and Day'. For two others he got a comment, 'He is not an impressive singer when he lets out—that's a cinch.'

Those criticisms hurt him then.

The late Manie Sacks, a hard-driving, aggressive young showman from Philadelphia, then head of Columbia Records, was approached about putting Frank under record contract if Frank decided to leave Dorsey. Sacks had to be sold on Frank. 'Bullets' Durgom was Frank's friend, and he gave it a hard sell.

'I don't want him,' Sacks said.

'But look how he can steal every show from Tommy!' Durgom argued.

'He could be a freak,' Sacks said.

Suddenly, however, Frank was Number 1 singer according to *Billboard*'s college poll. That was the dance crowd. He had knocked Bing Crosby out of top spot.

For Tommy, the news was both bad and good. The kid was going to be a hell of a headache. Dorsey wasn't even permitting the Sinatra name on his record labels. Instead the labels read 'Vocal Chorus'. That touched off an explosion by the Sinatra faction. It didn't change Dorsey until there were threats of a 'strike' by Frank. Dorsey gave in. Not long after, Dorsey said he would permit Frank to make solo records to his and Axel Stordahl's accompaniment.

Frankie was still unsure of himself at the recording sessions. The inside story was that Dorsey tricked Frank by arranging for his recording of 'The Song Is You' and other tunes to be brought out on Bluebird, a subsidiary label of Victor. They would be sold at half the Victor price, meaning half as much money for Frank. Frank wasn't wise enough to the business to have prevented Tommy from putting that over on him.

Frank soon sang his first solos: 'Night and Day', 'The Night We Called it a Day', 'The Song Is You' and 'Lamplighter's Serenade'. He was ecstatic when he heard them the first time in Hollywood, and he played them over excitedly. He was less than pleased, however, with the press comments; he didn't read anywhere that he was a singing genius.

But a disappointing review has never affected him long, and he went right on with 'There Are Such Things' a couple of months later. By Christmas 1942, when he was twenty-seven, that song had been on 'Your Hit Parade' for six weeks. Sinatra was almost unable to get off the bandstand whenever he appeared with Dorsey and the orchestra. The gossips around the Brill Building were saying that the situation had finally reached a breaking point.

Tommy's eyes got a steely look whenever he was up there on the stand playing for the boy to sing while the dancers he was playing for quit dancing. Tommy agreed with his proud mother, 'Mom' Dorsey, from the Pennsylvania coal mine regions.

'Anybody that can't sing with my Tommy playin' the trombone for him,' she said, 'ought to be shot.'

Tommy burned when he saw that in the minds of the song-pluggers Sinatra was getting to be more important than Dorsey.

'Do I really want to leave him?' Frank asked himself. 'I've got the best vocal spot in the business now!'

Frank liked Tommy and the battles and scrapes that made him colourful. (Once, Tommy and his beautiful wife, Pat Dane, got into a Hollywood fight in which screen actor Jon Hall's nose was almost severed with a knife and required thirty-two stitches. Nobody ever admitted anything. But Tommy grinned a lot and got considerable publicity.)

Frank consulted with black jazz band leader Sy Oliver, who was on the dance dates with Tommy. Predicting certain success for Frank, Sy encouraged him to go out for himself. 'Even then Sinatra had that spark and great belief in himself, and you knew he was going to be big. When he walked out on that stage, you knew he was in charge. Tommy was like that,' says Sy.

Sy Oliver watched Frank studying Dorsey's method of blowing the trombone seemingly without stopping to take a breath. 'Tommy never breathed where you thought he would breathe, so you never thought he was breathing. Frank learned to do the same thing from watching Tommy. I think it's a major reason for Frank's great success, and he got it from the boss.'

Years later, as a labour of love, Sinatra would do a recording, 'I Remember Tommy,' but in the summer of 1942, Frank was simply getting too big for Tommy. Tension increased. Dorsey broke house records, but it was due to Frank's fans, who screamed at him to stay onstage. It began to appear that it was Frank's orchestra and show, not Tommy's. And Frank's agents were already tentatively booking singles dates for him outside New York.

'Let him go,' shrugged Tommy. 'Might be the best

thing for me. Anyway, I got another crooner . . . Dick Haymes.'

'Frank and Tommy are finished,' was the word in Tin Pan Alley.

Frank suffered conscience pangs about going. Tommy had taught him much, including, he said later, 'how to be a doer instead of a talker'. He had a musician's respect—that word 'respect' again—for Tommy's command on the bandstand. He enjoyed Tommy's wild behaviour: squirting seltzer down the vocalist's bosom, leaving water-filled sponges on musicians' chairs, turning a garden hose on the band from the wings.

Years later Frank was to throw ice cubes at friends and squirt catsup or dump spaghetti on their new suits. He does it even today, and they pretend to like it.

After two and a half years, they split; Frank went out alone because he believed in Sinatra and thought his time had come. Frank was finally his own man, the Boss, the Star. In September 1942, he said good-bye to Tommy.

Tommy and his manager, Leonard Vannerson, worked out a financial deal that gave Frank his wish to be free. Tommy would get $33\frac{1}{3}$ per cent of his future earnings, and Vannerson would get 10 per cent. They took $43\frac{1}{3}$ per cent of Frank between them. Could he really give away that much of himself? Forty-three and a third per cent? Tommy was exacting his pound of flesh, and then some! Frank's ego was large enough that he believed he could overcome even that.

It was one of the best deals Tommy ever made for himself and probably one of the worst Frank ever made, but it left Frank free to start manoeuvring.

Did Frank call on 'friendly pressure' to get out of the deal later? A legend persists to this day that Frank succeeded in breaking his contract with Dorsey with the help of mobster friends. The thirty-year-old story goes that Dorsey refused to let him go.

'Somebody put a gun in Tommy's mouth and asked him whether he'd let Frank go. Under the circumstances, Tommy naturally said he would.'

That legend was incorporated into the movie, *The Godfather*. Although this story has been repeated many times, this author feels certain it is an untruth.

'It couldn't have been true,' says a source I trust. 'Frank was just a kid. He didn't know people like that. . . .'

Frank needed an agent. (A smarter artist would have lined up the agent before leaving Dorsey.) And agents, as always, wanted an established name. So when he went to MCA to ask them to represent him, he had to sit around waiting. It was Tommy's agency. They didn't want to upset Tommy by handling the kid who'd quit him. He got the message. They weren't fascinated by the chance to handle him

But Manie Sacks at Columbia Records, having been sold on Frank by 'Bullets' Durgom, was willing to help him and arranged for the MCA rival, General Artists Corporation, to represent him. Later on MCA would regret its chilliness to Frank and take him over from GAC and also help him buy out the Dorsey $33\frac{1}{3}$ per cent slice.

Finally, Frank was poised for his leap to grab on to Success.

Sinatra came to depend on Hank Sanicola, his solidly built, loyal pal from the Bronx, to help him in business. Frank once said, 'That son of a bitch would go down with the ship.'

Hank a couple of years older than Frank had strong fists, and though he didn't look for trouble, he didn't back away from it either. Word got around that Hank, carrying out what amounted to managerial duties, represented Frank fistically as well as fiscally. It was untrue. Frank was a bantam rooster himself. Hank hit like a mule and belted many a non-believer to the floor, but Frank was in there swinging, too.

In his dogged but unspectacular way, Hank Sanicola hustled Sinatra ahead. As the years went on, they started their own music company, bought into hotels and made investments that were enriching to both. They were eventually to part company after a difference that most of their friends thought could have been straightened out by mediators if the Sinatra emotions hadn't been involved.

When Hank Sanicola died at sixty in October 1974, a decade after their split, *Variety* said he was worth $4 million. At the peak of their quarrel, Frank had reportedly said, with a shrug, 'Give the —— the music company!' Four million dollars he gave him!

But that was to be a whole career away. In 1942 nobody was surer than Frank Sinatra that he would be very important. He had convinced Hank Sanicola and Manie Sacks, who were going to have rough days ahead. Worrying about his future, he remembered one day when two little bobby-soxers, trying to snatch his bow tie from his neck, got on either end of the tie and tugged, and almost strangled him. He'd have to depend on that fervour to make it now.

And he did. For nearly thirty-five years Frank's name has been in print somewhere, every day, and no year has passed without his name being in the headlines. Probably not an hour has passed without his voice being heard in song somewhere in the world. The movies he made when he was younger are constantly being re-run on TV. Some friends believe he fans the flames of the bad publicity and nurtures it to make Frank Sinatra 'bigger box office'. Nearly all these years, Frank has had the world on a string, and he did it all—or nearly all—by himself.

While on tour with Dorsey, Frank had grown gradually into a non-family man. With Nancy at home, he had other women. Partying was everybody's hobby—'Let's get some chicks, let's have a ball!' They were young, wild and healthy. At least they were usually healthy. Occasionally a musician got VD and was kidded about being temporarily out of action.

Hearing reports of these frolics, Nancy complained. Frank didn't deny them. He asked her if she wanted a divorce. From early in their marriage, he talked of divorce.

He was quite careless in his husbandly conduct. Once Nancy gave him a small ring. Much later, sitting one night in the Copacabana Lounge, she saw a ring suspiciously similar on the finger of one of the most beautiful Copa Girls.

'You want to hear what that son of a bitch did now?' she shrieked to girl friends. 'I'll kill him.'

But she loved him unreservedly, dieted for him, prayed for him and cursed him. She wanted to be more attractive for him, to be chic, and she got little encouragement from the husband who had a gift so great he probably wasn't aware of its potency.

Eventually, when divorce action was begun, Nancy was advised that locks on her home should be changed and that if she had intercourse with her husband even once, the divorce action would be negated. Days later she admitted she'd gone to bed with her husband.

'But you had the locks changed!' a friend said.

Nancy smiled and said, 'But I didn't lock the doors.'

'Frank's like an animal, a wonderful animal—a young bull,' one girl said. His sex adventures away from Nancy gave him momentary guilt feelings, but he attributed them to his unquenchable Italian thirst for more and more *amore*. His sex drive and his work drive were linked, with the sex drive powering the work drive. After the work, there would be more sexual gratification, and then more work. It was an endless treadmill, but a pleasant one for Frank. Sinatra knew little about Sigmund Freud, but he rationalizes his exploits by saying that he was the helpless victim of certain forces that were too strong for him to control. Although his infidelities bothered him, the hurt was minimal, because he had decided he couldn't help it. He learned much more about himself later in life when a psychiatrist told him he was a manic-depressive.

A SMASH AT THE RIOBAMBA—ALONE

Young Frank was flatpocket as he walked Broadway alone after breaking from Dorsey. Nobody rushed to offer him enormous salaries. He was ready to demonstrate how well he could do without Tommy, but there were no takers. He was scared that he might have jumped too soon.

Back across the river to New Jersey he went for his first important solo attempt—to the Mosque Theatre in Newark. He was surprised when squealy teenagers poured in, gushing that they'd heard him at Meadowbrook. When they went into their ecstasies, Frank grinned and said, 'This is my room.'

Bob Weitman, manager of the Paramount Theatre in New York, was coaxed into watching Sinatra work alone in Newark. He was impressed by the fans' enthusiasm. He'd only heard such squealing for Rudy Vallee. He knew Frank, of course, from his appearances with Dorsey.

Frank had been good, but not that well received, with Dorsey. Without the Dorsey paternalistic guidance, Frank was doing as he liked, and pleasing the kids more.

Coming up was the Paramount New Year's show to open 30 December 1942. It was to star Benny Goodman, the 'King of Swing'. Always willing to take a chance, Weitman asked Goodman if he had any objection to his booking Frank Sinatra as an 'Extra Added Attraction'. Benny showed he had no objection by asking, 'Who the hell is Frank Sinatra?'

After all, Frank was the leading vocalist according to *Billboard*, and he had replaced Bing Crosby in the polls.

He wasn't unknown. And so Weitman grinned his quiet grin and waited in the wings on opening day to see what would happen when Benny Goodman, without any long speech, simply said, 'And now, Frank Sinatra.'

It was school vacation time. The hundreds of kids rocked the theatre with their yelling, and Benny Goodman said, 'What the —— was that?'

What was that? It was the birth of a star.

Bob Weitman was to do a lot for and with Frank Sinatra from that day on. Frank was going to be bigger than Tommy Dorsey.

I was caught in these 'swooning' panics, or riots, as they came to be, in my reportorial duties and can attest that Frank generated as much sexual excitement among those bobby-soxers as the Beatles or Elvis Presley ever did. Moreover, I think the teenage girls were more in love with their Frankie. The Sinatratics, however, did not throw their panties or bras at Frank. They were too young for that.

The real Sinatra riots, which would make this first demonstration at the Paramount seem as nothing, came on Frank's return engagements. For this opener, however, he remained eight weeks—and of course the resulting publicity made Frank the hottest thing in Show Business.

One afternoon when Frank was playing the Paramount, I rode with him and a couple of members of his 'varsity' from the stage door to a radio rehearsal—in a taxi. (He hadn't yet attained limousine stature.) When I stumbled while getting into the cab, some little girls clawed through the open window, begging just to touch him, as though he were the Saviour.

A two-storey-high picture of Frank was displayed on the front of the Paramount. The cab driver, a Pentecostalist who didn't know who his passenger was, lectured us: 'Who are they glorifying?' he asked. 'Better they should glorify the Lord Jesus.'

In a couple of weeks, Frank had had four expensive suits ruined by the grabbing hands of the young adorers. With several shows at the Paramount each day, the radio rehearsal and radio show, plus occasional benefits, he often sang 100 songs a day.

He ate six or seven times a day—big dinners, desserts, French chocolates, sandwiches before singing. 'You gotta eat to belt those notes out,' he said. As a result of all the work and running, his weight sometimes dropped to 128, which made him only a shade fatter than the microphone. He liked sherry and Dubonnet before dinner. The only time his voice was weak seemed to be on misty days.

He hadn't much of a beard yet. 'Zoom, zoom, it's off,' he said.

Frightened at what could happen to him, Frank once ran into a liquor store on the corner. We barricaded the door. Later a cab driver drove up on to the sidewalk to load Frank inside to return to the theatre, to face another mob. Frank had to have a complete overhaul before going on-stage.

The girls waiting in the theatre let out shrieks when they heard he was on his way from his dressing room. A girl here or there would collapse and ushers would hoist her into her seat—a little roughly, because the ushers were getting disgusted with this conduct. It was hard work chasing the kids from the aisles back into their seats.

At last, Frankie came onstage with everybody standing, waving and yelling. From somewhere in the balcony came a male voice:

'Why, you can't even *see* the guy! He's so tiny, you can't even *see* the bum!'

And all the little girls would boo and hiss.

Frank had to devise strategies to avoid the kids. Once I rode with him in an NBC freight elevator. The kids hadn't discovered that yet. A car pulled up to the door of the big freight elevator, and we all jumped in.

A Broadway columnist for the Associated Press, the late George Tucker, wondered, cynically, whether somebody was paying for those squealy demonstrations for Sinatra and others. While he denied this and offered $1,000 reward to anybody who could prove the charge, press agent George Evans admitted that he had assembled the Sinatratics in the Paramount basements and coached them to yell and squeal when Sinatra bent certain notes.

'They shouldn't only yell and squeal . . . they should fall apart,' Evans said.

Frank crowed that he was just beginning, and the next time around at the Paramount he would have a riot that would knock them on their asses—a favourite expression of the 'King's' even then. Bob Weitman slapped Frank on the back and told him that Benny Goodman still didn't know what hit him, and gave him a hint that the Paramount would be paying bigger money next time.

Frank and Bob posed for pictures with arms around each other.

'What I want now, besides a good movie, is a big night-club,' Frank said.

The Copacabana would be a good spot for him, he thought. The Copa, a new basement club at 10 East Sixtieth Street, was playing such stars as Sophie Tucker, Ted Lewis, Jimmy Durante and Joe E. Lewis. The Copacabana management scoffed at the suggestion. 'Who ever heard of Frank Sinatra?' Frank got wind of that. Well, those bastards would hear of him.

A less brash kid than Frankie might have become discouraged because the best cafés told him to continue lullabying the bobbysoxers. But Frank was born with one of the big egos of history. He was as blushing a flower as de Gaulle, as reticent as Muhammad Ali, and he believed he had come along at the right time. The Bing Crosby adulation was waning; the time for Sinatra was ripe, and somehow Frank knew it.

America was deep in the war. On Broadway, there were soldier uniforms everywhere, the comedians were telling jokes about nervous draftees, and the shows would wind up with the song 'Praise the Lord and Pass the Ammunition'. When Frank Sinatra would walk into a club as a visitor, he saw workers from defence plants, who were making big money, spending their money on whiskey. Their wives were buying nylons, and their kids had money to spend on records.

Frank was lucky in having an agent who believed in him, the late Harry Kilby, head of the café department of General Artists Corporation. Kilby nicknamed Frank 'The Voice'.

' "The Voice," what the hell is that?' asked one of the café operators to whom Kilby was trying to peddle Sinatra.

'It's a gimmick,' admitted Kilby.

The clubs weren't buying him. Kilby got rebuffed a second time at the Copacabana. One turndown was so humiliating that Kilby didn't even tell Sinatra: The little Glass-Hat at the Belmont Plaza wouldn't touch him.

In his desperation, Kilby went to the struggling Riobamba Club on East Fifty-seventh Street, which he heard was near 'shuttering'. (That's the word we always used in those days. No club ever closed; it shuttered.) It had had a success with the popular and beautiful stuttering stage star, Jane Froman. But after some losing attractions, it was in trouble. The owners, sleek, slick, Artie Jarwood and quiet Linton Weil, resisted the Kilby sales talk about 'The Voice'.

One night Kilby was describing his grief to a Broadway press agent, Irving Zussman, who had been part-owner of a club with the late gangster moll, Virginia Hill. As Kilby moaned to Zussman that he couldn't even get the Riobamba to listen to Sinatra, Zussman had a thought. He and his partner, press agent Gertrude Bayne, were publicizing the Riobamba. If it closed, they'd lose a client, not to mention the back salary they had coming.

Partly to save the account, they pressed Artie Jarwood to hire Sinatra. Beautiful Gertrude Bayne was in her twenties, a Rita Hayworth look-alike, the girlfriend of the late Irving Hoffman, a publicist, play reviewer, columnist and artist, and an intimate of Walter Winchell. She could surely deliver some Winchell plugs for Sinatra.

'Sinatra's for kids,' Jarwood argued.

'No, he sings ballads. He can get the dames,' Zussman came back. Gertrude Bayne said Sinatra could bring in the ladies as Rudy Vallee had done at the Villa Vallee.

'I'll take a chance on him at $750 a week,' Jarwood finally said.

'You paid a hell of a lot more for Jane Froman and Benny Fields,' Kilby protested.

'But they're *Stars*!'

Kilby took it. The word got around Broadway that the Riobamba was going to take a chance on Sinatra. Some smart people were sceptical.

'This kid can hardly stand up,' they said. 'He holds on to

the mike like he was going to fall down if he doesn't.'

But Frank was the cockiest guy in town as he circulated the Fifty-second Street clubs getting ready for his début. The Riobamba management proceeded with caution. It booked a line of chorus girls called Russell Patterson's Cover Girls. Monologist Walter O'Keefe and singer-comedienne Sheila Barrett got top billing. That burned Sinatra. He was the 'Extra Added Attraction'. Sinatra, coming in to look the place over, said, 'They'll have to bust the walls of this joint.'

A great promotion campaign was launched—not for the stars, but for the 'Extra Added Attraction'. The newspapers were reminded that he had been the greatest thing that had ever happened to the Paramount. Bayne and Zussman called him 'Swoonatra', and the publicists promoted other variations of the name. 'He was an easy product to sell, because of the swooning connection,' they said later. 'Everybody went for it.'

One week before the event, I wrote in my column in the New York *Post* that 'Frank Sinatra, the Hoboken singer who has replaced Bing Crosby in some of the popularity ratings, begins an engagement at the Riobamba Thursday night.'

The big star of the New York nightclubs was Jimmy Durante at the Copacabana. Few of us thought that Sinatra would score against Schnozzola. But Sinatra won the town starting that March night in 1943, and a cute little seventeen-year-old brunette, Blanche Karo, a Sinatra fan clubber from Floral Park, Queens, whom I took to the opening, was a part of the show. The more sedate adults were not prepared for her hysterics. George Washington Hill, Morton Downey, Xavier Cugat, Sonny Werblin and Sherman Billingsly hadn't heard girls 'go on' as she did. Nor had Private Zero Mostel, who was in khaki.

'Ooooh, this is the most wonderfullll thing that ever happened in my life. They won't believe it,' she gasped. 'Oooooh, I won't be able to go to school tomorrow.' She was fighting for her breath. 'But I'll have to go so I can tell the other girls what happened!'

Frank was in a dinner jacket and was wearing a wedding

band. He had a small curl that fell almost over his right eye. With trembling lips—I don't know how he made them tremble, but I saw it—he sang 'She's Funny That Way' and 'Night and Day', and succeeded in bringing down the house, as we called it then.

A woman fainted. The reason she fainted, they still claim, is that one of the press agents turned up the heat so that somebody would be sure to faint.

Upon finishing the opening show, Sinatra came to my table and sat with my guest, Miss Karo. Frank turned her night into a dream by dancing with her.

It was a wondrous night for all of us who felt that we had a share in Frankie. Everybody seemed to like him—all those adults. The New York *Post*'s pop music critic, Danny Richman, leaned over to me and said, 'He sends me.'

Some of the oldsters—'the adults'—declared that not since Rudy Vallee had there been a birth of such a voice.

His fame snowballed. By Saturday, two nights after the opening, the Riobamba front door resembled the Paramount stage door when he was there. Autograph fans swarmed outside—unusual for a nightclub. Ethel Merman, Grace Moore and Gladys Swarthout went to hear him for themselves. The crush was so great that Broadway star Nancy Carroll had to stand near a telephone booth in the back.

Within a week, Frank Sinatra had changed from singer to national hysteria. I had to rush over to the Riobamba every night and try to squeeze in. I was witnessing one of the marvellous happenings of modern Show Business.

'What do I have to do to hear him sing?' fifteen-year-old Marjorie Wohl asked me by mail. 'I'm listening to one of his records now, and my heart is beating like a sledgehammer. Please tell me how I can get to hear him for my family is going crazy with me, I'm going crazy myself every time I hear "Night and Day" and "The Song Is You".'

His slenderness caught the public's attention. Comedian Jackie Miles said in his act at La Martinique, 'I was over to the Riobamba to see Frank Sinatra, and he's the only fellow in Show Business skinnier than I am. I also heard somebody say he was almost as ugly. He's so skinny that both of us are going to get together and do a single. Everybody applauds every song he sings and I know why. They think each song is going to be his last.'

His popularity soared. The papers and magazines were full of Sinatra. 'Your Hit Parade,' on which he sang, was booming. During the third week of his Riobamba engagement, he got word that he was going back into the Paramount Theatre in May at $2,500 a week. His last figure there had been $1,750 a week; his first had been $150 a week.

Romantic couples came to the midnight show. The women were mooning over Sinatra ballads. He had accomplished what the bosses had thought he could never do: he had won the adults.

He had also quite definitely made it alone—without Dorsey—first on the Paramount stage and then in a café.

Some astrologists have since contended that Sinatra, born 12 December 1915, and therefore a Sagittarius, is favoured by the stars. He fits the characteristics of the sign: a man of action, rebellious, sensitive to criticism, outspoken, generous, optimistic, annoyed at routine, never satisfied, always racing against time . . . inclined to bachelorhood.

His success at the Riobamba was due to the torrent of good publicity. Touching little stories were printed about his mother phoning from New Jersey to listen to his midnight show. Frank got a good press from the eight New York newspapers, the slick magazines such as *Life*, the *Saturday Evening Post* and *Collier's*, and the radio networks. Frankie did everything right. They liked him, they enjoyed him. He had needed the press; now he had the press. The press said Frank had humility.

Triumphant though the Riobamba engagement was for 'Skinatra', as one punster called him, it was disastrous for Walter O'Keefe and Sheila Barrett.

'Walter and I were supposed to be the stars,' says Miss Barrett, 'and opening night we could hardly get through the crowd that had come to see Frank. Walter was one of the best-known monologists, and he was pushed back by the little girls and almost had to beg them to let him through.

'Walter didn't like it. Frank's dressing room was filled with his managers, press agents and song-pluggers. The club was so crowded the chorus girls couldn't go on nor could a dance team booked first. I almost knocked the glasses off of Louis Sobol, the columnist, who was there with Jane Wyman.

'Frank was well prepared and very professional with his own sound system, own lighting, own conductor, Nat Brandwynne. The crowd was impatient for us to get off. The light would change, there was a hush, then big applause and there was Frank. They wanted Frank!'

Walter O'Keefe naturally couldn't stand Frank. Miss Barrett told him, 'Walter, it's a terrible thing to admit but perhaps for the first time an audience doesn't want to see us.'

O'Keefe began to thaw. Sheila Barrett grew to like Sinatra and today can't stand any criticism of him. They would have a drink at the tiny bar after the show, and Frank was pleased when she told him she'd worked the club before when there were black ties and no people. Now it was not black tie, but there were people. Frank used that observation in his act.

A chorus girl had a small engagement party they all attended. 'Frank,' Miss Barrett remembers, 'handed that little girl a box. Next day she was so proud of it. He had bought her a lovely little bracelet. The rest of us hadn't thought to do it.'

O'Keefe was also won over by Sinatra. He changed his introduction. 'When I opened here,' he told the crowd, 'I had top billing. But then a steamroller came along and knocked me flat. So now let me introduce you to the rightful star, Frank Sinatra!'

Frank's success at the Riobamba might never have happened. Two weeks before he went in there, he'd had a bad cold when he did a guest appearance at Benny Davis' Frolics and could hardly make himself heard. An advertising man for the Riobamba who was at the Frolics tipped off the others of the Riobamba that they might have booked a lemon, a turkey.

'Some lemon, some turkey!' he said later.

Caught up now in the swirl of success, Frank suddenly had new agents. He was parting from dear Harry Kilby. He was going to Hollywood to make a picture, and he was buying a $25,000 home in Hasbrouck Heights, New Jersey.

'So long, Artie,' Frank said to Artie Jarwood, as they embraced on closing night. 'After I finish my movie, you can have me again, if you want me.'

But by then the giants had to have Sinatra, and the Riobamba got bad news. Frank was next going to the Waldorf. His new management wouldn't honour his old management's contract. Lawyers advised Jarwood to sue.

'I never sued anybody, and I won't,' Artie insisted. 'Good luck, Frank,' Jarwood said. They remain friends to this day.

Milton Rubin, who'd been Sinatra's first press agent, remembers that he left Frank because Frank wanted an entourage and personal attention that Rubin couldn't give him. Frankie wanted to sit around Lindy's or the Stork Club, but Rubin was busy helping out Walter Winchell and gladly gave the job over to George Evans.

'Frank was already very proud. He liked to rush over to a New Jersey shirtmaker where he could get monogrammed shirts for five dollars. He liked to be recognized by the Holland Tunnel cops.'

Besides, there was the problem of Rubin's fifty-dollar-a-week salary. Frank got behind. Rubin asked one of the agents, Frank Cooper, to take it up with Frank. With some embarrassment, Cooper reported back, 'Nancy handles the money. She has a theory that if you keep somebody waiting for his money, he works harder till he gets it.'

Of that tumultuous time at the Riobamba, Irving Zussman remembers that one night a high-ranking police official wanted Frank's autograph for his daughter. One of Frank's stooges, one of 'the varsity', signed it. Zussman objected.

'In a case like this, couldn't you really have Frank sign it?' he said.

The stooge completed the autograph, reminding him, 'The King can do no wrong.'

INTO THE WALDORF AND OUT OF THE DRAFT

Within two weeks after closing his triumphant winter engagement at the Riobamba, Sinatra was booked at the Waldorf Wedgwood Room, the classiest supper club in America. The Copacabana now wanted him, and he could name his price. He was going to Hollywood. He was on the cover of *Life*. The intellectual and sophisticated magazines had discovered him. But press agent George Evans felt uneasy. The newspapers began asking about his draft status. Why wasn't he in uniform? And stories of Sinatra's romantic peccadilloes had reached the gossip columnists.

Frank began developing a toughness to criticism. But he was generally pleasant and modest, and he was being adopted by Café Society. He was seen dining now at the Colony or Stork Club or 21 or Voisin or Pavillon, although he was probably more comfortable with the sporting set at Toots Shor's. Toots called Frank a 'crum-bum' as he did all his close friends, and said, 'Don't tell anybody you eat here, Skinny, you're no ad for the joint.'

He began to give up the boyish-looking sweaters and bow ties, and wore impeccably tailored dark suits. He bought gold cigarette lighters at Dunhill's for special friends. He was a quick draw on a cigarette lighter himself, especially when he sat near a pretty woman. Sinatra got to know columnists Walter Winchell, Mark Hellinger and Ed Sullivan; and Phil Silvers, the comedian; Postmaster-General James Farley and the later Postmaster-General Bob Hannegan. He became a young man of the world.

Marilyn Maxwell, the beautiful, busty and very healthy blonde actress and singer, was the first woman mentioned in the gossip with Frank. 'Marvel' Maxwell had come to Show Business from Fort Wayne, Indiana, and titillated thousands of American soldiers when she toured with Bob Hope and USO camp shows. Living in one of the major New York hotels between pictures or tours, she saw Frank often.

Movie star Lana Turner was a formidable competitor. The public knew her as the heroine of a press agent tale that claimed she'd been 'discovered' while sitting at the soda fountain at Schwab's Drug Store in Hollywood. George Evans was alarmed that stories about their romance would break into print. One night while Lana Turner was waiting for Frank, who was busy with another admirer, she fumed, 'Where is the skinny little son of a bitch? I'll fix his wagon!'

Hollywood called him before he could get to the Waldorf. Arriving there for a concert with the Hollywood Bowl Symphony Orchestra, Frank was almost trampled by several thousand girls who had heard that he was trying to avoid them by getting off the Santa Fe *Chief* at Pasadena. Undoubtedly, the girls had been tipped off by Frank's fan club.

The newspapers screamed almost as much as the girls—about such a ridiculous thing as a crooner appearing with a symphony, and about Frank's sex allure. He sold out the Bowl, but there were Bronx cheers—even in California—from some of the males. Frank had grown accustomed to the furor in New Jersey and New York, but the shock of thousands of Californians trying to get to him, and thousands more screaming when he sang to them, left Frank more impressed with himself than he'd ever been, and also thankful.

George Evans was playing both sides of the street. He was getting stories printed that Frank was a love object and also a serious musician. George got one of the papers to print that the crooner's secret lure was love. He was a dreamer and a romanticist. At the same time, Frank said he had a hobby—collecting symphony albums, of which he had 500.

When Frank was trying to get nightclub jobs in New York

not much more than a year earlier, he had been called to Hollywood to do one song, 'Night and Day', in a film called *Reveille with Beverly* at Columbia. He didn't get billing. Now, however, after the Bowl concert, RKO was bringing him out as a star in *Higher and Higher*, and the celebrated tunesmith Jimmy McHugh was knocking out songs for him.

Frank cavorted with Michele Morgan and Jack Haley, tried to do a dance with the help of Paul Hartman and kidded around with Victor Borge and Leon Erroll. Believing he was making great strides forward, Sinatra was a little dejected when Bosley Crowther's review headline in the New York *Times* suggested that *Higher and Higher* should have been called *Lower and Lower*. It was no loss, however, for he returned to New York with a contract for another picture.

Frank tried to be philosophical when *Higher and Higher* was reviewed. Bosley Crowther, besides joking about the title, said Frankie 'is no Gable or Barrymore. He is graciously permitted to warble and ooze out what passes for charm'. Howard Barnes commented in the *Herald-Tribune* on Frank's 'ugly bony face'.

Frank finally met Bing Crosby, his hero, in Hollywood, and asked Bing what to do about reviews. 'Pay 'em no mind,' Bing said. Frank confessed his financial troubles—he had practically nothing left for himself after paying managers, ex-managers and taxes. 'What do I do?'

'Tell them that when you're nervous, you can't sing.'

Frank was also rocketing along successfully on records, despite a musicians' strike that forced the record companies to turn out songs with only vocal backgrounds. His friend Manie Sacks negotiated a contract with Columbia that got Frank $360,000 in advances. Frank plunged to work in the studio on 'You'll Never Know' and 'People Will Say We're in Love', and made both of them Number 1 on the Hit Parade. Later, Manie Sacks was to leave Columbia and go to RCA. Frank was to get into many disputes with Mitch Miller, later of 'Sing Along with Mitch' fame, who took over at Columbia.

Shrewd manipulator Manie saw Frank getting into big money, but handing most of it over to the Tommy Dorsey–

Leonard Vannerson partnership, which took 43⅓ per cent. Everybody was on a percentage.

'I don't have any per cent left for myself,' lamented Frank.

It took the best brains of several lawyers, working with Manie, to open the gates of riches for Frank. Manie manoeuvred for Frank to leave the management of General Artists Corporation and go to the Music Corporation of America, which would buy out Frank's contract from Dorsey and Vannerson for $60,000. Then MCA would represent Frank. MCA was the more prestigious and powerful. At last, Frank was into the big money and he was no longer in slavery to Tommy. There would be big movie possibilities. He would be able to do outside pictures, away from RKO. It seemed true, as the stooges said: The 'King' could do no wrong.

Although Frank in his later years has called himself the last of the saloon singers, he wanted to prove his serious musicianship when he was starting. 'I'm no damn freak; I've worked; nobody's worked harder,' he'd say. He wanted their respect as a musician, not just as Number 1 crooner. Experts now say he was, in his way, a singing genius. But in the forties there was scepticism about him, especially when he made a surprise starring appearance at the Lewisohn Stadium in New York as soloist with the New York Philharmonic Orchestra. It was a brave try. The critics, however, wouldn't take him seriously.

'An amazing phenomenon, more revealing sociologically than from a musical standpoint . . . a facet of American culture revealing itself in all its effete nakedness,' wrote Paul Bowles of the New York *Herald-Tribune*. 'He sang harmless Tin Pan Alley tunes to a chorus of hysterical feminine voices synchronizing their screams as he closes his eyes and moves his body sideways.'

Frank was unsure of the symphonic accompaniments. Trying to give it a light touch, he referred to the proud members of the Philharmonic Orchestra as 'the boys in the band'. The audience was extremely small—only about 7,000.

Continuing to try to prove he was more than a crooner,

Sinatra apprised Alec Wilder, the composer and 'musician's musician', that he wanted to conduct some of his compositions for Columbia Records.

'You're out of your mind,' Wilder laughed. 'You can't read music.'

'But I can do it, I can conduct.' Frank pressed his request on Manie Sacks, who also objected. But Frank got his way.

Arriving for the recording session looking nervous, he threw himself on the mercy of 'the strings'. In a burst of humility, Frank said, 'This is wonderful music. Let's do something with it. I can't read, but I'll follow the soloist.'

Responding gallantly to his appeal, the fiddlers gave their all. It worked. Frank had made long-hand notes on the sheet music with such directions as 'Enter Cello Here'.

The musicians applauded Frank. When the resulting music was brought out in an album, Sinatra protested that Wilder's name wasn't as big as his on the cover, and the cover had to be redone. The musicans agreed with Wilder that 'that was a nice guy'.

When Frank went into the elegant Waldorf on 1 October 1943, some of us who were his fans were worried about that engagement. It was very complimentary for a star to play two big New York rooms in six months, but it might also be dangerous because there might not be enough customers for two appearances. The Waldorf was more aristocratic, more sophisticated and harder to please than most other nightclubs.

I'm one of the handful of survivors of the two openings. They were both memorable and dramatic. A boy was fighting his way up to greatness.

The headline on my column on 2 October 1943, read:

SINATRA WINS THE SCEPTICS IN OPENING AT THE WALDORF.

Seldom had success happened to anybody in Show Business so swiftly.

Frank, without the curl down in his eyes, without as much of the sexy trill, walked before the mike in perhaps the haughtiest room in America and faced a non-swooning crowd, which included Will Hayes, Cole Porter, Clifton Webb, Ruth Draper, Larry Adler and Meyer Davis. The actress Constance Bennett was there. She added to the elegance of the evening.

Many people who went to convince themselves that he was some kind of press agent's dream left persuaded that he was great.

Frank took me up to his hotel room, along with his 'varsity', after he'd finished and admitted he'd been nervous.

'If I hadn't been, I'd be a self-satisfied guy, and that would stink,' he said. Frank said that while getting into a shower just before going on, he'd slipped on a bath mat and had come close to braining himself.

Frank's young admirers would have wanted more squealy stuff, but Frank accurately figured that the opening night Waldorf crowd would be ten to fifteen years older.

One punster said, 'No matter how important they were, Frank whittled them down to their sighs.'

People were talking about Sinatra, even in the other clubs. Comedian Joe E. Lewis at the Copacabana made numerous references to Frank, who had already become his friend. 'Frank Sinatra looks like an advance man for a famine,' Joe E. said. 'If he ever gets an Academy Award, it'll be for his sunken chest.'

One day I inserted a Poet's Corner in my column, printing a contribution by a young man named Larry Siegel, who today is a top comedy writer.

Oh Dear, What Can Sinatra Be?

A hanging curl, two dreamy eyes,
Looks that swirl to distant skies,
The unconscious girl sits and sighs.

A quivering lip
Blaring lovesick rhyme,
Her insides flip in double time.

A slender frame with sagging knees
Yet garnering fame with uncanny ease
The stricken dame pants the breeze.

Eyes of blue, two hands alike
Stretching forth true
Lovingly to strike
Close to you? No, his mike.

Although this lank's
The latest thing
He'll never outrank the 'groaning' king
You take Frank, I'll take Bing.

Elsa Maxwell, the party-giver, the columnist, the prophet of Café Society, glared at all this foolishness and deplored it. It was some kind of a disgusting epidemic. These 'emotionally unstable females were parading naked and unashamed for the drooling, crooning, goonish syllables of a man who looked like a second-string basketball player'.

George Evans got Frank to meet Elsa and arranged for her to hear him at the Waldorf. Elsa changed her tune about him. 'He has found a setting to show off the sweetness of his voice,' she said.

Another posh columnist, Cornelius Vanderbilt, braved the Waldorf to observe this emaciated-looking creature. 'His modesty and dignity are superb,' he wrote, 'his mike technique was reminiscent of Bonnie Baker.' When Sinatra sang the room was quieter than the Supreme Court, and even Lawrence Tibbett of the Metropolitan Opera 'had fallen under Sinatra's hypnotic call.'

The Waldorf had printed 36,000 menus with his picture to simplify the autograph problem. On closing night, the girls pressed forward with their menus. A flying wedge of waiters boxed him in, ready to rush him to his room. Frank said to them, 'Wait a while,' and went to greet his fans and sign his name. It was a human gesture by Sinatra, who laughed and joked with the girls who stood on tiptoe trying to reach him over the heads of the other girls.

One fan was waving her souvenir—Frank's pocket handkerchief—above her head. Announcing that she'd snatched it from his pocket, she said that it had some cologne on it, which caused several other girls to shriek, 'I want to smell it.' A Brooklyn girl ecstasized about her special autograph, 'To Gloria, Frank Sinatra, No. 35'.

She explained that it was the thirty-fifth time he'd given her an autograph and that he always remembered how many times he'd signed for her.

The girls who'd been fans for a couple of years were critical of the new Sinatratics. 'They think it's smart to pull his hair and ties and follow him in cabs and paw him and scream,' one of them told me. 'They spilled ink on his new camel's hair coat. I mean he spilled it on himself when they crowded him too much. I think they're rotten to him.'

In the beginning, the cops weren't sympathetic to the singer who drove women crazy. But Sinatra brought them records for their daughters and gave them Saint Christopher medals and went with them to Mass. And they were soon fans, too.

The female fans were getting wilder. One day Sinatra had just finished getting his hair cut at a midtown New York barber shop when some girls rushed in and persuaded the porter to give them the trimmings from Sinatra's hair—right out of the dustpan.

Every time a young girl ran away from home, some policeman thought she had followed Sinatra to Pittsburgh or Boston. George Evans set about to change his image—probably the first time that anybody tried to change Sinatra's image. A woman living on Park Avenue wrote that her 'indolent, lazy thirteen-year-old niece' would only do her school work properly if appealed to by Sinatra. Frank did make appeals for regular school attendance and diligent study.

Frankie became a fad, a fashion, a rage, a hurricane, a household word, a jest, a Cinderella story, a subject for columnists to dwell upon in 'think pieces', a subject for dinner table debates. He was the new wonder boy, the greatest thing in the entertainment business in recent times, and he was also a tough kid who had taken on many bigger guys and licked them.

Often he sat quietly thinking of the miraculous thing that had happened to him. He felt humble, and he expressed his thanks in one way he knew. He bought presents for those who had helped him. He would do it all his life.

*

In 1943, the draft board was waiting for Frankie.

He got his greeting in November: he was classified 1-A, and his induction was set for 12 January 1944.

Hysterical groans went up from the girl swooners. Frank didn't complain. 'I'll go any time they say,' he said. 'My wife is going to have another baby in a couple of months. I hope it's a boy.' Singer Jack Leonard had gone into service and disappeared. It could happen to him.

Sitting on some steps at Madison Square Garden one night in a checked sports coat, green tie and slacks, he said he had $300,000 worth of contracts he'd lose if the army took him.

'Just look at Joe DiMaggio and Hank Greenberg,' he said, referring to the biggest baseball stars. 'They both had a chance to make a lot of money, and they went.'

There to root for his prizefighter friend Tami Mauriello, whom he also helped 'manage' as a backer, Frank pretended to be unconcerned, but behind the scenes his manager and press agent were panicky. One or two big stars were rumoured to have pretended to be 'psycho' to get rejected. Sinatra was in good physical condition, intelligent, active, a good subject for the growing army. His managers and press agent had reason to be scared.

On 9 December 1943, the New York *Post* headlined:

THE ARMY SWOONS—SINATRA IS 4-F.

'Relax, girls,' wrote Naomi Jolles. 'Frank Sinatra was rejected for military service today because of a punctured eardrum.' The tone of most of the stories about his 4-F was that he'd been saved just for the good of the bobby-soxers.

He'd undergone an hour-and-fifteen-minute physical examination at the Newark induction centre. Leaving the armoury, looking weary after having travelled all night from Boston, where he'd broken records at a movie house, Frank said, 'It wasn't an ordeal. I found out a lot of things about myself that I didn't know and a few things I'd better take care of right away.'

'That "hole in my ear" I didn't know about.' He believed

that it was the result of a series of mastoid operations between the ages of three and seven.

Frank 'looked disappointed' about his rejection, the paper said, and they quoted him as saying, 'I was planning to ask for the Marines if they'd have me.'

Very little had been said about the punctured eardrum before his examination. His camp was more than relieved about the 4-F because the way was clear to great things—big promotions, big career, big money.

Frank was enraged at one comedian who asked on a nightclub floor, 'How do you get a punctured eardrum?' Frank didn't think that was fair. Hadn't he taken his examination like everybody else?

It didn't lessen his popularity, although in one theatre a boy threw a couple of eggs at Frank. One egg connected. Later it proved to have been set up so that a newspaper could get a picture of Frank being splattered. Frank's publicists said the egg-thrower was a boy who was jealous because his girlfriend was crazy about Frankie. 'If my gal swooned, I'd do the same,' Frank said.

At his most charming now, Frank was 'so disarmingly modest that he leaves a reporter shaken', Ted O'Gorman said after an interview in which Frank said he really wasn't a success yet.

But the girls were unshaken in their delirium over him. Two bobby-soxers went to his home and pleaded with Nancy to give them a pair of his shorts from the clothes'-line. Nancy declined the honour on behalf of his shorts. The girls thereupon begged for the clothes'-pin that held up the shorts. Mrs. Sinatra gave them The Clothe's-pin That Held Up Frankie Sinatra's Shorts.

Suddenly, and terrifyingly, for Frank, his draft status came up again. The New York *Daily News* needled him with a headline:

WHEE-EE! SWOON! FRANKIE'S NOW IN 2-A

Upon re-examination of his status, draft officials deferred him because he was in a profession 'necessary to the national health, safety and interest', and besides, he wasn't physically fit to serve. The Sinatra case had gone from

Newark to Fort Jay in New York to Washington, where army officials looked over the papers and decided that he was a 4-F in an essential job—a 2-A.

Though there was grumbling about the decision from show people in uniform, that was the end of it except for the snide remarks by Westbrook Pegler, who hated Sinatra because Sinatra adored Franklin D. Roosevelt.

Frank was looking forward to seeing something of his son now.

Nancy had given birth to Francis Wayne Sinatra, Jr., in Jersey City on 10 January 1944. The father was making a movie, *Step Lively*, at RKO in Hollywood. Some people around him wanted to play down the father stuff and references to Nancy. George Evans disagreed; he wanted Frank to keep a family-man image. While some said Frank was on an unstoppable steamroller with no room for a female, George Evans snapped, 'Nuts to that.'

THE GOSSIP IS HEARD

Frank Sinatra discovered power, the Hollywood kind. Nancy, Sr., saw her husband become a movie star and she was scared.

Every day was ego-building. Movie-making was vanity, and Frank already had enough vanity. One day Frank read an article in the *New Republic* by Bruce Blivens that said Sinatra was 'a genuine mass phenomenon', who with his sexy singing inspired 'an hysterical orgy comparable to the Children's Crusade'. Frank was surprised to learn that he was compared with an event in the year 1212 when French and German children undertook to recover Jerusalem from the Saracens and were mostly drowned or sold into slavery.

Bruce Blivens had written of the 'orgy' inspired by Sinatra after having seen the Sinatra 'Columbus Day Riots', which broke out when he returned to the Paramount Theatre in October 1944, during the time he was shuttling between New York and Hollywood. These unbelievable demonstrations gave Sinatra still more self-assurance.

Frank got into the empty Paramount Theatre at 6.00 a.m. Already a thousand girls were in line to buy tickets. Some had been there since 3.00 a.m. They were yelling 'We want Frankie, we want Frankie.' The theatre opened at 8.30 a.m. and was filled.

The bobby-soxers were there only to see Frankie. They paid no attention the the movie, *Our Hearts Were Young and Gay*.

The next day was much worse, because there was no school. Finishing up my column around 5.00 a.m., I ventured down to Times Square on foot and was literally scared away.

The police estimated that 10,000 kids were queued up six abreast on Forty-third Street, Eighth Avenue and Forty-fourth Street and that another 20,000 were running wild in Times Square, overrunning the sidewalks and cars, making Traffic movement almost impossible.

Over on Fifth Avenue, a Columbus Day parade was forming. Two hundred cops were taken off guard duty there and rushed over to the Sinatra riots. Eventually there were 421 police reserves, twenty radio cars, two emergency trucks, four lieutenants, six sergeants, two captains, two assistant chief inspectors, two inspectors, seventy patrolmen, fifty traffic cops, twelve mounted police, twenty policewomen and 200 detectives trying to control some 25,000 teenage girls.

Girls shrieked, fainted—or swooned—fell down, were stepped on and pulled up by their companions and resumed screaming. They rushed the ticket booth and damaged it. Windows were broken.

Sinatra was a prisoner inside. Food was brought to him from Sardi's famous theatrical restaurant next door.

The cries of 'Frankie, Frankie' were heard blocks away. And there was a rumble like distant thunder from those outside. Inside, most of the girls sat in their seats after the first show. They were going to stay for another show. They were going to stay the whole day.

'I won't be able to get out of here all day!' Frankie said gloomily.

'You'd be killed, you'd be torn limb from limb,' George Evans said.

'You started this with your swooning stories,' somebody told George Evans. George grinned, pleased.

'Who, me?' he said.

Everybody was probing into the personality of the 'Moonlight Swoonatra', the 'Prince of Swooning', the 'Doctor of Swoonology', the great 'Swoondoggler'.

The *New Yorker* magazine ran a series of profiles by E. J.

Kahn, Jr. Kahn found that the bobby-soxers read the gossip columns to keep track of their hero. 'Earl Wilson is their old reliable,' he said. 'He has maintained closer liaison with Sinatra than any of his competitors. So many Sinatra fans read Wilson that he prints intra-Sinatra bulletins like "Note to Sinatra fans: Don't try to mob Frankie when he arrives shortly. Let him alone, for he's busy".'

The E. J. Kahn series and his subsequent book, *The Voice*, revealed to me my standing. According to Kahn, Sinatra had spent thousands of dollars for gold cigarette lighters for close friends; to headwaiters, he gave gold money clips. That's what he gave me: a clip inscribed 'Oil, Youse is a Poil.'

Sinatra made his Hollywood entrance simultaneously with this newest hullaballoo at the Paramount. He was bucking up against a hardened world that would harden him.

Confronting the studio kings who had ruled for years and were rich, rich, rich, he was again the kid fighting the boy bigger than he was. They were annoyed at his advance hints that he was going to do pictures his own way just as he sang his own way.

The Hollywood gossip columnists were also waiting for Frankie. They even had spies in the dressing rooms and the ladies' toilets. Many a story of a glamour girl's sudden 'engagement' or 'elopement' was the result of a columnist's finding from a wardrobe mistress that the beautiful star had missed two periods and decided she'd better fall in love and get married immediately. These people were waiting to pounce on Frank.

Breezing on to the scene with his usual confidence and charm, Frank found immediate acceptance from the working actors.

'Prince' Mike Romanoff, the restaurateur, became a pal. 'Everybody' ate there. Humphrey Bogart boasted to Frank that he had made an investment in the restaurant and that Mike had never bought him a drink. Restaurateurs Dave Chasen and Charlie Morrison, of the Mocambo, liked Frank because he talked to them about spaghetti and clam sauce. He also tipped well. He became an intimate of MGM Producer Joe Pasternak, who told him the sex gossip he heard in the MGM dining room.

Anchors Aweigh with Gene Kelly, Frank's first important film, brought him his first collision with a studio. Determined that two friends, lyricist Sammy Cahn and composer Jule Styne, should do the music, he ran into resistance from the studio, which said Sammy Cahn wasn't known. They wanted a 'known'.

Embarrassed at being an unknown instead of a known, Cahn found himself becoming known. 'But,' he said, 'with everybody hating me, because I was the centre of the argument.' He told Frank, 'Look, I'll get other chances. If this is so big they want somebody else, let them have somebody else.'

Frank stood firm. 'Sam, you be there Monday morning, and you tell Jule to be there, or I won't be!'

The studio yielded.

Frank worked hard on the picture, getting along well with Gene Kelly and Kathryn Grayson. He knew he had a unique style. His secret was that he sang songs in a personalized way, in an unbroken flow, almost coddling the lyrics. He made the listeners feel that he was singing to them. He believed he could pull off the same trick on the screen.

Sinatra wanted to see some rushes and, now accustomed to getting his way, he asked for a screening.

'You can't see them,' Pasternak said. 'It's against studio policy.'

'Screw studio policy, I'm going to see them,' Sinatra said.

Pasternak liked rebels, he was rebellious himself. 'We never let actors see them,' Joe tried to explain. 'The reason is that they never like the way they look. They want us to shoot everything over and if we did that, we'd never finish the picture. It's for your own good that we do this, believe me.'

'I want to know how I look, and I'm going to see them!' insisted Sinatra.

Pasternak spoke to Sinatra in a lowered voice. 'Listen, I'm not supposed to do this, but I'll make an exception and let you see them. Just you, though, and nobody else.'

Sinatra felt the satisfaction of enforcing his power again, and he liked it. For the secret screening of the rushes, he arrived with six people. Pasternak exploded. 'No, you can't do it. I said just for you. Not for half a dozen.'

'I'm walking off the picture,' Sinatra announced.

'So walk!' Pasternak shouted. 'The studio'll back me up because it's got a strong rule about it.'

Sinatra 'walked', but he also walked back because he wanted this film. The press got word of the incident, and one columnist reported it with the inference that Frank was already getting a swelled head.

In the future he was to battle with one director after another, berating them for sacrificing spontaneity by shooting scenes over and over. It was very early in his career that they nicknamed him 'One-Take Charlie'. He accepted it—and liked it.

Nancy confessed to girlfriends her concern over their marriage. She had a new Cadillac and jewellery and luncheon dates, but she wasn't sure about Frank. Lacking the sophistication, worldliness and artificial beauty of some of the starlets and stars, Nancy frequently wasn't a good companion for the country's fastest rising star. She could no longer amuse him with a joke; he'd already heard everything before she did. She was no match for the half-dressed lovelies. She was part of Hoboken and his walk-up past. Nancy moved furniture from New Jersey to a new home in the Toluca Lake section of Los Angeles, not far from Bing Crosby's home. But it seemed shabby there instead of gay and bright and California-ish.

Nancy sometimes wondered whether Hollywood wasn't one big brothel. MGM was Number 1 studio, and the stories of sex adventures in the executive offices after lunch were lurid.

Edgy and irritable, Frank was also worried about the marriage. He was also very busy with deals and negotiations. He was seeing more display of personal power every day.

Then he met President Franklin D. Roosevelt at the White House and saw what power really was. His friend Toots Shor had long wanted to meet the President in private and mentioned it to a customer and friend, Democratic National Committee Chairman Robert Hannegan. In September, Hannegan notified Shor that the President was inviting him to tea. There would be about twenty people present.

'Could I bring Sinatt?' Toots asked, using his pet name for Sinatra. 'And could I bring Rags?' That was Rags Ragland, the big lantern-jawed comedian from burlesque who'd gone into pictures.

Hannegan asked FDR's secretary, Marvin McIntyre, whether he could bring these rather questionable characters and received approval.

The President knew of Sinatra's fame, and when Frank was presented to him at the White House, FDR looked him over and, noting his slimness, said to McIntyre, 'Mac, imagine this guy making them swoon. He would never have made them swoon in our day, right?'

When the three returned from Washington, I caught up with them at Ruby Foo's restaurant having a late supper—and celebrating.

The White House visit had made them elated, but quite humble. Frank was in the presence of his elders (he was not thirty yet), and he didn't interrupt as Toots described the tea, coffee and cake session with the President. Toots kept saying, 'I was nervous. I kept thinking, "A bum can go in and see the President. A crooner, a restaurant guy and a burlesque comic can go call on the Prez!" I kept eating cake to keep myself busy. It was damned good cake. I wish I could get the recipe for my joint. Sinatra did a Sinatra. He fainted.'

Of course Frank didn't faint. He interested FDR very much. The President asked Sinatra if he knew how he made women swoon, of how he 'revived the charming art of fainting'.

'No, I wish to hell I did know,' Sinatra said.

Sinatra's photograph with his two pals made page one in many papers the next day. They were shown at the White House, and the remark about 'the charming art of fainting' was printed. It was all to the good for Sinatra.

Rags Ragland said to Roosevelt as they were leaving, 'Well, Mr. President, it looks like Mr. Dewey's gonna be the next governor of New York.'

'He didn't answer but he smiled,' Rags told me. 'It wasn't anything great, but it was just something to get off with.'

There were repercussions from that White House visit. A Baltimore political pundit suggested it was 'a cheap little publicity stunt'. Some senators shrieked that FDR had more compelling and worthwhile things to do for the country than to be sitting around with crooners and saloonkeepers and burlesque comedians.

Sinatra immediately donated $7,500 to the Democratic party—a sum that he couldn't afford at the time.

Frank was exhilarated by that experience and transferred his political affections over to Harry Truman when he became President. He played a dirty little trick on Governor Thomas E. Dewey when he was on a vote-getting tour around New York four years later. Learning that Dewey was going to make a stop at the Waldorf Hotel entrance to receive applause, Frank arranged to get there simultaneously. Seeing Sinatra, the crowd lost interest in the embarrassed Dewey, who waved weakly and made no effort to compete. The trick angered anti-FDR columnist Westbrook Pegler, who increased his criticism of Frank and his friends. Frank threatened to punch Pegler, but it never got beyond scowls at each other in nightclubs.

Once Frank sat not far from then Vice-President Truman in Shor's. Truman was about to leave. There was an autograph crowd at the door. As the man soon to become President got to the door, the crowd groaned, in disappointment, 'Aw, we wanted Frankie!'

Anchors Aweigh was one of MGM's biggest money-makers and that convinced Frank of something he'd already suspected—that he was great movie material. It built up his already well-built self-confidence. Typical of his moodiness, he was soon telling everybody off: the columnists, movie companies, recording companies and networks. He was screaming at George Evans, who was trying to get him to be less public about his affection for Marilyn Maxwell.

Surprisingly, he had a misunderstanding with Toots Shor over Marilyn Maxwell.

(Frank had become saloon-broken at an early age; it was part of his maturing. He was his most natural self when he was sitting at the Copacabana listening to comedian Joe E. Lewis say 'You're my kind of people—drunks.')

Around the Sinatra home in Hollywood, there were increasing unhappiness and signs of an imminent break-up. It came out in the open with the approaching world heavyweight championship fight between Joe Lewis and Billy Conn. Since Conn was an habitué of Shor's, it was assumed that Shor would be there with his wife, and Frank and his wife. Toots was stunned to learn that Frank intended to take Marilyn Maxwell.

Protesting that this would be a virtually public announcement that Frank had abandoned Nancy, Toots refused to participate. Manie Sacks and George Evans joined in squelching Frank's plan by making a direct appeal to Marilyn Maxwell.

Frank sat with Marlene Dietrich and Joe DiMaggio at the fight. Miss Dietrich said later that Frank was a champion, too—a champion lover.

The Marilyn Maxwell incident did not chill his friendship with Toots Shor. Frank could not foresee that he would be in dismal decline in a few years and depend on Toots to appeal to Bob Hope to put him on TV. 'Don't worry about "Bones",' Bob said. 'I'll have him on my next show.' Frank never forgot that Toots and Bob helped him at a critical time. To round out history, Toots could not foresee that one day *he* would be broke and Frank would advance him over $300,000 to stay in business.

Now the rumour-spreaders were talking about Frank and Lana Turner as well as Frank and Marilyn Maxwell. Sinatra was on the verge of getting very rich. With an MGM $1.5-million-a-year contract, records and radio, he could make more than $40,000 a week! He was overworking, but loving it—he was also yelling at people.

The fact that something's always happening to Sinatra, something that goes counter to something that's just happened to him, intrigues those who follow his life. He's always very high or very low.

On 20 August, his friend Rags Ragland, who had just had an over-festive vacation in Mexico, died in a Los Angeles hospital with Frank and Phil Silvers at his bedside. His personal effects included a cigarette case inscribed 'From Riches to Rags—Frank.'

The Copacabana in New York had booked Ragland with Phil Silvers for a 5 September opening. The Copa insisted that Silvers carry out the contract. He didn't feel that he could. The club insisted.

'I'd come in, but I can't leave the picture,' Frank said. It was *It Happened in Brooklyn.* Phil Silvers understood.

Phil's dinner show was depressing. Sitting nervously in his dressing room waiting for the next show, Silvers looked up and saw Frank Sinatra standing in the doorway, smiling. He had flown in to be Phil's stooge. Frank sat at the ringside when the show began.

'Turn up the lights,' Phil told the electrician. 'If there's anybody here famous, I'll introduce them.' He looked over the crowd, directly at Sinatra. 'Turn down the lights,' he said.

Phil touched his tie—a prearranged signal. Frank strolled on to the floor, and the crowd jumped up yelling. Frank submitted to taking Phil's singing lesson—as part of the act Silvers slapped his pupil for being so stupid. Leaving the floor without taking a bow, Frank returned to his seat, to another ovation.

When he finished, Silvers called Sinatra to the mike. They bowed together. 'May I take a bow for Rags?' Silvers said. Men and women, including some supposedly hardened nightclub owners, cried openly. Frank looked grimly at the floor.

Sinatra was a hero again. *Variety* headlined its story:

SINATRA'S STOOGERY FOR PHIL SILVERS NITERY PREEM AN INSPIRED EVENT.

It said Sinatra's gesture 'understandably sets him in a niche all his own in the big sentimental heart of show business'.

But seeing his dear friend Rags leave him made Frank

extremely sad. He became so upset eventually by funerals that he could seldom attend them. He shrank from being a witness to death, from watching those close to him being wheeled by the pallbearers down that church aisle and out towards the cemetery. His sensitivity to funerals revealed a side of his character completely opposite the usual picture of a brawler. Years later when services were being held for one of his very dearest friends, comedian Joe E. Lewis, Frank pledged to attend and reiterated right up until the last hour that he would be there. The mourners waited in the chapel past the scheduled starting time until Frank finally confessed by phone that he couldn't do it. The service went on without him.

Back to the Frank-and-Nancy situation, which threatened to explode at any moment: It got worse.

Nancy patiently endured his restiveness. In the nightclubs where he sang so romantically, he was often snappish and easily annoyed, and not as polite to some of his boosters as we thought he should be. A few times he forgot the lyrics of his songs. In Hollywood, fellow actors claimed he took only half-hearted interest in his scenes and was generally uncooperative.

He was made more insecure by the fact that Bing Crosby had replaced Frank Sinatra as Number 1. Spike Jones, the slapstick band-leader, tried to start a funny feud between them. When Bing was briefly in a hospital, Spike sent him a bedpan. In the bedpan was a framed picture of Frank Sinatra. The feud never came off.

Hating the delays of moviemaking, forced to sit in the dressing room waiting to be called, Frank complained about his Hollywood labours. He was unhappy about his next film, *Step Lively*, at RKO, and between scenes he told Gloria DeHaven how he felt. The RKO executives shrugged. Frank's complaints were echoes of his previous protests at MGM, where they remembered Frank walking off the set or leaving before the day's shooting was finished.

Sinatra simply was always either 'difficult' or 'charming'. When he was charming, you loved the guy; and when he was difficult, it was easy to hate him.

Yet, as Frank said even in those days, talent will out; it will be recognized and rewarded, and eccentricities will be forgiven. A movie magazine polled its readers and named him the most popular screen actor of the year, topping new glamour boy Van Johnson.

Frank's chest swelled a bit at the dinner the magazine gave him because big MGM boss Louis B. Mayer presented him with a bust sculpted by Jo Davidson (reportedly for a $10,000 fee).

The marital split that we'd anticipated came almost at the same time. After another quarrel with Nancy, about his other women, Frank blew up and walked out. Nancy remained in their Toluca Lake house and he took an apartment. Frank confirmed the gossip that he wanted a legal separation. Lana Turner felt that she had to deny that she had broken up their home. The columnists, the press agents, the close friends, all hastened to explain that Frank was too busy to play lover to his wife of seven years and just didn't want to be married any longer. He was a unique talent and he was entitled to some emotional idiosyncrasies, they argued. Frank wasn't like other men.

Frank didn't enjoy his bachelorhood. He was tricked into returning to Nancy the next month. Phil Silvers opened at Slapsie Maxie's in Hollywood, and Frank was there 'solo', the columnists reported, while Nancy sat at Jule Styne's table. Frank got up to sing one song, and Phil Silvers seized that opportunity to lead him to Nancy; they fell into each other's arms and everybody had a good cry. Frank went back home. Phil Silvers and Jule Styne congratulated themselves when they saw Frank escorting Nancy around Hollywood and Beverly Hills again, and taking her to New York when he went back to sing at the Waldorf.

'We're definitely reconciled,' Frank said. 'Everything's fine.'

But of course it wasn't.

HE PUNCHES A COLUMNIST

Frank's first big disaster with the press was his fight with New York *Mirror* columnist Lee Mortimer just after he went to Hollywood. The Sinatra fans of today who think Frank is a bit extreme in his criticism of the media are mostly too young to remember his fights with columnists Mortimer, Robert Ruark, Dorothy Kilgallen, Louella Parsons, Hedda Hopper and Westbrook Pegler, all of whom are long dead.

Frank's umbrage was more violent in his younger years. It triggered him to punch Lee Mortimer at Ciro's in Hollywood in April 1947; the incident led to a trial. The punch probably cost Frank around $25,000, and in those days he thought it was worth it.

Lee Mortimer was amusements editor of the *Mirror* and an understudy for Walter Winchell; he was also a nephew of Jack Lait, editor of the *Mirror*. He had a violent hatred for gangsters and suspected Sinatra of having connections with mobsters.

Havana was the place to go for expensive fun in the late forties. The high rollers went to the Havana Nacional. Mortimer, who was fearless, reported that Sinatra had flown to Havana to deliver $2 million in small bills to Lucky Luciano, then very big in the Mafia, although the term Mafia wasn't commonly used yet.

No supporting evidence of such a Sinatra mission to Havana was ever offered by any authorities. In fact, one investigative body didn't even bother to ask questions about this legend.

A very much respected reporter, Robert Ruark of the Scripps-Howard chain, attacked Sinatra similarly. To Ruark, Luciano was 'Sinatra's buddy', 'Frankie's boy-friend'. (Several years later, Ruark recanted some of these accusations.)

Ruark, in a visit to Havana to see his hero, Ernest Hemingway, witnessed the excitement over Luciano. The tourists went to the Floridita restaurant or Sloppy Joe's and to the Nacional Casino, where Meyer Lansky's mob hung out. There were famous Havana brothels. Near the airport was one where the main attraction was 'Superman', who made frequent personal appearances.

Columnist Ruark wrote that Sinatra and Luciano 'were seen together at the race track, the gambling casino and at special parties. In addition, I am told that Ralph Capone was present . . . and so was a rather large and well-matched assortment of the goons who find the south salubrious in the winter or grand jury time.

'But Mr. Sinatra, the self-confessed saviour of the country's small fry, seems to be setting a most peculiar example for his hordes of pimply, shrieking slaves.'

That, and the Lee Mortimer columns, were the beginning of the charges that are still heard today about Sinatra's associations and affiliations.

As Frank eventually explained it, in a carefully prepared defence, he had happened to run into one Joe Fischetti when Frank was playing a Miami benefit for the Damon Runyon Cancer Fund. 'Where are you headed?' Frank asked. And the answer was Havana. And 'What a coincidence, why don't we all go together?'

'I was brought up to shake a man's hand when I am introduced to him without investigating his past,' Frank said.

'That night, I was having a drink at the bar with Connie Immerman, a New York restaurateur, and met a large group of men and women. . . . The introductions were perfunctory. . . . I was invited to have dinner with them and while dining, I realized that one of the men in the party was Lucky Luciano. It suddenly struck me that I was laying myself open to criticism by remaining at the table, but I could think of no way to leave the table without creating a scene.

'After dinner I went to the jai alai games and then, with an acquaintance, toured the night spots. We finally wound up at the Nacional Casino where we passed a table at which were Luciano and several other men. They insisted that we sit down and have a drink. Again rather than cause a disturbance, I had a quick drink and excused myself. Those were the only times I have ever seen Luciano in my life.'

That wasn't the whole story, however. Young Sinatra had wanted to meet some tough guys. It stemmed from his background; he grew up in an underdog neighbourhood where the boys' heroes were often rough characters who defied authority. Frank was not alone. The kids in the poor neighbourhoods of Brooklyn and the Bronx and Philadelphia didn't want to be mobsters, but they regarded them with awe.

Attacks on Frank came from all sides. Louella Parsons, in her column in *Modern Screen*, warned him that he was going to be dropped by MGM for pouting over publishing rights to a song and for being in general a very difficult boy on the lot. Louella claimed that Frank 'isn't a well boy. And I bet that when he's feeling well again, we'll hear no more about his temperament.'

But Sinatra especially seethed over Lee Mortimer's criticisms. Sinatra told me and others, 'I will belt him sometime.'

Nightclub violinist Joe Candullo, who accompanied Sinatra in his nocturnal adventures, was asked by Sinatra to 'give Mortimer a message'. The message was, 'If you don't quit knockin' me and my fans, I'm gonna knock your brains out.'

Candullo, who was also a friend of Mortimer's, didn't want to do it. Sinatra persisted. 'He hangs out at the China Doll?' asked Frank. 'Take me over there and point him out, and I'll give it to him. Just let me know it's him, and I'll take care of him.'

'Don't do it, Frank,' Candullo cautioned him.

'I'm doin' it,' Frank said.

But when Mortimer heard about the threats, he scoffed at Sinatra. 'I'm not afraid of him,' laughed Mortimer. 'I'm not going to quit writing about him. Tell that to him and his cheap hoodlums.' He wrote that the dishwasher, the busboy and the clean-up women sang better than Sinatra.

'He's going to beat you up, Lee,' Candullo warned him.

'He doesn't scare me,' Mortimer said.

On 8 April 1947, Lee Mortimer and Frank Sinatra were both having dinner at the then popular Ciro's on Sunset Strip in Hollywood. Each was the centre of a group of friends, and each detected the presence of the other.

It was a ridiculous fight. Frank later claimed that he was in a sufficiently friendly mood to nod greetings to Mortimer across the room and that the columnist returned an insulting, drop-dead look. Mortimer maintained that as he was leaving, Sinatra barged into the foyer and clipped him from the back with the snarled warning, 'Next time I'll kill you, you degenerate.' And that three of Sinatra's buddies leaped on him while he was on the floor and pummelled him.

Sinatra also claimed, 'He called me a dago and I saw red. I was all mixed up from being called a dago.'

Mortimer denied he'd used such language; in fact, when he thought it over, he decided he didn't even know Sinatra was there until he got hit.

Frank brushed himself off after the battle and returned to his table. Mortimer went to a doctor, and a lawyer. Deciding he was suffering from wrist and neck bruises and the blow behind the ear, Mortimer swore out a warrant for Sinatra's arrest on assault and battery charges. Mortimer was enjoying all this just as much as Sinatra wasn't.

The police picked up Frank while he was at a radio station and trundled him off to Beverly Hills District Court, where he pleaded not guilty and requested a jury trial. Bail was set at $500. Frank went through his pockets and his wallet and didn't have $500. The Sinatra buddies, courtroom hangers-on and others helped raise the bail.

Everybody with access to a microphone or column made jokes about the Non-Battle of the Century. Mortimer said that what hurt him most was that he would 'have to go through life admitting that Sinatra knocked me down'.

As it all built up towards a trial, the press went wild with headlines and special stories. The Hearst organization, powerful in Los Angeles, moved in to knock Sinatra down and got the District Attorney's office excited. Frank had slugged a whole newspaper chain when he hit Lee Mortimer.

'Why did he call me a degenerate?' asked Mortimer. 'Because I didn't like his singing? His voice is all right if you don't like singing.'

The Broadway crowd generally agreed that Frank was in the wrong. I wrote this in my column. The next day, my wife and I were in the Copacabana Lounge when Frank came in and greeted both of us warmly. He wasn't objecting to my piece, but still said he'd done it because Mortimer had called him a name.

'Did you have to hit him?' I asked Frank.

'He was coming towards me. I thought he was going to hit me.'

'He said you belted him from behind.'

'I hit him on the chin! To hit him on the chin and hit him from behind, you got to be an acrobat.' Frank's eyes lit up with excitement. 'When he said what he did, I said to myself, "Here goes," and I let him have a good right hook. I felt very good about it afterwards. Somebody pinned my arms behind me—there was an awful tussle all at once, people coming out of walls.'

What did he resent most in Mortimer's writings? That about his fans being moronic was one of the things—he'd always been loyal to them as they had been to him. (Mortimer had said they were 'imbecilic, moronic, screemie-meemie autograph kids'.) And, curiously, he hated references to his being an overnight success.

'Don't make me laugh! All the cream cheese-and-nut sandwiches I ate when I was living on about thirty cents a day, working on those sustaining programmes. Nancy was working in a department store and used to slip me a couple of bucks. We weren't married yet. One station paying me, in fact the only station paying me, was WAAT, Newark: seventy cents a day for car fare.

'The coldest nights I walked three miles because I didn't

have the bus fare. I wasn't getting anywhere, I was giving up, but after I got married, I got lucky.'

The approaching trial was very serious, and Sinatra could have gone to jail for six months.

The newsreels—this was just before television—wanted to cover every scowl and grimace of the belligerents in the courtroom.

The District Attorney's office had investigated and concluded that Sinatra had no right to jump Mortimer. Sinatra had been the attacker.

'Settle the damn thing,' advised the late Louis B. Mayer, head of MGM. Sinatra rebelled. He didn't want to settle. He couldn't see himself giving in.

But on 4 June at six o'clock, he went bitterly and reluctantly into court and acknowledged that he had erred. He had been told by an acquaintance that Mortimer had referred to him as a dago, but now he decided that Mortimer actually hadn't said it and that there was no reason for him to have struck Mortimer.

Enjoying the moment to the fullest, Mortimer stood in the same court and, with a triumphant smile, read a statement that he was contented with the apology and the settlement he was getting.

Charges against Sinatra were withdrawn by Mortimer, with Sinatra agreeing to pay the fifty dollars' court costs. Sinatra actually paid Mortimer $9,000 additionally, and his legal expenses, trips, etc., were considerable.

Sinatra was most unhappy. Mortimer had cost him at least $25,000 and much shame and humiliation. He would have to watch himself in the future. As for Mortimer, *he* wasn't happy, either. He'd wanted to go after Sinatra more forcefully. Well, he would—in future columns. And he did.

The fact is that Mortimer had considered the trial quite a show-offy opportunity for him. He had bought four new suits for his 'personal appearances' in the courtroom.

Lee Mortimer came out better than Frank in the public's opinion. There was a party for Mortimer, given by Sophie Tucker at the Latin Quarter (he was, after all, still writing a column on amusements in New York), at which Milton Berle said, toasting him, 'You're the first fighter to lose a decision and win a purse.' The Scandinavian singer Carl Brisson, father of Fred Brisson and father-in-law of Rosalind Russell, offered to go into the ring against Frank, proceeds to the Cancer Fund. Frank's advisers winced at such remarks.

Stirred up by Westbrook Pegler, some papers struck out at Sinatra, going back into a seduction charge brought by a woman of thirty who had an eight-year-old child. Ed Sullivan went to bat for Frank, pointing out the stupidity of this allegation—the case had long ago been dismissed.

There was a report that Frank, after his visit to Luciano in Cuba, had obtained a gun permit, and the suggestion was that Lucky had helped him get it. I had access to the facts and reported that Frank had obtained the permit two or three months before going to Cuba. He carried largish sums of money late at night; hardly anybody disputed that he was entitled to carry a gun.

But he wasn't doing well. He was booked into the Capitol Theatre rather than the Paramount, which hadn't scored with him lately, and while his columnist friends such as Winchell and myself trumpeted his return to Broadway, the fact was that something had happened to his appeal.

Mortimer was sniping at him from the paper, suggesting that Sinatra was finished, and Frank rose to the occasion and said he didn't mind the $9,000 settlement for the one punch: 'It was a pleasure to pay it.'

Lana Turner was in town, and many were the stories of Frank entertaining her between shows. He was working . . . maybe too much. He had never been quiet in his demands, and now there was a difference of opinion about the string section of the Skitch Henderson band, which was to play for him when he went into the Copacabana in a few weeks. Frank wanted more strings. That has been a battle between singers and nightclubs since it was discovered that an inadequate voice can be made to sound adequate if there are enough violinists covering it. His agency, MCA, agreed to pay the difference so he could have more.

The trial and settlement of the Lee Mortimer case did not end Mortimer's hostility towards Sinatra nor Sinatra's hostility towards columnists. Editors of several Hearst papers, in their loyalty to fellow worker Mortimer, constantly attacked Frank.

While Sinatra was appearing at the Capitol, one of the New York *Mirror* critics, Harold Conrad, was assigned to review Sinatra. Conrad, who later became a fight promoter associated in Muhammad Ali battles, knew that Jack Lait, the *Mirror* editor, hated Sinatra because his nephew Mortimer hated him.

'But I liked the show and wrote a good review,' Conrad recalls. 'The next day, George Evans phoned me and wanted to kill me. I hadn't seen the paper yet. I said, "I thought I gave the kid a good review."

' "GOOD? You murdered him! Listen to this." And he read me a review that I hadn't written at all. Jack Lait and Lee Mortimer rewrote my good review into a rap and printed it under my name! There was nothing I could do about it.'

Later, another columnist, Dorothy Kilgallen, would be turned loose on Sinatra. And for a woman, she played rough.

(In fairness to Sinatra, it should be pointed out that Mortimer never attempted to prove his charges that Frank carried money to hoodlums, and the charges were generally discounted in later years. Mortimer wrote a book, *New York Confidential*, listing call girls' phone numbers, which resulted in dozens of lawsuits. Mortimer was later hit with a sneak punch by another nightclub figure, and the papers said 'The list of suspects had been narrowed down to thousands.' Mortimer didn't mind being disliked—he enjoyed it.)

FRANK'S BIG NOSEDIVE

Mysteriously, Frank's career went into a slow decline that quickened and became a historic nosedive for the hero of the great American success story.

Pretending to be happy again at their Toluca Lake home after many battles, Frank and Nancy were actually miserable. On radio Frank heard his popularity being whittled away by a new sound that to him was shrieking, ear-splitting and horrible: Johnnie Ray singing 'Cry' and Frankie Laine singing 'That's My Desire'.

I visited Frank at this black period in his life. He was holding his head up courageously. 'When you're on top, you're everybody's target,' he said.

Everybody went for his throat, and his money. Most demanding were the income tax collectors. He owed thousands. He told columnist Sidney Skolsky and me, 'All I am or ever hope to be, I owe.' He worried that he'd overspent on a Palm Springs house he had built for $150,000. Some columnists gloated about his tailspin and said the little bobby-soxers had now grown up and gotten some sense. Music tastes were changing. 'It's because he's been telling everybody to go to hell since 1943,' others said.

Frank gloomily admitted that he was no movie box-office smash. *The Kissing Bandit* was a hodge-podge; he wondered if he had a film future. He couldn't come up with a good record, although Frankie Laine and Johnnie Ray could, and so could Nat ('King') Cole and Vaughn Monroe.

'Your Hit Parade' replaced him with opera star Lawrence Tibbett, which was doubly irritating. He by then hated the programme and the songs he had to sing; it was demeaning to be fired but to be replaced by an opera star was too much. Some of his lingering bobby-soxer fans, however, proved their loyalty by writing angry letters to George Washington Hill, one of the highest salaried men in America and the head of American Tobacco Company, sponsors of 'Hit Parade'. One letter said, 'You ought to be ashamed of yourself! What were you, anyway, before our Frankie made you?'

He had a few more programmes to do and the idea made him sick to his stomach. Everybody seemed to know he was in a decline. His engagement at the Capitol Theatre was received tepidly. Frank suffered new anxieties when he walked to the stage door and saw no mob of screaming fans. He was smoking and drinking too much, and that was hurting his voice.

On a Sunday in the summer of 1948, the Sinatras invited my wife and me to dinner at their Toluca Lake home. Frank was playing daddy. He played and joked around the water with Nancy, Jr., and Frank, Jr. Nancy, Sr., superintended the preparation of the dinner. There was a pretence of domestic tranquillity that day.

Before dinner, Frank told me that he was very hurt by the sharp criticisms of his movies and records. 'What do you think is happening?' he asked.

'It's a pendulum; it'll swing back,' I said.

'I'm not throwing in any sponge to Johnnie Ray!' he said. 'JOHNNIE RAY!' He laughed at the thought of Johnnie Ray being bigger than Frank Sinatra.

Showing me around the house, he said, 'I've taken up painting.' He studied a book, *The Techniques of Oil Painting*, desperately looking for some new interests to soften the disappointments he suffered in his nosedive. Proudly, Frank exhibited a painting of a clown that he'd done. It was one of the first of the Sinatra clown paintings, which are greatly cherished today.

Frank then presided at the dinner in as pretty a family picture as you could find anywhere. The children were happy at having daddy home. He was always running, working. Actually, right at that moment, at the family dinner, he was restless. He wanted to move on.

The marital crises were continuing. 'You and that—— broad!' George Evans kept saying. Evans had tried so hard to preserve the image of a home-loving, tolerant, kindly crooner, and he couldn't stand to see it wrecked. He had sent Frank on a USO tour to beat down the punctured eardrum jokes. It had been a little precarious for Frank, who couldn't forget the time he walked into the 3 Deuces on Fifty-second Street and heard some Marines shout, 'Hey, wop, why aren't you in uniform?'

'Frank grabbed something off the wall, hit one guy over the head, and he and two music publisher friends chased them out of the place,' the black female singer, Bricktop, told me. 'It was some brawl and Frank won it.'

Evans also scheduled numerous speeches where Frank spoke in favour of tolerance. He overloaded Frank, who said, 'You've got to get me out of this one,' and George would yell, 'You're not getting out, damn you, you just want to be with *that* broad.' (And 'that broad' wasn't Nancy!)

Evans would yield, and choose a later date, and make it sound doubly important because of the delay.

Evans, Manie Sacks and some of the agents were concerned about Frank getting literally sick over the crisis with Nancy and the criticisms he was getting. Where were his little fans? Had the parade passed him by? He looked frail and discouraged. One disappointment was the reaction to the film *Miracle of the Bells*, in which he played a humble priest. *Time* magazine went after him with claws: 'Sinatra plays the priest with the grace and animation of a wooden Indian.'

Frank toughened under this. He didn't want to go to a charity première in San Francisco, but they wouldn't let him out of it. Louella Parsons said he bought clothes at the film company's expense, had a piano delivered to his suite at 4.00 a.m. and insisted on being driven all the way to Palm Springs by chauffeured limousine.

Everything was going badly. Sinatra told me of his

constant searching for books and stories to be filmed. He had been pleased with his singing of 'Ol' Man River' in *Till the Clouds Roll By* until *Life* magazine pointed out that he sang 'You and me . . . we sweat and strain' while 'wearing an immaculate white suit' and called it the year's worst moment on the screen. His film *Take Me Out to the Ball Game* also failed.

Whatever Frank did was wrong, and whatever he rejected was brilliant if somebody else did it.

'Why can't I find some decent songs?' he asked.

And why was Frankie Laine suddenly so popular and Frank Sinatra suddenly so unpopular? Frank was getting reviews that he could hardly bear to read, and he called the critics ignoramuses whose opinions nobody read or cared about. But he cared very much because he is in his own way a perfectionist. He might insist on filming a scene in one take, but it's only because he really believes he does it best in one take.

His remaining 'Hit Parade' performances got blasted, too, as sounding the worst yet, and of one picture a critic said, 'While his songs aren't bad, his acting is'. They said 'the Hoboken Hummingbird was on the way out'.

More disasters crashed around his head. The 'King' was cancelled off other shows, and the nightclub offers weren't tempting. When Mitch Miller of Columbia Records persuaded him to do a song with bustaceous Dagmar on a record called 'Mama Will Bark', Sinatra complained to non-critic George T. Simon about it. He was losing respect for himself by doing such songs. 'How low can you get?' Frank asked. He no longer had confidence in his own judgement; that had always been his strength.

He was voted the Least Co-operative Star by the Hollywood Woman's Press Club. He was battling with just about everybody, especially with columnist Erskine Johnson, a veteran Hollywood observer. Frank warned him that if he kept printing lies, he'd hit him in his 'big mouth'.

He got into a furious dispute with United Press correspondent Hal Swisher over an interview in which he supposedly said, 'Pictures stink'.

'Most of the people in them do, too,' he was quoted as

saying. 'I don't want any more movie acting. Hollywood won't believe I'm through but they'll find out I mean it. It's a good thing not any of these jerks came up as rapidly as I did. If they had you couldn't get near them without running interference through three secretaries.'

This was such a shocker that his advisers had to jump in and pull him out. First Sinatra was going to demand a retraction and sue, but Swisher declared Sinatra had said all that, and more.

A spokesman made a believable explanation. He said it was the hottest day of the year, the temperature was 104, and Frank was in a hot navy uniform with the sweat pouring off him. One of the crew had asked Frank what he thought of Hollywood and motion pictures now. Sinatra apparently did say, 'Pictures stink', and went on from there.

MGM insisted that he quit talking about suing the UPI and make it clear that he regretted his words. He eventually did say, 'I think I might have spoken too broadly about quitting pictures'.

The studio directors discovered then that Sinatra had a cold and a temperature, and should be put to bed and made to quit talking about it. Frank never did quite concede that he made the controversial assertion. Seldom has he apologized for a remark.

Deeply depressed, Frank knew that he had to leave Columbia Records. Columbia Records convinced itself that it had to leave Sinatra.

It hurt Sinatra that Johnnie Ray had scored a hit at the Copacabana. Although some critics thought Ray sounded like a case of acute bellyache, he drew big crowds reminiscent of Sinatra's successes.

Something had to be done for Sinatra. But who could admit to being a has-been at only thirty-four? Frank heard that description applied to himself, and it gave him a weak stomach. He threw up. He could hardly stand to read newspapers any more.

EMPTY SEATS AT THE CAPITOL . . .
WHATEVER HAPPENED TO SINATRA? . . .
THE VOICE'S FANS CRAZY ABOUT NEW KID SINGERS.

Frank looked around for a friend, but he found very few. Nightclub bosses who had fought each other to book him now looked away. Finally he got a singing job at the French Casino in the basement of the Paramount Hotel; not the theatre, the hotel. It was a comedown. I did as much as I could in print to make it sound respectable.

A dreary and dismal scene awaited the few Sinatra fans who went to see him. What had once been Billy Rose's Diamond Horseshoe, filled with champagne, perfume, girls and laughter, was now a sad, dark, rather large cellar with an atmosphere of gloom. One walked down the winding stairway and was shocked to see a 'crowd' of forty nondescript people. Even the club had a has-been look.

Frank needed the job. But word got around that he had bombed again.

Frank asked himself, 'What the hell am I doing wrong?' (It wasn't easy for him to admit he must have been doing something wrong.) 'Is the taste in singing changing?' he wondered. By God, maybe he *was* a has-been and in need of a new style.

He was no longer the sensation he had been at the Stork Club, sitting with Walter Winchell at Table 50 in the Cub Room. He wasn't big at Madison Square Garden. He couldn't seem to get anybody to say anything good about him in the papers.

Then he, or somebody in his group, hit a man in an inconsequential incident at a party in Palm Springs and it got in the papers. Frank became even more depressed.

And there it was again in the papers:

FRANKIE IS WONDERFUL . . . FRANKIE LAINE, THAT IS . . . WHO'S SORRY NOW?/SINATRA.

It got to be a joke, almost a stale joke.

Seeing finally that everybody seemed to believe he was passé, Sinatra adopted a new posture: modest, unassuming, non-egotistical, sweet to everybody—even to photographers and reporters. He was a new and humble Frankie. Few people really believed it.

Frank swallowed a bitter pill when he realized that he

had to explain to the people that he was really a nice guy—merely misunderstood. It was foreign for him to say such a thing, and he got a professional writer, Irving Fine, the late Jack Benny's press agent and business partner, to put the words together.

Ready now to say almost anything to gain sympathy, Frank approved a version that said he was highly strung, emotional and impulsive, and often did things without thinking them through. He bowed to the press, saying that without its help he would never have done so well financially or professionally.

As for Nancy Sinatra, the signed story that had been written for him said—surprisingly to most people—'I realized that I had mistaken our friendship for love.'

He was conceding that he had been very foolish and very human, and some of the public accepted it, but much of the hard-boiled press believed he deserved his scars, and to hell with him.

Some of them liked to keep repeating that they liked Frankie—Frankie Laine—but not the Hoboken Hummingbird.

'Anyway,' one editor said, 'I don't care for the humility pose. I liked him better when he was nasty.'

George T. Simon, writing for *Metronome*, found Frank in deep despair. He was upset about the industry and what it was doing to him.

In his discouragement, Frank still clashed with Mitch Miller over material. He was nervous about his choice of songs when he was hoping for a comeback. Frank declined 'Tennessee Waltz', which Patti Page made into a top record. He conceded later that he'd made mistakes and blamed it on his emotional life. Now he was broke, so everybody said. His readiness to order a chartered plane whenever he felt like it contributed to his financial embarrassment.

'I'll get an advance,' he had always said before.

When he was hot, it was easy to borrow against anticipated record royalties or other moneys soon to be earned. But his disastrous experiences with Columbia were such that Columbia was trying to get back the advance it had already given him. The movie studios were also frigid. They had been so generous when he was on top!

One night at the Copacabana, I found George Evans in a grave mood. 'I make a prediction,' Evans said across the table in the lounge. 'Frank is through. A year from now you won't hear anything about him.'

'Come on,' I protested to the man who'd done more than anybody to make him famous.

'He'll be dead professionally,' Evans said. 'I've been around the country, looking and listening. They're not going to see his pictures. They're not buying his records. They don't care for Frank Sinatra any more!'

'But you're the fellow that's supposed to whet up that yearning for him, aren't you?' I asked.

'I can't do it any more,' Evans said. 'You know how much I've talked to him about the girls. The public knows about the trouble with Nancy, and the other dames, and it doesn't like him any more.'

'I can't believe that,' I said.

'In a year,' Evans reiterated, 'he'll be through.'

Sinatra faced new trouble. His throat hurt. He had laryngitis more frequently. The disc jockeys, less friendly now, found he was singing unevenly. He knew it. He was physically ill, but wouldn't admit it, because he always hated to admit an illness.

Frank asked Nancy again for a separation.

All his problems, mental and emotional and physical, had crashed in on him at the same time.

In May 1950, while singing at the Copacabana, Frank lost his voice.

He had a problem just as big or bigger: Ava Gardner. George Evans didn't know that she was one Sinatra girl-friend he couldn't shush or put aside.

Though he tried to be jaunty and confident, he had hardly ever been lower in morale. He was a whipped dog.

The story of his recording of 'I'm a Fool to Want You', a torch ballad, has become a lugubrious legend embellished by each teller of the tale. He had contributed to the lyrics out of his own sadness, so the story goes. He was so taut and wrought up over a woman—he didn't say what woman at that time—that he could only sing the song once. Then he almost ran from the studio, seeming to be close to tears and collapse. It was a masterpiece of emotional singing, and to have cut it a second or third time would have seemed a false note to Frank. His colleagues watched him bolt to his car and take off quickly. Sinatra's contribution to the song was eventually acknowledged in the credits. His co-writers, Jack Wolf and Joel Herron, are among a handful of writers who have shared a songwriting credit with Frank Sinatra.

There were other hurts. Today, Milton Berle and Frank are close friends, but in those days they had been rivals and it was difficult for Frank to accept Berle's rule, 'Anything for a laugh.' Having been dropped by CBS-TV, Frank was sensitive to references to his flop programme. He could only laugh very weakly when Berle said on his own programme, 'Here are some people who have never been on TV—they were on Frank Sinatra's programme.'

After having been dropped even by his own agents, MCA, Frank was glad to pick up $1,500 for a one-nighter singing at the Click Club in Philadelphia. He needed the money.

Frank bit his lip, took a drink, lit another cigarette and brooded about the problems that faced him and his little circle of believers, especially Hank Sanicola and Jimmy Van Heusen. He remembered how he had met them when they were piano players demonstrating songs in Tin Pan Alley and they had slipped him sheet music that they should only have given to important singers. They and Manie Sacks and his lawyer Henry Jaffe would have to see him through this storm if they had the strength. If *he* had the strength.

THE FRANK AND AVA SOAP OPERA

Finger-snappin' Frank tried to sing off his blues around his thirty-fourth birthday in December 1949. The little old roulette wheel of life hadn't been hitting his numbers. Low in spirits because Billy Eckstine was now Number 1 singer (Frankie Laine second, Sinatra fifth), he grew increasingly sophisticated and thick-skinned. Going into a little time-step at a cocktail party in New York, he said, 'What the hell?' and mentioned that his movie *On the Town* was a record-buster at Radio City Music Hall. All was not lost. Maybe he could pull himself out of the worst tailspin of his life.

Along came Ava Gardner—just when he needed her least.

Their stormy 'courtship'—it doesn't seem the right word because on Frank's part it was extramarital—and their on-again-off-again wedding, with Frank offering to knock every photographer on his ass, are chapters in one of the wildest, weirdest love stories ever told about a Show Business couple.

It was a two-year soap opera, with screaming fights heard around the world. Their Reno-begun divorce wound up in Mexico. For Frank it brought agony, the greatest sadness of his life. He was tortured; he threatened—or pretended to threaten—suicide. He shot off guns, he threw Ava out of the house, he repented, he wooed her back. As violent as the Elizabeth Taylor–Richard Burton affair, it ended with Ava still his fan, his admirer, his friend, occasionally still his date and, for whatever it might mean, his occasional house guest.

It took two years for their romance to get started and the same length of time to wear itself out.

Howard Hughes, then the 'big operator' (an expression that today would be translated into 'swinger' or 'stud'), was dancing in a Palm Springs restaurant with Ava Gardner. Frank danced with Lana Turner. Changing partners, Frank enjoyed the switchover and so did Ava.

As the Palm Springs historians tell it, Frank and Ava left in his car, followed by a sound that resembled a gunshot. It was probably Frank indulging in a favourite prank: flinging a cherry bomb out the window.

'An authentic sex goddess with the hidden but smouldering charm of a Jean Harlow' was *Time* magazine's description of Ava in a cover story titled 'The Farmer's Daughter'. A woman of some mystery, a feminine riddle who'd given much of herself to ex-husbands Mickey Rooney and bandleader Artie Shaw, Ava still had much more to give. Frank Sinatra could truly sing 'I'd like to make a tour of you . . . the east, west, north and the south of you' to Ava, a sharecropper's daughter from the Carolinas.

Once I interviewed her when she was just getting good parts (this one was in *The Hucksters*), and she exclaimed over the tasty old-fashioned a waiter set before her. 'You'll like it even better,' laughed Robin Harris, the publicist who'd brought her, 'when they put bourbon in it.'

Alluding to her sex life, *Time* claimed 'the men are mostly tight-lipped about their memories of the green-eyed, reddish-haired young woman in the bare shade of 30', whose mouth was a little too large and figure too slender and legs just average. She didn't brag about her acting, but considered herself a singer. She made $2,000 a week and had a Cadillac reputedly given her by Frank Sinatra, who was rumoured to be working in a Reno nightclub to finance a divorce from Nancy Sinatra. She often swore like her Southern antecedents and liked to go barefoot.

Ava's discoverer was a clerk, later to become a New York policeman, named Barney Duhan. Ava, at seventeen, had come from North Carolina to visit her sister Beatrice and the latter's husband, photographer Larry Tarr, who shot many pictures of the beautiful kid sister-in-law and displayed them in his window. Impressed by her beauty, young Duhan, who worked in the Loew's Inc. legal department, posed as a Metro talent agent. Borrowing all available photos, he harangued the MGM talent operatives into giving her a screen test and subsequently a fifty-dollar-a-week contract. Duhan became a cop, studied law, and today is an attorney quite amazed at what he started.

Indifference was Ava's charm. She'd never fawn over producers, directors—or lovers—and she didn't give a damn about being an actress. She had gone to business school and would make a good secretary.

Playing the free soul who didn't need anybody, Ava continued to enchant bachelor Howard Hughes, who had more time and money to spoil her than Frank, who was still married and in financial trouble. When Ava's mother was ill, Hughes sent a plane with medical specialists.

Seen frequently around Hughes' hotel suite, Ava always looked cool, confident and interesting. Hughes, she smiled, was her 'personal pilot'; he flew her around the country. But her eyes lit up with an interest in Frank that she didn't have in Hughes, who was somewhat deaf and wore sneakers, even in El Morocco, because he had a bad foot.

Covertly, Frank and Ava kept in touch, and kept it quiet, until 1949 when Frank got the love bug very bad.

Before that, there had often been parties with Frank in the centre and Ava on the fringes, and the two of them together afterwards. But in 1949, mingling with the champagne-quaffers at a party for the opening of Carol Channing in *Gentlemen Prefer Blondes*, were Ava and Frank. They were snuggly, laughing and enjoying each other.

Beautiful Ava was also on the fringes of a birthday party given for Frank at the Copacabana by Jack Entratter, the manager. They said it was his thirty-third birthday because they'd been going along with a publicity claim that Frank was born in 1916 (instead of 1915).

Taking a sleeper plane to go back home for Christmas, Frank was indefinite about his future. But first he had to play the Shamrock in Houston, Texas. Unable to keep away from Ava, unable to keep his hands off her, Frank asked her to go to Houston, an indiscretion that was the start of a long war. A Houston columnist, Bill Roberts, finding them trying to have a quiet dinner, tried to get a photograph. Frank leaped at the camera to smash it. The story was out.

It became an open scandal. Returning to Hollywood, embarrassed by the publicity, Frank told Nancy that he and Ava had been almost inseparable for eighteen months, they'd gone to Europe twice, he was virtually commuting to be with her, and he wanted a divorce to recover from the frustrations that were affecting his work. He was ill, and he was being held back in his struggle to regain his leadership in his field.

For weeks, Nancy weepingly refused on religious grounds, saying they'd been happier when he was with Harry James. Finally in April 1950, Nancy told me, 'I'm giving him a separation—not a divorce. Yes, I'm giving in that far.'

Frank felt elated for the first time in months. He was confident that he would get a divorce eventually. Scheduled to open at the Copacabana that very month, Frank saw no reason why he shouldn't have Ava attend. The newspapers were speculating whether Ava would face another barrage of gossip.

Ava went, in a no-shoulder gown. She was twenty-six and at the peak of her beauty. She sat considerably back from the ringside and clapped her hands furiously. Frank was a happy bachelor in a celebrating mood. He wore a coonskin cap, swung a whip and blew a duck call as a takeoff on 'Mule Train' and 'The Cry of the Wild Goose', the popular songs sung by Frankie Laine. He repeated a dance he did in *Take Me Out to the Ball Game.*

'He's using stunts to conceal that his voice has slipped, and he's letting the orchestra drown out his inability to reach the romantic peaks of his songs,' some critics said.

They were probably right. His voice was weakening. Frank took the offensive. He attacked the Hollywood columnists who were criticizing him and Ava.

'My voice was so low the other night singing "Ol' Man River" that I got down in the mud and who do you think I found throwing mud down there? Two Hollywood commentators! They got a great racket. All day long they lie in the sun and when the sun goes down, they still lie.'

In his dressing room on opening night was a good-luck telegram from Nancy and the children.

Ava was being pictured as a home-wrecker. She was furious and gave me a statement saying, 'Since Frank is still officially married, it would be in the worst possible taste to discuss any future plans. One thing I'm sure of is that Frank's plans to leave Nancy came into his life long before I ever did.'

Hurt by the continuing criticism, Ava decided to go to Spain to film *Pandora and the Flying Dutchman* two weeks earlier than she'd planned. Frank asked me personally if I would write a story presenting Ava's side of the controversy.

Sitting together, holding hands, Frank and Ava said they were in love and couldn't help it. Ava had been subjected to vilification from letter-writers who said they hoped her plane would crash going to Europe.

'They even claim I'm pregnant,' Ava said. 'I could sue.'

Ava went off to Europe, and Nancy celebrated her birthday with a new mink coat from Frank.

With Ava away, Frank wasn't really idle. He had dates every night. He was singing hard, the crowds were applauding 'Nancy with the Laughing Face'. His headlines about Ava had awakened new interest in him.

Bob Hope got $40,000 for a TV show. Fred Allen said Frank Sinatra was entitled to $10,000 for a burp. Frank did a guest appearance for Hope and CBS signed Frank for a series at $10,000 a show.

(Jackie Gleason was signed as a guest star on Frank's TV show, which was to 'buck Milton Berle', who was called 'Mr. Tuesday Night'.

Frank and Ava were the main topic of conversation, and Gleason wouldn't let the Ava Gardner angle rest. Inviting Frank to a hospital where he was dieting, Gleason showed Frank a faked autograph picture. It read: 'To Jackie, I can never forget you. With all my love. Ava.' Gleason also said, 'I get a new Cadillac as my guest fee and I understand

Ava comes with it.' Sinatra was still slight of stature. To his nurse, Gleason bellowed, 'Did you send back my tray? I think Sinatra was on it.')

Extremely highly strung now with Ava away, Frank projected a programme with veteran Broadway stage producer Max Gordon and magazine writer Paul Dudley that was to have taste and creativity rather than vaudeville sketches. It was 'live' and also wild, with all the mistakes in it. After it was withdrawn, Frank contended it should have been done on film. Twenty-five years later Frank had a reverse opinion. He declared the only way to do TV was 'live'.

Ava was reported having dates in Spain, Nancy was holding out against a divorce in Hollywood and Frank's throat was scratchy in New York. He was over-trying in his effort to regain his former position in the field. He was pressing himself to do charity benefits, and he made a call on a sick little girl who thought a visit from her hero would help her get well.

A new drama was awaiting Sinatra. On Wednesday night, 26 April 1950, Frank opened his mouth to sing at the Copacabana and, as some said later, 'nothing came out but dust'.

For the first time he'd lost his voice. It was another headline. Billy Eckstine went on for him. 'Frank promised he will be back tomorrow,' the Copa said.

The second day of his breakdown, as it was getting to be, found him worse. I wrote in my column: 'He winced with discomfort and was unable to appear at the last two shows. Managers were deciding what to do about his daily radio programme and his scheduled opening at the Chicago Chez Paree on 12 May.'

It became official!

> FRANK SINATRA SUFFERS THROAT HAEMORRHAGE, CANCELS CLUB SHOW
>
> Sinatra was ordered by Dr. Irving Goldman to take a two-week rest. He leaves today for an undisclosed vacation place.

It was submucosal haemorrhage of the throat.

Frank romanticized the incident in later years and said he had to go on a forty-days-of-silence period. Terrified as he was at losing the voice with which he'd made millions, he was quite airy about it as he flew to Miami Beach.

A week and a half later, Frank turned up in the little Spanish town of Tossa Del Mar, and who should be there but Ava Gardner.

Frank, miraculously, was talking plenty, and so was Ava. To this day there are some who think it was less a throat haemorrhage and more a desire to see Ava. A press statement issued on his behalf said that Frank's 'voice vacation' would take more than two weeks. 'He and Ava will be well-chaperoned,' one spokesman said, giving everybody a titter.

Newspapers leaped on the story. Would they try to get married in Europe? Reached by the overseas operator in Tossa Del Mar, Ava, in her most colourful language, denied as fictitious the reports coming from special correspondents that Frank had flown off in a huff to Paris because a Spanish bullfighter, Mario, was issuing bulletins about their love.

'Honey, it's all a big lie,' Ava said. 'He left because he's got to get back for a TV show.' Did she give him a good-bye kiss? 'Honey, I'd give *you* a kiss in Tossa Del Mar. We're closer than we've ever been.' Did he bring her a $10,000 necklace? Ava replied, 'Holy Christ, Frank brought me six bottles of Coca-Cola and some chewing gum.' Had she sunk into bullfighter Mario's cape? 'I'll kill those bastards,' Ava howled. 'They take what's happening in the picture and pretend it's really going on.'

When I got to Sinatra in Paris, he and Jimmy Van Heusen were at the Club Lido and Frank was loquacious. Indignant about the claims of bullfighter Mario, Frank said in a voice that sounded like a yell, 'He is nothing to her, nothing, NOTHING! Don't you understand? The Spanish press is trying to make a hero out of this guy because it would be a feather in their cap if they could show that this girl was interested in him. This girl has had nothing to do with this boy.'

Continuing to shout above the sounds of music in the nightclub, Frank said he and Ava were closer than before, 'and there's something else I'd like to get across. Ava and I have kept this as clean as anybody could. We were chaperoned all the time. ALL THE TIME! Just like at a high school dance.' And not a word—'NOT A WORD'—about getting a divorce. 'Everybody's talking about us getting married but us,' he insisted fiercely.

How was the throat? How was the silent treatment the doctor ordered? 'It helped. I got away from a lot of things. I forgot work for a while. The pipes are okay again—I hope.'

On the wing once more a few days later, Frank flew back to New York, then boarded another plane for a six-hour visit to Los Angeles—to see if Nancy was yielding on the divorce. (She wasn't.) Airborne again, he arrived in New York, did a slick performance on Bob Hope's show, and was immediately invited to reopen negotiations to appear at the Palladium in London in July. The money was good, and Ava would be in London at the time.

It was surprising to me that every day there was a new twist to make a suspense serial of this love affair.

Artie Shaw was going to London! Was he going to see Ava, who frankly said she frequently went to him for advice? What would he tell her? To marry him or not to marry him? On a trip to London, I saw Ava at Shepperton Studios in the English countryside.

'Artie's one of my greatest friends and always will be, but the love thing is past,' she said. She spoke of Frank with tenderness. 'You know how I feel about Frank.'

Ava's quiet and leisurely beauty and sex appeal were undeniable. In her dressing room, she was wearing a towel-like bathrobe. She'd just done a scene in which, according to the script, she'd swum nude to a yacht to see James Mason. In another scene, she fell into Mason's arms and kissed him tempestuously. It was easy for me to see and understand Sinatra's fascination with her.

When she had a chance, she talked to Sinatra. She was teaching her London camera crew some of his slang, but they were slow. Frank called objectionable people 'creeps'; the camera crew called them 'creepers'.

'I think Frank is a wonderful person, I like him as a human being as well as for his talent,' she said. Yes, she'd still be in London July 10, when he went into the Palladium. And of course she'd be there.

In those years, the best people travelled in double-decker Boeing Stratocruisers, which had a cocktail lounge below and berths above the seats. Ava was flying from London to New York after Frank's successful Palladium engagement and so was I. At a fuel stop in Shannon, we talked. Frank was coming by another plane. 'I'm so anxious to get home I've got butterflies,' she said.

Reporting on the conversation, I said there was nothing to report, 'but Ava didn't conceal the fact that she and Frank are closer than wiener and schnitzel'.

Frank was nervous when he arrived at Idlewild. Walking to his limousine, he explained that forty musicians were waiting for him to record and he was two hours late. He motioned to the chauffeur to get going. The car door was still open. It sideswiped a couple of photographers, breaking someone's film holder. Nobody was hurt. After a momentary stop, the car continued to the city.

But there were other cliffs in the cliff-hanger. Just when Frank was ready to break up his home, Hollywood reported Ava was having dates with British actor Richard Greene. Frank couldn't figure why Ava was interested in another man. He was temporarily deranged over one of the most beautiful women in the world. However Ava soon quit being naughty.

Later Sinatra and Ava were back in town!

But not for long. They disappeared. Ten days later they were going from one hideout to another in Beverly Hills. Ava had a pink stucco house on a mountain-top. Her trunks were in the garage, but the shades were drawn and telegrams were piling up on the doorstep. Her private phone was cut off, and she'd cancelled the answering service.

Conferences with lawyers and a few friends were in progress. Good friend Manie Sacks was making more visits to Nancy. On 15 February 1950, I had printed with Frank's consent that he had asked for a divorce so he could marry Ava.

More than a year later, on 29 May 1951, I wrote: 'Nancy Sinatra has thought it over since Valentine's Day, 1950, and decided to give Frank Sinatra a divorce so that it'll be possible for him to marry Ava Gardner. Nancy and Frank reached the next-to-last step in their fourteen-year-marriage in a series of quiet, friendly, dignified talks in Nancy's home in Hollywood.'

There would be no bitterness. Frank said Nancy was the ideal mother of his children.

Frank looked pale and drawn when he flew in a chartered plane to Las Vegas to get the divorce. He engaged in a row with the press. The headline said:

BELLIGERENT SINATRA GETS DIVORCE, SCORNS REPORTERS

Calling the reporters 'newspaper bums', he said, 'Why should I give the newspapers anything? I ought to give a cocktail party for the press and put a Mickey Finn in every glass.'

Less than twenty-four hours after Frank got his divorce, he and Ava made a futile attempt to get married in Philadelphia. They left the Hampshire House in New York by car, Frank hoping that influential Philadelphia friends could get a friendly judge to waive the three-day cooling-off period so they could marry immediately at the home of Isaac M. (Ike) Levy, a close friend of Manie Sacks. Despite the pressure and the excitement of dealing with glamour folks, Orphans Court Judge Charles Klein refused. The earliest they could get married would be the following Monday, 5 November.

Frank and Ava returned to the Hampshire House in a sulk. It was a tempestuous weekend, with several lovers' quarrels, highlighted by Ava getting pre-wedding jitters and throwing her diamond engagement ring out the window in an outburst of jealousy. Ava threatened to kill herself. Frank said he would also kill himself.

In a true sense, Frank had sacrificed everything for Ava, and now his bride-to-be wouldn't even let him into her room. He was shaken to his soul. He believed in love. Such tragic experiences enabled him to sing about it with conviction.

'The wedding's off,' Frank gloomily informed intimates, 'and what was to have been a celebration is a shambles.' He was drinking. The reports of Ava cancelling the marriage and showing her contempt by throwing away the engagement ring were heard in the Colony restaurant and other chi-chi spots that they and their friends visited.

Their war cooled down. On Wednesday, 7 November, I learned that the most romantic event of the decade was on again. I reached the Hampshire House just as they were walking out, hand in hand, to get into their limousine to go to Philadelphia for the ceremony. They were giggly, obviously very much in love and sober.

I congratulated them and wished them eternal happiness. Frank threw his arm around me; Ava gave me a kiss. They slid quickly into the backseat of a limousine with two friends in the frontseat, and waved to me. Some photographers who had been waiting for them were unable to move quickly enough to get pictures, and that delighted both.

When the couple arrived at 5.30 p.m. at the new site of the wedding, the home of Lester Sacks, a cousin of Manie Sacks, in West Germantown, Pennsylvania, Frank saw some photographers waiting and he began screaming.

'How did these creeps know we were here?' he demanded and then insisted that only CBS cameramen would be allowed to take pictures. One photographer thumbed his nose and said he'd get his own pictures. 'I'll bet you $500 you don't get a picture, and if you do I'll knock you on your ass,' bellowed Frank.

Ava had told me with a laugh as we walked away from the Hampshire House, 'Frank's had this thing about photographers for years. He's very ingenious at lousing up newspapermen. He had one idea. He wants to stick chewing gum in somebody's camera. Instead of a picture, they'll get a big blob of gum.'

It was for a few minutes more a war than a wedding. It was rainy, it was dusk and Ava was scared and doubtful. Frank had wanted this woman more than anything in his life, and he switched off hostility and turned on tenderness at about 7.00 p.m. when Ava started downstairs on the arm of Manie Sacks, while Frank's close friend, arranger Dick

Jones, played the 'Wedding March' and then 'Here Comes the Bride'.

On the stairs, Ava lost her footing and started to fall, but Manie caught and steadied her. Frank flashed her a smile and held his head up with such a look of strength that Ava felt tears coming into her eyes.

True to the music profession, Frank had his bandleader and arranger, Axel Stordahl, as best man, and Stordahl's wife, the popular singer June Hutton, was matron of honour. It was mostly 'family' and intimates.

'Well, we finally made it,' Frank grinned, after Police Court Judge Jose Sloane married them, following an exchange of rings. Frank kissed Ava several times, she kissed him, and then Ava rushed into the arms of her new in-laws, Martin and Dolly Sinatra. The women cried and Mrs. Ike Levy toasted the newlyweds with champagne. Ava, wearing an eggshell tinted wedding gown cut low in front, with a starched white collar, personally sliced the seven-tiered wedding cake, assisted by her new husband, who wore a white carnation in the buttonhole of his handsomely-tailored dark suit.

By chartered plane, they flew from Philadelphia to Miami and then on to Havana for a honeymoon. They appeared to be wondrously happy in a picture taken of them while walking on the beach barefoot, holding hands.

But there were always snipers waiting for them. Had Ava paid for the honeymoon? That was one newspaper report. Why was Frank perpetually angry at the press? George E. Sokolsky, the conservative columnist for the Hearst newspapers, blasted Sinatra for his treatment of photographers.

'Frank Sinatra evidently craves privacy,' he wrote. 'When a man resents having his picture taken it should not be taken. If the name Sinatra never appeared in a single paper, would the world sink back into Stygian blackness?

'When these theatrical folk are on the make, they curry favour and seek notices and hire publicity men to spread interesting and exciting tales about them, true or untrue. Then they try the gag of seeking privacy, which some believe is of human interest. If it is privacy that Frank Sinatra wants he should be kept out of the public eye permanently.

Perhaps the day might come when he would like to be remembered.'

Just a month after Frank and Ava got married, Nancy Sinatra, in a luxurious mink, had dinner at the 21 Club in New York with movie producer Freddie Kohlmar. She told an amusing story. Flying from California, she had been booked on the same flight that Frank and Ava were on, but 'something happened to their plans and they switched planes', Nancy said. Clearly, somebody at the airlines had tipped off Frank that his ex-wife was going to be aboard, and that was why he took a later flight. (What a chummy flight that wouldn't have been—and wouldn't it have been a field day for the photographers!)

And so Frank and Ava were happy, but not forever after—just for a few months. They went to England, where they were victims of a jewellery robbery. Ava complained about Frank's outbursts against the press and his strong words about knocking photographers on their asses. She accused him of being lackadaisical about his vocalizing. He twitted her about Artie Shaw and Mickey Rooney. She twitted him about Marilyn Maxwell and Lana Turner. Because of their work commitments, they were often apart. The press was always bombarding both of them. Frank still had some guilt feelings about Nancy. It wasn't working out.

Frank the married man got touchier and tougher. His fame made privacy impossible. The press played up anything suggesting marital discord. While they were in London, Ava had promised to sing a duet with Frank at a benefit. Later she thought better of it. The papers believed there'd been a quarrel about it. Frank exploded—at the press—and didn't sing his best. The papers reported that the audience yawned.

Career setbacks made him irritable. He was, according to his old friend, theatre manager Bob Weitman, 'knockin' on doors'. Some people said 'Frank's down on his ass and he deserves it. He's out of style. Nobody feels sorry for him.'

Sammy Davis, Jr., told of seeing Sinatra in Times Square alone and unrecognized. He was the Forgotten Frankie; Sammy hesitated to say hello to him, afraid that Frank would be humiliated.

Frank brooded through sleepless nights, using sleeping pills to get some rest, wondering what he could do to get back his lost popularity. Maybe the Paramount Theatre, which had been lucky for him? He phoned Bob Weitman, who was vacationing in Florida. 'When you comin' back? I'm in trouble.'

Frank wanted to go into the Paramount with his newest movie, *Meet Danny Wilson*, and stir up the old enthusiasm again. But it wasn't a Paramount picture and the Paramount usually played only their own product.

'What are you starting up with that guy again for?' Barney Balaban, the Paramount Pictures president, asked.

'But Frank was a friend and we knew he had talent,' Weitman says. 'We took a chance on him for two weeks with Frank Fontaine, June Hutton and Buddy Rich.'

As one of his surviving and loyal friends in the press, I tried to create excitement for him. The Paramount gave me a couple of rows of seats for VIPs whom I got out for the opening on 26 March 1952. Jackie Gleason, Phil Silvers, Ted Lewis, Jimmy Durante and the columnists stood up in the audience and sang out greetings to Frankie, and I reported it in the papers: 'Jule Styne reached for his handkerchief when Frank sang "The Birth of the Blues".'

I wrote about him almost every day: He was singing better than ever. . . . He was reconciling with photographers. . . . He was the talk of Show Business. . . . 'Ava has a flock of new clothes and may be seen on stage with him. . . . Ava has been in Europe and was so happy to be reunited with him that they dashed right off to a hotel from the airport—forgetting all her bags.'

Despite my extravagant praise for Frank, his competitor Johnnie Ray was a bigger sensation opening at the Copacabana in April 1952. Frank and Ava seemed happy again at Johnnie's opening. When I asked Frank what he thought of Johnnie, he said, 'I'd like to tell you, but my girl won't let me.' Everything was 'Honey' and 'Darling' and 'Baby' between them, and Ava said she was signing all her autographs 'Ava Sinatra'. She'd been late that evening 'because my old man got into the bathroom first'.

Frank's mood was cheerfully optimistic. 'We're over all

our crises now,' he said. 'We have nothing to worry about any more.'

It was over-optimism on Frank's part. The Paramount engagement was only 'okay'. The *Meet Danny Wilson* picture was based on a story Harold Robbins had written to pay the rent. The producer, Universal International, didn't pick up Frank's option. His records weren't improving. He was jolted when some radio shows were cancelled.

His big $250,000-a-year five-year CBS-TV deal got off to a dreary start. Jack Gould, the TV sage of the New York *Times*, said, 'Sinatra walked off the TV high dive but unfortunately fell into the shallow end of the pool.'

But the most resilient man in Show Business, Frank Sinatra, wasn't knocked out yet. He would bounce and bounce and bounce again.

'I remember,' says Bob Weitman, 'that Sinatra was talking around that time about a book he was reading and saying, "If I can get into a picture they're doing from this book, it will start me up all over again." It was James Jones' *From Here to Eternity*.'

After the Paramount engagements, Frank stuck his chin out for more blows, and he got them. He had just conceded to Ava that he had been overly harsh with photographers and would make himself available to them when a couple of the photographers brushed by and said, in unison, 'Fuck you.'

He worked the Chez Paree Club in Chicago, where they could amass only about one-tenth of a crowd for him. His agency, MCA, didn't want him any more; he owed them $40,000 in commissions. CBS was sorry it had put him on TV, as he turned out to be a million-dollar loss. He couldn't get any records going.

Sinatra blamed Mitch Miller for 'ruining' his career, but Mitch said Sinatra was an ingrate who was responsible for his own failures because he had approval of all songs.

Once, flying off from Hollywood to meet Ava abroad, Frank made a stop-off in New York to record two songs. But after reaching the studio, where the musicians were waiting, Frank began shaking his head 'No' when he listened to the demos. 'I won't do any of this shit!' Frank announced. 'It's the worst kind of crap.'

Miller couldn't persuade him. 'He left in a huff to meet Ava in Africa,' Miller says. 'To save the session, I got a fellow named Al Cornick, later known as Guy Mitchell, to record them. Both became hits, "My Heart Cries for You" and "The Roving Kind".'

Miller, who had eleven 'Sing Along' gold albums on his own said Sinatra 'screwed himself up and blamed others for it'.

A few years later, during a congressional investigation of payola, Sinatra telegraphed the committee that Miller had favoured BMI songs and taken kickbacks. An accusation that was never supported. 'It's a lie,' Miller said. 'Of the songs I recorded for Columbia, 97 per cent were ASCAP.'

Mitch Miller is completely without awe for Sinatra's fame and renown and maintains that Sinatra's recording failures then were due to the Ava Gardner scanda, land that he had to serve penance for it. 'Columbia Records had advanced him $150,000 to pay his taxes, and it was my job to record songs that were profitable so Columbia could get its money back. I would not select unpromising material deliberately. I would be defeating my own purpose.'

When Frank got popular again, several of the songs that had been flops for him became successes when re-released, which leads Mitch Miller to say they were good songs all along. Long after their blow-up and Sinatra's departure from Columbia, Mitch Miller saw Sinatra in Las Vegas. He extended his hand to Sinatra and said, 'Let bygones be bygones.'

'Fuck you,' snapped Sinatra. 'Keep walkin'.'

'Sinatra is such a contradiction in personality,' declares Miller. 'I have seen him belittle an employee in front of people and reduce him to excrement. And the next morning there's a Cadillac in front of his door.

'Anyway, the whole idea that to be able to sing thirty-two bars entitles you to be a dictator, a little Rasputin, is a misreading of Show Business rights. Take away their microphones and electronic equipment, and most of today's singers would be slicing salami.'

'But Sinatra is a very generous man. He gives away enormous amounts of money,' I said.

'So what!' retorted Miller.

But the big spectacular chapter of the Frank and Ava love story broke in the newspapers 21 October 1952, just two weeks short of their first wedding anniversary.

FRANKIE THROWS AVA OUT

was the headline in the New York *Post* written by Paul Sann, the executive editor.

Though Frank was trying to keep it a secret, the Palm Springs police were talking. They said Frank called them to put Ava, Lana Turner and other friends out of the house after a loud quarrel. Frank had overheard some remarks about him that he bitterly resented, according to the police.

Another police version was that Frank became enraged when he found Ava had invited Lana to share their home while Lana was looking for a new house. Lana had recently been carrying a big torch for movie actor Fernando Lamas, and Ava had been 'holding Lana's hand', according to Hollywood gossip, trying to console her.

To fit the pieces together, I tried to reach Sinatra in Palm Springs at the home of Jimmy Van Heusen, where he'd gone after the quarrel. Jimmy, of course, wasn't discussing it. 'Where's Frank? Can I talk to him?' I asked Jimmy.

His exact reply was, 'Frank's in the bathroom throwing up.' That was Frank's reaction to many emotional crises.

The Sinatras had been battling since their marriage, just as they had battled before. Two weeks earlier, after a quarrel, Frank returned to his hotel room in New York to find a farewell note from Ava, and her wedding ring. He promptly lost the ring.

He couldn't pursue her because of his nightclub engagement at the Chase Hotel in Saint Louis. He was getting vaccinations to accompany her to Africa, where she was going to be making a movie for at least a year. He got a duplicate of the wedding ring and was trying to patch things up when he returned to Los Angeles to appear on the Jimmy Durante TV show.

And that's how it stood after the show. He returned to Palm Springs. 'And he found his former girl friend, Lana, and his wife, Ava, cutting him up,' one friend explained.

What they were 'cutting him up' about never got explained. With Ava and Lana in Sinatra's home that early Sunday morning were Ava's manager, Ben Cole, and Ava's sister, 'Bappy'. The police chief, August Keppman, a former football star, said some neighbours complained of the noise.

'It wasn't just another battle of the Battling Sinatras, it was more like a war,' one neighbour said.

After he expelled the two celebrated beauties from the premises, Frank picked up suits and shirts and moved in with Jimmy Van Heusen. Lana and Ava found their own hiding-place.

A peculiarity of this friendship was that both Ava and Lana had been Sinatra romances, and both had been wives of supposedly great lover Artie Shaw. They had a lot to talk about.

'Frank's in bad shape,' one of his group told me afterwards. 'Maybe he got a bad reaction from the vaccination shots he was taking. He hasn't been himself.'

And so began a war of nerves between Frank and Ava: Frank was insisting on certain terms in any peace that could be arranged; Ava was saying that unless Frank apologized for his bad temper and accompanied her to her family in North Carolina and then to Africa, everything was off.

One reason for their battle seemed to have been an argument about another girl friend of Frank's, Marilyn Maxwell. The blonde, willowy, voluptuous Miss Maxwell had been in the audience at Bill Miller's Riviera nightclub a month before when Frank opened an engagement there. Ava was in the audience, too, and she wasn't happy about seeing Miss Maxwell, especially since her previous romance with Frank was no secret. Probably half of the audience knew about it and was watching them. Ava accused him of 'putting on a special show for Marilyn Maxwell'.

'Some of your cute little gestures were intended especially for her,' Ava insisted.

Frank kept denying it, and told me that he 'never so

much as looked at another gal' since their wedding the previous November.

For a week, the war of nerves continued. Frank went to Las Vegas for three days; Ava moved back into the Palm Springs house. On 27 October, Frankie was ready to surrender. 'After a week of considering it,' one of his friends told me, 'he realizes he loves her more than anything and he must do everything to get back together.'

A humorous sidelight was that the late Governor Adlai Stevenson was said to be rooting for a reconciliation of the Battling Sinatras. Both Frank and Ava were supporters of Stevenson's presidential candidacy. They were scheduled to appear at a movie stars' rally for Stevenson. Ava, in fact, was scheduled to introduce Frank at the rally. One of the comedy writers said that the way things were going, somebody would have to introduce them to each other.

It was at that rally, publicly, openly and dramatically, on the stage of the Hollywood Palladium, that they made their reconciliation official just a week after the Palm Springs explosion.

Arm in arm they stood there, hugged and kissed and adored each other while cameras recorded the end of the great battle.

In a strapless black satiny gown and a mink jacket, Ava introduced Frank just as planned. 'I can't do anything myself,' she said into the mike, 'but I can introduce a wonderful, wonderful man. I'm a great fan of his myself. Ladies and gentlemen, my husband, Frank Sinatra!'

The reporters leaped for the phones.

FRANKIE, AVA KISS AND MAKE UP.

Frank spoke out for Stevenson's candidacy (he was wearing a Stevenson button). He looked drawn and thin-faced, but was smiling and posed willingly for the cameras as he put his arm around Ava's bare shoulders and pulled her to him. He sang 'The Birth of the Blues' and 'The House I Live In' to a crowd of stars that included Janet Leigh and Tony Curtis.

Before the rally, they had had dinner at Frascati's, a Wilshire Boulevard restaurant, and had arrived at the

Palladium just in time for their appearance. They had kept the officials guessing right up to the last minute whether either would actually appear. And they stepped out of the car hand in hand, calling each other 'Honey'.

'They have Stevenson in common,' Sidney Skolsky, the Hollywood columnist, commented. After they left and went home together, it was the most natural thing to say, 'Politics makes strange bedfellows.'

THE FALLEN SHALL RISE AGAIN

After their spectacular reconciliation, the Swinging Sinatras soon broke out into more big battles about Frank's deteriorating public relations, his declining prestige, his impossible financial condition—and his desperate need to achieve a comeback.

Ava never got proper credit for helping her husband make his first great climb back up. It had cost her worry, effort, tears, money (which she eventually got back) and her marriage.

The destruction of a marriage bought at such an emotional price was sad to see. I talked to Frank about it probably fifty times. They were both young—Frank, thirty-seven and Ava, thirty. They were too sophisticated, too much like movie stars, to back down. It *is* true that movie stars get to believe their own publicity.

Insecurity was the problem of each. Frank was motivated by an urge, not uncommon among men, to own his wife exclusively. He was jealous of her occasional wanderings and displays of independence. She was an early Women's Libber, refusing to be owned. But she, too, was insecure, believing that Frank preferred other women to her.

Frank, notwithstanding his celebrated sexual attractiveness, doubted his hold on her. He burned when he called their residence of the moment and got no answer. 'Where the fuck is she? Out with Artie Shaw?' Flying into a rage, he promised to 'beat her brains in and kick her ass out'.

When Ava phoned back a few minutes later and said she'd been in the tub, he dissolved completely and said, 'I love you, Baby.'

Ava often turned a bare and cold shoulder to Frank's commands. She was not one to greet him in tears. Who the hell did he think he was, ordering her around? What about some of *his* disappearances?

It was jealousy, part of the Sicilian pride he got from his father, who taught him he should never permit anyone to walk over him. One night when Artie Shaw was playing at Bop City, Ava made what was intended to be a clandestine visit to see him. An employee of the club tipped off the papers, and some Sinatra followers, that Ava was there having a drink with Shaw. 'Get her the hell out of there or there's going to be a murder,' the Sinatra camp warned the Shaw camp.

Frank's love of Ava was almost classic. He had a collection of Ava's photographs that resembled a small art gallery in his den, softly lighted as in a shrine. One night in a fit of anger, he tore his favourite picture of her into small pieces. Friends later found him on the floor trying to put the picture back together—but her nose was missing. His guests got down on the floor with him and tried to help him find the missing nose. They couldn't find it. Later, a liquor store delivery boy, in opening the door, discovered the missing nose stuck under the door. There was an appropriate celebration.

In his continuing nosedive, Frank became increasingly cynical. 'Dear friends' for whom he'd done favours and given his celebrated gold lighters were always 'in a meeting' and would call right back, but didn't.

He would sit up brooding aloud over his financial condition.

'I've pissed away eight million dollars,' he said one night in their Palm Springs house.

'Quit talking about it,' Ava said.

Frank insisted on talking about it to an overnight guest: 'I'm flat on my ass. All the houses, cars, clothes, chartered planes, salaries for help, jewellery, furs. Gifts for friends.'

He had bought literally thousands of dollars worth of

cigarette lighters. He tipped almost as lavishly as the big spender, columnist Mark Hellinger, and like Hellinger, he tipped when he didn't have it to tip. Because it was now expected of him, it was his way of life.

'You sit up and talk about it; I'm going to bed,' Ava said after one such recital, and left with a glass in her hand.

Next morning, Frank discovered Ava and her car were gone. She was being independent again.

Their battles frequently were caused by a need for reassurance of the other's love and respect. During a stay in London, where they had such loud quarrels in an apartment that the neighbours complained, Ava demanded that Frank accompany her to Spain on a vacation. Frank demanded that she accompany him to Atlantic City and vacation there while he made an appearance for his friend, Skinny D'Amato, owner of the 500 Club. While he wasn't making much money on the date, it was 'a favour for a friend'.

That was one of Ava's complaints. He was always doing favours for friends, but not for her. This battle was so fiery that Ava went out with Italian actor Walter Chiari, with whom she had a romance later.

In the forefront of Frank's mind at that time was a desire to play the Italian-American GI, Maggio, in the movie based on the James Jones bestseller, *From Here to Eternity*. It was a 1000 to 1 shot. It was an intensely dramatic role. Between quarrels, Ava agreed with Frank that he could and should play the part. She encouraged him to go after it.

Frank was unemployed. Ava was going off to Nairobi to film *Mogambo* with Clark Gable. Frank was going along, but Ava was the breadwinner. That was bad for the ego of a man in a tailspin. Brooding about how to get the part, Frank determined to go directly to Harry Cohn, the dictatorial boss of Columbia Pictures, which would be making the film. 'This little guy Maggio was like a lot of Italian guys I knew in Hoboken,' Frank later told columnist Norton Mockridge. 'He wasn't unlike me.'

Frank's long-time publicist and friend, George Evans, was no longer around to help. Evans had died of a heart attack. He and Frank had broken up over Frank's romance with Ava Gardner, but there had been an attempt at a reconciliation the night before he died. Deeply distressed over Evans' death, Frank overcame his dislike for funerals and spoke, feelingly. One of the mourners hadn't seen Frank so moved. 'We thought,' he said, 'he'd never stop talking.'

Evans' forecast to me a year earlier that Sinatra would soon be through had almost come true. Evans' associate, Budd Granoff, took over the publicity account, but found it was hard to get space for Sinatra because he would lash out at the press or get into a new scrape with the photographers or a bodyguard would threaten to put a hole through a reporter.

'I should take a salary cut,' Granoff said. Sinatra took that almost as an insult. He had his pride. He has always had it.

But he sacrificed some of it when he began a campaign for the Maggio role. It was a sad time for Frank. Eddie Fisher was a big record seller with 970,000 discs of 'Any Time' already sold, while Al Martino had a big hit in 'Here in My Heart'. Sinatra was trying to sign with RCA-Victor. It was 1952 and 1953. Gen. Dwight D. Eisenhower was being inaugurated President and Queen Elizabeth was having her coronation. When Frank Sinatra was flying to Africa and then back to play a nightclub date in Boston, nobody in the press was interested.

Even I wasn't much interested. I noted that when he arrived at the airport, Frank needed a haircut.

Frank persuaded Harry Cohn to have lunch. Sinatra hinted that he had something of major importance to tell him. Cohn, who was interested in girls, money and pictures, anticipated something different. This is the true story of what happened, despite many other versions. It comes from Cohn himself to a dear friend and associate.

Sinatra candidly said, 'Harry, I want to play Maggio.'

'You must be out of your fuckin' mind,' Cohn said. 'This is an actor's part, not a crooner's.'

'Harry, you've known me for a long time,' Frank said, and again this is the way Cohn told it. 'This part was written about a guy like me.' He added, 'I'm an actor. Give me the chance to act.'

Cohn wasn't impressed. Frank knew Cohn was a hard-bargainer. He knew Cohn appeared to have a piece of some gambling casino. In Las Vegas, he was always carrying big bills in an inside jacket pocket.

'I've been gettin' $150,000 a week,' Frank said. 'Well, you can get your Maggio for my expenses.'

What did he mean expenses? 'A thousand a week . . . $750 a week . . . for nothin',' Frank answered. 'I've got to have it.'

Cohn was finally impressed by the money angle. 'You want it that much, Frank?'

'I told you, it was written for me.'

'Well, we'll see, Frank, we'll see,' he said.

He had to test some top character actors. One was Eli Wallach, who was being stuffy about the salary. 'I'll think it over. It's pretty crazy,' Cohn said.

'You're not turning me down then?'

'I was, but let's see, let's see. It's a wild idea.'

Cohn's office phoned Frank that he would get a chance to be tested. They would let Frank know the date. Frank waited and waited for the call. He didn't get it. Ava was nudging him, and he returned to Africa with her.

Frank could not know that Cohn was haggling with Eli Wallach over salary. Cohn had budgeted $16,000 for the role—$2,000 a week for eight weeks. Cohn summoned Wallach's representatives and lectured them. 'Whoever plays this part is going to get an Academy Award,' he argued. Cohn had a riding crop on his desk that he sometimes thumped for emphasis.

Wallach's agents insisted that Wallach wanted $20,000.

In Africa, Frank was brooding. Ava kept Frank hoping. Cohn said subsequently that Ava had communicated with him personally by phone during that period and said, 'You've got to give that part to Frank. If he doesn't get it, he'll kill himself.'

He was at his lowest. 'I was way way down,' Frank later told columnist Mockridge. 'I'd barely come back to Africa before I got a cable to report to Hollywood for the test! I got a plane, flew to Hollywood and made the test. I'll say this, I made a hell of a test. More than 27,000 miles just to make a test of a few minutes. I didn't even need a script.'

Frank had worried so much about getting this part that he felt he *was* Maggio when he did the test.

The producer was Buddy Adler, of the Adler elevator shoes family of New York, husband of blonde film star Anita Louise and later the head of 20th Century-Fox Studios. He was astonished when Harry Cohn proposed Sinatra for the Maggio role; so was the director, Fred Zinnemann. But it was an interesting thought.

Harry Cohn hammered the desk and thumped the edge of it with his riding crop. He was as sold on Sinatra's crazy idea as Sinatra was. 'Have you ever seen this little guy without a shirt on?' Cohn demanded. 'Well, this is a thin little guy with a heart! When you see this little guy up against Fatso [the sadistic sergeant in charge of the stockade], you're gonna see an actor!'

But Hollywood was silent for days. Frank figured he'd lost out. Ava told him not to give up. She agreed with him that it should be his role. She called Cohn from Africa again.

One day Frank was with Ava on location for her picture and returned to their hotel, alone. The gloom was deep. There was nobody around even for him to talk to.

Then the phone rang. The William Morris office in Hollywood was calling.

'You got the part!'

He shouted and sang congratulations to himself and he had some drinks, alone, and got a little tipsy, but there was one thing wrong: 'I wanted to tell somebody but there was nobody around to tell it to! I thought I'd go off my rocker.'

But he was apprehensive. He didn't have his voice to fall back on this time, and who the hell knew whether he could act? He was worried: he was a little song-and-dance movie actor up against the heavyweights. Maybe he would be a laughing-stock. Maybe he would blow whatever he had left—whatever that was.

A little guy who didn't have the plane fare for all those trips. . . .

Frank left Ava in Africa with Clark Gable—a cheerless thought—and returned to New York and Hollywood, then went on to Honolulu for his big gamble, his big crapshoot, a throw of the dice 1,000 times more important to him than leaving Tommy Dorsey's band to go out on his own.

On the beach in Hawaii, Frank the dramatic actor was not the usual Sinatra with a mike in one hand and a cigarette and glass in the other. He was intent and determined, and in awe of Burt Lancaster, Montgomery Clift and Deborah Kerr. From his reading and re-reading of the novel he knew the outline of his part before the cast assembled. He had learned one drunk scene even before his test, and he displayed a familiarity with the story that brought the others close to him and made them want to help him. They felt his urgency.

Around the Waikiki hotels, where he was still regarded as a top singer, Frank heard gossip about himself. Zinnemann and Adler were saying that he was going to be good in the picture. Did they mean it or was it 'somebody bullshitting me'? It was the first good news in a year. The bad news was that he had to pay the government over $100,000 in taxes and was practically working for free. He'd made ten times this salary in small nightclubs.

He heard more rumours. They liked him; not only liked him, they loved him. The publicity department went further: 'Sinatra's sure to be nominated for an Oscar as best supporting actor.'

He was playing the Hoboken Italian kid that he was and the pros marvelled that he could really act. It had taken him six months to land the part. They were getting a bargain for the $2,000 a week they were paying him for eight weeks. When he finished the filming, the publicity department raised its sights: 'Sinatra will definitely win the Oscar.'

Frank turned buoyant and charming again. But he and Ava battled. She was in a nervous state from a miscarriage that had put her in a London hospital. During a tour of Europe, he got testy and walked out on audiences.

On 6 August 1953, my wife's birthday, we were at the Savoy in London, and by previous agreement, I phoned the

Sinatras to remind them that they were to celebrate with us. They came up from the lobby and were in a merry mood. We celebrated until morning, frequently calling the all-night room service for replenishment. Ava and my wife sat on one bed; I sat on the other bed. Frank moved a chair to the foot of the bed the ladies occupied; Ava later sat barefoot on the floor.

Ava adored barefootedness. She often walked barefoot around dressing rooms during rest periods or interviews. But once when I referred to her as a sharecropper's barefoot daughter (which was a publicist's slight exaggeration of the facts), she got angry with me. Strangely, *The Barefoot Contessa* was later one of her major films.

Barefoot that night in our room, Ava appeared to have Frank docile and under complete control, even when we discussed the reports of his success in *From Here to Eternity*.

'He doesn't know whether to believe all the talk,' Ava said when Frank went to the bathroom. The picture was yet to be edited, previewed and premièred. Maybe what he thought was so good—the death scene—would be considered overacting.

Frank was torn about what attitude to take about all the build-up. Should he be humble or, as one of his realist friends said, 'should he start getting that old shitty feeling towards everybody who'd helped him?'

There was a series of senseless quarrels with Ava. What were they mad at each other about?

Returning to New York from London one night, Ava hadn't found Frank there to meet her, which he said wasn't his fault because she hadn't notified him she was coming. Ava flounced off to her own hotel and wouldn't talk to him. In another display of independence, she pointedly ignored his opening at Bill Miller's Riviera and went to a theatre opening instead. However, he wooed her with words on the phone, took her home to Mother for an Italian dinner, escorted her in grandeur to his show and played the show to her.

It was bliss regained. Frank had been singing 'I Get a Kick Out of You', getting a laugh out of pretending that love, represented by Ava, kicked him in the behind. With

Ava watching, he dropped that from the song, and they were happy again—for a few weeks.

Ava recalled that he soon became nasty again after a few drinks and warned her, 'Don't cut the corners on me too close, Baby, that's the way it's gonna be from now on.'

More quarrels broke out, and then suddenly Frank went into Mount Sinai Hospital 'for observation'. Frank was suffering from his old complaint: 'Gardneritis.'

Ava returned to Hollywood.

My wife and I, pitying Frank, believing we understood at least a part of his vulnerability, participated with other friends in some efforts to bring them back together. Our efforts were as childish as was their determination to stay apart. During a period when they weren't talking to each other, we resorted to the hoary device of getting one on the phone and saying the other was calling. It didn't work. They got connected on the phone all right, but resumed screaming—frequently at us.

Leaving the hospital after three days of observation, against the protests of a doctor who couldn't keep him there because he just had to see his wife, Frank took a plane to Hollywood, carrying sleeping pills to help relax him. His aim was to reconcile with Ava and dissuade her from carrying out the threats of divorce she'd made such a short time after we saw them seemingly happy together at the Savoy in London.

Again the crisis in their romance was about as secret as a press conference, and Frank woke from his sleeper ride—they had beds on some planes in those days—to find headlines greeting him in the Los Angeles papers. The word of Galahad's return had reached Ava, whose press agents encouraged the lovers to take another chance.

AVA TABLES DIVORCE, DATES FRANK TONIGHT.

They made love and made love some more.

Another woman has said, 'When Frank's on the make, there's nobody so ardent, there's nobody quite so persuasive. He really comes on big and strong.'

Whatever their troubles were, sex was never among them. Ava even told the famous black singer, Bricktop, who relayed it to me, 'It was always great in bed; the troubles were all out of bed. Great in bed, but the quarrelling started on the way to the bidet.'

On the way to the bidet! The secret of their non-success. Ava loved him, loved their sex life, but with her need for independence, began battling with him after she got her clothes on.

The advance comments of his performance in the picture confirmed to Frank that he had scored a great comeback. His crowd of hangers-on irritated Ava, who could remember when many of them were ignoring him and she was picking up the tabs. It was back-slapping time, and Ava saw her old man, as she called him, getting to be impossible to live with because of his ego. When her own picture, *Mogambo*, opened at Radio City Music Hall, they attended the première together because MGM had arm-twisted them both. Nevertheless, they were arm in arm there, and also arm in arm when they returned to Hollywood.

Whenever they were arm in arm, there was likely to be trouble ahead.

Back in Palm Springs with the old bunch of Sinatra enthusiasts, who could see no wrong with the 'King', Ava sized up the future and decided she didn't have one with the 'Comeback King'.

Just when all appeared serene, with a reconciliation seemingly having been effected, there was another explosion.

MGM issued a 'joint announcement' on behalf of both in October 1953, that Mr. and Mrs. Frank Sinatra were divorcing.

We all leaped to our typewriters to write that we'd known it all along. We had, in fact, but Frank and Ava, with their tiresome break-ups and reconciliations, had thrown us off. Ava made a remark that would become famous. 'Now that he's successful again,' declared Ava, 'he's become his old arrogant self. We were happier when we were on the skids.'

As one who had followed the case closely, I undertook to be a love expert. The break-up after less than two years of marriage was due to the facts that Ava was on the verge of a nervous breakdown, that Frank was suffering the strain of career worries and that he was domineering and Ava wouldn't accept his bossy treatment.

Frank agreed to speak to me about his side of it, going beyond the 'joint' statement, which seemed to indicate that the statement was really Ava's and that she had hoped he would want her so much that he'd force her to withdraw her thoughts about a divorce.

'If it took seventy-five years to get a divorce, there still wouldn't be any other woman for me,' Frank said gallantly.

Pouting, Ava said, 'Frank doesn't love me. He would rather go out with some other girl, almost any other girl.' She said that when she tried to get together to discuss peace, Frank brought some of his chums along. 'Maybe if I'd been willing to share him with other girls, he'd have been happy.'

Ava, one of the great sex symbols, believed that Frank preferred less attractive women to her. What was the cause of her insecurity? According to her psychiatrist, she had a marriage-failure complex. 'I don't believe if I were a man I'd like me,' she said.

The progress report from the studio was 'Ava is leaving for Europe next week on a loan-out picture, *The Barefoot Contessa*. She still plans a divorce, though no date has been set.'

'Things are looking up,' Frank confided to me.

Frank flew to Rome to join her for Christmas just in time to find that she'd taken off for Madrid, despite Frank's telling her he was arriving. Pursuing her to Spain by chartered plane, he got to her in time to sing Christmas carols and spent the next day in bed with a bad cold and a worse hangover.

The day after New Year's 1954, it didn't look good.

From Rome, Reynolds Packard, New York *Daily News* correspondent, cabled his paper: 'A downcast and lonely-looking Frank Sinatra sneaked out of Rome this afternoon on a New York-bound plane after a five-day attempt to win back his wife, Ava Gardner.'

Frank would only say, 'There are still problems.'

Ava wasn't with him. She was busy posing 'in a chilly studio without much on' for the well-known Roman sculptor Assen Peikov, who was doing a statue of her for *The Barefoot Contessa* movie. He had to get a good idea of how to mould the Gardner curves, so he asked her to pose in a skimpy slip.

'She was very nice and very co-operative,' Peikov said, and added with a frown, 'But a little square in the shoulders.'

Ava had found a new love: Spain, Spaniards and flamenco dancing.

Later, visiting her in Madrid, we were invited to one of her flamenco parties. She made half-hearted inquiries about Frank. Her long stays in Spain had made her less close to her husband. She had become bored with his swinging ways and his entourage. In Rome and Madrid, she had dated men with smooth manners and sweet talk, and she preferred them to the rough characters with Frank.

'Some of that's kid stuff,' she said. 'They're playing games.' Once it had enchanted her, but she had grown more sophisticated.

The week before the Academy Awards, Frank Sinatra was in a jubilant mood as he had dinner at La Scala on West Fifty-fourth Street in New York with Jimmy Van Heusen, Hank Sanicola and music publisher Jackie Gale. They'd had dinner there every night for a week. Although this was during Sinatra's low period, he was always picking up cheques and tipping with twenty-dollar bills. As Sinatra and Jimmy Van Heusen left for the airport to fly to Los Angeles, the others called to him, 'Bring back that Oscar!'

'I'm gettin' it,' Sinatra promised them, but he had his fears. He was up against Eddie Albert, in *Roman Holiday*; Brandon de Wilde, in *Shane*; Jack Palance, also in *Shane*; and Robert Strauss, in *Stalag 17*. They were all pros.

Frank worried about the film community's feelings about him. He knew that many actors didn't like him and would vote for the popular Eddie Albert or Jack Palance. He'd heard it said, however, that his performance was so good it might overcome the dislike some felt for him.

Jimmy Van Heusen cautioned Frank to keep calm and warned him, 'Anything can happen. There are a lot of upsets in these contests.'

Frank's own suspense increased as ex-wife Nancy, Nancy, Jr., and Frank, Jr., gave him their own miniature gold Oscar in the form of a Saint Genesius religious medal at dinner the night before. It was inscribed: 'Dad, we'll love you—from here to Eternity.'

On the big night, the Pantages Theatre was full of tension as Mercedes McCambridge prepared to read the names for the Best Supporting Actor category. Frank was nervously rocking back and forth in his seat as he waited with his daughter and son beside him.

This was it.

He was sitting towards the back to the left on the aisle, figuring out the logistics. If his name should be called, he would have to get from the left side to the centre aisle and then run down to the stage.

Everybody in the audience watched as Mercedes McCambridge read the nominees' names. When she said, 'And the winner is . . . FRANK SINATRA!' the crowd roared its approval long and lustily. There was a special burst of applause from Frank's section as he sprang up, kissed Nancy, Jr., and jogged to the centre aisle and to the stage, the proudest man in the world at that moment. As he took the trophy from Miss McCambridge, he hugged it, clutched it to him and looked a little bewildered. He smiled and waved, inspiring another outburst of cheering. He said his thanks simply and quietly, mentioning Cohn, Adler and Zinnemann.

He was thirty-eight years old, and he had come back.

He said later that he had to fight back the tears, and he realized that his whole life changed in those few seconds, that it was the greatest thing that had ever happened to him.

Frank knew, too, that luck had been riding for him. The part had been offered first to Eli Wallach; if he hadn't turned it down, Frank Sinatra wouldn't have been there that night.

Frank was at his most sentimental. He phoned his mother in New Jersey and let her do most of the talking. He phoned Nancy, Sr. There is no evidence that he phoned Ava, who had been so helpful and encouraging and who was in Europe.

I pointed out in my column that Frank in his happiest moments seemed to want to be unhappy. In moments of triumph, he courted disaster. This was the manic-depressive emerging. Frequently he was deliberately masochistic.

His comeback story tempted every Show Business writer to mention again and again that he'd worked for $8,000, violating the Show Business rule that an actor should never lower his salary.

Frank carried home an Oscar for Best Supporting Actor. *From Here to Eternity* also won Best Picture for Buddy Adler and Best Supporting Actress for Donna Reed. (William Holden won Best Actor for *Stalag 17*, and Audrey Hepburn for *Roman Holiday*.) Some carpers said that Maggio was a part that would have won an Oscar for anybody, but Buddy Adler and Fred Zinnemann disagreed. They declared that Sinatra had beautiful timing and made contributions to the dialogue that showed a director's touch. Sinatra, and Cohn, had been right.

'The greatest comeback in the history of show business,' they said. Yes, they said it over and over until Frank finally objected to the word *comeback* and said, 'Just call it "The Rise and Fall and Rise Again of Frank Sinatra".'

He was still cocky. The people of the press who loved the drama of comebacks were eager for Frank to ascribe it all to luck.

'Luck is fine,' he said in an interview, 'and you have to have luck to get the opportunity'—in this case, to get the role—'but after that,' he said, 'you've got to have talent and know how to use it.'

It was just one of several times that he boasted of his talent. He'd been unable to get a job, but suddenly he was the oracle, handing down to the masses his philosophy of success.

So many offers and propositions came in that Frank's friends said, 'He's got to have a whole new staff just to say no.' It was only a short while since he had been summoned to Hollywood for tests and he had to get the plane fare from Ava.

The movie companies, of course, were suddenly delirious about his talent. They dangled *Pal Joey* and *Pink Tights* (with Marilyn Monroe) before him. He had a hit song, 'Young at Heart', which shot to the top. TV and radio just had to have him again, and his financial problems suddenly seemed to be easing. Somehow he was acquiring two points (a 2 per cent interest) in the Las Vegas Sands Hotel. Everything in the world was going well except his marriage.

Still, there was a slender hope for even that. Ava found a ranch for him when he came to Spain to film *The Pride and the Passion.* When he arrived in Spain, he had a young lady with him, beautiful Peggy Connolly, a starlet and singer he'd been enthusiastic about for a couple of years.

Ava was irked; Frank was cocky. When he was asked if they might reconcile, he was reported to have replied, scornfully, 'Are you kidding?'

The next year, when Ava came to New York to plug *The Barefoot Contessa*, Frank stayed out of the city.

In July 1954, Ava established a residence in Nevada, preparatory to getting a divorce after Frank had won the Oscar in March. Frank's lawyers told Ava's lawyers to hurry it up *please!* Frank wanted to get it over with. But Ava didn't seem to be in any hurry. She was up in the woods near Reno and Lake Tahoe, while Frank was singing at the Sands in Las Vegas.

Rita Hayworth was in the neighbourhood, sitting out a divorce from Aly Khan, before marrying Dick Haymes.

In the Sierras, at a place called Cave Rock on Lake Tahoe, in the general neighbourhood of Mount Rose, my wife and I found Ava's divorce cottage, and Ava *and* the bullfighter, Luis Miguel Dominguin.

'Hi, Honey,' Ava said, and introduced the slim, youthful, handsome bullfighter who'd been swimming and fishing with her for a couple of days. He kissed my wife's hand. 'Miguel's only staying a couple of days, he's going to the Philippines and then to South America, where he has business,' she said.

Characteristically hospitable, Ava suggested that Miguel give us a drink. 'Get a piece of ice,' she told him. With a laugh, she added, 'A piece of *ice*—that's not the same as a piece of *ass*. He's trying to learn English,' she explained.

Beyond telling me, 'It's over or I wouldn't be here,' Ava did not discuss Frank.

However, without following through, Ava suddenly departed Lake Tahoe with a very famous private pilot—Howard Hughes.

Ava went off to Cuba to visit Ernest Hemingway at his farm outside Havana. She came back to New York with Dominguin. Ava went to the Copacabana with him to attend Joe E. Lewis' show. She did not encounter Frank; he remained in Las Vegas.

It was another year before Ava actually filed for divorce—and then it was done in Mexico City and not in Nevada. By this time, the Spanish bullfighter had dropped out of Ava's life and the new man was the fun-loving Italian actor, Walter Chiari, with whom she had gotten romantic in Rome.

Chiari flew to New York to do the Ed Sullivan TV show, and Ava went with him to the studio to help him with his English. Then she took him with her to California. I asked whether she might marry him. Ava said, 'I cannot talk of marriage as I am still married to Frank Sinatra.'

I asked Ava if there was the slightest chance of reconciling with Frank.

Ava smiled but she was very final and definite: 'Give it up, Earl,' she said. 'It's over.'

The marital experts delved into their brains, and vocabularies, to new depths, endeavouring to explain the break-up. There were never any sex problems between the sex symbols. They were both competent in their own way, according to well-informed leaks from their boudoirs. Therefore, the experts blamed the split on Ava's 'complexes', which she allegedly nurtured with fifty-dollar visits to psychiatrists. Frank also saw a psychiatrist, who kept their conversations confidential.

Frank was guilty of trying to be a caveman, according to one expert who had interviewed Ava's psyche. His strutting and peacocking had eroded whatever small self-confidence she had left. Ava had been testing her strength with Francis Albert Sinatra just to make sure she had some. He hadn't responded the way she felt he should, so Ava felt weaker instead of stronger.

Amazing to me now is how freely their friends discussed and analysed the Sinatras with other reporters as well as myself, and how much we wrote and how much the papers were willing to publish of a really private matter. To be quite fair, however, the newspapers thirty years later printed just as fully the stories of the very personal problems of Elizabeth Taylor and Richard Burton.

Now Frank blew out the torch and began living the happy life of a swinging bachelor.

(Because of his comeback, there was in fact a 'new Sinatra' singing in Las Vegas. Walking through the Sands Hotel casino one day, I heard a voice paging 'Mrs. Sinatra'. It blared out again: 'Paging Mrs. Sinatra.'

The high-rollers didn't notice. I did, and wondered if Ava had come here to visit Frank.

The voice sounded again. 'Paging Mrs. Sinatra . . . Mrs. Ray Sinatra!' Ray Sinatra was his cousin, the Sands' bandleader.)

Frank kidded himself about his torch songs in his performances. When he sang, 'All of Me', he threw out his bony chest and made fun of the word *all* as he sang 'Why not take *all* of me?'

'ALL,' he would shout scoffingly.

When he came to the line 'Take these arms,' he would hold out a skinny forearm and say 'arms?' questioningly.

Frank was being so light and airy about the whole thing that some people thought he was trying too hard to prove that he wasn't really brooding about Ava, whom he never mentioned.

It had been Frank's fate to have two extremely different wives. Nancy would get tears in her eyes when the photographers asked her to smile for a picture when they broke up; Nancy said, 'No, I don't feel like smiling.' She took it very seriously. 'What do other girls do for him in bed that I don't do?' she asked her girlfriends.

Ava could be flippant. She would have smiled for the photographers. When Frank fired shots into the mattress to scare her, she didn't get scared. She laughed.

In July 1956, after two years of legalistics, Ava told me when I saw her in London in a trailer dressing room at Elstree Studios that she and Frank had just then formally ended their marriage.

'I just signed the bloody thing this morning,' Ava said, nodding towards a brown envelope which contained the agreement. 'And I couldn't care less.'

Was there any kind of a property settlement with Frank?

'Ha! You know I don't want anything. But let's don't go into THAT!'

'So, then, it's absolutely and positively over?'

'Oh, Earl,' she sighed, 'it's been over for years!'

Still, Ava in the next few years continued to see Frank from time to time and under happier conditions than when they were married. She often stayed at his apartment, home or whatever place he was living, and often declared that she had been married to one of the great men. What had gone wrong? It was Frank's uncontrollable rages that she couldn't accept and it was her own temperamental anxieties that caused her doubt. It was partly his Sicilian temper.

Twenty years later, the singer Bricktop said to me, 'I think they're both still in love with the other. Ava's still around Frank whenever she can be. I think she still likes to rub up against him—you know what I mean?'

Ava not long ago laughingly said to Nancy, Jr., 'Ask your dad if he remembers when he pushed a television set out the window at the Hotel Fontainebleau.'

HIS 'MARRIAGE' TO LAUREN BACALL

With Ava Gardner now part of his past, Frank Sinatra could have settled down in the late fifties and swinging sixties into a life of peace. But that is not His Way. He never wants peace. He enjoys conflict. He is a warrior, an unhappy warrior.

He prospers, yes, prospers—even commercially—on brawls, lawsuits and headlines. The conflicts make him a bigger box-office attraction than all the happy singers. Sinatra knows exactly what he is doing. By protesting that his privacy is being invaded, he gets free advertising for his egocentricities—and his bookings. He lures great crowds into paying record prices to see and hear him. In that sense he has made dupes of the press for thirty to forty years. The press give him free space to blast the press. It has found no way to refuse him space for his outbursts because he is colourful and controversial, and a story about him may be the most interesting thing in the paper. An occasional editor has played down his temper tantrums, but usually Frank is soon back in the paper on page two or three with stories that always mention where he is currently appearing!

After Ava, Frank was, for a while, between women. He entered the swinger, Ring-a-ding-ding phase of his life that had preceded the superstud phase. Candid sex was taking over America. There was a new language, and Frank contributed to it. Some was shocking, at first. The expression 'balling', for copulating, was used even by young ladies. To call somebody a 'grabber' was to compliment him. The incestuous expression 'mother' came down from Harlem, and Frank was soon calling people 'mothers' or 'those mothers'. Generally, he would accompany it with a laugh, and that made it a ribald compliment.

Having made his comeback and landed back on the money train, Frank realized one of his ambitions: to be a Casanova, a womanizer. Many women became quickly fond of him, among them Judy Garland. An uncommon number of beautiful and famous young women seemed to be waitin' for Frankie.

Frank sat in the bar at the Copacabana Lounge one night, his head down, looking gloomy, talking to a pretty woman of my acquaintance. 'Quit looking like that!' she said. 'You should be the happiest man in the world. What are you so down about?'

His hand squeezed her knee. It wasn't Ava he was gloomy about, he said. He kept thinking of that black period of his life, when he was in his nosedive and so many supposed friends hurt him by rejecting him when he needed help. The Sicilian in him would not let him forget the way they'd hurt him. He wanted to 'kick them in the balls' just as they'd kicked him. The nosedive period had hardened him and was to guide his future behaviour.

Frank's hand remained on the pretty woman's knee.

The woman had been in psychoanalysis for several years, and she could not resist trying to straighten him out. She found to her surprise that Frank was conversant with the subject. He knew that he was ambivalent, having conflicting hate and love feelings simultaneously.

'Where did you find out so much?' the woman asked. Frank replied that he was a late-night reader. He admitted he could be a mean bastard to those who had been mean to him, but he had his principles and there was a lot of underdog left in him. He would never pick on anybody too little to be a match for him. He did not go around punching little people.

'You defy authority, you don't conform to society?' The woman had all the questions.

Frank, whose hand was still on her knee, agreed that

sometimes he got a little crazy about that. He was inclined to pick on the biggies.

Yes, Frank, unable to forget all the hurts he suffered in his down period, had developed a defiance of society that reinforced his childhood thinking and influenced the rest of his life. He would forever after be the little guy fighting the System. He would seem to be somewhat psychotic about it, and there were people who would question his sanity and say, 'The man is crazy, he is unbalanced.' But the way he saw it, he was being honest: He had been a hurt person; why couldn't he hurt other people if they hurt him, especially if he had won the battle and was on top now?

His disappointment in 'friends' who hadn't helped him during his nosedive period was deep, and he was going to remember them. He felt they were part of the 'Authority', the 'Society' that he didn't like when he was a poor kid in Hoboken, and he didn't like them now.

The woman did not have a romance with Frank. She regretted that. While they were talking, somebody interrupted, and Frank left the table—and her knee.

'One of Frank's pals,' she told me several years later, 'said, "I can see what's happening. You don't want to become just one more girl in his entourage, just one of the mob." ' He had steered her away from Frank's table.

'In all honesty, I have resented Frank's pal's protective instincts in my behalf all these years since,' she said. 'Frank and I could have had a very interesting time together. I would not have minded being a member of the entourage for a while!'

Frank's rebellion against authority was on and off in the years to come; he loved it one day, hated it the next. When he was throwing cherry bombs from hotel windows, firing off guns, telling police he didn't know who did it, he was—so he thought—rebelling against society. He often behaved like an undisciplined brat. 'They threw me to the dogs,' he rationalized 'They didn't mind ruining me.'

The 'new Sinatra' was so hot in the actor-singer marketplace that United Artists bankrolled him as an independent producer—he who'd once worked for less than one dollar a week. He was offered lush offices, chauffeurs, expense accounts. Nightclubs hinted at salaries up to $75,000 or $100,000 a week, counting the 'under-the-table'. He accepted *Suddenly* as his first picture after *Eternity*, and the happy reports on it inspired him to remark, 'I feel eight feet tall.'

Even his vocal cords co-operated in his brilliant ascent. He'd been forced to accept an unfavourable recording contract from Capitol when he was down, after his break with Mitch Miller at Columbia when nobody really wanted Sinatra. But things were breaking his way now, and he got Nelson Riddle to become his arranger-conductor. Riddle, a top trombonist with the big bands, had played with Tommy Dorsey. Frank bragged later that he raided Dorsey and stole Riddle.

Sinatra respected Riddle's musicianship and his sense of adventure and non-conformity. Riddle's technique was to tell a complete story in a song, not a new idea in music, but one that hadn't been employed much lately in popular music. Soon Frank Sinatra's songs were on the air again more than Eddie Fisher's and Frankie Laine's. Frank had hits in 'My One and Only Love', 'I've Got the World on a String', 'Come Fly with Me' and 'Young at Heart'. It was all to the good for Capitol Records.

But Frank failed to stay out of brawls. Rather comically he emerged as a defender of pure American womanhood. In a fight in a parking lot at the Crescendo Café in Hollywood, he took it as an insult to chivalry when press agent Jim Byron asked him who his 'broad' was that evening.

'I dumped him on his fanny,' Sinatra was quoted. Byron said he didn't put it that way but was trying to get a news item. The girl was Judy Garland, whom Frank happened to be escorting that night for Judy's husband, his friend Sid Luft, who was in New York. It came out later that Judy actually had love tremors for the 'King' and burst into tears once when Frank stood her up. Frank blasted at Byron. 'You're either a cop or a reporter. I hate cops and newspapermen.'

The papers printed it, playing into his hand. Editorial writers excoriated him. Police itched to run into him speeding. But they never did. Frank was too smart. He was careful. He drove so slow that one passenger with him asked, 'Why are you crawling?'

His swinger reputation built up. Bosomy Anita Ekberg from Sweden, such a choice morsel that Bob Hope took her on a USO trip, boasted that Frank paid her fare from Hollywood to meet him at the Copacabana in New York, where he was starring. When she arrived at the club with another date, Frank ignored her, joined another table, and letting no opportunity pass by, began a flirtation with socialite heiress Gloria Vanderbilt, whom he had met just then. Her marriage to ageing conductor Leopold Stokowski was breaking up.

He introduced his sweep-them-off-their-feet technique to Society in late 1954 and early 1955. Lunch, drinks, dinner . . . he rushed Gloria to the opening of the Truman Capote–Harold Arlen musical, *House of Flowers*, left her to do his show at the Copa, picked her up and returned her to the Copa, then to El Morocco for breakfast.

FLASH: Miss Vanderbilt will have a part in a Sinatra movie!

NEXT DAY: Miss Vanderbilt will not be in a Sinatra movie. There was a misunderstanding about the size of the role. She thought it would be bigger.

Newspapers wondered whether Sinatra broke up her marriage. Sinatra asked me to clarify that. He delicately referred to her as Miss Vanderbilt. He said, 'I didn't meet Miss Vanderbilt until less than two weeks ago. It's pretty silly to call that a romance.'

Whatever had happened was finished.

One of Frank's eccentricities is his hatred of people pawing him. He wants to keep a well-pressed look. When somebody merely touches him or puts an arm around him, he flares up and angrily squirms out of the grasp. It is a foible so well known that his best friends keep their distance. This has been interpreted as being part of a God complex.

Frank's lawyers sued *Look* magazine for $2 million for invasion of privacy and straightened out a well-known story that pictured him as being rude to Speaker Samuel Rayburn at the 1956 Democratic Convention, where he'd sung the national anthem. A story was told that Rayburn reached out as Frank was leaving the platform and said, 'Aren't you going to sing "The Yellow Rose of Texas", Frank?' whereupon Frank snapped, 'Take the hand off the suit, creep!'

Sinatra produced a telegram from Speaker Rayburn denying that he did it.

Frank glanced around the set of his *Pal Joey* film one day and warned director George Sidney that if *Time* magazine reporter Ezra Goodman (doing a story about Frank having dates with Kim Novak) remained there, he wouldn't. Goodman left.

If Frank wanted adventure, he got it in the celebrated 'Wrong Door Raid', the next upsetting chapter in his life. It brought him into conflict with his long-time close friend, Joe DiMaggio. They were about the most prominent Italian buddies in America and could call each other 'dago', without offence being taken. They shared a bizarre experience.

Few people knew the true story. 'Joltin' Joe' DiMaggio of the New York Yankees, the hero to baseball that Sinatra was to popular singing, was carrying an unextinguishable torch for his wife Marilyn Monroe. Joe suffered as severely as Frank had suffered over Ava Gardner. It was a coincidence: two Italian heroes, both on their knees to their ladies.

Marilyn had locked the door on Joe and was hiding out in hotels and apartments. When she was staying at the Ambassador Hotel on Park Avenue in New York, he asked some of us to get her room number so he could find her. He was suspicious of Marilyn being with other men. He appealed to some of us to help him get to her and plead with her to take him back.

Joe—like Frank when he was trying to get Ava back—was not quite rational. The big, moody Yankee star was sometimes close to tears. A private detective who was reportedly following Marilyn's Hollywood activities, had said that the blonde sex symbol was having a narcotics experience in Los Angeles with a lesbian.

I've got to break in and find out,' Joe said.

It was a dangerous business, breaking in. Frank understood Joe's torture, it was the same as his had been. He could not easily say no when Joe asked him to join their expedition to hunt the suspected hideout.

'It was the worst organized raid I ever heard about,' one of the private eyes said later. It is not clear what part Sinatra was to have had, if any, beyond joining the party.

The intrepid raiders found Marilyn's car parked on Waring Avenue in Beverly Hills. Now all they had to do was break in and snatch Marilyn from the arms of her lesbian lover. Somebody crashed down the door.

They didn't find Marilyn. They found an indignant woman whom they'd awakened. The raiders had gone to the wrong door. Marilyn Monroe had been visiting another apartment.

The 'Wrong Door Raid' became acutely embarrassing to all. It might have passed over, but the awakened woman claimed she'd suffered acute hysteria, and sued.

The scandal magazine *Confidential* published the story; suddenly everybody was investigating the farcical raid.

Frank's mere presence in the group gave it headline value. He got two subpoenas from California state senate investigators demanding he explain his alleged trespassing. Denying indignantly that he'd trespassed, he maintained that he hadn't participated; he'd stayed in the car, he said.

The image of Sinatra the battler staying away from a battle was hard to accept. One of the investigating committees declared that Sinatra had not remained in the car. Sinatra stood firm on his story and was cool and convincing. Two grand jury sessions pumped private detective Barney Ruditsky (the chief of the 'search') and accepted his sworn word that Sinatra had remained in the car a block away.

Sinatra was held innocent. The District Attorney tried to find perjury, but couldn't. The 'Wrong Door Raid' soon became one of Hollywood's forgotten flops.

Students of the Sinatra character and conscience have noted that Frank, for all of his supposed defiance of authority, has always remained within the law. Here was another instance when he was found 'clean'. But Frank did suffer, and those old enough to remember will always wonder whether he was or wasn't in the raid.

Worse, the friendship of Frank and Joe perished.

'Joe should have spoken right up and cleared Frank in this thing,' the Sinatra camp said, while the DiMaggio side replied, 'Joe was out of his mind and didn't know what he was doing.'

Their palship ended. Frank quit speaking to Joe, and Joe now ignored Frank in restaurants. Efforts to get them back together failed dismally.

There was increasing bitterness after Joe and Marilyn divorced. Floundering around Beverly Hills and Hollywood, Marilyn took up with the Peter–Pat Lawford set, which then included Frank. Becoming one of Sinatra's many girlfriends, Marilyn was a guest at his home for weeks. Frank said he was just trying to help her get out nights, and he joked about her infidelity. 'She's staying at my house and going out with other guys,' he said.

Marilyn, believing in her giddy way that she was in love with Robert Kennedy or John F. Kennedy and not quite sure which, once rushed to Las Vegas to sit ringside at a Sinatra show and pretend she was his Number 1 girl. Joe DiMaggio watched all this with increasing anger. Even though he was by then her ex-husband and powerless to change the course of events, he believed that Marilyn's associations with the drinking Hollywood swingers were leading to her ruin.

When Marilyn died six years after the 'Wrong Door Raid', her ex-husband, Joe DiMaggio, took iron-hand command of the funeral. Frank and the Lawfords were stunned to learn that they were among the first he barred from the services.

Frank's friendship with Humphrey Bogart dated from his beginnings in Hollywood and Bogie never turned his back on him when Frank was down. Sinatra the actor liked to have people compare him with Bogart, both as a performer and person. Bogart was a 'natural', too, one of the 'No Crap' school of stars without affectations or pretensions, a man who would use four-letter words if they seemed to be the ones needed at the moment, and in Bogart's conversations, they often were.

In Romanoff's restaurant during one drinking session, a Sinatra girlfriend said to him as he sat with Bogart, 'You know you sound like Bogie sometimes.'

'Don't remind him, Sweetheart,' Bogie snarled. 'The poor bastard's tryin' to kick it.'

Sinatra added some of Bogart's attitudes of independence to his own collection. Together they were a defiant duo. Bogart constantly pretended not to take his acting or his profession seriously. His first thought was, 'Let's have a drink.' His second was, 'Now, who can we louse up today? Let's get started.'

They formed a fast friendship after Frank bought a $250,000-house in the Holmby Hills area of Beverly Hills, near Bogart's residence. Frank surrendered the house to Nancy, Sr., when they divorced, but he got accustomed to Bogart, and to Mrs. Bogart, and the exclusive neighbourhood where high walls were built around the pools and the grounds to protect the children and the animals and the owners.

Bogart joined in the applause—although mutedly, because he played everything down—when Frank rose higher and higher after his comeback. Another Bogart type, Robert Mitchum, shouted praise for Frank, declaring that he had saved the film *Not as a Stranger* with his own special acting touches. As a notorious bar-room brawler, who was bigger, taller and sturdier than Sinatra, Mitchum commanded respect when he said he'd hate to fight Frank: 'Sinatra was so resilient he'd keep slugging and getting up and slugging until somebody'd get killed,' he said. Frank grinned over that tribute more than over some of the comments about his acting.

The Sinatra singing style was definitely back in fashion. Look who was Number 1 in the *Metronome* and *Downbeat* polls due to 'Violets for Your Furs', 'My Funny Valentine', and Nelson Riddle's arrangements. Not Eddie Fisher!

It was no secret near the end of 1956 that Humphrey Bogart was dying of cancer. Bogart was the leader of the Holmby Hills 'Rat Pack', a do-nothing organization devoted to non-conformity and whiskey-drinking, which, of course, numbered Frank as a member. Lauren Bacall, then only about thirty-one, accidentally gave the group its name, referring to the bunch as just that, the 'rat pack'. Bogart grabbed the reins and announced the purpose of the non-organization was to stay up so late and loud that neighbours raised hell. The Rat Pack, which never did anything except get written up, included Judy Garland, Sid Luft, Irving Lazar, Paul Douglas, Joey Bishop and almost anybody who dropped in. Frequently the members assembled on Bogart's sixty-five-foot yacht *Santana*.

With Bogart very ill, the shock of seeing his physical decline was severe on everybody. Bogart himself was blunt about having cancer. 'Nothing to be ashamed of like some other diseases I could have had,' he said. 'Why not talk about it?'

Sinatra and all the other friends waited sadly for him to go. On Christmas Day 1956, Lauren Bacall did not give her usual holiday party. Paul Douglas and restaurateur Dave Chasen visited Bogart for only a few minutes on New Year's Day. A week passed with Bogart getting lower, and then one night Bogart gave his wife a kiss and a pat on the cheek and said, 'Goodbye, Kid'.

The entire country was saddened. Frank suffered an emotional upset at the Copacabana where he was starring. He was troubled about what he should do. He phoned Lauren Bacall that he had cancelled two appearances at the Copacabana due to his own grief and had explained to his agents, 'I can't go on. I wouldn't be coherent.' He might fly to the funeral. But he was developing laryngitis. He would have to cancel more shows.

Three thousand people lined the streets outside All Saints Episcopal Church in Beverly Hills, where John Huston delivered the eulogy. But Frank remained in New York.

Huston complimented Lauren Bacall's bravery saying, 'She was gallant; she knew death was there every hour of the day and night. And out of the power of her love she was able to hide her grief and go on being her own familiar self for Bogie—a flawless performance.'

A tiny gold whistle was placed in the receptacle for Bogie's ashes: a memento of their film *To Have and Have Not*, with the words from the film inscribed on the inside: 'If you need anything, just whistle.'

One of Sinatra's charming qualities is his comforting of people in grief. He is Italian-descended, after all, and emotional, and sincerely sympathetic. He especially 'has a way with widows', it has been said. He is the first to hold their hand and let them cry on his shoulder. He is understanding and soothing. His talent to enchant bereaved women and ease their suffering and sadness has been remarked upon by many men who have seen Sinatra work his magic, and wished they could do the same.

Lauren Bacall Bogart had some painful weeks. In the summer months after the funeral, it wasn't surprising to see that Frank Sinatra and Lauren Bacall occasionally had dinner together. Why not? They were both unattached now, both lone, single survivors of the Rat Pack that was no more; and Sinatra had been Bogart's best friend.

Now it was little Manie Sacks who was dying.

It was a year since Bogart's death. Manie was fifty-six; Frank was forty-two. Manie was the quiet saint of Show Business, the bachelor NBC vice-president of TV programming, who'd crossed countries or oceans to keep Frank from divorce or suicide or to help get him new recording contracts. Broadway Show Business took a day off to go to the funeral in a Philadelphia synagogue. Frank walked slowly ahead of the casket, looking thinner than usual, biting his lip and near tears.

Frank, in all the glory of his new success, was shaken. He had known Manie was dying longer than anybody except Manie. Little Manie knew for three years that he was dying of leukaemia, which had also killed his friend, pianist-bandleader Eddy Duchin. Manie remained silent to keep it from his mother, who was in her eighties.

Frank was one of the few who knew that Manie knew. Even at the funeral, when the rabbi said Manie 'had known', almost every head went up. They all thought that Manie hadn't known. Perry Como, Tony Martin, Cyd Charisse, Sid Caesar, Imogene Coca, Leo Durocher were all amazed.

Frank and some other mourners discussed it back in New

York that night at dinner at the Colony restaurant. Frank sat with Lauren Bacall, by now his frequent date. Dinah Shore remarked that Manie 'knew Frank and me since we were just babies'. Frank said that Manie learned in 1954, while getting a blood count after a flu attack, that he had leukaemia. He didn't immediately tell Frank.

But Sinatra suspected: 'You're sick,' he said to Manie. 'Let's figure out what it is.'

'What I've got,' Manie told Frank, 'you're never going to be able to figure out.'

Manie and Frank lived with the secret for about a year. The last thing Manie saw in Show Business was Frank Sinatra on a TV show. Then, knowing his own fate, he broke into tears.

'What bothers me is that when I holler for help, he ain't gonna be there any more,' Frank said that night after the funeral, as he and Lauren Bacall said good-night to the others.

Frank and Lauren Bacall had become best friends. Nevertheless, it was a jolt to all of us when London *Evening Standard* columnist Thomas Wiseman reported 14 September that Sinatra and Miss Bacall would marry within six months, 'barring an act of Providence or Ava Gardner'.

'I understand Sinatra is anxious to keep his marriage plans a secret and that he will probably deny it . . . but you can take his denials with a pinch of salt,' the story said.

Wiseman had caught the Hollywood columnists by surprise. At first they denied it. They had considered it indelicate to suggest a romance. But Betty (she was usually referred to as 'Baby', Bogart's name for her, or Betty, but seldom as Lauren) was young and attractive and shouldn't be expected to stay home alone. She eventually flew to Las Vegas with friends for one of Frank's openings. Later, Frank and she went out alone. Louella Parsons wrote that it was part of Frank's friendship with Bogart 'to see that she didn't mourn in loneliness'.

There was a circusy atmosphere to the journalistic follow-up that made Frank uncomfortable. He was put on a spot.

On 12 March, 1958, about fourteen months after Bogart's death, Louella Parsons wrote flatly that they would marry. Frank had been overheard proposing to her at dinner at the Imperial Gardens. Betty hedged when asked about it and said, 'Why don't you ask Frank in Florida?' But she finally admitted he'd asked her and said she had accepted. Despite the tradition that a reporter doesn't reveal sources, Louella admitted that Irving ('Swifty') Lazar, the literary agent, told her, 'Yes, it's true, they'll marry.'

But Walter Winchell wired from Miami Beach, where he had been having dinner with Sinatra, that 'Frank Sinatra and Lauren Bacall will not be married in the near future or at any time.'

Winchell quoted Sinatra with one of the unlikeliest remarks ever attributed to Frank: 'How can I ever get married again? There's nothing left of my heart.' Obviously it was a line Winchell composed himself.

Yet despite being in the middle, Sinatra enjoyed being cast in the role of a romantic. Marriage was far from his mind, he said. He and Betty were 'very, very dear friends'. After his successful opening at the Fontainebleau Hotel, he sang torch songs at a private party and said, 'This one is for Betty.'

Some of his friends suggested that he didn't want to get married again because he feared the effect on his children. But after all, hadn't he married Ava Gardner? What about the effect on the children then?

They didn't marry. They broke up. Winchell got it from the horse's mouth, and the horse was Sinatra.

Betty tried to maintain her sense of humour about the rebuff. 'I'm not going to talk about Frank Sinatra,' she announced on a trip to New York. She had her feet up on a long coffee table and was looking at me with a grin over the top of a glass. Actors deserve a little privacy, she said. She'd never sought publicity, never had a press agent. She wasn't going to say anything about Frank Sinatra.

Columnists predicted that they'd get back together, but they didn't. A month later, Betty wasn't finding it funny any more. Frank was opening at the Las Vegas Sands, and she attended a Dean Martin opening at the Coconut Grove in Los Angeles.

'Why aren't you attending the Sinatra opening in Las Vegas?' a columnist asked her.

'Do me a favour: never mention me again in the same breath with Frank Sinatra,' she said.

The truth was that Frank rebelled against being pushed or hastened by friends who tried to run his life. Again he was doing it His Way even if it meant defying conformity or what his friends expected.

(Seventeen years later, when Lauren Bacall was out of the movies and a big stage star, she was discovered in a party with Frank Sinatra one night at the Hotel Carlyle bar in New York, listening to Marion MacPartland at the piano. Frank had requested, 'Last Night When We Were Young'. Was it possible that Frank and Betty were reviving their romance in 1975? I phoned Miss Bacall, who laughed. 'We weren't together,' she said. 'I was one of about ten people in the party. We're friends. We don't see each other any more because he's there and I'm here.'

Delicately I said, 'Funny you should say that because you were once quoted as saying "Never mention me in the same breath again with Frank Sinatra." '

Coolly and with a light touch, she said, 'Well, I might have said that fifteen years ago, but later on it's not important. Anyway, this was nothing . . . and thanks for checking.')

BUILDING A KINGDOM

Frank is a driven person, according to behavioural scientists.

He has style, flair, charm and charisma, but above all, he has drive. When he was nearing forty, he was flattered to be asked to explain his success and he enjoyed expanding upon his earlier theme that he'd had an unhappy childhood in Hoboken.

'My old man thought anybody who wanted to go into the music business was a bum,' he told one interviewer. 'So I picked up and left home for New York, quitting high school to do it.' He had to prove to his father that he could make good as a singer.

Now that same drive pushed him on to make him rich—and also poor again (by his standards) for a brief period.

He was going to do big things. Play big, spend big, give big. He was going to live and with dash. He would be a brilliant businessman. He would be bossy and even dictatorial, nasty at times, ruthless, sentimental, unbelievably kind and generous, flashily flamboyant; he would defy convention and flout the rules. What he didn't know was that he'd constantly need to be reassured that he was important and would require obeisant friends around him to massage his ego.

He'd continue being 'One-Take Charlie' on the movie lots, refusing to do scenes over and over. Frank maintained that the first take was natural and adequate. 'But you're reducing some great actors to shit out of deference to you,' some performers argued. But Frank retorted, 'They *can* rehearse—I *can't*.'

Many couldn't wait for Frank to stub his toe. But one friend, Burt Lancaster, was cheering. Lancaster had seen Frank working hard on *From Here to Eternity* even while he was so unhappy about Ava Gardner. 'And Frank's voice came back at the same time he got the Oscar,' Lancaster pointed out. 'He was champion again in both departments.' Lancaster, an obvious fan, said Sinatra's album, 'Swing Easy', popular in the mid-fifties, was one of his greatest.

Frank suddenly discovered Big Money. He was amazed at how much Sinatra the Oscar-winner could earn. Leonard Goldenson, the American Broadcasting Company president, flew to Hollywood and handed him a cheque for $3 million for twenty-six half-hour TV shows and two spectaculars.

'It's a good capital gains deal,' Frank said. He accepted the cheque with a Show Business flourish. Photographers found him, for once, very willing to pose for pictures.

Frank began having dreams of empire. He was the most ogled customer in Romanoff's restaurant, where he had his own table and his own phone, from which he was always making deals (or dates). He played baccarat at $2,000 a hand. He had previously used chartered planes, but now, he and some friends acquired a twin-engined Martin with an electric piano, tape machine, conference or card section, and a bar. Robin Douglas-Home, a young English writer who visited Sinatra, was puzzled at the name of his plane, which he believed to be *Eldago*.

Frank laughed and explained it was *El Dago*, his name for himself.

Having made a prestigious purchase of the old Al Jolson home in Palm Springs for $90,000, he also picked up, for $200,000, a Broadway play, *A Hole in the Head*, to make into a movie. In his next movie, *Suddenly*, he would of course have star billing. He had so many movie offers he didn't know which to do.

With his over-confidence running away with him in the early fifties, Sinatra said nobody was going to tell him how to do his ABC TV show, and he was red-faced soon afterwards because critics hopped on his questionable taste, objecting to use of such words as *broads* and *mother-grabbers* and *your bird*.

Everybody gave him advice; he didn't want it. He became bad-tempered; ABC wanted to bail out. The show was an admitted flop.

Frank just didn't come over on TV as he did in pictures, concerts and nightclubs. He wasn't as smooth or amusing. The fact is, Frank never did quite achieve the success he wanted on TV.

Finally, Frank surrendered. The show had lasted about a season.

He was sick of it. He quit with a parting blast at the rating system. The only good thing about it was the capital gains, which saved him on income tax. But he'd be back. As he often said in those days, he'd show the mothers!

In Las Vegas in the fifties, they were learning to pamper people, and Sinatra became one of their first and most willing subjects. He was going to get subservience, almost worship, and he was going to love it. In 1952, Big Jack Entratter arrived from New York, where he'd managed the Copacabana, to take charge of entertainment at the new Hotel Sands. A close friend of Sinatra's, Entratter began building a realm for the 'King'.

The Sands was colourful with the president, Jakie Friedman, from Dallas, hustling around the casino in his western togs and sombrero, betting and sometimes losing $100,000.

The astute Entratter wanted Frank Sinatra, and he knew Sinatra's need to be Number 1. But Frank was starring at the Flamingo. The atmosphere wasn't too cheery there. Owner Gus Greenbaum and his wife had just been mysteriously slashed to death with a large carving knife at their ranch house outside Phoenix.

'There's an understanding among "the boys" that you never murder anybody in Las Vegas,' they would tell you there. 'It would give the town a bad name.'

Greenbaum evidently knew too much about somebody. His wife must have known the killer, and so, in this never-solved case, both were murdered.

But not in Las Vegas.

Big Jack waited till Frank worked out his contract, then set up the Sands opening for his pal for the autumn of 1953, just when Frank was the hottest attraction in the country, thanks to the enthusiasm for his role in *From Here to Eternity*.

Frank was given the best living quarters, the luxurious three-bedroom Presidential Suite on the ground floor with a private swimming pool protected from the outside world by a stone wall.

The subservience to Frank began as soon as Entratter brought him from the airport. 'Sinatra's here!' everybody seemed to be saying. Out raced the motorized luggage carts. Their drivers piled Sinatra's bags aboard and whizzed past the regular swimming pool to the Churchill Downs building. (The buildings were named for race-tracks.)

After acknowledging some excited greetings from people who'd caught a glimpse of him, Sinatra stepped into a special cart, which seemed larger than the others, and rode with Entratter to his new home-away-from-home. It was dominated by a bar well stocked with Frank's beloved Jack Daniels. They had a good-luck drink, and Frank looked out at the private swimming pool with a smile and nod of satisfaction: This was class.

It was the right way to treat a guest. Of course, the suite was complimentary. The food, the drinks, the service were all free, not only to him but to his guests, who often stayed overnight and sometimes for several days. Anybody trying to compute Frank's payment from the Sands would have to add $300 to $500 a day for this set-up. It certainly was flattering. It surely was pleasing to the recipient.

Just a whisper, a murmur, and Frank had one of those carts speeding to him to service his latest desire. Steam room, sauna, health club, massage, of course! Sleep till mid-afternoon. Read the goddamn papers.

Entratter had his own dreams. Using Sinatra's strength, he brought in the team of Dean Martin and Jerry Lewis to star in the Copa Room. They had drawn crowds as big as Sinatra's at the Copacabana in New York. He also wanted Sammy Davis, Jr., but it took Entratter a couple of years to pull in the Will Mastin Trio 'starring Sammy Davis, Jr.'

Frank remembered that it was way back in the 1940s when he saw the black Will Mastin Trio performing in Harlem. Will Mastin and Sammy Davis, Sr., were good, but that little Sammy, Jr., was a dancing, drumming dynamo. A couple of years passed, and when Frank did some Army Special Service shows in 1945, he saw Sammy in line in his GI uniform waiting for an autograph.

'You're the kid that works with your father and uncle,' Frank said. 'When you get out of the service, come and see me.'

Following through, Frank asked an agent to find Sammy, but didn't remember the act's name. But Sammy was found—in Detroit—and Frank pushed the act ahead. Once Frank got the act to substitute for him onstage when he was out with laryngitis. They were a smash. They became Frank's protégés.

When Frank became a power in Hollywood, he told Sammy, 'I'm putting you in pictures. You're getting $100,000 in films. You're with Dean and me. The billing is going to be me, Dean and you.'

'Man!' gasped Sammy.

Sammy said later, 'Frank cared when nobody else did—before it became popular.'

Nevertheless, Sammy also had flashes of independence and indignation. Some of Sinatra's hot-and-cold indifference hurt him. Sammy was emboldened to criticize the 'King' in an interview with radio chatterer Jackie Eigen in Chicago.

'I love Frank and he was the kindest man in the world to me when I lost my eye in an auto accident and wanted to kill myself,' Sammy said. 'But there are many things he does that there is no excuse for. I don't care if you are the most talented man in the world. It does not give you the right to step on people and treat them rotten. That is what he does occasionally.'

Jackie Eigen says Sammy didn't mean to rap Sinatra, but that his honest observation came out as more of a blast than he intended.

Sinatra went into a chair-throwing act when he heard

about it. Sammy wanted to apologize, but couldn't get through to the 'King'.

Sinatra soon opened at the Miami Beach Fontainebleau, and Sammy opened next door at the Eden Roc Hotel. Frank suspected that Sammy would try to make peace from next door. 'Frank left word at the front door of the Fontainebleau,' recalls Eigen, 'not to let Sammy into the hotel.'

Sammy seriously repented his words. Frank, who had put him in pictures, took him out of pictures. Sammy never said precisely what Sinatra had done that was 'rotten', but Sammy was notified that he was no longer in the movie *Never So Few*, which Frank had had rewritten so there'd be a part in it for him. Frank cracked Sammy sharply across the knuckles. Steve McQueen went into the role that had been Sammy's.

Brooding about it, Sammy suffered for months. Frank had been his greatest booster and benefactor. One night at a Los Angeles charity benefit, Frank was the master of ceremonies and Sammy performed. They fell into each other's arms.

Dean Martin witnessed the reconciliation. 'Seeing those two make up was a disgusting display,' Dino said.

There would be more chilly times between them later.

Sinatra's sexual activity was increasing—if that was possible. Swingin' Frank became an international Casanova, a connoisseur of feminine beauty. Dean Martin made the pungent observation: 'When Sinatra dies, they're giving his zipper to the Smithsonian.'

An old story about Errol Flynn and Dick Haymes was modernized. Supposedly Sinatra had placed a list of Hollywood beauties on his dressing room wall and checked off the conquests one by one: 'Finally he had checked them all off and had to get a fresh list!' Frank did tell some reporters, 'If I had all the affairs you gave me credit for, I'd be a jar at Harvard Medical School.'

With a mischievous smile, Sinatra was stealing girls out from under Howard Hughes (literally). Hughes would put new beauties under movie contracts and set them up in apartments for future reference. But Sinatra never went to all that effort; they usually came to him.

Columnist Dorothy Kilgallen, who at first liked him and

then hated him, wrote repeatedly of the ease with which he lured beauties to his boudoir. Sinatra retaliated at some of his nightclub shows by referring to a Kilgallen facial weakness. 'Dotty Kilgallen couldn't be here tonight,' he said, 'she's out shopping for a new chin.'

'You're being too rough,' friends cautioned Sinatra.

'I'm not being rough enough,' he answered grimly.

Sinatra was so busy in the boudoir that he sometimes got his schedule confused. One night, after inviting composer Jule Styne to stay at his Beverly Hills house overnight, he withdrew the invitation. 'I've got a date with somebody that you know. She wouldn't want you to know she was here,' Sinatra said. 'Go to the hotel for the night.'

Styne agreed, but was fascinated. 'Some great chick that knows me?' he thought.

He couldn't sleep for wondering who it was and found he didn't have sleeping pills because he'd left them at Sinatra's house. He got up, got dressed, returned through the night to Sinatra's house, entered through a side entrance without being seen, and peeked.

'There was Frank with this girl in his arms on the steps. There was love-making music—a Sinatra ballad.

'He was going to take her upstairs. He was reciting poetry to her . . . (Oh, some awful garbage!) . . . I got a look at her. It was our manicurist!'

Frank courted some most respectable ladies. He developed a pattern of having a headline romance between professional crises. It was time for another one.

He chose an acquaintance of mine, Lady Adele Beatty of London, who had been Adele O'Connor from Texas and California, former press agent for the Colony restaurant and certain chic social clients. She and Lord Beatty were separated. Lady Beatty was regarded as one of the classic beauties by London society writers. The New York press was self-conscious about her because it had never placed her upon such a lofty pedestal.

With Frank now climbing the ladder socially, it was natural that he would romance a titled lady. They had met in Hollywood, and when Frank went to London to introduce acts at a charity première of *Me and the Colonel*, he was soon giving Lady Beatty the same rush he had given Gloria Vanderbilt.

After all, he didn't have much time.

It was lunch, tea and dinner with Lady Beatty, and often breakfast, too, in some club. The British press made the same assumption it had with Frank and Lauren Bacall: that such steady company-keeping meant marriage. Since I knew both parties in this new romance, I went to London where I found reporters and photographers shadowing Frank in the belief that he and Lady Beatty were going to marry. One paper actually printed a marriage announcement.

Frank was courteous about it all, but irritated because he was receiving stacks of mail, both for and against, from the British public, which likes to write letters.

'That so-called announcement,' he said, 'has embarrassed the lady and my children.' He made the same complaint in the Lauren Bacall situation! 'I love London more than any city in Europe, but they are going to drive me out of it.'

From his continual talking about reports concerning himself and Lady Beatty, it was clear that he momentarily enjoyed being spotlighted with aristocracy. It was he who kept the gossip alive. When he thanked the crowd at the benefit for its ovation, he said in the presence of the Queen, 'I did not come here to get married. Some of your papers would have me marry as often as King Farouk, and I'm not even as fat as he is.' Danny Kaye howled, but some British writers said it was a vulgar thing to say before the Queen.

Some of the American press was good—especially my home paper, the New York *Post*, which said,

MAYFAIR FLIPS ITS CRUMPETS OVER FRANK SINATRA.

It was true, as John Mills, proprietor of Les Ambassadeurs, was saying: 'Sinatra in London is bigger than God.' I was invited to a small party Frank gave at the expensive Harlequin Suite at the Dorchester Hotel during the Lady Beatty period. Sinatra had a servant who said to the early arrivals, 'Mr. Sinatra is still in the bawth.' He had invited only a dozen guests. He came out still inserting studs in his shirt, and said, 'Hey, there's food out there,' and he led the way to the caviar, shouting, 'My father and mother brought me up on this sort of food.' The guests discussed singing with him, and he said, 'Vic Damone's got the best set of pipes of anybody singing today.' Thinking about the party later, I decided there wasn't a great difference in his manner from the days when he was Tommy Dorsey's band singer in Meadowbrook, New Jersey, except now he was rich and world-famous.

With Frank returning soon to New York, the stately Lady Beatty realized she wouldn't be getting his exclusive devotion indefinitely. He plunged into more movies and more money-making. He repeatedly took a dozen or so guests to dinner. An attractive singer named Diana Trask, whom he'd discovered in Australia, was starring at the Blue Angel. Escorting a stunning actress, Judith Meredith, he took fifteen people to see and hear her. Any woman would have to love that.

(For the record, Frank's romance with Lady Beatty was declared *finis* within a year. On the night of her subsequent marriage to film director Stanley Donen, she received a cable with a one-word message: 'WHY?' The Donens believed Sinatra had sent it.)

Again the Sinatra fans—an older group now—screamed after him. In Atlantic City at the 500 Club, I saw a woman of seemingly mature years give twenty dollars to a bandleader to bring her a cigarette butt Frank had just stamped out on the floor. She tucked it in a napkin to take home as a souvenir.

Sinatra became enormously generous to women as he got richer. Just before my wife's fiftieth birthday, I asked Frank if he'd send her a telegram. Getting bolder the next day, I asked if he'd allow me to have his signature inscribed on a small disc I intended to buy for her charm bracelet.

'I'll take care of all that jazz,' Frank said.

It arrived: a beautiful gold bracelet, and dangling from it was a large 14-carat gold disc inscribed: 'To Rosemary—Happy 50th—Frank Sinatra.' On the other side was sketched the calendar of August, and within the figure 6 was a diamond measuring one quarter of a carat. I tried valiantly to pay for it. It had cost several hundred dollars.

When he was acting in a movie on location, Sinatra was a law unto Sinatra. Restless and bored, he would argue that much of the filming could be done just as well at the studio. 'One-Take Charlie' could get as mean as a boa constrictor.

Simply because he's Sinatra, Frank can shake up a town, or even a country, and start an uproar merely with his normal conduct. When he and Dean Martin moved into Madison, Indiana, in 1958 with Shirley MacLaine and director Vincent Minnelli to film *Some Came Running*, they quickly raised hell.

Girls were brought in to entertain the stars. Strolling the streets with a drink in his hand, Frank commented picturesquely about the native girls, saying he preferred the importees. Declining to visit the local country club, he crossed the river into Kentucky with Dean Martin to hunt a floating crap game.

In the morning 'his eyes would look like two urine spots in the snow', a studio publicist said, 'and when I saw his hangover look I would keep walking.'

Frank was said to have referred to local women as 'broads, finks and old hags'.

Actress Martha Hyer, who was in the film (and later married director Hal Wallis), defended Frank's conduct, saying that 'Hello, you old bag' was accepted language in Romanoff's and Toots Shor's. Hundreds of women had waited in the streets of Madison to see or touch Frank, she said. Miss Hyer wondered about such women and the state of their sanity.

Because he was Sinatra, Frank was accused of ripping phones off walls, pushing people and other misbehaviour that was never proved.

Director Minnelli became upset when Sinatra kept saying, 'Let's blow this joint'. Producer Sol Siegel flew to Madison to try to make peace between them. The 'One-Take Charlie' argument arose again.

In a final scene, Frank was supposed to get killed. Frank proposed a change so that Shirley would get killed instead—it would fatten her part. In the filming, Shirley from eight feet up, leaped on Frank as he lay on the pavement, and he said he thought she'd hurt him.

'Retake!' commanded Minnelli. Frank, all aches and pains, couldn't believe it. They did it over five times. Minnelli later said that he usually got what he wanted from Frank, tense though the atmosphere was, and that though 'feisty as a rooster, he was a dependable friend, especially during hard times'.

Knowing about Frank's assistance to people in need, Minnelli said, 'He's prone to tell friends how he'll help them rather than to ask how he can help . . . but that's the prerogative of any leader of the clan.'

Sinatra and Martin—and Madison, Indiana—were glad when that adventure was finished. The picture was well received. Sinatra and Martin went on to many more projects together, they became millionaires together; they also got into some fights together, but not against each other.

A few years later, Minnelli had some difficulty in obtaining permission to use a Sinatra-owned song in another picture. Minnelli phoned Sinatra, then in the Orient.

'Don't worry, you got it, it's yours,' Sinatra told him.

'What do I have to do?' Minnelli asked.

'IT IS YOURS!' replied Sinatra. And it was.

Producer Howard Koch, long the head of Paramount Studios who made seven films with Sinatra and remained his friend had difficulty with him on the first, *Sergeants 3*, made at Knabe, Utah. 'Sinatra requires little sleep, gets bored quickly and demands bigger excitements,' says Koch, 'but he's conscientious.'

Koch and an advance unit had been shooting for a day when Sinatra arrived unexpectedly early at the film location and announced he wanted to see the rushes. Some stars only want to see their own rushes, some don't want to see any. Caught by surprise, Koch said he didn't have the equipment available yet.

'I want to see them,' Sinatra said.

Koch replied, 'I'd say it's almost impossible.'

'That word isn't in my vocabulary,' Sinatra said.

'I'll show him!' thought Koch. Remembering that Kirk Douglas had a unit in New Mexico, Koch reached him with several phone calls and arranged for a plane and pilot to pick up a projection unit there and show Sinatra the rushes in Knabe about four hours later.

'Since that day, the word *impossible* isn't in my vocabulary either,' Koch says.

Frank gave his good friend, director Mervyn LeRoy, some headaches over the rehearsing problem while filming *The Devil at 4 O'Clock* on the Hawaiian island of Maui. Spencer Tracy wanted to do scenes over and over; Frank wanted to do everything in one take. LeRoy tried to keep them both happy. One day he told Sinatra he wanted to do another close-up. It got to be an argument.

'Do you really think that we need it?'

'Yes, I do.'

'Well, I don't.'

'Well, I do.'

Frank acquiesced, but he wasn't happy. He asked if he could leave the set and go home even though he was supposed to work two more hours. LeRoy gave him permission. It was tense around the set. Back at the hotel, LeRoy found a note in longhand from Frank saying he'd been wrong, adding, 'I'm cooking a spaghetti dinner for all of us.'

After the dinner, Frank sat on the piano bench with a drink in one hand and cigarette in the other and sang for almost an hour.

Their friendship went back to *The House I Live In*, the short that had been Sinatra's idea, for which LeRoy got an Oscar. 'Sinatra's a much-maligned, misunderstood man; his greatest joy is doing things for others,' LeRoy said. 'Many times I've come into my office and found a box of cigars on my desk—no card, no name—but I knew it came from Frank. It isn't a big thing, but it's typical of the way he operates.'

(Giving boxes of cigars to men who can afford to buy their own is, incidentally, still one of Frank's generosities.)

During the shooting of *The Devil at 4 O'Clock*, Sinatra was overheard saying he had never seen the picture *From Here to Eternity*. Publicist Bob Yaeger arranged a 'delayed world première' on Maui—almost a decade after its release—with local officials enthusiastically greeting Frank while native girls danced and put leis around his neck. Frank and his date for the evening watched the film from seats towards the back.

Halfway through the picture, Yaeger looked around. Sinatra and the girl had gone.

The local officials were dumbfounded.

Frank never explained why he'd left or where he'd gone. But a friend pointed out, 'After his death scene, he probably figured, "Why should I hang around?" '

Sinatra carried himself off well in a picture with Marlon Brando.

Frank was never a devotee of Brando's itch-and-scratch school of acting and was credited with giving Brando the nickname 'Mumbles'. When they co-starred in the film *Guys and Dolls*, based on the Damon Runyon story that was a Broadway stage hit, everybody anticipated a clash. Brando had his partisans, too. If Brando was 'Mumbles', Sinatra was 'Jumbles'.

'Let me know when "Mumbles" has finished his five-hour rehearsal and I'll give you what you want from me in about half a minute,' Frank would tell director Joseph Mankiewicz at the Samuel Goldwyn studios in Hollywood.

Frank was already angry, not at Brando, but at Sam Spiegel, the yachting fancier, and at Horizon-American Pictures. Claiming they'd promised him the star role in *On the Waterfront* and were to pay him $55,000 and a percentage, he accused them of breach of faith in eventually giving the role to Brando. He sued for $500,000, but what was more embarrassing was that Brando was already in line for an Oscar for the part. As Frank took over the Nathan Detroit gambler role and Brando portrayed Sky Masterson in *Guys and Dolls*, the women in the picture, Jean Simmons and Vivian Blaine, wondered when there would be an explosion between the two giants.

'Although we had respect for Brando, I was more in awe of Sinatra,' Vivian Blaine remembers. 'It was exciting, and distracting, too, hearing the talk about whether Marlon would get an Academy Award.'

Vivian and Sinatra got to be known as the 'One-Take Kids'. 'We always did it fast. Brando, on the other hand, was slow. He once took 135 takes. Nobody could believe it.'

Brando was trying to do a song that had been taken from Sinatra, 'A Woman in Love'. With all the synchronizing of lip movements, and the singing itself, Brando was in agony. Of course, he got no sympathy from Sinatra. Although not a singer, Brando did sing the song himself, without dubbing, according to Miss Blaine.

Due partly to Brando's refusal to be hurried, the picture ran over budget. Mankiewicz tried to speed it up. One day at about 5.30, after Vivian Blaine had been working all day, he ordered a series of close-ups of her.

Frank stepped in. 'WAIT A MINUTE,' he insisted. 'It's too late to start this.' Mankiewicz yielded.

During the filming of *Guys and Dolls*, Brando won the *Waterfront* Oscar. Sam Goldwyn, never a great diplomat, aggravated the situation by sending Brando a gift—a small European car.

The film, which took almost six months to complete, was favourably reviewed, but Samuel Goldwyn's efforts to promote it got Sinatra into a celebrated rhubarb with Ed Sullivan, the columnist and TV host. It was another display of Frank's feeling for power. It was also an unfortunate misunderstanding.

Years before, when columnist Westbrook Pegler attacked Sinatra, columnist Sullivan had defended him. Frank sent him a watch and a message: 'Ed, you can have my last drop of blood.' Now the Screen Actors Guild was acting against 'personalities' with TV programmes who got actors to perform free. Goldwyn wanted Sinatra to go on Sullivan's show to promote the film. Sullivan's show did pay actors—but Sinatra thought he was being asked to work for nothing.

Sinatra surprised Show Business by taking ads in trade papers: 'Dear Ed, You're sick (signed) Frankie. P.S. Sick, sick, sick.'

'Liar,' retorted Sullivan in another ad. His programme had paid $5 million to actors. 'Aside to Frankie Boy. Never mind that tremulous 1947 offer, "Ed, you can have my last drop of blood." I don't wear wristwatches . . . furthermore, it's on its way back.'

Although it turned out that the Screen Actors Guild was really sniping at columnist Hedda Hopper instead of Ed, the comedy of errors continued with Ed claiming that Frank was offended because he preferred Marlon Brando and Jean Simmons on his programme.

'Brando, of course, is the hottest thing in Show Business,' Ed said. He added, cuttingly, 'Sinatra is not exactly a TV novelty.'

They feuded for a couple of years. Frank found a way to make an honourable peace when Sullivan was seriously injured in an auto accident and was confined to bed at his home in the country. Going on Sullivan's show voluntarily, he announced that he loved Ed and that the feud was a misunderstanding. Frank got no money, and Red Skelton, substituting as master of ceremonies, read a letter of praise for Frank that Ed had written in his sickbed. Frank didn't sing; he had a sore throat. He just stood there and got embarrassed as Skelton told him that Sullivan thought he was great. He did, however, get a plug for his then current movie, *Johnny Concho*.

Clearly, Frank thought he was doing his duty for actors in the Sullivan conflict, and he tried to do it again on *Carousel*, the Rodgers and Hammerstein musical. Twentieth Century-Fox was going to shoot it in both Cinemascope and Todd-A-O. Sinatra argued that each scene would have to be done at least twice and maybe more often, and if the actors were going to make two pictures, why shouldn't they be paid for two instead of one?

He walked off the picture at Boothbay Harbour, Maine, and let them sue him for $1 million. They blasted him for standing up the company. Passing up $150,000 worth of work for what he thought was a principle, he shrugged as his long-time friend Gordon MacRae replaced him.

A month later, Frank won the argument. The studio decided it would only do the picture in Cinemascope and the actors would not play the same scene twice.

This was a time of victory for Sinatra because he also won another Oscar nomination—for Best Actor in *The Man with the Golden Arm* in 1955.

'Frank has told me he considers this his best picture,'

says producer-director Otto Preminger. Sinatra portrayed a card dealer trying to beat narcotics to become a jazz drummer. The critics said Sinatra's own creativity was evident in his portrayal of the addict.

Preminger got Sinatra to rehearse and do scenes over by telling him gently that he wanted him to help actress Kim Novak with some of her lines. 'When he was working with beautiful, blonde Kim, Sinatra didn't seem to be so eager to get away from the set,' Preminger says with a smile.

'He was very patient,' recalls Preminger. 'Sometimes he would do twenty-five or thirty takes with Kim!'

Ernest Borgnine won the 1955 Oscar for *Marty*. Along with Frank, the other nominees were James Cagney, James Dean and Spencer Tracy. Frank won the British Kinematograph Award. Regardless of what non-Method, non-acting, non-rehearsing technique Frank was using, he really had become a thespian.

By 1960, there was a lot of mythology about Frank's wealth and where it came from. He had to be very rich.

His original two points interest in the Hotel Sands had grown to six or eight points as Entratter became increasingly influential in the management. Frank had made almost twenty-five pictures. He owned pieces of some of them. He always got top salaries in nightclubs, reportedly with 'special deals'.

For example, at the Sands, particularly, he had almost unlimited credit, and it was rumoured that the management sometimes tore up his IOUs because it was good business to have him in the casino since he would bring in hordes of people to gamble also. He worked at a furious pace between clubs and films, squeezing recording sessions in between. He was almost always in the first five among pop record sellers. Why shouldn't he be rich?

Yet, he told Robin Douglas-Home in 1961, 'I have been rich twice and poor twice—I wonder how it'll work out.'

Still, there were critics who blasted him for his cocky approach to some of his recordings and said he was getting boring. The drive that pushed him ahead in films was to push him forward again in records.

'I want my own record label,' Sinatra said. Unhappy with Capitol Records, which he felt wouldn't let him sing as he wished to, he plotted to get out of his contract. He also dreamed of setting up his own talent management company, with the artists controlling themselves and getting most of the money. He conceived his own conglomerate—although it wasn't yet called that.

Out of this came Reprise Records.

Frank chose Morris Ostin of MGM-Verve Recording Company to be his vice-president. Walking along Vine Street one day past the circular Capitol Records Tower, a landmark, Sinatra remarked to Ostin, 'I helped build that, now I'm going to build one of my own.'

Enjoying the prospect of a good fight—the underdog against the Establishment again—he announced he would be a 'new, happier, emancipated Sinatra, untrammelled, unfettered, unconfined'.

Capitol Records executives were burning up. When Sinatra announced a Reprise album, 'Swing Along with Me', Capitol went to court to claim it was a steal, by Sinatra, of a Sinatra album he'd just done for Capitol, 'Come Swing with Me'. Sinatra rushed out an explanation. 'Album titles are hard to come by. The title "Swing Along with Me" is the theme for my record company, the main line being "Swing Along with Reprise." '

The courts sided with Capitol and commanded Reprise to change the title and cover. Frank changed it to 'Sinatra Swings'. Capitol offered a 15 per cent cash discount on its album; Reprise jumped the gun on a scheduled release date of its album.

Personally romancing the disc jockeys with phone calls, parties and visits, Frank was really tending and diapering the new baby and getting tremendous promotion for Reprise. He was also having fun.

He felt he was making music history. He was. The musicians around him sometimes cheered him or gave him a standing ovation after a song was played back. They liked his spirit and his enthusiasm. He was, however, over-confident when he cut 'I Remember Tommy' in tribute to Tommy Dorsey. 'That'll do $800,000 or $900,000,' Frank prophesied.

It didn't.

The battle with Capitol went on. Frank and Reprise brought a $1-million suit charging that Capitol was offering twenty-one Sinatra albums at drastically reduced bargain rates that endangered the new company's future. The fight raged on with both companies turning out Sinatra albums and with the USA getting more than an earful of Frank Sinatra.

Frank was singing well and became more famous and controversial, if possible. But, so he said, he was losing money. He confessed that he lost $1.5 million on Reprise before he started making a profit. 'All of it was out of his own kick at the start,' one of his associates told me. 'He didn't ask anybody for help. He wanted the company set up just the way he wanted it. He didn't want to owe anything to anybody else.'

This was when Frank was poor the second time.

Three years later, Frank turned Reprise Records over to Warner Brothers, became part of Warner's himself and also became very rich.

He was a tycoon of respectable size who had truly, honestly and industriously worked his way up to become the 'Emperor of Tinsel-town'. He ruled his corporations from the City National Bank Building on Sunset Boulevard, Hollywood. Reprise, Essex Films, four music publishing companies, his Las Vegas and Lake Tahoe gambling interests, his radio station partnerships with Danny Kaye, his real estate holdings, all grossed more than $20 million a year. He was gaining more and more influence. And some people were afraid that because of his changing moods, switching from a friend to enemy in a few seconds, he was a dangerous power figure.

Frank, of course, never understood that. He was comfortably off, and he was worried about a couple of things. He meant to enlarge his realm, but he hoped his vocal cords would hold out. He was also concerned about his hair. The balding patch on top was getting larger.

KAYOED BY THE KENNEDYS

Frank Sinatra's political romance with John F. Kennedy resembled some of his own love stories. First the lovers were very, very warm; then hot and hotter; then they exploded in their passion—and then they turned colder than New Year's Eve in Bad Axe, Michigan.

He was kinging it very big when he got into it, all because he wanted to be a President-maker, and he never foresaw that he would be jilted. He discovered that in spite of his mounting importance, there was a power bigger even than he was. It burns his backside even to this day.

Frank was mentally and spiritually wounded by the chill he got from the Kennedy family: 'Old Joe', the 'Ambassador', the father; brother Bobby, the Attorney-General, and, to a lesser degree, the President, who eventually jabbed in the stiletto they had sharpened for him.

They cut him down because of the reputations of some of his so-called friends in the Nevada gambling world. He was regularly accused of having Mafia connections, but he found himself in battle with Bobby Kennedy's Irish Mafia, which could be as devastating as any Italian Mafia. The experience hardened Frank and toughened his hide for his next encounter with a power figure.

And it was just when Frank was getting points for being a Nice Guy.

He was becoming closer to actor Peter Lawford, who was married to Patricia Kennedy, the daughter of former Ambassador Joseph P. Kennedy, and was the brother-in-law of the handsome young Senator from Massachusetts, John Fitzgerald Kennedy. Peter was blithe, blasé and British, and an agreeable bloke. It was always 'Peter' or 'Peetah,' and almost never 'Lawford'. Peter was sort of a member of the 'Clan'.

Frank emphatically denied that it was an organization and declared it was merely a name. Sammy Davis said, 'It's just an ordinary bunch of guys who get together once a year and take over the whole world.'

But it was young Senator Kennedy, aspirant to the presidency, who fascinated Frank. He was on the rise. He was handsome, witty, rich, Harvard-educated, charismatic and clever politically. He was also a dedicated swordsman, as they called studs in those days, just as Frank was. The young senator was married to a socialite named Jackie, but that didn't deter him from discreetly dating the new beauties of any city. Because young Kennedy was a Catholic in a country that had never elected a Catholic to the presidency, he was also regarded as an underdog—and Frank liked that.

Frank and Peter Lawford discussed the Kennedy presidential hopes in the summer of 1958, when Frank was being a most docile, most co-operative movie star. Their talk about Kennedy, who had been beaten for the vice-presidential nomination in 1956 by Senator Estes Kefauver, shaped some of Frank's future—and Peter's, too.

As the star of a luxurious press junket to Monte Carlo for the world première of his not-very-good movie, *Kings Go Forth,* Frank was a model of good behaviour during three days of partying, feasting and drinking in the kingdom of his old friend, Princess Grace of Monaco. There was no time for politicking on this pleasure safari.

The London writers commented rather loftily about Frank, the band singer from Hoboken, and Grace Kelly, the bricklayer's daughter from Philadelphia, putting on this display of Show Business regality over in Monte Carlo for benefit of the UN Refugee Fund, which was headed by the Princess.

As the star attraction, Frank was, as usual, pushing the girls away. The rush for his body had started before he arrived.

Learning of his visit, the French-Polish blonde bombshell, Bella Darvi, protégée and long-time mistress of Darryl Zanuck, rushed from Paris hoping to capture him on his way down the ramp, but found him in the hands of other ladies. She sulked and visited the casinos, where she was a famous gambler.

Princess Grace summoned Frank to her palace to be received officially, and he then returned to his Hotel de Paris suite to give parties that lasted till the sun came up over the Mediterranean. He slept most of the day.

I had never seen him more gracious to the press and the guests, although he *should* have been gracious, since they were being worshipful and plugging his picture. Acting as host at a garden party, he gladhanded everybody and signed autographs.

I chanced to be sitting with Ludwig Bemelmans, the writer, painter and world traveller, and I asked him where he'd like most to live. 'Weehawken, New Jersey', he said, to considerable laughter.

Seriously, he explained that the light over Weehawken was fine for painters, and that 'from Weehawken', south of the George Washington Bridge, 'you have a perfect view of New York City—you look down on Forty-second Street.'

By coincidence, Frank Sinatra, the host, circulating among the guests, was nearing our table.

'Listen to this,' I said to Sinatra, 'Ludwig Bemelmans says Weehawken, New Jersey, is the garden spot of the universe.'

'You're tellin' me!' Frank said. 'I used to take that Weehawken Ferry over to New York. My dad and mother have a house two blocks away from where you're talking about. I've been trying to get them to move to California with me, but they won't leave beautiful Weehawken.'

One night Frank went with the press crowd into the small nightclubs, and he sang in one of them. He weekended, however, with a titled beauty, the shapely blonde Marquessa de Portago. Like Lady Beatty, she was an American—the former Carol McDaniels of South Carolina and New York.

The Marquessa—her sizeable diamonds and emeralds, and exciting figure—had caught his attention long before in Rome. Now the lovely lady took over the 'King' for the weekend.

Saturday night was a night of triumph for Frank. The première was done stylishly, with Princess Grace in her jewels and Prince Rainier in his medals. Nearly all of the Princess' Monégasque subjects pushed forward to try to touch Sinatra and compliment him. Playing a white soldier soon to marry a black, portrayed by beautiful Natalie Wood, he may have contributed to some advanced thinking about mixed marriages.

We went from the première to a klieg-lit midnight gala, where the sad Marquessa sat across from my wife and me. Princess Grace had snared Sinatra for her own guest-of-honour table. The 'King' sat with the Prince and Princess.

It became almost a testimonial to Sinatra. Noël Coward spoke smooth words of praise that Frank would never forget. Sinatra, he claimed, had never offended with bad taste. 'Putting it musically,' he said, 'Mr. Sinatra has never sounded a wrong note.'

The Prince and Princess returned to the palace, and the partying resumed in Sinatra's suite. With several press people there, Frank and his close friend, Hollywood writer Harry Kurnitz, exchanged newspaper stories. Kurnitz once had given a columnist what he called an 'exclusive story'.

'That story was wrong,' the columnist subsequently told Kurnitz, who answered, 'It may have been wrong—but it *was* exclusive.'

'I love that story,' Frank said, 'maybe because I don't like the columnist. He's not a stand-up guy. He should have stood up for me once and he didn't.'

Politics was discussed. President Eisenhower's campaigners had used a slogan, 'I Like Ike.' Sinatra said he liked John F. Kennedy.

'I like me,' Harry Kurnitz said. 'I'm going to bed. I don't want to get sunburned with my dinner jacket on.'

After I had said good-night—or good-morning—Sinatra and his accompanist, Bill Miller, plotted a practical joke on fellow columnist Leonard Lyons and me. We had both asked Miller, who was returning to New York next day, to take back envelopes containing our next columns. It was

Frank's sadistic idea to have Miller open the envelopes and switch the contents, so that Lyons' column would appear under my name and mine would appear under Lyons'. Thank God they didn't do it.

It was Sinatra's Era of Good Feeling. He survived the première without one fight or one broken camera. We left with a lot of new friends—he had strewn big tips along the way. Those stories from America must have been true—Frank Sinatra tipping a parking lot attendant $100!

In California, not long afterwards, Sinatra leaped into the campaign to elect Kennedy President. Always a Democrat, he had gone to Saint Patrick's Cathedral to pray when FDR died. He liked to tell how his mother Dolly demanded that he back her for party chairman saying, 'You supported Franklin D. Roosevelt and you won't support your own mother!'

The dashing, swinging young senator from Massachusetts was well known on the Las Vegas scene. He attended a memorable event at the Hotel Sands, which its president, Jack Entratter, called a summit meeting. Taking advantage of headlines about international summit meetings, Entratter brought his biggest stars on stage together and allowed them to go wild with impromptu material. Sinatra, Dean Martin, Sammy Davis, Joey Bishop—and Peter Lawford—gave unpredictable performances, which they enjoyed as much as the audience and, in some cases, when they were drinking, more than the audience.

In January 1960, the young senator, his sights on the presidential nomination, was introduced from the Sands audience by Sinatra. As John F. Kennedy arose, smiled, waved and took his bow, Dean Martin lurched from the wings. 'What did you say his name was?' asked Dean.

Joey Bishop called Sinatra and Dean Martin 'the Italian bookends', and Dean 'the stoned Martin'.

At one point, Dean Martin picked up Sammy Davis bodily and carried him across the stage. He pretended to hand Sammy over to Frank. 'This is an award that just arrived for you from the NAACP,' Dean said.

Frank and his Clan, who were filming *Oceans 11* in Las Vegas during the day, had had very little sleep; none the less, they sat up with Kennedy prophesying that he would be President. Sammy Davis said one night, 'Senator, when you get to the White House, can I be Ambassador to Israel?

'I mean, of course,' he said, with a bow to Sinatra, 'after Our Leader becomes Ambassador to Italy.' During this work marathon, Sammy collapsed from lack of sleep and lack of oxygen and went briefly into a hospital.

On Sunday night, 10 July 1960, during the Democratic Convention in Los Angeles, Frank Sinatra sat at the side of Sen. John F. Kennedy at a banquet table, talking confidentially. Frank talked, Kennedy nodded. Frank, then forty-four and a half years old, described to Kennedy, two months over forty-three, how he was going to raise money to help elect him President just as soon as he got the Democratic nomination.

As Frank grew more animated, the young senator smiled and nodded more vigorously. Sinatra told how he would get the biggest stars to join him in Kennedy rallies, to raise funds and get out votes.

Sinatra and Kennedy were sitting on the dais at a $100-a-plate dinner at the Beverly Hilton Hotel. It was so well attended that it required two ballrooms, two daises, two foyers and two toastmasters: Milton Berle and George Jessel.

Judy Garland, Sammy Davis, Mort Sahl and Sinatra entertained in both rooms. Frank and Judy were the most ogled names at the dinner and the biggest stars. Judy was the belle of the party. She sat on the dais alongside Sen. John Kennedy, Sen. Lyndon Johnson, Adlai Stevenson, Sen. Stuart Symington and Eleanor Roosevelt.

On the dais, too, sat Peter Lawford, laughing about a joke just then going around: 'Would you buy a used car from Richard Nixon?' The convention was like a big holiday. Kennedy was still 'Jack' to Lawford, Sinatra and others.

Comedian Joe E. Lewis told Kennedy he was out till 6.00 a.m. wearing a Kennedy badge. Kennedy fell into the trap. 'Where's the badge now?'

'Oh, I'm sober now,' Joe E. said.

This happy crowd tried to believe that Jack was going to be President, but since they knew him by his first name, they were nervous about it. Peter Lawford was worried about talk he was hearing concerning the function of the Sinatra Clan members in case Kennedy got nominated and elected. He was the first to sense the danger.

'There's nothing to all that talk about the Clan, but the opposition could make something out of it,' Peter said to me. Nevertheless, he repeated a line he'd heard: Dean Martin would be Secretary of the Cabinet—the Liquor Cabinet. Frank would be in charge of international affairs and all other affairs, especially his. Peter Lawford was seriously concerned, he said, about a suggestion he'd heard that he would become Kennedy's Robert Montgomery. (Veteran TV and movie actor Montgomery had coached President Eisenhower and hadn't done much for him, in Lawford's opinion. When Montgomery heard about it, he replied, 'Mr. Lawford is entitled to his opinion, worthless as it is.')

Lawford was right in worrying about the Clan getting into print. The jokes grew into serious news stories. Frank told me, 'There is no Clan. It's some guys that like each other and get along together. There are no membership cards or anything like that. This whole thing is silly.'

On the day Kennedy was nominated, I went down on the convention floor, where Peter Lawford's wife, Patricia, was marching in a Kennedy demonstration, and discussed with her the contentions of some columnists that the Sinatra crowd might be trying to burrow into the White House.

'That whole thing is preposterous,' she said.

'There's even a report that the Ambassador wants Jack to renounce Sinatra and the whole crowd,' I said. (The Ambassador was Joseph Kennedy, her father.)

'I never heard it, and I don't believe it,' she said.

Columnist Dorothy Kilgallen, notoriously anti-Sinatra, later wrote that Senator Kennedy claimed that he objected to being linked to Sinatra.

It was rumour. But where do rumours come from? Somebody starts them. Who would have started this one? Somebody who was afraid of Sinatra hurting the senator. Bobby? Old Joe? Somebody very protective of the senator!

'He's no friend of mine,' Dorothy Kilgallen quoted Senator Kennedy as saying. 'He's just a friend of Pat and Peter Lawford.'

Dorothy Kilgallen said she knew better. The senator had attended a private soirée given by Frank after his nomination. 'Why try to kid the press?' she asked.

The Sinatra crowd purportedly was embarrassing Kennedy from another angle: black Sammy Davis' forthcoming marriage to white May Britt. They had planned to marry before the election, but 'practical politicians' wondered if it couldn't wait. No need to add that to the Kennedy problems of being a Catholic.

Sammy wasn't fearful of his personal reputation suffering from marrying a white girl. For all he cared, 'our baby can be polka-dot', he said.

Sammy consulted Frank about it. Frank told Sammy to be happy—to go ahead and get married. But Sammy declined. He invented some alibis: His new house wasn't ready; in fact, it wouldn't be ready . . . well . . . how do you like that? . . . until just after the election. Sammy and May postponed the marriage until 13 November. Sammy was 'negotiating' with Frank to be his best man.

Sinatra was in a rage at the reported Kennedy chill because he had worked so hard for Kennedy. But Peter Lawford assured him that the stories weren't true, or if they were true, the difficulty was entirely with brother Bobby Kennedy, not with Jack, who after all was Number 1.

As October arrived, with the election about a month off, Sinatra hurriedly finished a movie, *The Devil at 4 O'Clock*, in Hawaii, and rushed back to the mainland to lead some glamourites-for-Kennedy in a campaign invasion of the Eastern Seaboard.

Bobby Kennedy, managing the campaign, was ruffled, but he knew that Sinatra was a big draw, particularly in New Jersey.

'We're bringing in a party to Governor Meyner's rally in Newark a week from tomorrow,' Frank informed me on 18 October 1960. The invaders included Tony Curtis and Janet Leigh, who were then married, and Peter Lawford.

It was one of the most tumultuous meetings in New

Jersey history—and an enormous success from Frank's standpoint. The Newark Armoury held 10,000—and 40,000 were there, most of them shouting, 'We want Sinatra!' The principal spellbinder was supposed to be Adlai Stevenson. When he saw the mood of the crowd, he diplomatically cut his speech. As Frank walked on stage, the crowd in the armoury surged forward. Some eager people from the audience climbed on the press table—and it collapsed. Columnist Barbara Lewis, who reported the event, remembers it as a political rally that turned into a personal riot for Sinatra. He proved himself to be a mighty man in his home state.

Sinatra was stirring up riots slightly smaller than that all over the country, always raising money for the campaign.

And so it happened. A young senator, a young Catholic, handsome, swinging millionaire, was elected President over Richard Nixon in the late hours of 8 November 1960. He opened the way for the great Inaugural Gala, and the move-in of the Clan to the White House—the move-in that never took place.

During the post-midnight excitement, with Nixon tearfully conceding after losing by such a close margin, one of the Broadway quipsters at the Copacabana asked, 'Never mind how Kennedy's doing—is Sinatra carrying Hoboken?'

Joey Bishop wired Sinatra, 'Remember, you said I could be postmaster of Englewood.'

On to the Inaugural! Here comes Hollywood!

Frank had won a 'stack'—many thousands—betting on Kennedy. Sinatra's friends, who had been calling him the 'King', now called him the 'King-maker'. They were still calling Kennedy 'Jack' and discussing 'that old Jack Magic'. The ladies were ordering gowns for the Inaugural Ball: Janet Leigh, Mrs. Milton Berle and, of course, Pat Lawford.

Some performers who had been steamed up into working for Kennedy by Sinatra took the unrealistic view that Frank had won the election single-handedly. That didn't please Bobby Kennedy, who thought that his own brilliance and his father's money had much to do with it.

Comedian Don Rickles said on a nightclub floor,

'Kennedy's boss—that's Frank Sinatra—said to Kennedy, "Jack, Baby, you see? It turned out just like I told you it would. Listen, Jack, Baby, now about Italy." '

To Peter Lawford, this bespoke a danger, for he knew Bobby Kennedy's moods. It was rumoured that Peter would move into the White House, that Sinatra would be a regular visitor. 'Not a chance of me moving into the White House,' Peter said. 'Jack doesn't need any court jester.'

But Sinatra was not out of the controversy. Returning to the Copacabana, he was challenged to produce a cabaret card, a permit from the city to entertain in New York. To get one of those, the entertainer had to submit to fingerprinting. Somebody evidently wanted to embarrass Frank, and he didn't want to be embarrassed. It was not likely that he had a police record. If he had one, surely somebody would have noticed it by now. It became another, but very small, *cause célèbre*. Frank never got fingerprinted in New York.

Frank won that small battle, but the menace of Bobby Kennedy was always before him. Crusading Bobby, the all-powerful Attorney-General, known as ruthless and unstoppable, was determined to oust the mobsters from Nevada. He was going to run the Mafia out. Bobby Kennedy wrote a book, *The Enemy Within*, which revealed that he knew the inside workings of the Mafia and its insidious influences.

Sinatra was a friend of many strange gambling types. Some were within the law, but just barely within it. Sinatra's best friend in Las Vegas, Jack Entratter, was 100 per cent clean all his life. But Entratter knew about the other world because he had a brother, Charley Green, who was killed by the Vincent ('Mad Dog') Coll mob in the post-Prohibition era and was found under a bridge.

The Copacabana itself had been partly supported by Frank Costello, the long-time Mafia boss. It was difficult to be around the nightclubs and Las Vegas hotels without being friendly with some *mafiosi*. Many carried guns—a few of them even had permits to do so.

And often they were very charming acquaintances with

whom Sinatra enjoyed having a drink or dinner. They were not convicted criminals. They were not in jail. They were not under arrest. They were colourful characters.

They were not funny, however, to Attorney-General Bobby Kennedy. He was a serious young man, eleven years younger than Sinatra.

Bobby was a hero to many, and he had his own cult, much more serious than Sinatra's cult. Bobby wore his hair so long that, at one movie première, it was noted that his was longer than Elizabeth Taylor's. Barbers publicly said he should get it cut or change the style. Bobby joked about it. But Bobby, though only thirty-six and boyishly coiffeured, was quietly working his way towards keeping Sinatra out of the Washington scene.

For once, Frank wished he'd been less hostile to the press, but he'd been nasty, and now some of the press was out-nastying him, giving the worst possible interpretation of the silly old Clan.

Frank seethed at Bobby's suddenly becoming so moralistic. He knew Bobby to be as much a swinger as Jack, and both got it from their father, Old Joe, whose sexual proclivities, extramaritally, had been celebrated his whole lifetime. Kennedy, Sr., had been a whiskey baron. Historically, the whiskey business is as sinful and corruptible as the gambling business. So what was Bobby yelling about?

Of course, Bobby was yelling about organized crime—the Mafia—and Frank kept declaring, 'What's the Mafia? I don't know anything about any Mafia.'

Feeling put upon by the conspiratorial Machine, the System, Frank swaggered bravely into a new fight. Ignoring advisers, he hired Albert Maltz, one of the blacklisted 'Hollywood Ten' writers, to do the screenplay of the controversial *Execution of Private Slovik*. There was such an uproar that Frank was afraid to take phone calls.

'They're calling you a fucking Communist,' Harry Cohn screamed at him.

Maltz had been fined and imprisoned for refusing to answer questions about his Communist sympathies, but that was long past. Evidently, however, the Hollywood establishment wanted Maltz never to work again. Frank took ads saying he believed the Bill of Rights gave him the privilege of hiring a man who had paid his debt; besides, he believed Maltz was capable of writing the best screenplay.

'They're not only saying you're a Commie bastard, but you tried to hold off announcing you hired him for fear you'd hurt Jack in the election—and you will,' a top Democrat warned Frank.

As each phone call got sharper and each editorial got more personal and virulent, Sinatra's bravery weakened. Finally, one day came a message that the Ambassador said he should drop Maltz or get off the Kennedy team.

Frank boiled. After almost three weeks of hell, he gave in, saying that the American people had convinced him he was wrong. The conservative press acclaimed him as a hero; the liberal press said he should have had more guts. However, those who'd been witnesses to all the concentrated pressure on him didn't see how Frank could have taken much more.

In late December 1960, Frank and Peter actually went to work producing the Inaugural Gala to be held the night before the Inauguration. 'Quality' people would be there: Leonard Bernstein, Carl Sandburg . . . and, of course, Jack Kennedy and Vice-President Lyndon Johnson. With seventy-two boxes going at $10,000 a box, in addition to less expensive seats, it would be the greatest take in history.

'One million-nine—first time a man has gone into office clean—with all debts paid up,' Peter Lawford said.

Having set up headquarters in New York at the Conrad Hilton Suite of the Savoy Hilton Hotel, Frank was sitting at a desk with a beer and a sandwich in front of him, on 4 January, talking on the phone to Fredric March.

'Freddie,' he said, 'I was wondering whether you would be available to help us in Washington. We wondered if you'd do that farewell speech that Lincoln did off the back of the train in Springfield. Just before Helen Traubel closes the show? You know the piece?'

March was heard saying that he was occupied doing a movie in New York, *The Young Doctors.*

'Who's the producer?' Frank asked. 'Stuart Millar? He's

a good friend of mine. Maybe we can get him to spring you.'

Stuart Millar, indeed, was the son of Mack Millar, who had been Frank's press agent. Frank phoned Millar. He put his foot on his desk and pulled up his sock. 'Hello, Stuart,' Frank said. 'I wonder if we could steal Freddie for a few days. It's very important.'

March himself was anxious to do it. He called Frank back and said, 'Florence [his wife, Florence Eldridge] wants to know, "What kind of dress shall I wear?" '

Frank later said, 'Gene Kelly's coming in from Switzerland to dance for only four minutes. Ella Fitzgerald's coming from Australia. Nelson Riddle and the whole orchestra are coming from Australia.

'When I called Eleanor Roosevelt,' Frank said, 'she was so cute. She said, "What could I possibly do with all those stars?" Well, she's going to be an actress that night!'

Frank was sure that President-elect Kennedy would be in the armoury at curtain-raising time, even though he had agreed to appear at a Washington symphony concert half an hour earlier.

It was the 'Million-Dollar Gala', the grandest in history. Hollywood couturier Don Loper tailored a flashy tailcoat and Inverness cape for Sinatra—in fact, he made two, in case Frank spilled something on one of them. By Wednesday, 18 January, Hollywood and Broadway stars were arriving on chartered planes and rehearsing all night—from Mahalia Jackson to Pat Suzuki to Eleanor Roosevelt. They were quartered at the Washington Statler-Hilton.

About 2.00 a.m. I went across the street to a diner. A little man came in and said, 'Gimme three dozen hamburgers. Sinatra told me to get about seventy-five dollars worth, but I figured this would be enough.'

Sinatra enjoyed being Number 1 man, next to Kennedy. Who wouldn't? Kennedy's sister Mrs. Stephen Smith gave an 'exclusive' sit-down dinner at her Georgetown home—for two hundred. Kennedy and Sinatra talked at times in confidential tones, and laughed together, probably about some of the guests. Kennedy's hair was mussed. They made jokes then about his hair being dishevelled.

On a TV show, a comedian playing Kennedy was to

have said to his wife, Jackie, 'Fix your hair,' and she snapped back 'Fix YOUR hair!' The censors considered the Kennedys' hair a sensitive area and deleted it.

Details of the Mrs. Stephen Smith party were kept such a secret that society editors phoned Sinatra for information. One woman said bitterly, 'Fine thing when you have to call Sinatra to get information about the next President!'

Frank had to grin about that. Frank had brought Nat ('King') Cole, a long-time friend, Jimmy Durante and George Jessel. Jackie Kennedy was still in Palm Beach. When she did arrive, there was no notable there to greet the in-coming First Lady. They were all with Sinatra or the other VIPs.

Mostly Frank was with the Gene Kellys, Tony Curtis and Janet Leigh—and the actress and dancer, beautiful, leggy Juliet Prowse. She laughed and laughed when I asked her whether her friendship with Sinatra meant they were going to get married. Miss Prowse had on a new mink coat and was carrying another on her arm. 'I bought them both myself,' she said.

The Sinatra contingent had rented an entire floor, and it was like a big house party. I was impressed by the easy mingling of the whites and blacks on the Sinatra floor. Nat ('King') Cole was everybody's beloved as the stars laughed and joked and ran around with drinks in their hands. Sinatra was in and out of many parties. Vice-President-elect Lyndon Johnson gave one for Texans, at which there were sixteen bars operating. Lyndon Johnson, incidentally, was perhaps less a celebrity that week than the 'King', or 'King-maker', Frank Sinatra.

Succeeding in getting a pass to the rehearsal at the Washington Armoury, I found Sinatra in complete charge on 'Gala' afternoon. 'I'm so excited, I'm shaking,' he said. 'We actually passed the million mark. It looks like there won't be an empty seat in the joint. This is going to be a great night for Kennedy!'

At that point, only the musicians and a few entertainers were there. 'You know the "Merm" is coming?' Frank said. Making a deal with the producers of *Gypsy*, he agreed to do a benefit for one of their charities in return for them allowing

Ethel Merman to take a night off from her hit show to come to the Gala. And she was a Republican!

Frank rushed off to look into details in which he'd developed a curious interest. He was concerned about the presidential box being properly fireproofed. He had it sprayed with some heat-resistant chemical that he'd recently learned about. He wanted to be certain the presidential box was properly lit. He didn't want the next President to be sitting in the dark, yet for security reasons, John F. Kennedy should not be too exposed.

But he was also helping Gene Kelly direct.

Joey Bishop was going to sing a special-material song referring to the defeat of Richard Nixon. 'Fellas, wait,' Frank said. 'We won. Everybody knows that. Why do we need to make such a point out of that?'

As I got into a cab to return to the hotel and get into a dinner jacket, the driver said, 'You're just in time. There's a hell of a snowstorm.'

By 6.00 p.m., it had become one of the worst blizzards in Washington history. Cab drivers went home. The VIP limousines that were to have taken us to the armoury were stalled or blocked somewhere in the snow.

'There are buses that can get through,' somebody said. My wife and I slogged through the snow and climbed into a bus, and there, well towards the front, sat a lady in furs calling out a loud hello—Ethel Merman. It was Gala Night, Thursday, 19 January 1961: 'The Show Must Go On' and 'There's No Business Like Show Business'.

With some of the armoury crew unable to report, Frank Sinatra himself was at the stage door checking people in when we arrived. Due to the storm, Frank faced a sad failure and it didn't seem fair. Would the whole thing have to be called off? No, they couldn't return the tickets for those $10,000 boxes!

'The snow's lettin' up,' Frank said. 'They're comin' in.'

It got to be 9.30, then 10.00, then 10.30—no time to start a two-hour show! Then it was 10.40—twenty minutes to eleven—and just then Leonard Bernstein's seventy-piece band struck up John Philip Sousa's 'Stars and Stripes Forever'. To one-third of a house (the police estimate was

6,000), the all-star cast stomped, swung and sang through an exciting show just as Frank had rehearsed it. Helen Traubel sang a special song to Jacqueline Kennedy concerning son John-John, who'd been born after the election.

Everybody knows, Mrs. K, the baby is quite a hit . . .
But if you'd had him earlier, it might have helped a bit.

The Kennedys arrived via back streets about 11.30, and Jackie left at about 1.00 a.m. As I watched the show, I marvelled at the spirit of the performers playing to a third of a house. Joey Bishop said, concerning the weather, 'Those Republicans are sure sore losers,' and Milton Berle said, 'Mr. President, we'd rather have snow with you . . .'

It was 1.30 when Sinatra at last introduced John F. Kennedy, who stood up to a long, long standing ovation from the snowbound souls still there.

'I know we're all indebted to a great friend, Frank Sinatra,' the President-elect said. 'Long before he could sing, he was pulling votes in a New Jersey precinct. . . .'

He didn't say it, but I got the impression that the President-to-be meant that Frank wasn't above stuffing ballot boxes for the party.

During the speech, Kennedy, with his characteristic choice of words, said, 'We have seen excellence tonight. . . .' It was a touching phrase to Frank and to those of us who were carefully listening. 'It is now Inauguration Day,' Kennedy continued. 'I hope that all of you will join Lyndon B. Johnson and myself in committing us all to the defence of the Constitution of the United States.'

The President-to-be's capsule encomium, 'We have seen excellence tonight,' was seized upon immediately by those with ears attuned for Kennedyisms. One with such ears was Sinatra, who subsequently asked me to call *Variety* and reserve the back page for an ad thanking the performers, with 'We have seen excellence tonight' as the top line. He would pay for it. During this discussion, Frank himself turned headline writer and wrote a proposed headline to fit the *Variety*ese style.

On a piece of paper, he wrote:

PREZ PRAISES PROS.

Well after 3.00 a.m., barely nine hours before he would be sworn in, JFK was seen dancing at a party for Frank Sinatra's guests at the restaurant known as Paul Toung's.

The Ambassador, Joseph P. Kennedy, was the host to Frank's imported stars. The Secret Service agents were watching from the kitchen—JFK wouldn't be President until around noon. The President-to-be arose at one point during the steak-and-lobster supper to dance.

'This is his last night out with the people before he takes over; he's entitled,' was the general attitude.

Sinatra, still happy about the gala show, said to me, in answer to some questions, 'I only wish my kids could have seen it. I can't find the words . . . I'll never find the words.' He and the President posed for a picture Inaugural Night, which he treasured.

His warmth for the President was at its greatest. Eleanor Roosevelt was happy she'd participated, but was a little surprised at all the drinking, although she shouldn't have been, considering some members of her own family.

It was 'Happy Days Are Here Again' for the Democrats and the Sinatra crowd. Everybody was talking about 'Jack' and 'Bobby'—and even a few were talking about 'Jackie'. The atmosphere was electric, and leading hostess, Gwen Cafritz, said there would be more parties than ever before and that youth would be in charge.

A close friend said JFK was high on hi-fi. Frank and Peter Lawford would obtain the best hi-fi and stereo system in the history of hi-fi and stereo for 1600 Pennsylvania Avenue, if JFK just gave the word.

Frank and Juliet Prowse told the current Kennedy stories. One concerned a White House guard shouting, 'Hey, you kids, off the lawn! Oh, excuse me, Mr. President.'

The blacks got treatment at the Inauguration such as they'd never had before, due, in part, to Sinatra's influence. Harry Belafonte told me he had a suite at the Carlton 'much bigger than I needed'. He repeated the current anecdote: the black leaders, Lumumba and Kasavubu, said, 'Did you ever hear such a funny name as Kennedy?'

Sinatra was the typical cocky Sinatra on Inaugural Night, when the President's father gave another party. The

Wedding portrait of Frank's parents, Anthony Martin Sinatra, now dead, and Dolly.

A seven-year-old Frankie decked out in his stylish knickers.

Frankie, eight, sits front row right, in front of guitar-playing Mom, during a 1923 vacation in the Catskill Mountains.

Frankie autographed this picture in 1938 for his Aunt Marge and Uncle Babe.
(*Courtesy of Mr. and Mrs. John Garaventi*)

Frank (right) is one-fourth of the Hoboken Four as they appeared on the Major Bowes Amateur Hour on radio in 1935.

TOP At a rally for Brooklyn volunteer workers in the 1944 Red Cross War Fund campaign. From left: Red Barber, campaign chairman; Borough President John Cashmore; Sinatra; and Ed Sullivan, producer of the rally. (*Pictorial Parade*)
BOTTOM With Bing Crosby, hamming it up on NBC radio, 1945. (*Pictorial Parade*)

TOP Frank's the center of attraction at a party at Toots Shor's in 1945. Manie Sacks, his friend and counsel, is in the audience (left, with hand on chin).

BOTTOM Director Richard Whorf (left) talks to Frank on the set of *It Happened in Brooklyn*, 1947. Others gathered around are (from left) Whorf, publicist George Evans, personal manager Bobby Burns, and Sinatra. Peter Lawford, on the telephone, is on the extreme right.

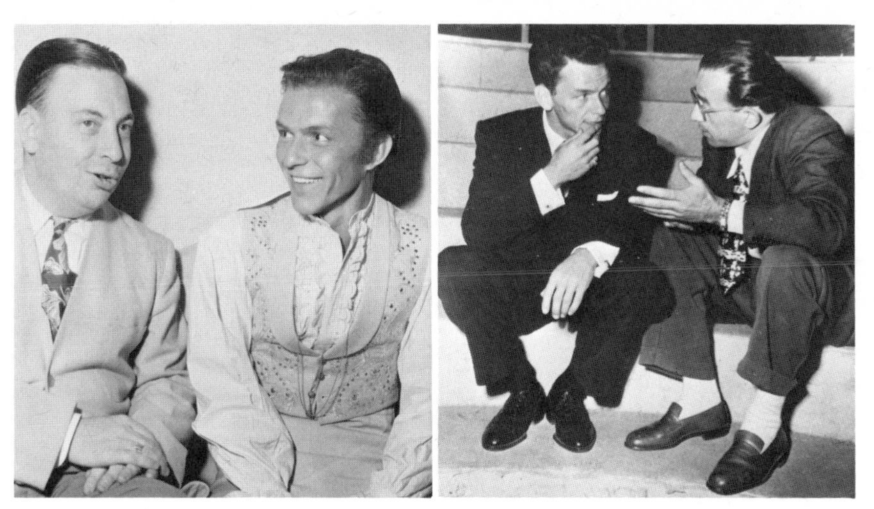

LEFT An early Earl and an early Frank on the set of *The Kissing Bandit*, 1948.
RIGHT Frank holds an earnest meeting with his publicist, George Evans, to plan publicity strategy in 1950.

Irving Berlin encouraged the young Sinatra in the late forties.

A familiar threesome—the groom, the bride (Ava Gardner), and the wedding tier (1951). (*Pictorial Parade*)

The day after they were married in Philadelphia on November 7, 1951, honeymooners Ava Gardner and Frank take a barefoot stroll on a lonely stretch of Miami Beach. (*Pictorial Parade*)

A teen-age Nancy, Jr., with her father in his dressing room when she made an early appearance on his TV show in the mid-fifties. (*Pictorial Parade*)

Escorting Lauren Bacall to the Hollywood premiere of *Sayonara*, 1956. (*Pictorial Parade*)

A grim Sinatra arrives at the Los Angeles County Grand Jury in 1957 to testify about the famous wrong-door raid on Marilyn Monroe. (*Wide World*)

Frank stands close by as Stuart Symington, Lyndon B. Johnson, John F. Kennedy, and Adlai Stevenson shake hands on their political future at the 1956 Democratic Presidential Convention in Chicago. (*Pictorial Parade*)

The welcome sign at the gate post of the Sinatra house in Palm Springs in 1959.

With American-born Lady Beatty, who was divorced from Earl Beatty, leaving hotel in South Kensington for a party in Mayfair, 1958. (*Pictorial Parade*)

Stewardess Judy Bennett joyfully escorts Frank Sinatra, Sammy Davis, Jr., and Peter Lawford off the plane in Chicago where they arrived for business meetings in 1960. (*Pictorial Parade*)

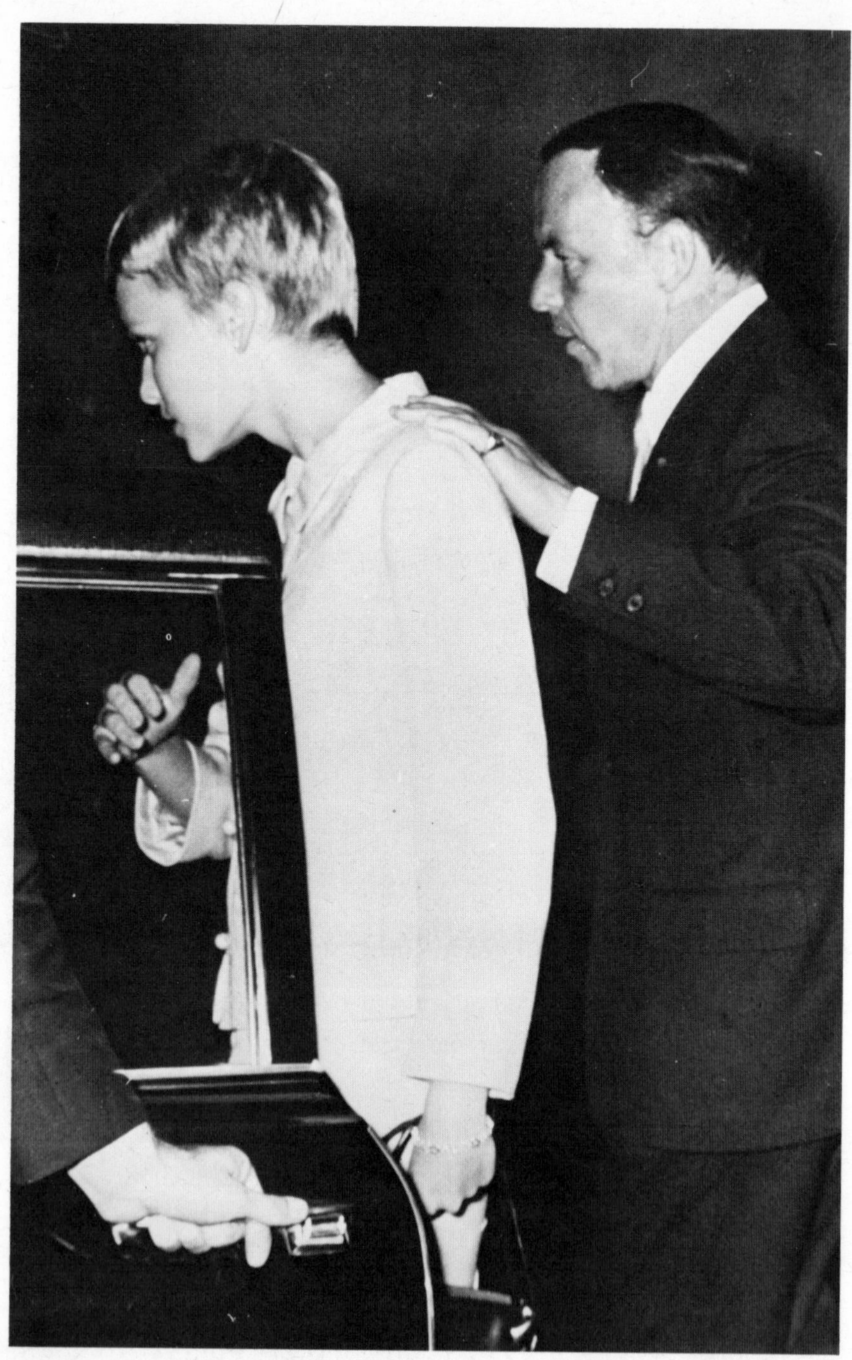

Taking Mia Farrow out on the town in 1966. (*Pictorial Parade*)

Before doing a benefit for the blind in 1962, Frank visited the Sunshine Home for Blind Children in Northwood, England. (*Pictorial Parade*)

Sinatra and Mia Farrow leave their honeymoon party held at the 21 Club in New York, 1966. Photographer Jerry Engel claims Sinatra swung at him, knocking off his glasses, right after this picture was taken. (*Jerry Engel*)

Nancy Sinatra (right), twenty-six, in London to record the theme song for the James Bond film *You Only Live Twice*, has girl talk with her sister Tina, eighteen, in 1967. (*Pictorial Parade*)

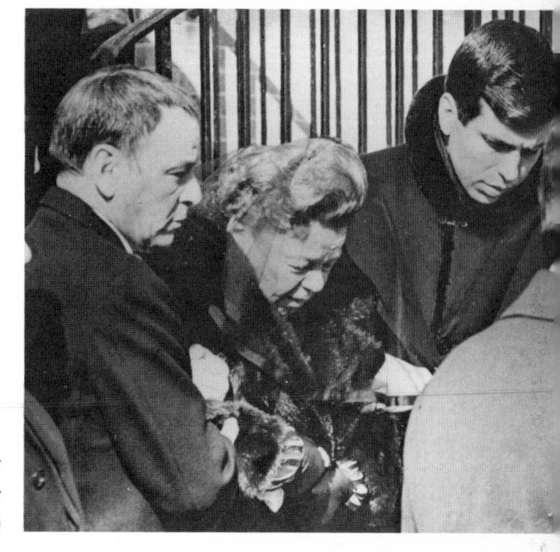

Frank Sinatra and Frank, Jr., assist Dolly Sinatra from church following the funeral for Frank's father in 1969. (*New York* Post)

Frank Sinatra, Jr., escorts his mother Nancy, Sr., at the wedding of Nancy, Jr., to Hugh Lambert in Palm Springs, 1970. That's Jilly Rizzo in the background. (*Pictorial Parade*)

Arrival in London following the brouhaha in Australia in 1974. (*Pictorial Parade*)

Jilly Rizzo runs interference for Sinatra and Hope Lange as they leave the Bistro in Hollywood, 1974. (*Frank Edwards/Fotos International*)

Tina Sinatra Farrell (left) and Barbara Marx arrive at James Cagney tribute in Hollywood, 1974. (*Frank Edwards/Fotos International*)

Sinatra Inaugural Gala group, relaxing after its show the night before, was having its own party. Peter Lawford burst in on the Sinatra party. 'The President would like to have you join his party,' he said.

'Tell him we're eating,' replied Sinatra, spurning the royal command.

Frank's quick answer shocked at least one guest, Edward G. Robinson, who predicted to a dinner companion: 'You're going to see a wop get nailed to the door.'

He was wrong. The President of the United States came to Sinatra's party and said, 'I'm sorry, I didn't know you were eating.'

'*That's* class!' Frank said later.

For all the chuminess between Frank and JFK, Frank had been considered a political liability from the start of the campaign, though he didn't know it. Political winds and windbags change. When some of Robert F. Kennedy's official documents were opened to public inspection in 1974, it was disclosed that Sinatra was regarded as a problem back in 1960.

There was to have been a Constitutional Rights Conference in 1960, sponsored by the Kennedys, in New York, and Sinatra was scheduled to appear. But a nay note came from Harris Wofford, the Kennedys' civil rights adviser. He recommended to another Kennedy aide, John L. Seigenthaler, that candidate JFK not meet Sinatra 'in public'.

The Associated Press quoted an undated Seigenthaler memo: 'It is hoped that Sinatra would realize his own worth and keep his distance from the senator.'

But 'the aide also said Sinatra would help with a voter registration drive in Harlem, "where he is recognized as a hero of the cause of the Negro".'

Bobby Kennedy was increasingly suspicious of Frank's curious friendships. His special agents woke people at night, asking about Frank. They inquired whether Frank had put Phyllis McGuire into the movie *Come Blow Your Horn* because she was the girlfriend of Mafia mobster Sam Giancana, one of the overlords of organized crime.

(This was the same Giancana whom the CIA approached

about assassinating Fidel Castro and who was himself murdered at the height of the investigation of the CIA in 1975. And he was the same Giancana who was linked again with Sinatra and with—ironically—President Kennedy during those investigations. It was December 1975 and Sinatra, just turned sixty, made the front pages, again. Next to an old picture of him chatting with President John F. Kennedy was one of his frequent house guests, murdered Mafia mobster Sam Giancana, in dark glasses, handcuffed to a chair. And then another picture, of Judith Campbell Exner, a one-time playmate of Sinatra, whom he had introduced to both President Kennedy and Sam Giancana. Put them all together—the President, the murdered mobster, and the girl who kissed and talked about it—and they spell Sinatra.

Later, at a press conference, Mrs. Exner said, among other things, that she gave up sex with Sinatra because he had 'kinky' tastes. Frank replied pungently in eleven words, 'Hell hath no fury like a hustler with a literary agent.')*

'I think Frank put her in the picture thinking she'd be a good addition to the cast,' one friend said. Bobby didn't believe it. Bobby's agents brought in tapes in which Giancana was heard implying that he had Sinatra under control. To Bobby, this association with Giancana, who was blacklisted by the Nevada casinos, was bad for his brother, and Bobby reported his fears to the President.

Bobby also probed the ownership of the casinos. Frank and Hank Sanicola controlled Cal-Neva Lodge and its casino. They weren't supposed to permit Giancana on the premises. He was there; it endangered their licence. Bobby couldn't actually link Frank with mob money. The FBI had a dossier on Frank, which included some things in his favour.

Back during the Kefauver Committee investigation, in 1951, they wanted to question him about the old story that

* Early in 1974, I first exposed John F. Kennedy's 'swinging White House' and Kennedy himself as 'the sexiest, swingingest President of the century', saying he kept his many dalliances secret from his wife Jacqueline with the help of friendly co-conspirators who served as 'beards'.

Now I can add that Jack and Bobby Kennedy's brother-to-brother sharing of Marilyn Monroe (and other girls), passing between them, caused a big White House 'inside' scandal. JFK, Sinatra, and Sam Giancana seemed to have had similar sharing arrangements.

he'd carried money to Luciano. Sinatra argued that to be shown all over the TV screen in an inquiry about an obviously untrue story would be ruinous. He was convincing. The committee believed him and didn't call him.

Bobby's agents questioned Italian-Americans of dubious reputation about how well they knew Frank. The comedians had said Frank was now called the 'Pope'. (They had another line: 'The real Pope made Frank a cardinal and now we only have to kiss his *ring*'.)

Known *mafiosi* were asked whether Sinatra was in the Mafia. 'We wouldn't have him,' replied one. 'He'd be too much trouble. He'd be too easy a target.'

Bobby decided he had to go.

The din in the press about Sinatra's closeness to the White House increased. One day Joseph P. Kennedy was inviting Sinatra and the Clan to visit him on the Riviera; a few days later it developed that he didn't have room for them all: the visit was off. The White House was believed to have advised the Ambassador to cool it for a while.

Suddenly, just when backstage voices were saying Sinatra was not a proper buddy for JFK, came an announcement that Sinatra was going to have President Kennedy as his house guest in Palm Springs. The social coup of the year! The President would be living in the Sinatra compound on Frank Sinatra Drive in the world of swing and ring-a-ding-ding. Sinatra was so honoured that he began building a new wing for the President and the guest houses for the Secret Service. This two-bedroom house had grown into a compound with a dining room for about forty. The anticipated arrival of President Kennedy threw the millionaires into a state of excitement that reached all the way up the coast to Pebble Beach.

Just as suddenly—while Frank was proceeding with plans to be the extravagant host—came another announcement: President Kennedy wasn't coming to Sinatra's. He would visit Bing Crosby's Shadow Mountain residence in Palm Desert instead.

It was the Secret Service's decision. The explanation for the switch given out on 25 March 1962, was that the Secret Service apparently felt that Bing Crosby's stucco-and-wood three-bedroom bungalow fifteen miles from downtown Palm Springs was more defensible than Sinatra's sprawling compound.

It was an astonishing slap in the face for Sinatra. Wasn't Bing a Republican? He had probably voted for Nixon. Frank was bitter. Bobby had shot him down with that Secret Service explanation, which Frank didn't believe. Frank saw Bing getting all the attention he'd wanted.

And the smiling face of Peter Lawford was in all the photographs. That terminated Frank's long friendship with Peter. After the break-up, when Frank no longer spoke to Peter, Frank's intimates said, 'Peter should have delivered Jack.'

There'd already been a small misunderstanding over a picture partnership involving the Clan members—Frank was supposed to work for less, but his managers asked for $1 million for his services—and that had led to a blow-up.

But this JFK switch to Bing's was treachery as Frank saw it, though Peter said he personally couldn't have influenced the Secret Service. 'The Secret Service was afraid the security available at Frank's place was just not adequate,' he said. 'Bing's place was better from that standpoint. And Jimmy Van Heusen's house nearby was excellent for the security headquarters.'

Considering some of the places the President *had* stayed, Frank had a right to be offended.

The President, it can be said now, had wanted to stay at Frank's. A man of magnetism himself, he enjoyed Sinatra's charisma and liked gossiping with him. They had some women in common. Afraid that Frank was offended, the President personally placed a call to Sinatra from Bing's home and asked him to come to Bing's to see him.

Sinatra declined.

He was 'on his way to L.A.'.

He was sorry he couldn't make it now.

Frank said no to a presidential summons.

Peter Lawford was with the President when the call was made. Frank never knew the behind-the-scenes begging that Peter Lawford engaged in, imploring the President to save their relationship by calling him, inviting him over.

'Get him on the phone,' the President finally said.

Frank's feelings were too hurt to have it all glossed over. While he was 'nice', he also explained that he had 'some people' waiting for him in Los Angeles. The 'people', it happened, included Marilyn Monroe, one of his house guests, and subsequently an intimate friend of the President's.

Sadly, Frank realized that a successful propaganda campaign had been waged against him for months. He claimed not to believe the papers, but they had been right. The gossip columnists had repeatedly reported that JFK was going to dump him. They had said that Jackie Kennedy didn't want to be contaminated by him (probably a lie, because Jackie liked him) and that Bobby, Old Joe and Jack's political advisers wanted to sack Sinatra. Sinatra had been licked, and good.

Some of the Sinatra contingent thought that all this only proved the truth of the gags going around about Old Joe and his sons. Sinatra had told them himself, in good humour at the time:

Old Joe, the Ambassador, had asked Jack, 'Son, what do you want to be?'

Jack said, 'President.'

Old Joe said, 'No, no, after you grow up?'

And Jack had explained why he appointed his brother Attorney-General: 'I thought he ought to have a little experience before he goes into private practice.'

Comedians Marty Allen and Steve Rossi did an 'interview' with Bobby Kennedy:

'Are you happy as Attorney-General?'

'No!' (stomping his foot).

'Why not?'

'I wanted to be President!'

'Why do you think you're entitled to be President?'

'My father promised it to me.'

Sinatra was enormously shaken by the assassination of the President. Friends hadn't seen him so depressed and low in spirit. He felt little rancour towards the President, but much towards Bobby. Frank still treasured an autographed picture, and in the Palm Springs compound there was a plaque: 'John F. Kennedy Slept Here November 6th and 7th, 1960.' Those were happier days.

Documented correspondence gathered a dozen years later shows that the President wrote to Sinatra in June 1962, three months after switching plans to be his house guest, thanking him for 'the floral rocking chair that you so thoughtfully sent me for my birthday'.

Sinatra telegraphed Kennedy's press secretary, Pierre Salinger, in August that he wanted to send him a print of his latest movie, *The Manchurian Candidate*, adding that 'a print will be available any hour, night or day for viewing by the President'. There were other letters from the President thanking him for similar gestures.

Sinatra was not seen at the Kennedy funeral. He did phone the White House from California to offer his condolences. The call was taken by Patricia Lawford.

ENGAGED, 'DROWNED' AND REVOKED

Frank the lover wanted a wife as he saw middle-age coming around the bend. He needed an obedient hostess to run cosy little dinner parties for fifty or sixty, a sexy bride intelligent enough to make all the guests laugh as she presided over the 'King's' palace.

It seemed like everything happened to Sinatra in those three or four years, in the sixties. He became engaged; he was reported drowned; he was classified as one of the Bad Guys by the state of Nevada, which moved to take away his gambling licence and then he was reclassified as one of the Good Guys by recipients of his widespread charities. He reached the age of philosophising and revealed himself as very confused—like everybody else. Sinatra was at that time divided, the most split split-personality he had ever been—but it was probably the most interesting period of his life.

'I don't like my image,' he told the publicity agency he employed. 'What's wrong?'

'You are,' he was told.

The jokes got under his skin. Readers were chuckling over a fictitious story in the scandal magazine *Confidential* claiming that the secret of his sex prowess was that he ate the 'Breakfast of Champions', Wheaties, all day and all night long while he was entertaining a woman for the weekend. He couldn't get too mad at that. It was complimentary.

But he kept telling the press to go to hell.

Columnist Jim Bacon wrote, 'Frank Sinatra was reported to have slapped a photographer in Palm Springs. This was a vicious rumour started by some reporter that Frank had ordered his chauffeur to run over.'

When he's showing the charming side of his dual personality, Sinatra helps people. He likes to make stars, as he did with Sammy Davis, Jr. Now he wanted to help Juliet Prowse, the beautiful red-haired dancer from South Africa he'd been escorting since Shirley MacLaine introduced them. Frank was intoxicated by her legs. He advanced her career by casting her in his movie *Can-Can* and putting her on TV. She was often at his side as he whipped around Hollywood in his Dual-Ghia.

One night in January 1962, Frank told comedian Joe E. Lewis as they sat in Romanoff's that he had bought Juliet an engagement ring.

'Romeo and Juliet Prowse!' exclaimed Joe E., who later told me that he quickly said to Frank, 'Let me call Earl Wilson and tell him.'

Frank said, 'No, I have other plans.' He saw it on a much bigger canvas. He was going to make it smashing.

Juliet had told me a whole year before this, 'I love Frank and am going to marry him.' Now she was in New York making publicity noises. She was going to bolt 20th Century-Fox studios because Spyros Skouras, the board chairman, wasted her talents, gave her bad pictures. She charged that he played games with her, trying to get her to help get Sinatra to do a remake of *Blood and Sand*, the Rudolph Valentino picture, by subterfuge. She claimed Skouras said, 'We wouldn't want Sinatra, his legs are too skinny,' and she believed that was intended to bait Sinatra into wanting to do the film.

Two days after showing the ring, Sinatra announced that they were engaged. Sammy Davis was shocked that Frank was giving up bachelorhood. He asked an audience, 'Let us observe a moment of silence for Our Leader, who has left us.'

As plans steamed ahead for the wedding, with Juliet racing off to South Africa to invite her parents, the question arose whether Juliet would continue to work.

'After working this long and hard for a career, I can't see myself giving it up,' she said.

Frank was filming part of *The Manchurian Candidate* at Madison Square Garden in New York. I asked him about reports that Juliet was insisting upon working. 'The people who are saying those things are irresponsible,' he said. 'She's not going to do any work. I'd rather not have it.'

He seemed to think that settled it. He said she had to do a television show with Arthur Freed, and that would probably be her last job. As Mrs. Sinatra, Juliet would ascend to the loftiest heights of Hollywood society and Frank would spend his nights at home, a tamed tiger.

But Juliet still wanted that career. Some sceptics in the press said that Frank was merely trying to help her make a big name. When Frank heard that Juliet had asked the advice of her friends and parents, he said irritably that she would quit work any day. To him, getting married wasn't something you talked over with your parents. You were either in love and wanted to get married, or you weren't.

Forty-three days after the engagement was announced, it all came crashing down with another communiqué: 'Juliet Prowse and Frank Sinatra today disclosed that they had called off their wedding plans. The pair in a joint statement said, "A conflict in career interests led us to make this decision. We both thought it wiser to make this move now than later".'

'Frank's had longer engagements in Las Vegas,' said Sammy Davis, Jr.

And so it was really true that Juliet Prowse didn't want to give up her career. In trying to be a star-maker, Frank had only partially succeeded. He hadn't been able to bend her will to his. But she had earned his respect. 'She could have been dishonest, agreed to give up her career, then changed her mind later,' a friend quoted Sinatra as saying after the break-up.

Juliet gave back the ring. 'It was the only thing a lady could do,' she said. She claimed that she had made the right decision: 'How could I retire at twenty-five?'

It did not end their friendship. They would see each other at parties or Frank would be on the phone and say,

'Hi, let's have dinner.' Frank took her to a big charity party as his date a couple of years later. Juliet played nightclubs, getting close to $50,000 a week in Las Vegas, and also went on summer theatre tours at good salaries.

And she continued to make news. Ten years later she and choreographer-musical director John McCook were on their way to get married, but made an emergency stop in Stateline, Nevada, where she went into Barton Memorial Hospital to give birth to a son she named Seth. This delayed the wedding for a month.

Today Frank and Juliet continue to speak highly of each other. Frank enjoys the remark that Dean Martin made: 'Frank and Julie broke up. Julie wanted Frank to give up his career, but he wouldn't.'

The old story that Frank was the buddy of mobsters broke out again. It had caused the split with the Kennedys; now it would hurt him again, and more.

Frank has known many mob bosses intimately, but there is no proof he has had any dealings with them or that he owes them anything. He puts them down as he puts others down, and if the toughest one asks him for an unreasonable favour, he can easily say, and does say, 'Fuck 'em'.

He has friends as tough as any of them, and he can be fearless. He has socialized with some of them—having a drink or a meal. It is a peculiar fascination of his. But Frank has been too well advised by attorney Mickey Rudin to have any business deals that would be suspect.

In 1963, Frank was enjoying high-living days at his Cal-Neva Lodge at Lake Tahoe. He was romancing beautiful Jill St. John, the former daughter-in-law of Barbara Hutton. Jill had been the wife of Lance Reventlow. Jill was getting the 'A' treatment from Sinatra. She was gorgeous and sexy, and a few years later she would be romanced by Henry Kissinger. But then she was the 'King's' girl and he flew her in his own plane to New York for concerts and benefits and squired her over to New Jersey for a home-cooked Italian dinner prepared by Dolly Sinatra. That was always one of the important stops in a Sinatra romance. Frank wanted his mother's opinion of the current candidate.

The Cal-Neva Lodge was giving Frank headaches, and there were reports that Eddie Fisher, flying very high in those days, might buy it.

Suddenly, Frank was too busy to see Jill St. John. He was busy with lawyers.

The Nevada Gaming Control Board charged that mobster Sam Giancana had checked into one of the cottages in Cal-Neva on 17 July, and remained until 28 July. He was there with Phyllis McGuire, of the singing McGuire Sisters, who was appearing at the club. Giancana had been given one of the 'chalets', as the cottages were called. It was registered to Miss McGuire rather than to Giancana.

The chalet Sam Giancana shared with Phyllis McGuire was in a wooded area away from the hotel proper. It overlooked beautiful Lake Tahoe, and it was because of the snowcaps high up in the Sierras that these cabins were called chalets.

Giancana was a Mafia boss. Sinatra knew of his unsavoury reputation and defied the board by saying he was going to continue to see him and be his friend. The Gaming Control Board thereupon began action to revoke Sinatra's gambling licence, on the ground that he had played host to a notorious underworld figure.

Frank at first claimed he hadn't known Giancana was there. 'How in the hell could I know the name of everybody registering at my place? I wasn't even in town at the time,' he said.

Then the board charged that Frank, in salty and obscene language on the phone, dared them to do anything about it. It further charged that one of Frank's employees, Paul ('Skinny') D'Amato, had clumsily attempted to bribe one of the gaming board members, offering $200.

With his usual bravado, Frank said he couldn't say any more until he consulted his lawyers, but he threw out a couple of quips, including: 'Anybody want to buy a hot casino?'

I stayed in one of those chalets, or log cabins, when Giancana was quietly visiting there. We heard that 'somebody big'—'Sam' or 'Momo'—had sneaked in. But the name Giancana meant little to us then, and we never suspected that in 1975 he could be murdered in his basement kitchen in Oak Park, Illinois, as he prepared sausages and spinach for a supposed friend who shot him in the back of the head.

Sam was a popular mobster. Fifty-five, quiet and inoffensive, he was like an uncle to women I knew, whom he took to dinner or who cooked dinner for him. He was generous and kind. Those who knew about the Mafia understood that he was as powerful in his world as the President of the United States was in his. The word was, actually, that Sam's crowd 'ran the world, including the government'.

A graduate of the Al Capone school of crime, Sam enjoyed flashy ties, black silk suits, pretty women and nightclubs. Frequently questioned about suspected gangland killings, he was never convicted. He was close-mouthed, never a squealer and, of course, rich.

The New York *Times*' crime expert, Nicholas Gage, an indefatigable exposer of the Mafia, wrote that Bobby Kennedy had a nineteen-page FBI report saying that gangsters had called Sinatra at his unlisted number and that he had performed special favours for them. Once Sinatra did a singing commercial for an auto dealer—free.

'The report quotes Sam Giancana as bragging to friends that he owned a piece of Cal-Neva through Sinatra,' Gage wrote in his book, *The Mafia Is Not an Equal Opportunity Employer*. The insiders said it was Sam's hotel. The insiders sometimes said it was Sinatra's hotel, but no effort was made to prove these assertions and they were believed to be untrue and another part of the Sinatra legend.

Sinatra had developed a special court or entourage for Cal-Neva. One member was one-armed 'Wingy' Grober, a fast-talking casino boss, dealer or manager, a likeable character who made Sinatra laugh and who kept his mouth shut about the presence of Sam Giancana. From Atlantic City, Frank had brought 'Skinny' D'Amato. There were also two massive gentlemen called 'Pucci East' and 'Pucci West'. Often they were joined by 'Swifty' Morgan, the so-called millionaire tie salesman, who hustled Frank's friends for ties and jewellery of dubious value. He claimed that the jewellery was hot. It was all a joke, and because he was a friend of Sinatra, people gave him $100 for merchandise of little worth. Everybody had lots of $100 bills.

Frank was about twenty pounds overweight and trying to slice it off in the steamroom. Cal-Neva Lodge was a small-time operation compared to the giant gambling enterprises in Las Vegas or even Reno. The guests gathered at a pleasant circular bar before going to see the show that night. Lake Tahoe is a showplace that was at that time just starting to build. When a celebrity came up the driveway, the entire Cal-Neva community knew about it. If they didn't know it, it was because somebody like Sam Giancana wanted it kept secret.

Sinatra defied the Gaming Control Board and offended Edward A. Olsen, its chairman. Sinatra believed he had the right to have any friends he wished, particularly outside the state.

Frank made jokes about the fact that the California–Nevada state line cut through the hotel and the swimming pool. 'It's the only place where you can walk across the lobby—and get locked up for violating the Mann Act,' Frank said.

Olsen argued that having an association with gangsters reflected on the state of Nevada. He said Sinatra offered to have dinner and 'talk it over', but Olsen refused. Olsen wanted Sinatra to appear and answer questions. Sinatra refused.

Olsen said the board could subpoena him. Sinatra, according to Olsen, replied, 'You subpoena me and you're going to get a big fat fucking surprise.'

The issue of 'guilt by association' was raised. Attorney Greg Bautzer spoke up in Sinatra's behalf. 'I don't think it should be possible that an individual can lose a property right by virtue of having a friend,' Bautzer said. 'I can even have a convicted individual as a friend, and there is no law that says I cannot.'

Sinatra was going to take on the state board, it appeared. Amazingly, he had some supporters in the press. Why was anybody surprised at Giancana staying at Cal-Neva? Everybody knew Giancana had financial interest in Nevada casinos, and it was presumed to be mob money. Wasn't the gaming board being naïve?

Frank made uncomplimentary remarks about the board and said he'd win. The board wasn't yielding. It gave Sinatra two weeks to answer the charges.

He backed down.

Surprising everybody by his action, Sinatra announced, just before the two weeks were up, that he had decided not to contest the board's attempt to revoke his licence. It was an unusually pacific surrender by Frank.

'No useful purpose would be served by my devoting my time and energies convincing the Nevada gaming officials that I should be part of the industry,' he said. He was going to give up all his Nevada holdings and devote himself to new duties at Warners in the making of pictures and records, he said. Jack L. Warner had suggested this.

The Gaming Control Board revoked his gambling licence, stating he had brought discredit on the gambling industry. He was commanded to get out of the gambling business by 5 January 1964. It meant disposing of property valued at $3.5 million. There is no doubt that Frank was hurt hard by this order. It was a severe financial setback, as well as a blow to his ego and to his belief that he could do as he liked.

But he was spared from answering questions about Giancana and others and their interests in casinos. Sinatra has, many times, regretted losing the licence and wished he could get one to operate in Las Vegas. His supporters see little chance of that in this century, but he keeps hoping to do it.

Surprisingly, columnist Robert Ruark, of the Scripps-Howard newspapers, spoke out for Sinatra in the licence squabble. Ruark and Westbrook Pegler had denounced Sinatra back in the 1940s for being friendly with Lucky Luciano in Cuba. Now Ruark confessed that he had been 'unduly severe' with Sinatra. He said that a state like Nevada that lived off gambling and its by-products, such as 'harlotry', had little right to 'bust' Frank. Ruark said Sinatra had got 'a bum rattle'.

Some papers, however, did gloat about his getting kicked

out. There was a current joke about it after an earthquake in Nevada: 'That'll teach them,' some comedian said, 'to fool around with Frank Sinatra!'

How did Frank feel about the mobster talk?

The popular contention that Frank is the friend of mobsters is one that he will just have to live with. As one of his friends explains, Frank is fascinated by them; he says as he sees some of them, 'There but for the grace of God, go I.' He and Dean Martin have softened the charge somewhat with jokes. Dean told one audience when he made an appearance with Frank, 'Don't clap so loud, you'll wake up our Mafia partners. They're trying to sleep.'

Andy Williams said that when Sinatra opened in Caesar's Palace in Las Vegas, 'A lot of the audience put their hats over their faces. There was 500 years off for good behaviour on the first row.'

On Sunday, 10 May 1964, a Hawaiian radio broadcast the report that Frank Sinatra had drowned.

It was one of the most dramatic in Frank's lifetime of dramatic occurrences. He actually was almost drowned, and according to witnesses with whom I have talked, he did say, 'I'm drowning. I'm gone. Let me go and save Ruth.' He was referring to producer Howard Koch's wife, whom he had been trying to save.

Trying to become a film director as well as a producer and star, Frank had brought a company to the beautiful island of Kauai to shoot *None but the Brave*. As always, there was a party atmosphere with plenty of drinking, and girls flying in to amuse the star and director. Producer Koch, who knew Sinatra's moods and whims from previous films, began to notice that Sinatra was getting restless. He feared Sinatra would soon say 'Let's get the hell out of here,' and the picture wouldn't be finished.

They were on the beach in a little cove on Wailua Bay on a Sunday noon. Swimming was discouraged, if not actually forbidden, because of a strong undertow. But the Sinatra company fanned out from a beach-front house that he had leased and did just about as it liked. The Coco Palms Hotel nearby was the centre of activity.

'Sinatra was getting itchy,' Koch remembers. 'I told my

wife Ruth I was going back to the desk to do some rescheduling to see if we couldn't finish sooner. I reminded her to stay out of the water.'

Big, muscular movie actor Brad Dexter also was fearful of the undertow. 'I decided to go up to the house to get some drinks and bring them back,' he said. 'I took Murray Wolf, a record man who was a close friend of Frank's, with me.'

Minutes later, Brad Dexter looked out the big bay window of the house and yelled. He saw that Sinatra and Ruth Koch were being sucked into the ocean. They had been standing with their backs to the waves. Suddenly, a huge one engulfed them and the undertow pulled them into the roaring surf.

Brad Dexter bolted from the house at full speed, with Murray Wolf following.

A phone rang on Howard Koch's desk. 'Your wife has drowned and Frank Sinatra is drowning!' It was the voice of a unit hairdresser.

Koch, a large-shouldered, big-chested fellow, blasted out of the building on to the beach. 'I was running and it seemed to me like I was running in a slow-motion picture . . . running and not getting anywhere.'

Dexter came flying in ahead and plunged into the surf. Sinatra had told Ruth Koch, 'You'll be all right, I'll get to you,' but the waves pulled him in and down.

'He looked like a goner,' Brad Dexter remembered ten years afterwards. He said to me, 'Save Ruth, I'm going to die.'

Dexter was trying to hold both of them afloat. Sinatra was in the worse condition. He was already suffering from anoxia (deprivation of oxygen).

'Look up at the sun,' Dexter cried at him, but Sinatra said, as Dexter tried to hold him against the undertow, 'I can't see anything. I've gone blind.'

Koch saw his wife's orange bathing cap and Sinatra's bald head bobbing in the waves. He heard Frank say, 'I'm gone. I'm going to die. I'm going down for a third time.'

But the hairdresser who had phoned Howard Koch had also phoned for help.

'I held one up and then the other for what seemed like twenty minutes,' said Dexter. 'I knew we would eventually get help. And finally they came, those giant Hawaiians on their surfboards, from the fire department and the police and the shore patrol. They got hold of Ruth and Frank, both of whom had passed out with water in their lungs.'

In the excitement of saving Frank and Mrs. Koch, the rescuers forgot about Brad Dexter, who was still battling the undertow. By the time the surfboard crew pulled him in, he saw Sinatra being taken back to the hotel on a stretcher. Frank, now revived, waved to him weakly and said, 'Hi.'

That was about as much thanks as he could manage at that time.

'I suddenly felt a terrible fatigue like I was going to die as Frank had said he was going to,' recalled Dexter. 'I said to Murray Wolf, "I want a drink". I drank an entire glass of scotch and couldn't feel it.'

When the terrible scare was over, there was a return to the conviviality of noontime. Brad Dexter was toasted as the man who had saved the lives of Sinatra and Mrs. Koch. It led to considerable publicity for Brad Dexter, not all of it welcome. The late comedian Jack E. Leonard used to salute Dexter as 'combination producer and lifeguard'. Joey Bishop wired Frank, 'Did you forget yourself? You could have walked on the waves.' Frank dismissed it with, 'Just got a little water on my bird.'

People in the movie industry believed for a time that Frank rewarded Dexter for saving his life with movie deals and producerships, but Dexter refutes this.

About three years later, they were filming *The Naked Runner* with Dexter as producer, and he sided with the director, Sidney Furie, in a dispute over the amount of work Sinatra, the boss, should do.

'That's why Sinatra wasn't making good pictures then,' says Dexter. 'He wasn't putting in the time.'

Dexter soon found himself no longer with Sinatra Enterprises. Dexter married Mary Bogdanovich, heiress to the Star-Kist tuna fortune, and now makes his own pictures. 'Sinatra is a great guy,' he says. 'I got nothing materially from him and wanted nothing.

'Once when he got sentimental he said there's a Chinese proverb that whoever saves one's life is responsible for that person afterwards. I told him I didn't agree with that and that I wasn't going to take care of him forever. I always felt that there might be a love–hate relationship here and maybe he didn't want me around to remind him that I'd saved his life.'

The cynical comedians wouldn't accept that. They said that 'Sinatra got even with Dexter for saving his life. He dropped him.'

Dexter would never accept that theory. 'I saw him once at Chasen's,' Dexter told me. 'We embraced and he said, "We must get together. I'll call you. . . ." '

Dexter would never forget running into the surf, reaching Sinatra, flipping him over, slapping him on the face, hearing him say he was dying. 'I was part of him,' Dexter says. 'I was a great friend of his great friend, Jack Entratter. I was never a camp follower, but I would never let Frank get hurt. I was protective.

'Afterwards,' says Brad Dexter, 'we just kind of went our separate ways.

'I always have a feeling that some day we will get back together. I think he knows that if I were protecting him, he'd never get into these troubles.

'I also felt that Frank meant it when he said I should save Mrs. Koch and not worry about him. I felt that Frank wouldn't care if he died. Because he'd lived a great life. Frank had been there and back.'

But Fate, or the waves, had willed that Frank would live on and get into more wars.

Sinatra was loved in the islands, but hotel people were puzzled by the habits of some of his movie actors. They had to change not only sheets but mattresses because they were cigarette-burned, scorched by firecrackers and pummelled out of shape. On one visit, a stopover on the way to Australia, Sinatra arrived sartorially perfect, bowing, waving and patting children on the head, but he erupted like a volcano when he discovered that an aide travelling with him had only tourist accommodations. Sinatra cancelled the trip, publicly blaming an airline. He later changed his mind and went, but not until he'd raised hell as only he can.

He was remembered for singing at a party—at which Katharine Hepburn and Spencer Tracy held hands—to celebrate the sixtieth birthday of Mervyn LeRoy during filming of *The Devil at 4 O'Clock*.

Spencer Tracy jammed his hands in his pockets, congratulated LeRoy on joining the exclusive 'Sixty Year Club', and told Frank, 'It's not enough to look sixty—you've got to be sixty.'

A girl was playing the piano softly. Sinatra began singing, cigarette in one hand, drink in the other, and continued for half an hour.

Columnist Eddie Sherman of the Honolulu *Advertiser* was under instructions to write nothing of the party, held at Kula Lodge at Mount Halakala. But the one-man Sinatra show in the Hawaiian setting with the lights twinkling below was so picturesque that Sherman asked LeRoy if he could report it; it would be helpful to the eighty-three-year-old operator of the lodge, Frank James, and his new wife.

'No, I promised,' LeRoy answered.

Sherman appealed directly to Frank, who said, 'You can print anything you want to.'

Sinatra once phoned from Los Angeles and asked his close friend Buck Buchwach, executive director of the Honolulu *Advertiser*, for some Maui onions, reputed to be the sweetest in the world, 'the kind you can eat like an apple'. They were out of season.

'I'd better put something in the column,' Eddie Sherman said.

His boss, Buchwach, said, 'Anything for Frank.' A farmer forthwith sent two twenty-pound bags he'd stowed away in his cellar. Sinatra soon had his Maui onions—thanks to two newspapermen.

'When Frank finished a picture or project in Hawaii,' Eddie Sherman said, 'he gave away everything left . . . TV sets . . . radios . . . whiskey . . . food. He'd give it to the maids and waiters. He likes to cook and sometimes he would make spaghetti for them. They really love him here.'

*

Sinatra added new gold nuggets to his fortune. He disposed of his film and music holdings to Warner Brothers for $7 million with a capital gains deal that set up a genuine Frank Sinatra estate. The *Wall Street Journal* began to take note of him. He was getting $1 million plus percentage per picture and was asking for ownership of the negative after seven years, a financial manoeuvre that had been used by Cary Grant and others.

Colourful Jack L. Warner enjoyed Frank's flash, dash and gambling spirit at Las Vegas and at Monte Carlo, and thought of Frank as a possible future president of the Warner corporation. 'Wouldn't that be a hoot?' thought Frank, remembering the days when Louis B. Mayer was the head mogul and usually talked only to superstars.

Looking ahead, Frank said, 'Someday my pipes will quit on me, I have little time left as a singer and probably not much more as an actor.' He admitted he was getting a little tired. He would like to do more behind-the-scenes things—and finance fascinated him. He and fellow-investor Danny Schwartz and attorney Rudin were reported to be partners in ownership of a $400,000 racehorse. Frank let his mind travel to real estate investments down Mexico way around Acapulco and a townhouse in New York and ownership of office buildings. 'Not so bad for a bum that didn't finish high school,' he had to admit.

With his new wealth and his thankfulness at having been saved from drowning, the Good Guy Sinatra re-emerged. He became increasingly the friend in time of trouble who said, 'How much do you need?' He was the 'whip-it-out' guy who gave away millions in his public appearances to benefit children's charities and a fortune through his private generosity, which he seemed actually to try to keep secret. His fortune, later to be estimated at $50 million, would have been much larger if he hadn't been so free with money and gifts.

He was a giving man, a giving giant.

Frank's generosity was demonstrated when George Raft's income tax delinquencies became news. Raft, the movie gangster, the hoofer, had known Frank since he was the highly paid star and Frank was the beginner.

'I was going with Betty Grable, and I went with her to see Tommy Dorsey at the Palladium in Hollywood,' Raft recalled. 'As a hoofer, I wanted to dance. But nobody got up to dance. They just listened to this new kid sing.'

Twenty-five years later, the situation was reversed. Having made millions and flung them away, Raft owed the IRS. 'Sinatra was the first one to help me,' Raft said. 'He called and said, "George, what do you need?" '

Sinatra sent him a signed blank cheque.

'Fill this in for any amount up to $1 million,' Sinatra said to him, according to Raft, who had tears in his eyes as he told it. 'My lawyer wrote in ten thousand dollars. Lucille Ball called me too. I said to her "Frank called me," and she said, "He always gets there ahead of me".'

Charlie Morrison's widow, Mary, told how Sinatra helped when her husband died broke while operating the smart Mocambo nightclub: 'Charlie had thousands of friends, but we had about four dollars,' Mary recalled. 'I prayed for God to help and He sent me Sinatra.

'Frank called me up. He said, "Mary, I don't have anything to do for two weeks. How about me coming into the Mocambo with Nelson Riddle's orchestra?"

'I said, "What can I say?"

'He said, "Don't say anything."

'He had never sung in any club in Hollywood and it was like New Year's Eve every night. We took in over one hundred thousand dollars in those two weeks, and I gave old Charlie a millionaire's funeral. It kept me going for a year besides. Celebrities were shoving against celebrities, and the waiters were able to pay off the mortgages on their homes.

'I like to tell the story,' Mary said, 'and I've noticed that people like to hear it.

'Afterwards, when Frank would come in, I would not give him a cheque, but he always tried to pay.

'One night he arrived with his own champagne. He said 'You don't give me a tab, so I brought my own booze".'

Singer Sylvia Syms has her own story of Sinatra's generosity. 'He's why I'm alive,' she says. 'When I was in the hospital with respiratory trouble, I couldn't leave the place until I had a very special respirator, and they were not only hard to get, they were expensive.

'A day before Christmas, a doctor arrived in my room at the hospital. Here was this respirator made up like a travelling unit, put up in a portable carrying case. That was way back in 1950. I've been using it since.

'In 1951, when I had an auto accident and busted my legs, he brought me a pair of skates!

'He gets very shy. He doesn't do any of this for publicity. He sent me a note saying "You're always saying things about me on TV. If you don't stop it, I'll be forced to punch you right in the pants." '

In the days when Toots Shor was the king of saloonkeepers, the king of crooners would swing in as a customer and permit Toots to reach into his pockets and extract loose bills. Toots would toss them around to his help as tips. Frank never objected, but enjoyed watching the action.

But the money wasn't always given away frivolously.

When Sinatra was filming in Knabe, Utah, he flew from Las Vegas to Knabe and used the Knabe schoolyard as a landing field. 'I want to do something for those school kids for using their playground,' Sinatra said to Chuck Moses, then his press agent. 'Find out what they need.'

Moses prepared a list of fifteen or twenty items. 'We can pick out one or two,' Moses suggested.

'Give them everything on the sheet,' Sinatra commanded.

'But that would come to $5,000,' said Moses.

'I said *everything* on the list.'

Lying in bed in a hospital after a heart attack, Lee J. Cobb was astonished to get a call from Sinatra, whom he hardly knew, asking if he might visit him. Sinatra moved into his life, sending him flowers, books, candy, moving him finally into his Palm Springs home, where he encouraged Cobb about resuming his career. It was very hot in the summer in Palm Springs, so Sinatra moved Cobb into his Los Angeles apartment. Of course, Sinatra paid all the bills. When Cobb recovered, with Sinatra's help, they said good-bye; Frank was not needed any longer.

Bela Lugosi said that when he was committed for drug addiction, 'Sinatra was the only star I heard from. . . .

'I'd never even met him and it gave me such a boost for him to encourage me,' Lugosi said. Columnist Kendis Rocklin found out about Sinatra helping Lugosi and reported it, saying that 'Sinatra rarely speaks of the generous things he does. He's too busy alienating reporters and hating cops.'

Concerning Sinatra's gift of giving, one who has seen examples of his generosity said, 'Frank thinks he's God.'

Buddy Rich, 'the world's greatest jazz drummer', came off the bandstand one night and told me about their friendship. 'Frank broke away and made it on his own. I went into the army and after I got out, I went back with Dorsey, but I wasn't happy. I went to see Frank in his office one day and he said, "What do you want to do?" I said, "I want my own band."

'He gave me $25,000. No letter, no contract, no notes to sign, nothing. I paid it back when I could. That's the kind of guy he is.

'I'm sure you'll find other samples and here's another one. When I had my heart attack in Atlanta in 1959, he phoned and took care of the hospital bills, and not only that, but he sent me a cheque for $1,000. He didn't know whether I was working or not. He gave about twice what I needed. I really think he's a wonderful human being.'

Toots Shor, always in financial trouble, often nicked Frank for several thousand dollars to meet a current emergency.

Toots learned that once, when Frank was young and had lent him several thousand, Frank had had to borrow because at that time he was broke too. This is what the Toots Shor crowd called friendship.

'Over the years,' Toots confided to me, 'Frank has given me $150,000.

'One time he'd been gamblin' and he won $10,000. He turned to me and said, "Here, you need this more than I do." '

Twice, Toots said, Sinatra lent him $50,000. Toots told Frank of his desperate need one night. Next morning, a Sinatra lawyer sent a $50,000 cheque.

Father Bob Perrella, in his book *They Call Me the Showbiz Priest*, confirms that Frank is known in Show Business as 'the world's softest touch'.

'When tragedy struck the lives of the Judy Garlands, the Ethel Barrymores, the unlucky ones never knew the identity of the man who paid their rents and bought their food,' the priest said.

Frank has friends among the Los Angeles and Palm Springs priests who always know where they can get help for a proper cause. When he worships, it's in private just as he does almost everything else—in and out a side door, into a chauffeured limousine.

Like other philanthropists, Frank likes to think that the idea for his display of generosity is his own. The recipients of his gifts know that it is not wise to ask for something; it's best to 'have him think of it first'. The idea is 'planted' with him or one of his staff.

Unlike some Show Business philanthropists who travel at the expense of charities, Sinatra personally pays all his expenses—even a world tour for children's charities that was quite costly to him.

The results of that tour were monumental. He supplied facilities for five orphanages in Japan and helped build an educational hall in one; he raised money for an orthopaedic hospital in Hong Kong, created a youth centre in Nazareth, provided money for a nursery in Athens, helped a home for crippled children in Paris and the Boys Town of Italy in Rome.

In a London home for blind children, a most poignant event occurred while the children were singing for him. It was a windy day, and a girl about eight years old approached Frank and asked, 'Mr. Sinatra, what colour is the wind?'

The people with Frank hoped he would have an answer.

He did. 'You see, sweetheart,' he said, slowly, 'the wind blows so fast you can't see the colour.'

'In one three-year period, through appearances for which he personally absorbed all expenses, he raised more than one million dollars for a dozen charities in St. Louis,' wrote Father Bob. The Teamsters Union vice-president, Harold Gibbons, who had headquarters in Saint Louis, succeeded in getting the country's leading stars there, with Sinatra's presence as the main lure.

In Palm Springs, he is of course the biggest man in town, with the Martin Anthony Sinatra Medical Education Centre, a tribute to his father, and the Christina Sinatra Teen Centre for high school students, which he endowed.

Once, Frank happened to be reading newspaper accounts of the murder in South America of American diplomat Don Mitrione. With a phone call, he set up a concert in Richmond, Indiana, the diplomat's hometown, flying there personally to raise more than $100,000 for the Mitrione's widow and family.

Sinatra, the 'mayor' of Cathedral City, a suburb of Palm Springs, once got a letter from an Indian girl asking for a toy for her baby brother. The letter said she had no father; he had just taken off and left her and her mother to take care of themselves and the baby brother. With a couple of days' beard and a ragged jacket, Frank personally visited the Indian shack and found that the girl's story was true, except worse. The place wasn't fit for pigs. Frank talked to the girl and her mother never revealing to them who he was. A few days later, the shack was filled with new furniture and toys, clothing and canned goods such as its occupants hadn't imagined possible.

One night while playing blackjack in Las Vegas, Sinatra heard a baby crying—an unusual sound in a casino. Leaving the game, he found the baby in the arms of its mother, who was asleep. He proceeded to buy the baby a teddy bear from a souvenir shop. Waking the mother, he handed her the teddy bear and some bills so she could get home, and courteously suggested that she quiet the baby so a guy could play a little blackjack in peace.

Sinatra completely astonished producer–writer–director Mel Shavelson in the late sixties by accepting a small two-day part of an Italian-American plane pilot in the film *Cast a Giant Shadow*, which was shot in Israel.

'Tell Frank he doesn't have to come to Tel Aviv. We can shoot it in Rome,' Shavelson said.

'Unless I can come to Tel Aviv, I won't do it,' Sinatra replied.

After the shooting, Sinatra told Shavelson, 'Now you've got to do something for me. You have to go with me to Nazareth. . . . They're dedicating an Arab-Israeli Youth Centre to me there. I gave them most of the money, but I don't want any publicity about it.'

Sinatra made a moving speech, which Shavelson remembers. It was a formidable speech considering that the man who delivered it had arrived in one of the few jets that had a piano and a cocktail bar aboard.

'I'm not old enough to understand adults,' Sinatra said, 'but I think I know enough to understand kids. And I think if we can get the kids together, maybe we'll be able to keep them together when they get to be adults. . . .'

'Dolly Sinatra, Frank's mother, got a semi-private audience with Pope Paul on a visit to Rome,' says Father Bob Perella, and adds that the Pope whispered, 'I know all about the charities of your son throughout the world. God bless him.'

When Sinatra turned fifty in 1965, the music trade press hullabalooed it with special editions, hailing him anew as the 'King', the wonder man of Show Business. They fed his giant ego, and he stood back and looked at himself. What he beheld was a 'new' Sinatra, a thinker, a philosopher delivering opinions on war, communism and religion.

Generally, he decided, he was happy, but if he was a philosopher from Hoboken—a Hoboken Hegel—his personality was as hard to understand as Hegel's philosophy. He could not comprehend the paradoxes of his personality, nor the inner conflicts of a man who was at times inordinately sad and the next minute inexplicably blissful.

'Life has been very good to me,' he admitted. 'Enough has happened to me, more than I deserve. I have everything I need for the rest of my life. Now I would just like to have a little peace of mind.'

But doesn't everybody want peace of mind? The press was his *bête noire* and kept him from having peace of mind. But the instances when he would throw an improperly cooked hamburger at an employee had nothing to do with the press.

'The trouble with the press is they think they're God,' he complained. 'Fifteen years ago I said I wasn't going to talk to the press any more. It became an undeclared war. And I got my brains knocked out, and they're still knocking them out.'

But even as he voiced these criticisms, the music trade press—a legitimate part of the press—was blowing trumpets about his fiftieth birthday.

Acutely conscious of his own lack of formal education, Sinatra picked up a superficial literary glibness through reading and listening to such friends as editor Bennett Cerf, screenwriter Harry Kurnitz and restaurateur Mike Romanoff, who was constantly employing such Oscar Wildeisms as 'Work is the curse of the drinking classes'.

Frank became a 'closet' reader and looked up words. When pressed, and with a dictionary nearby, he knew the difference between ambience, ambivalent and ambulance. Some of the 'Charlies' (as sharp people were called) who tried to pass as intellectuals didn't know half as much as he did, and he knew it.

Bennett Cerf and his wife, Phyllis, got Sinatra into deeper reading. Frank was always reading scripts and bestsellers and story outlines, and could boast that he read more than Cerf, who didn't have a lot of time to read—he was always writing.

Romanoff had his own attitude, which was to pretend that he was right on every subject and to brook no argument. Sinatra adopted the Romanoff method. (Sinatra showed his appreciation of Romanoff later when his restaurant closed. Frank got him consultant jobs on films at $750 a week and took him along to Europe.)

'I don't think I'm always right,' Frank confessed one day while having a drink with Joe E. Lewis.

'That's a hell of a story,' Joe E. said.

Maybe he wasn't right, for example, when he tried to buy a Los Angeles hotel because its owners wouldn't let him land his helicopter on the roof.

'I was being insecure,' Frank said.

'You was being drunk,' Joe E. replied.

When *Playboy* magazine asked him to do a running

interview taped over a period of several days, he consented. It would give him an opportunity to explain the new Sinatra, the thinker, the philosopher. The published interview was fascinating because it revealed Frank Sinatra using such words as *concomitant* in casual conversation and reminding us that the Sermon on the Mount was in Matthew 5:7.

Upon investigating this literary exercise, which for the first time displayed a bookish Sinatra, I found that the interview had been 'produced', or arranged. Sinatra and his press agent made notes at his desk—he even made some notes on a bedside pad—and worked out questions and answers ahead of time. He reminded himself to speak of Albert Schweitzer, Bertrand Russell, the Spanish Inquisition, the witches of Salem and the Prince of Peace.

He thought that anything that got you through the night was good, even if it was Jack Daniels sour mash whiskey. He didn't think you had to go to church every Sunday, but he believed in his kind of God. He thought he would be able to help relations with Russia if he could go there with Count Basie and Ella Fitzgerald. He thought of himself as a self-effacing philanthropist and a potential goodwill ambassador.

One could not read this without thinking, 'Sinatra's really a very serious guy and a very nice guy.'

Well, that was Frank's purpose in doing the interview.

Characteristically, Sinatra got into a tiff over the publication of the interview. Sinatra controlled all rights to it: it could not be published anywhere without his permission. When it appeared without his okay in serial form in a London newspaper, he was furious. *Playboy* claimed it was innocent. There had been a 'misunderstanding' and the blame was placed on a literary agency.

Sinatra repeatedly acknowledges that he is a bundle of contradictions, all a part of his periods of elation that are followed by deep depression. One of these contradictions is his tendency to throw an ashtray at an underling while rushing out to buy a gift for some notable.

Through the Cerfs and Harry Kurnitz, Sinatra grew more interested in art. He was, after all, a painter himself, of clown subjects. He became intrigued with the last Edward Hopper oil, entitled 'The Two Comedians', and succeeded in buying it from Irving Felt, then head of Madison Square Garden.

He sat for a painting by the Chinese watercolourist, Dong Kingman, for the cover of a programme when he was named March of Dimes 'Man of the Year'. He was co-operative and went to Kingman's New York studio, but Kingman found himself unable to paint Sinatra.

'He was as nervous as a cat, he couldn't hold his face still,' Kingman recalled.

Kingman did the painting from a photograph, and Sinatra congratulated him on it being 'the best likeness of me'. (Frank was being nice; actually, it looked slightly Chinese.)

Finding one of Kingman's watercolours pleasant, Sinatra bought it for $5,000 and hung it in his Palm Springs home.

'Where's my painting?' Kingman asked on a visit to the compound.

'Oh, some girl liked it and I gave it to her,' Frank said.

The Kingmans were friendly with actress Irene Tsu, a former Miss Chinatown of San Francisco. She carried a beautiful Italian leather bag with a gold chain that she said had cost $1,500. Mrs. Kingman inquired about it. 'Frank Sinatra gave it to me.' She said she and Sinatra had been close friends for more than a year and that when she visited Hong Kong, he called her from Los Angeles to chat.

'Irene Tsu was his Chinese period,' Dong Kingman said.

One Sinatra contradiction is that while he believes he is almost universally loved, he is often protected by bodyguards.

Still, the crowds I've seen around him have been worshipful. They lose control in their awe at seeing the 'King'. He is meticulous about neckties, claiming no woman chooses the proper cravats for him. One day, tie-shopping alone in a Fifth Avenue store, he caused a near-riot. Customers forgot their own purchasing, salesgirls forgot their stations, scrambling to see him. Soon neckties were strewn all over the counters and on the floor, with women pushing and shoving to get near him—to see him. Nobody wanted to hurt him. They just wanted to get near. He needed no bodyguard that day.

He is a tireless purchaser himself, although he usually gets a secretary or other aide to shop. One of his devoted admirers is Broadway actor Martin Gabel, husband of actress Arlene Francis. Arlene once told Sinatra that Martin admired his evening pumps.

'Somehow he got my shoe size and sent me six pairs of evening pumps like his,' says Gabel. 'He must be the most generous man in the world. I am going to be well shod for life.'

FRANK, JR., KIDNAPPED!

Sinatra had another problem: his son, Frank Sinatra, Jr. —'Frankie.'

Although Frank, Jr., sometimes went for a month or two without seeing his dad, he idolized him and tried to emulate him.

Sinatra was busy being a corporation executive, movie-maker, international star and swinger. Frank, Jr., was only four when his parents parted. His father visited the children —it was always an event—and kept in touch.

Sinatra has a telephone compulsion. He phones the family, including his ex-wife Nancy, from New York, from abroad, to report in and hear about them. His phone bills are stupendous. He also had the 'goodness'—they called it that—to phone well ahead when he was making some announcement about getting engaged, or married, or divorced, so they wouldn't be shocked.

'I'm not home much, but I'm a pretty damned good father,' Frank said. He thought it was the mark of a successful man. He'd had his own difficult moments growing up.

'But it's not easy for me. People are always criticizing: I'm pushing Frank and Nancy too much, or I'm not pushing enough. Either way I'm wrong.'

It was true. Because Frank was so influential, one faction said, 'You'd think he'd get the kid a good record contract.' Others said, 'Without his old man's pull, where do you think he'd be?'

Frank, Jr., was slim and serious, and at nineteen was a

freshman at the University of Southern California, majoring in music. He had been studying his father's singing style as he grew up, mostly by listening to his records. His father wasn't sure that his son should be a singer. He didn't have his father's drive or ambition, but he was a pleasant young man and he could read music. He was likeable, and he was having the usual trouble of being a famous man's son and being compared with him.

'Get your college degree and then go into Show Business,' Frank told his son.

The boy told friends, 'Dad says if I don't get a college degree, I get a third degree from him.'

Frank, Jr., tried out his voice publicly in the summer of 1962 at Disneyland, and nobody paid much attention. A few weeks later he returned, and he was publicized. A girl fainted; that was enough. Frank, Jr., was working part-time at his father's Reprise Records and Essex Productions, but he was determined that from then on he was going to be a full-time singer.

In early 1963, he signed a contract to tour with the so-called Tommy Dorsey band (the remnants of the original organization), but 'just for the summer'. Frank, Sr., approved, since it was just for the summer.

In August, a year after his first appearance at Disneyland, he went back there with the reincarnated Dorsey band and delighted the crowd, especially the teenagers. The young girls followed him when he left the stage, and the older people said he was spindly and sounded a lot like his father. He played the piano and said he did his own arrangements. He was good—although there was no denying he was copying his father. But who would you expect he'd copy? Johnnie Ray?

He made his New York début at the Hotel Americana Royal Box in September 1963. He was adopted by his father's old buddies: Jackie Gleason, Alan King, Joe E. Lewis, Jack E. Leonard and me. The comedians cheered him. When they tried to bring him back out for another bow, one comedian said, 'He's like his old man, he's already left with a broad.'

Although he looked like his father, to me he seemed more

like his mother at times: quiet, serious and gentle. His mother could be proud of him. His father didn't attend the opening, not wishing to take away attention from his son, but went later on in the engagement. 'Frank is better musically now than I was at twenty-five,' he said.

Both Frank, Jr., and Nancy, Jr., swore they were going to make it without their father's help. Nancy appeared in a picture, *For Those Who Think Young*, made by her father's film company. She point-blank asked the producer, Hugh Benson, whether he was giving her the part because she was Frank's daughter. Of course, Benson said he wasn't.

Frank, Jr., had been offered more lucrative jobs than touring with Dorsey, but he said he wanted that seasoning. He, too, asked prospective employers whether Sinatra, Sr., had asked them to give him work. They all assured him he hadn't.

Frank Sinatra was at his Palm Springs compound the first week of December 1963, brooding over the fact that he was getting older. He was going to be forty-eight on 12 December. The assassination of John F. Kennedy had shaken him up, and his son had noticed an uneasiness in his father's manner when the family had had Thanksgiving dinner the previous week. Frank, Jr., said it was the first time he'd remembered his father acting distant and he attributed it to his shock about the Kennedy death.

NBC was going to do a tribute to Frank on its 'Monitor' radio programme on his birthday: a taped interview with Frank, Jr.

'Hi, dad!' the teenage son said on the tape. 'This is me; it's Frankie. I just wanted to wish you happy birthday. I'm sorry that I can't be with you, but the fellows were good enough to give me this opportunity.'

The interviewer asked, 'What kind of a father is Frank?'

'We were as close as possible in a situation where the family is separated and dad was away on the road so much of the time,' his son answered.

'What kind of a relationship did you have?'

'It's really rough to say. He was, shall we say, strict with me, but always open-minded.

'But my really great experiences with him came in the

late years. He's never been too busy that he couldn't talk with me about the movie industry, about religion, about philosophy or anything.'

'Your father is known as such a swinger, he's always so relaxed, it's part of his personality. Did you ever see him otherwise?'

The only time he hadn't seemed relaxed, Frank, Jr., said, was at the Thanksgiving dinner.

The interview was ready to be played on Sinatra's birthday.

A snowstorm hit Nevada the afternoon of Sunday, 8 December, and it was freezing cold at Harrah's Lake Tahoe Casino, where Frank Sinatra, Jr., was appearing. The roads were glassy with ice and traffic was slow on Route 50, which was surrounded by the 12,000-foot peaks of the Sierra Nevada range. Frank, Jr., was having dinner in his motel room across the street from the casino. He was living in Harrah's South Lodge, operated by the owner, Bill Harrah, for his entertainers and personal guests, and it was actually on the California side of the state line.

In a couple of hours Frank, Jr., was to do his show.

Having dinner with him was John Foss, a trumpeter with the Dorsey band. It was quiet, due to the snowstorm. About all that happened was that Frank, Jr., took a phone call. Foss remembered it later and thought it might have been significant.

'Not here,' Frank, Jr., said into the phone, and not much more than that. 'Wrong number.'

About 9.30 p.m. there was a knock on the door. 'Who's there?' Frank, Jr., asked.

'Room service. I've got a package for you.'

Foss opened the door. A man in a brown jacket walked in with a large package and put it on a table.

Swinging around suddenly, the man pulled from the box a blue-steel revolver with a four-inch barrel and told Foss and Sinatra to lie down on the far side of the bed.

A plaid-jacketed man also carrying a revolver entered the room and joined the gunman in the brown jacket. He bound Foss' wrists behind his back with surgical tape while the other bound young Sinatra.

At first, the gunmen acted as though they were bent on robbery. 'Where's the money?' one demanded.

The two victims had only the money in their wallets, about twelve dollars.

'We better take one of these fellas with us,' the brown-jacketed gunman said, as Foss recounted it later. The man clearly knew with whom he was dealing. He turned to Sinatra and said, 'Get some clothes on.'

Frank, Jr., knew by this time that it was a kidnapping. He got into a white T-shirt, grey slacks, brown moccasins and a blue windbreaker. They gave him no time to put on socks. The kidnappers tossed a dark grey overcoat over his shoulders and then blindfolded him with a sleep mask.

Leaving Foss there bound, one of the gunmen said to him, 'Keep your trap shut for ten minutes or we'll kill him. If we don't make Sacramento, your pal is dead.'

As a parting gesture, one gunman pulled the telephone cord from the wall. Outside, a third man could be heard saying, 'We've got him—let's make it to Sacramento.' Foss also heard an automobile's tyre chains crunching in the snow. The abduction of Frank Sinatra, Jr., had taken five minutes.

Foss wriggled and tore himself free of his bonds within a few minutes and ran screaming to the telephone operator, who called police. Then he ran to Tino Barzie, Frank, Jr.'s, manager, who occupied a room in the lodge. Barzie believed he had seen somebody go past his window, but he had paid little attention.

It fell to Barzie to phone the awful news to Sinatra in Palm Springs.

'Oh my God, I can't believe it,' was Frank's response.

By then police had arrived and were swarming into Frank, Jr.'s, room. Foss got on the phone and gave the details to Frank, Sr. The kidnappers didn't have much of a start.

'I'll be there as quick as I can fly it!' Frank shouted. He'd flown it many times. But his private plane wasn't available; it was in Los Angeles. He had intended to base it at Warners, where he was to start filming *Robin and the Seven Hoods* the next morning. Quickly getting another plane, he flew to Reno, which was about sixty miles from Lake Tahoe, and tried to drive to Tahoe with District Attorney William Reggio. They couldn't get through the snow and ice and dejectedly returned to Reno, where Frank went into seclusion at the Hotel Mapes. He anticipated that there would soon be ransom demands and he would make the hotel his headquarters. His press agent, Jim Mahoney, arrived.

On Sinatra's behalf, Mahoney issued a statement quoting Frank: 'I'd give the world for my son.'

Mahoney said, 'Sinatra is willing to make a deal with the kidnappers and no questions asked.'

Frank sat at the phone, Mahoney said, chain-smoking, waiting for the call. The FBI came in with twenty-six men because kidnapping becomes a federal offence when state lines are crossed. About 100 local police were spread out over the area. Sinatra was jumpy and unwilling to eat.

The headline stories and the broadcasts compared the abduction to the Lindbergh kidnapping and to snatches of other offspring of famous persons. It was an international story because of the father's fame. Police were asked whether there was danger to Frank, Jr.'s, life.

Of course there was!

Nancy, Sr., was frantic as she remained in her home in Bel Air, trying to keep a phone line free in case she got a ransom call. Tino Barzie tried to do the same at the motel.

Nancy, Jr., was in New Orleans, where her husband Tommy Sands was singing at the Hotel Roosevelt. Worried about her grandmother Dolly Sinatra and her grandfather Marty Sinatra, she asked Jilly Rizzo to go to their Fort Lee, New Jersey, home and assure them that 'all is being done that can be done'.

(The close friendship of Sinatra and Jilly long mystified the Sinatra set until it was accepted that Jilly was unquestionably the most devoted follower Frank has ever had. They met about 1958 in Miami Beach and liked each other immediately. Jilly, a New Yorker, had helped his father deliver ice to cafés and hoped to have his own café. He became a bartender, manager and finally owner of a West Forty-ninth Street bar, which then moved over to 256 West Fifty-second Street between Broadway and Eighth Avenue.

He called it Jilly's and gave it a distinctive look on the outside front. It appears to be an onion-shaped pagoda, or maybe it's bell-shaped. It's striped. Above is a somewhat smaller globe with the name 'Jilly's' on it.

Inside there's a piano bar where Judy Garland had been known to sing while having a drink. The inside décor, designed by Jilly's former wife Honey King, is largely ivory, black and orange. Honey was noted for her dyed blue hair.

Friends say Jilly has almost given up his profitable saloon business in New York to be with Sinatra. Jilly's is sort of a throne room for Sinatra, with activity reaching a fever pitch when he arrives between eleven at night to three o'clock in the morning. He likes the Chinese food, and there he meets worshippers who can shake his hand and remind him that they love him. Jilly's has become known to the whole nation as Sinatra's favourite hangout, and he and Frank are that close that when Jilly had a back ailment, Sinatra, with typical generosity, insisted that he do his recuperating at Frank's home.)

Nothing much could be done except worry and wait . . . and go back over what had happened.

The kidnappers' remarks—'Let's get to Sacramento'—were intended to mislead, the police said, for they traced the tyre chains through six inches of fresh snow heading eastward towards Carson City, Nevada.

It was a sleepless night for Frank Sinatra, Sr., because there was an important development. The police broadcast an alarm for two suspects—bank-robbers who had simply walked away from the California State Prison Facility at Tracy, California, stolen a car and gone on a robbery spree. It was just a possibility that these were the kidnappers.

Sinatra paced the room at the Mapes, seldom straying far from the phones. 'Why do things always happen to me?' Frank asked, looking more and more worried. The presence of Jim Mahoney was logical, but it suggested to some people that this was a publicity stunt to further the boy's career or even to gain public sympathy for the father.

Could it be underworld revenge for something Frank had done? Columnists asked that and other questions. Sinatra was sure it was for money; nobody disliked him enough to want to hurt his son. Summoning that old drive of his, getting his second wind, he said grimly that by God, he'd get Frank, Jr., back. They wanted money, and he had that!

He wished he'd been closer to his son. He wished there had been time and that Frank, Jr., had been more communicative and more relaxed.

It was between nineteen and twenty hours after the kidnapping, about 4.45 p.m. on Monday, that Frank got an abrupt call at the Mapes Hotel. FBI agents listened in on an extension.

'Is this Frank Sinatra?' a voice asked.

'Speaking,' said Frank.

The other party said, 'It doesn't sound like Frank Sinatra.'

Sinatra said, 'Well, it is.'

The voice asked, 'Can you be available at 9.00 a.m. tomorrow?'

Frank said, 'Yes, I can.'

The caller said, 'Okay, your son is in good shape. Don't worry about him.'

Now Sinatra could swing into action. Now he could begin functioning. He got word that the two bank-robber suspects had fizzled out. John Foss couldn't identify them as the men who'd snatched Junior. They were let go.

Again Frank went through a night of nail-biting, pacing and chain-smoking. The next morning the promised call came, the first of a series commanding him to get up $240,000 in 'used money' and prepare to deliver it to the kidnappers in Los Angeles.

'Right', Frank said.

Suddenly Frank, Jr.'s, voice came on the wire—the first time he'd been heard from! The FBI taped the call. When the tapes were played back later in court, they revealed Frank, Sr., anxiously asking his son, 'Frankie, how are you? Are you warm enough?'

Sinatra was irritated by the extremely complicated instructions. He was to go to Nancy, Sr.'s, house in Bel Air and wait for another call. There he was advised to go to a gas station at Camden and Santa Monica boulevards.

There he got another call telling him to have a courier bring the money to a pay telephone booth at Western Airlines at Los Angeles Airport at 11.00 p.m. The courier was to use the name Patrick Henry. The man meeting the courier would use the name John Adams.

From his close friend, Alfred Hart, president of the National City Bank of Beverly Hills, Frank procured the $240,000 in bills of varying denominations, 12,400 bills in all: $70,000 in $100 bills, $35,000 in $50 dollar bills, the remainder in other denominations.

Frank's own tension mounted when he was told in the call to the Western Airlines terminal to go to another gas station eight miles away in West Los Angeles and wait for another call. The federal agent with him, Jerome Crowe, asked, 'Can I speak to Frank, Jr.?' He wanted to be sure the boy was still alive.

'He's not here, we've got him someplace else,' the voice said.

Sinatra and the agent were then instructed to leave the money, in an attaché case, between two parked school buses at a deserted gas station near a cemetery on Sepulveda Boulevard.

The voice said, 'We'll release the kid about four hours after you drop the money. We'll need that much time to get going.' Frank, Jr., would then phone his mother of his release and could be picked up at Mulholland Drive and the San Diego Freeway.

The attaché case containing the money was placed between the buses at around 12.25 a.m. Frank, Sr., was over-anxious to reclaim his son and went barrelling off to find him. But he was not to be found. He had not been heard from, nor was he delivered.

'Double-crossed!' Sinatra shouted. He lost his calm for the first time. 'I act in good faith, and the bastards cross me up. They got the dough, and they also got Frank!'

While Frank was still exploding, Frank, Jr., was having his own problems.

About two and a half hours later, a private policeman in the Bel Air Patrol, driving along Roscomare Road, thought he heard somebody yelling, 'Hey!' The policeman thought at first that the slender youth he saw was a hitchhiker. Then he saw the sleep mask dangling from around his neck and realized that this must be Frank Sinatra, Jr. He had been released as promised, but had been walking from the drop-off point, hiding in the bushes, bound for his mother's house, where he wished to be taken now. He said one man had stayed with him while another went for the ransom, and he had persuaded his captor to free him immediately.

It was after 3.00 a.m. 11 December 1963, when Officer George Jones delivered Frank, Jr., to his father and mother, who were waiting hopefully for some such development. Frank, Jr., never very demonstrative, told his mother he was fine and that she shouldn't cry. He and his father embraced and Frank, Jr., said he was sorry he'd caused them so much worry. Frank, Sr., gave his son another hug.

'How'd they treat you? Could you identify them? Where do you think they have their hangout?' Frank, Sr., and the reporters who'd also been waiting asked many questions. Frank, Jr., replied that he'd been able to peek out from under his mask and had made some calculations.

'How long did they hold you?' He figured it out—about two and a quarter days, around fifty-four hours. It seemed like two weeks. Frank, Sr., thanked the private policeman for bringing his son home and gave him $1,000.

'By the way, dad, happy birthday,' Frank, Jr., said.

The next day was Sinatra's birthday. NBC had decided, during the period when Frank, Jr., was being held, not to play the tape of the interview, feeling that it would be in bad taste. Now that Frank, Jr., was back with his family, they would play it. After all, Frank, Jr.'s, return called for a celebration!

The Sinatras held their own celebration at the Las Vegas Sands, where Dean Martin was starring. Frank was claiming to be forty-six (he was really forty-eight), but Dean Martin said 'You're forty-nine, daddy. You were forty-six when Broadway was a prairie. My mother used to take me to see your movies.'

Red Skelton said, 'I can't gamble. Frank's got all the money marked.' Frank howled, and so did Jill St. John.

There was also a celebration up at Harrah's Club at

Tahoe when Sam Donahue, leader of the band, told the audience that Frank, Jr., was safe. The band played Christmas songs, and some of the listeners cried and patted each other on the back. Drummer Tommy Check wept openly on the bandstand, and Helen Forrest sang 'Almost Like Being in Love', which begins 'What a day this has been, what a rare mood I'm in'.

Frank, Jr.'s, troubles were not over. He had to help the FBI find his abductors, and he had to help dispel the growing suspicion that the kidnapping was a publicity hoax.

Frank, Sr., was proud of the way he'd gotten his son back. 'I was the only one who talked to those people on the phone, the only one,' he said. One man who seemed to be twenty to twenty-five years old spoke 'with a firm voice between a baritone and a tenor and articulated well', Sinatra said. He used words like *discretion* and *demeanour*, while one of the others was uneducated and vulgar.

Frank, Jr., told his father, 'I spent most of my time in the trunk of the car. I think I rode most of the way from Tahoe to Hollywood [about 485 miles] in the trunk.'

'Frankie showed plenty of guts,' his father commented proudly.

'I think they were a bunch of amateurs,' Frank, Jr., said. 'One of them chickened out before they made the pick-up and gave up the whole deal. They were more scared than I was.'

With Frank, Sr., having played his role well in making the contact and paying the ransom, the FBI moved in, interviewed Frank, Jr., twice, and got from him a detailed account of what he'd heard while being prevented from seeing much.

Together, the agents and Frank, Jr., figured out that the kidnappers' hideout, from which they conducted the ransom negotiations, was a one-storey house back from the road in the Canoga Park section of Woodland Hills, Los Angeles.

It took the FBI a surprisingly short time to solve the case. Within two days after Frank, Jr.'s, release and five days after the kidnapping, a man named John W. Irwin, forty-two, a house painter, got increasingly fearful that the FBI would find out about his part in the kidnapping and told his brother James that he believed they were on his trail and he wanted to give himself up.

'We'll be caught in just a matter of time,' he said.

The leader, the man with the idea to kidnap Frank, Jr., was Barry W. Keenan, twenty-three, a drifter. He was the man with the blue-steel revolver. One confederate was Joseph Clyde Amsler, twenty-three, a prizefighter and fisherman. Keenan and Amsler had perpetrated the kidnapping, leaving Irwin in Los Angeles to make the contact with Frank Sinatra.

At first, they were ecstatic over their success in collecting the ransom and displayed the pile of currency to some friends. They kicked the money around like they were playing football, and they asked if there was a Monopoly game around so they could play Monopoly with real money.

But they were scared, and Amsler contemplated suicide after they seized Frank, Jr., and were holding him for ransom.

Irwin notified the FBI that he wanted to give himself up. When the agents picked him up, they also picked up $47,938 of the ransom. When they arrested Amsler, they found most of the rest of the money in his Culver City apartment, bringing the total recovered to $239,832.29.

Barry Keenan, the 'brains', also arrested for kidnapping and held like the others on $50,000 bail, turned out to have been a classmate of Nancy Sinatra at University High School in Beverly Hills. He had also briefly attended Santa Monica College.

Along with the ransom money, the FBI recovered a ring with the initials FS. Frank, Jr., had taken it off while he was held as a hostage. The kidnappers had never attempted to hurt Frank, Jr., who said he tried to be co-operative so they wouldn't hurt him. Their captive was the only one who got any sleep; they gave him sleeping pills to keep him quiet while they drove back to Hollywood.

The sudden dramatic end to the case brought more relief to Frank, who was still at Nancy, Sr.'s, house with Frank, Jr. 'Thank God, it's over,' Frank, Sr., said. 'I'm gonna sleep for a week.'

And, at 2.00 a.m., he left Nancy's house and drove away—to a date, the papers said, with Jill St. John. Frank was back to being charming with the columnists, who were hoping that his sweetness would last.

As Frank, Jr., returned to singing at Harrah's, with his billing somewhat larger now, Frank, Sr., and Jim Mahoney put the perfect icing on the cake. It was Frank's idea of doing a gracious thing.

Frank issued a statement: 'Credit must go to the FBI for a masterful operation,' he said. 'Our only hope is that the rapidity with which they were apprehended will act as a deterrent to others with such thoughts in the future.'

Then began the joint effort by father and son to prove that the kidnapping was not a fake and a hoax.

Frank, Sr., is—generally—truthful. He's not a liar, he's not dishonest. Sadistic, yes; a blow-top, yes.

Thus Frank, Sr., blazed with indignation when he saw the three defendants' lawyers planting the suspicion that it was all a hoax when the trial began in federal court in February 1964. A crowd of Sinatra fans lined the corridors, and to some observers it seemed that Frank, Jr., rather than the kidnappers, was on trial.

Sinatra knew that he'd had no part in any hoax, and he was convinced that his son hadn't. If he had, wouldn't he have been brought into the 'hoax' so that he wouldn't have been worried half to death? Wouldn't his own publicist have been brought in to help the publicity plotters? Frank, Jr., wasn't stupid. Shy, maybe, but not stupid.

It began with a Los Angeles *Times* headline,

DEFENCE SAYS KIDNAP ENGINEERED

quoting Clyde Amsler's lawyer as saying Amsler learned during a prison interview with Barry Keenan that the abduction was a scheme concocted by a mystery man named West over a Las Vegas crap table, that it was a 'crazy gag', and that the stunt was to have been pulled at the Arizona State Fair in October.

Federal Judge William G. East had warned the defendants

against such interviews, and he was indignant. He denied a motion for a mistrial. The defence tried to say that Frank, Jr., was co-operative to the point of almost aiding his own abduction.

'By action, inaction and words, he went along with the game,' one lawyer said. 'He was enjoying it, this was exciting to him. He was consenting. Because of his consent, no crime was committed.' Therefore, said the attorney, this was a trial without a crime.

Everybody in the press and in the line of fans waiting to get into the courtroom wanted only to see the Star, Frank, Sr., when he took the witness stand. He was somewhat of a disappointment—he didn't have a tantrum, he didn't lose his temper, he didn't tell the cross-examiners to go to hell.

Deeply tanned and quietly dressed in a dark suit, he spoke 'civilly', one paper said, using no ring-a-ding-ding language. He emphasized that he believed the kidnapping had been genuine, relating that in one of the eight calls he received, one of the kidnappers practically apologized.

'The kidnapper-caller said to me, "Something has gone wrong."

'I said, "We have done everything you asked us to do."

'The voice then said, "No, not you. Something has gone wrong here. They haven't returned here. I just dropped your boy off at the San Diego Freeway and Mulholland. I wish to hell I hadn't got into it, but it's too late to get out. I'm sorry." '

Frank was, of course, very respectful to the prosecutor, who was on his side, hoping to prove the three men guilty of a crime.

'To the best of your knowledge, was this a kidnap hoax of any kind?' the prosecutor asked. 'Did you in any way arrange for your son to be taken from his motel at this time? Did your son ever tell you that this was a hoax?'

To each, Frank answered a polite but firm 'no'.

As Sinatra left the stand, he heard the applause from his fans, and he knew that he had given a colourless but effective performance. By not being his usual belligerent self, he had convinced the jurors, especially three housewives on it, that he and his son were gentlemen. If he had been nasty, he could have blown the case for the kid.

Did he have permission now to go to Japan on business? Certainly!

'I feel very good about the way it's going,' he told his son. 'These guys will go to the can, we got you back, we got most of the money back.' As he ascended into his limousine to depart, he admonished Frankie: 'Play it cool, don't let them upset you, don't lie. They could get you for perjury.'

For Frank, Jr., there was rough going. His voice broke when he clashed with Gladys Towles Root, a defence counsel, who said, 'The apple does not fall far from the tree' and then referred to 'your little kidnap plot'.

Why hadn't he tried to attract the attention of a policeman they saw when they were stopped at a roadblock?

'I didn't want it on my conscience, Mrs. Root, to make a sudden or idiotic move on my part, because I was afraid this man, who was already stupid enough to kidnap me, might blow the brains out of an innocent policeman.'

The woman lawyer smiled. 'The truth is, you would have wrecked your little kidnap plot which you arranged, and it would not have been successful,' she said.

'That is not true!' shot back Frank, Jr.

He gave sharp negative answers to questions about it being a hoax.

Hadn't he, the woman counsel pressed on, made up stories in the last few years that he had suffered trauma by being 'victimized' by strange persons?

'I don't understand that word *trauma*,' Frank, Jr., said. 'Would you explain it, please?'

They kept hammering at him. Why hadn't he made an effort to seize the car key from his captors?

'I felt I might get my intestines blown out,' he answered.

Hadn't he told defendant Irwin that he and his father never had any family feeling for each other? Hadn't he said that the 'publicity' for the kidnapping got out of hand? Wasn't there a connection between the kidnapping and his father's movie, *Robin and the Seven Hoods*?

Frank, Jr., tried to be cool as he answered 'no' to each disturbing question. Hadn't he shaken hands with his two captors when they released him and said, 'I know you won't believe it, but I hope you guys get away with this. You guys have got guts.'

Yes, he had.

Hadn't he said, 'Well, it's sure too bad that we couldn't have met under different circumstances.'

Yes, he had done that, too.

Hadn't he told them, 'You guys don't have to worry about me. I'll help you in every way possible.'

Yes, he had. They hadn't hurt him. He still didn't want to get shot.

Finally, Frank, Jr., protested when they called him to the stand a second time, 'The seeds of doubt have been sown on my integrity and guts and will stay with me for the rest of my life.'

The judge agreed with Frank, Jr., and excused him from further questioning, at the same time rebuking the defence for recalling him.

Finally, it went the way that Frank, Sr., had believed it would. Federal Judge East told the jury, 'I must comment that there is no direct evidence in this case by Frank Sinatra, Jr., or persons in his behalf that prearrangements were made for his abduction.'

In short, it was no hoax, no fake, no publicity stunt.

The jury brushed aside all the defence's claims and quickly found all three guilty of kidnapping. 'Your verdicts are fair and just,' the judge told the jury. He sentenced Keenan and Amsler to life imprisonment plus seventy-five years and put off immediate sentencing of Irwin, who hadn't participated in the actual kidnapping and had also given himself up.

Neither Sinatra was in court when the verdict came in. The father was returning from Tokyo after completing a deal to film *None but the Brave* in Japan, and the son was in London with the Tommy Dorsey band.

It was a big triumph for the Sinatras, although Federal Judge East later trimmed the kidnappers' life terms from life plus seventy-five years to twenty-four years and five months.

Assistant United States District Attorney Sheridan

objected, saying that Frank, Jr., would always suffer from having people 'slide up to him, poke him in the ribs and say, "Wasn't it really a hoax?" '

And that did occur. The very next year, Frank and Frank, Jr., won substantial damages against London's Independent Television News because two men discussing the case on a programme said that it was for publicity purposes.

'We've got a hell of a libel case,' Frank, Sr., said. 'We paid the ransom, the guys went to jail.' A British judge agreed with Frank that he'd been libelled, but did not reveal how much damages were paid. The TV programme apologized to the Sinatras.

Frank asked that the money he'd been awarded be given to a Variety Club charity called The Sunshine Homes for Blind Babies.

Frank, Jr., never talks about the kidnapping any more. He has steadily improved as a singer, and also added to his reputation as a swinger. He 'went out on his own' soon after the kidnappers' trial, leaving the Dorsey band to become a single act. He plays the best supper clubs from Boston to New York to Miami Beach to Las Vegas and gets generally excellent reviews. He gets even better reviews from his girlfriends. He has never married. His father would be proud of the reports of some of his son's performances in the boudoir.

For Frank, Sr., the kidnapping and his own 'drowning' were the most frightening experiences of his life. The terror over his son's kidnapping lasted so much longer. If he'd been the big man with the underworld that his enemies charged, his 'gangster connections' would have hustled his son back to him within a couple of hours. In both experiences, Sinatra, Sr., was simply a very, very lucky man—as always.

MAD, MAD, MAD ABOUT MIA

Frank's romantic caper with thirty-years-younger Mia Farrow when he was already fifty was an effort to keep up with the young. It was another movie scenario in itself, laid in a setting of yachts, big money and Beautiful People. A rebellious, unglamorous, unsexy-looking teenager captivated and then captured one of the most desirable males in the world.

Intimates were aghast at Frank romancing this thin little girl with the boyish look who was five years younger than his daughter Nancy. But it was an incredible era. In 1965, Lyndon B. Johnson was picking up beagles by the ears at the White House. The star performer at the Latin Quarter, Edie Adams, was giving impressions of Lady Bird, saying, 'Ah've been spending quite a lot of time in Washington since Mr. Johnson and I became President. Ah made mah husband what he is today—rich.' Sinatra and Joe E. Lewis were getting $115,000 for two weeks at the Miami Beach Eden Roc.

From meeting 'Mr. Sinatra' while she was tomboying around the 20th Century-Fox studio while doing the 'Peyton Place' television show, little Mia became his steady date. His friends alibied, 'He's just doing the father act.

'He digs her brain,' they said. She was getting recognition as star of the TV series. Mia, daughter of actress Maureen O'Sullivan and the late director John Farrow, was unlike the deep-cleavaged sex objects in Frank's starlet stable. She'd been booted out of two convent schools by the time she was ten for challenging the religious teachings of the nuns and priests.

I knew a little about Mia. Interviewing her mother a couple of years earlier, I had been admonished to pay attention to her talented daughter, whose picture smiled from a coffee table. I said, 'Yeah, yeah, everybody has talented daughters.' Maureen's theatrical lawyer friend, Arnold Weissberger, was giving a party and wasn't anxious to have a teenager among his sophisticates. 'Please let her come, she won't eat much, she's very thin,' Maureen begged. She was allowed to come providing she didn't get fat in the meantime.

Mia met the sophisticates of the sophisticated, becoming a friend, for example, of Salvador Dali and his free-soul set. At nineteen, she was more worldly than many three times her age.

Whenever Frank had a few dates with a woman, some press agent—or goddamn columnist—started a marriage rumour. Mia was a non-sleeper (four hours a night; she says sleep makes you senile) while Frank was a can't-sleeper. From their being seen together late at night came the marriage speculations.

Those who were close to the throne, of course, didn't want to see some young girl take away their power. They endeavoured to plant the idea that Nancy, Jr., and Frank, Jr., would be embarrassed having a stepmother younger than they were.

Maureen was cautious. As the mother of seven, Maureen, the woman who had said 'Me Jane' to Tarzan back in the thirties, knew that a negative word to her independent-thinking daughter might bring an instantaneous reverse action. Maureen exclaimed to a friend, 'Marry Mia! He should marry *me*!' Frank was only four years younger than she was. 'Me, not Mia!' said Maureen.

Even Bing Crosby, then filming *Stagecoach*, was intrigued by the gossip. 'Sinatra . . . boy, he's pretty hard to coop up,' Bing laughed.

Just eight years before, Bing and Kathy Grant had been the subject of the same speculation—the older star and the younger actress.

Bing gave Frank the go-ahead: 'I've certainly been happy. Mia must be a great little girl, she's got a wonderful mother and her father was a fine, talented guy. . . .'

Frank was being charming. One day during the Mia period, he invited his estranged partner, Hank Sanicola, to lunch at Warners in Hollywood—and they were friends again.

His film *Von Ryan's Express* was getting a build-up, and he was zipping around in a new eight-seater Lear jet, making personal appearances. He enjoyed the thought that he could leave New York, fly to Detroit or Chicago or Saint Louis, and return to New York in time for a drink at Jilly's at 2.00 a.m.

Gifted film director Mark Robson still smoulders at mention of Sinatra a decade after they made *Von Ryan's Express*. It was a matter of money.

Having created, developed and nursed the picture, Robson was to get a percentage of the net profit—if there was any—while Sinatra was to get a percentage of the gross, the amount taken in at the box office. Sinatra was a big winner no matter what happened.

Any little delay would add to the cost and cut down Robson's net profit. Sinatra developed an aversion to going from Italy to Spain for scenes that Robson had considered necessary. Sinatra refused to set foot in fascist Francoland. He was wooed by the studio with a free yacht vacation and he was pampered with pleadings by phone. Frank earned about $2 million on the picture and Robson feels his own share was enormously reduced by Sinatra's temperament.

Adding spice to the speculation about Mia, Frank showed up around New York one night with Nancy, Sr., and daughter Tina. It was Tina's seventeenth birthday. Frank took them to the old Basin Street East to hear Trini Lopez, who credited Frank with giving him his first big-time job, at Cal-Neva Lodge. The Sinatra crowd clapped hands and shook their shoulders to Trini's beat. Then the family proceeded to Jilly's, to end the night and greet the morning.

Frank backed off a little from Mia. He was the 'King of Show Business', he was cover boy on the major magazines with stories about his success in his middle years. He won a Grammy for his 'September of My Years' album, and was basking in CBS and NBC TV documentaries about his fascinating life story.

He didn't like the jokes the comedians were telling about his courtship of the teenager: 'He's got *ties* older than she is.' 'He has to diaper her before they go out.' 'She's still teething.' 'He'll soon be carrying her books home from school.' 'He just loves her braces.'

Nancy, Sr., gave him a fiftieth birthday party, and, naturally, Mia wasn't invited. Later the columnists claimed that Mia, in a rage at being left out, chopped off her hair. Mia snapped back that it was a lie and that she'd cut it because a TV role required it. And anyway, she had a date with him right after his birthday party—so there!

Frank could hardly take her with him on a trip to Israel with his lawyer Mickey Rudin and Teamsters Union vice-president Harold Gibbons. They joked about the reason for the trip: 'I want to visit Sammy Davis' birthplace.' Actually he went to appear briefly in a Yul Brynner movie.

He was becoming more controversial. Some Sinatra-haters didn't like the TV shows about him. 'I'm turning this thing off, it's spoiling my dinner,' a man said in Gallagher's restaurant where I was watching the show.

At another restaurant, Danny's Hideaway, Mia Farrow watched, exclaiming, 'Fascinating, fascinating!' Frank was in L.A.—telephoning. Mia went with her mother to Arthur, the new Sybil Burton discotheque where they did the frug, and took a call from him. They went to El Morocco with the Fred Brissons, Bette Davis and Van Johnson, and she took more calls from Frank.

'I'm crazy about Mia,' Frank told them in turn.

But Mia wasn't around when Frank Sinatra & Co. (which included Frank's moustached, penguin-shaped friend, Count Basie) went on a concert tour. She wasn't in the entourage—yet. She was sick in Beverly Hills.

Then Frank's tour headed for the Forest Hills Music Festival, where he got $125,000 for three nights. (The Beatles got $90,000 for two nights.) Frank was still the 'King', still needed police protection after a quarter of a century. Three grown women bolted out of the Forest Hills crowd to kiss him.

He was proud—justifiably—of his continuing popularity.

Soupy Sales, who had exploded on the TV scene as a sudden star through the device of hitting celebrities in the face with a pie, was at Jilly's one night when Frank was also there. Frank started for the men's room, and a woman fan leaped up from a nearby table and tried to follow him in. Soupy got up and steered her back to her table.

The Frank Sinatra & Co. eight-concert tour played to 90,000 and grossed $600,000, breaking records all along the way. In Washington, Frank went to visit the grave of John F. Kennedy. He thought of going to Vietnam to entertain the GIs.

Frank was looking for adventures—something romantic. He was on top of the world again.

At the end of July 1965, Frank and Mia jetted in from Los Angeles. Mia had recovered from her brief illness and looked healthy despite her perpetual appearance of fragility. They boarded Frank's rented 165-foot yacht, the *Southern Breeze*, for a thirty-day cruise along the New England coast.

'The Good Ship Sinatra' took off from Flushing and picked up passengers. Fred Brisson, who'd been in Europe, flew back and joined Roz Russell and others, getting aboard at Westport, Connecticut. Debbie Deutsch, daughter of wealthy Armand Deutsch and Benay Venuta, joined her father (a good friend of Sinatra's) at Cape Cod. Sinatra himself planned to leave the yacht occasionally for meetings.

For the first time, Frank began to bristle a little at the marriage rumours. 'What's all the fuss about?' he wanted to know. He was taking his girl along on a yacht with about a dozen chaperones, so what? They had envisaged some pleasant shore trips, but there were reporters and photographers and a mob scene every place they docked.

The cruise was to have been a love idyll, with the older marrieds smiling as they watched Frank restoring his youth with his little teenager.

Like everything else good in Sinatra's life, it didn't last.

Ten days after the cruise started, a crewman, returning to the yacht from the shore, was drowned when his boat capsized. It shocked Frank and Mia, and he ordered the yacht turned back to New York. The news stories called attention to the fact that Mia was with Frank. Maureen O'Sullivan thought this wasn't good publicity for her daughter, and she advised her to go back to their home in Westport to rest from the yachting trip and then to go back to work in 'Peyton Place'. And Frank decided to leave the yacht and return to Hollywood—alone.

That disposed of the marriage rumours . . . for the moment.

There wasn't any quarrel. In fact, the guests had a night on the town in New York, with Frank and Mia as the host and hostess, at the Seafare of the Aegean restaurant and then to Jilly's for a nightcap. And then back to Frank's penthouse overlooking the East River.

Frank and Mia weren't talking about marriage, and Maureen made it clear there wasn't going to be any just then. 'She was doing three shows a week and that's very rough, and besides she burned her eye and her doctor ordered a rest. That's how she happened to be on the yacht,' Maureen said.

'One misconception,' she said, 'is that Mia was on the yacht unchaperoned. Why, all those guests were there, and they're all friends of mine, they would take care of her, if she needed any taking care of—which she didn't.

'As for the age difference, age hasn't anything to do with romance,' Maureen O'Sullivan went on. 'I know people who are antiques at thirty-five and those who can frug at seventy. Frank was absolutely sweet the last time I saw him at a Hollywood party with Mia a couple of months ago.'

Frank and Mia were again around New York, usually in a pack of a dozen or so, having dinner, Frank at one end of the table, Mia at the other end acting the hostess. Then on to Jilly's—Frank sometimes dropping Mia off at his place, then going on with the crowd. They could get no privacy. They went to see *The Roar of the Greasepaint*, the Anthony Newley show, and left at intermission when they were discovered by photographers and reporters.

'Where's your yacht, Frank?' somebody heckled him.

He'd used it only about one week, but had paid rent on it—in advance—for thirty days at $2,000 a day.

Frank and Mia went over to Fort Lee, New Jersey, one night for one of Frank's mother's famous home-cooked Italian dinners. They were accompanied by the Hollywood elder statesman, the young-at-heart Jack L. Warner, the millionaire picture-maker. He was frequently with Frank then. It was an interesting age set-up: Mia twenty, Frank fifty and Warner seventy-two. Maureen O'Sullivan was right: Age didn't have anything to do with anything.

Princess Margaret and Lord Snowdon were visiting America, and 'Charmin' ' Sharman Douglas gave two big parties. Frank Sinatra was the one man that Princess Margaret wanted to see on her visit to California.

'Frank's been asked to do a "command performance" for Margaret,' reported Bill Rosen, owner of Gatsby's restaurant and a close friend of Frank's.

But that never took place. First, there was a big black-tie Sunday night dinner at the Hollywood Bistro. Richard Burton, Elizabeth Taylor and all Hollywood royalty were invited—and accepted. Frank decided the seating was wrong. He wanted to sit with friends. 'And so he did a horrible, unforgivable thing,' according to one of the social arbiters of Beverly Hills and Hollywood. 'He walked out of the room. He left the party before Princess Margaret left. You are never supposed to leave a party before royalty leaves.'

'Oh, well, in Hollywood,' one deep thinker explained, 'Frank is not a mere prince or princess—he's king.'

Frank cancelled his acceptance of the 'command performance', explaining it interfered with a TV special. None the less, Princess Margaret didn't think less of Sinatra nor reduce her admiration for his ability to live under stress and pressure. She asked him, 'Don't you have any nerves?'

He answered, 'Had them taken out years ago.'

There were more jokes:

'Hear about Frank Sinatra, Jr.'s, torrid romance?'

'No, who with?'

'He's going to marry Maureen O'Sullivan.'

Who should show up at Basin Street East to catch Frank

Sinatra, Jr., but Maureen O'Sullivan! She applauded him and then got introduced to the young man. Maureen didn't appreciate the jokes.

'It's just that I like to encourage young talent,' she said. 'I know Nancy, Sr., of course, and I know Frank, Sr., and I'd have come here to see Frank, Jr., to hear him even if they weren't his parents.

'And I would be very happy,' Maureen said, 'if they would come to see my children.'

A witness to this conversation cracked in a low voice, 'I understand, Maureen, that one of Frank, Jr.'s, parents is already coming to see one of your children.'

But Frank kept the followers of this love story—the affair of the hippie and the country's top swinger—in suspense. Mia wasn't fully appreciated yet. We didn't know she was capable of shrugging off her glamour world and flying off to India to meditate with the Maharishi Mahesh Yogi, nor that she had the spunk and spirit to spice up a police court hearing in London by blurting out the most vulgar word she could have chosen. Part of the time she was pink-tweeded and in double-strand pearl necklaces, but on one occasion she wasn't allowed into the Plaza Hotel's Edwardian Room because the harem pants she'd made herself didn't quite satisfy the maître d'.

Again the romance floundered. Frank went on the wagon for New Year's and also quit smoking cigarettes. He was having some worries about his throat.

Nancy Sinatra, Jr., suddenly became a world-famous singer at twenty-five with the Number 1 hit record, 'These Boots Are Made for Walkin' '. It was the top song in both the US and England, and the first time a Sinatra song had topped the charts in England in more than a decade, and the first time any American soloist had been Number 1 in England since Connie Francis made it in 1958 with 'Stupid Cupid'.

'You can imagine how proud my dad is,' Nancy said. 'If you know anything about Italians, you will understand how closely knit a family we are. My father's always encouraged me, but it's a big name to live up to. So much is expected of you.'

Independent like her old man, Nancy, Jr., refused alimony when she and Tommy Sands divorced. When she decided to resume her career, she went to photographer John Engstead in Hollywood and said she needed some pictures now that she was going back to work.

'I can't afford to pay you much,' she told him.

The pictures, showing her looking very seductive in a black garter belt outfit, were most helpful.

Nancy explained an anecdote that was going around:

'I was recording "Boots" in one studio and in the next studio, daddy was recording "Moonlight Sinatra".

'There was the usual horseplay in my father's studio, and I went over and said, "I don't know what you guys are doing in here, but we're making hit records."

'I guess they all thought "Isn't she cute saying things like that?" But it was true. Our record took off and went over a million.'

What had happened to Mia Farrow? She seemed to be out of Frank's life. Frank was sick. Appearing at the Miami Beach Fontainebleau, he was flattened by a virus, had a 101-degree temperature, missed some shows and flew to New York to consult specialists about the Golden Throat. He was worried. He was drinking and smoking again.

He was crazy about Mia, but where was she? On a Saturday night, Sheila MacRae gave a party for her husband Gordon's forty-fourth birthday. Frank wasn't with Mia. He escorted beautiful brunette Peggy Connolly, a long-time girlfriend.

The columnists hinted that Frank and Mia must be finished. Sinatra's friends, his advisers, had talked him out of it, they decided. Spring came, Frank was healthy again, Frank the swinger went to London to film *The Naked Runner*—and he was living at the Playboy Club, with beautiful Bunnies all over the place.

It's very easy now to see what was happening. Friends advised Frank to drop Mia, to forget about marrying her, and while he nodded politely, he was thinking, 'I'll do as I damn please.' He reacted just as he did when they told him not to drop Nancy and not to marry Ava.

On a Sunday night in July, Mia limped into P. J. Clarke's

come-as-you-are saloon and restaurant on Third Avenue in New York on two crutches. She had painfully cut one leg below the knee when she sat on some scissors in her mother's apartment. She was wearing a dazzling nine-carat diamond ring, which she said was a 'friendship ring' from Frank Sinatra.

P.J.'s is not a good place to hide anything, and maybe she didn't mean to hide it.

'This is it, it's definite,' one of Frank's close friends told me.

Our copyrighted story in the early editions of the New York *Post* was headlined:

SINATRA BUYS MIA THE RING.

Later:

OFFICIAL: MIA TO WED FRANK.

'Frank Sinatra is formally engaged to marry twenty-one-year-old Mia Farrow, her mother, actress Maureen O'Sullivan, announced today.

'Although no wedding date has been set, Miss O'Sullivan said she thought the two would be married between Thanksgiving and Christmas.'

One personality, who wouldn't let his name be used lest Frank accuse him of talking out of turn, said, 'Frank wants to end his loneliness.' That was why he always had an entourage of six to twenty and enjoyed the company of this woman younger than his daughter Nancy.

Mia hobbled into Jilly's on only one crutch a couple of nights later. Frank was flying to New York to meet her. He took a pack of celebrities, including the Bennett Cerfs, Arlene Francis, Pierre Salinger and Buddy Greco, to Jilly's Sunday night. I ventured near and thanked him for confirming my scoop.

'It was a pleasure,' he said.

Frank was tricking us that weekend.

On Monday night they went to a nightclub, Bill Reed's Coney Island, where Frank carried out a very effective deception.

'I'm going back to London tomorrow morning to go to work,' he told Billy Reed. 'Be gone about two months.' Arm in arm with Mia, whom he called 'My baby', Frank seemed relaxed. With him was Jack Entratter. At 3.15 a.m., he said good-night, adding, 'See you in about two months.'

Instead of flying to London, Frank boarded his private jet and flew to the Las Vegas Sands where he met Mia, who'd first flown to Los Angeles and then to Las Vegas. There, in Jack Entratter's suite, he was married—for the third time in his fifty years—to Mia in a five-minute single-ring ceremony. The wedding date was 19 July 1966; the marriage was performed by Judge William Compton. The best man was film producer William Goetz and the matron of honour was his wife Edie.

The ruse that he had concocted to keep the press away delighted Frank. 'I think I handled that pretty good,' he said.

Continuing the game, Frank said he and Mia were going to New York, but went to Palm Springs instead. None of Frank's or Mia's family had been at the wedding. Frank, Jr., didn't believe his father had married a woman younger than he. He didn't believe he had a new one-year-younger stepmother. The gossips said the ring cost Frank $100,000. Mia hadn't given Frank a ring. She blinked and said, 'Thank you' to the champagne toasts. She was a very strange kind of a bride.

Who believed it would last? Nobody!

Flying back to New York a few days after the marriage, they were given a honeymoon reception and dinner by Bennett Cerf and Leland Hayward. It was *intime* and held at the 21 Club.

The revellers kept revelling until about 1.40 a.m. Then Sinatra and Mia came out and Mia slid into a waiting limousine—but Toots Shor's was a few doors away and Frank remembered he'd told Toots he would be in to say hello to him and to his comedian friend Joe E. Lewis.

The photographers pounced on Frank, and there was a clash. New York *Post* photographer Jerry Engel phoned me later. He reported that Sinatra swung, knocking his glasses off and breaking the lenses, at the same time yelling that Engel was a 'parasite'.

At first the lovers were very happy.

On the night of Thursday, 12 January 1967, Frank gave a sixty-fifth birthday party for Joe E. Lewis at Jilly's South in Miami Beach. It was the wettest party I ever attended.

The little bride, Mia Farrow, was the hostess. At times she sat on Frank's knee. Frank and Mia made a tour of the room, greeting personally each of the 150 guests, talking with them for a few minutes, making them feel welcome.

'Have you met my girl?' Frank asked the guests, tweaking her on the cheek. He said he would be back in New York in midsummer to film *The Detective*.

What would Mia be doing? No films in Europe! 'I don't want to leave my fella,' she said, holding his hand.

The happy Sinatras went island-hopping in their private jet, but came back in a week, with Mia denying rumours that she was pregnant and letting it be known that she would make her first major movie with a starring role, *A Dandy in Aspic*. She would play a post-deb who became a photographer. Sinatra could tell her a lot about photographers.

A rather rough picture of Sinatra was painted in the New York *Post* by Fern Marja Eckman a week after the marriage. She was describing their wedding photograph.

> The groom, his retreating hairline camouflaged by one of his sixty toupees, his face tanned almost to the bronze of Max Factor's theatrical make-up Number 11-N but a trifle jowly, his chin just visible in duplicate, was beaming.
>
> His bride, her champagne-coloured locks cropped as short as his, her eyes demurely lowered, wore a beige silk jacket, a knee-length skirt and a glow of satisfaction.
>
> Arthritis has stiffened Sinatra's finger joints and rubbed some of the velvet from his baritone. But age, coupled with a spectacular success attained by few and sustained by even fewer, has enhanced his sex appeal rather than diminished it. His romantic exploits arouse

in men a glint of admiration and a hint of sullen envy. On occasion, that blend irks Sinatra, but it also fortifies his ego.

Honeymooning now at his home in Palm Springs, Frank Sinatra's still got the world on a string. Maybe this time he can hold fast to it.

However, columnist Dorothy Manners of the Hearst Headline Service foresaw trouble in Paradise because of little things. Frank entertained golf stars at their home and Mia sat in the corner needlepointing . . . and needlepointing and needlepointing.

Now and then she looks up and smiles at one of the regulars. She's a quiet girl who suddenly looks like a young boy with her sheared haircut and her slacks.

It's time for dinner, and the group follows Frank into the dining room.

Mia decides to finish the row she's working on before putting down her hoops.

Everyone must be seated by now. And suddenly, there's Frank.

There's no anger in his face. Just sort of blank patience, as if he had played this scene many times.

'Are you going to join us?' he asks, 'or are you going to eat that stool?'

When Frank gave her a twentieth birthday party, she didn't want to go—but the invitations had been sent. Frank was at one big table, Mia was at another.

Maureen O'Sullivan's optimistic predictions that the age difference meant nothing were not entirely accurate. Mia was still very independent and individualistic, and she was uncomfortable in the age group that Frank revelled in.

The frug was then the popular dance in the discotheques. Mia loved to go frugging at the Factory in Hollywood or at Arthur in New York. Understandably, Frank did not enjoy the blasting music nor the athletic gyrations of the fruggers so much younger than he. Frank couldn't wait to get out of such places.

Mia, therefore, went to the discos with Roddy McDowall, writer Lenny Gersh, Laurence Harvey and some other friends, while Frank went his own way.

Mia was lonely when she was away from Frank. She collected a menagerie of eleven dogs and several cats, watched TV and took long walks, and explained that she and Frank had each other and didn't need much else: 'It's the greatest thrill when you love someone and that person loves you back. I can't understand, though, why Frank chose me when he could have almost anybody.'

Why *did* Frank choose her? What did he, who could have had, and had had, the sex queens, see in this one so unsexy-looking? His friends asked themselves the same question. If it was youth—and she *was* young—there were many young women prettier and more voluptuous than this waif-like child who appeared to have an ironing-board figure. Frank, I think, was attracted to her newness on the scene, to her freshness and to her independence. She was unfettered and unbossed. Frank was acting according to form: Ava Gardner had been unbossable, so had Juliet Prowse. He had picked another one of the same mould, and he was wondering whether he had been wise.

But they seemed to be so much in love. Frank gave her a car, a horse, diamonds; he also gave her fame, and her picture price went up to $200,000. They rented a house that had belonged to Anita Louise and her husband, Buddy Adler, producer of *From Here to Eternity* and later head of 20th Century-Fox. In a subsequent law-suit, Anita Louise charged that Mia's dogs had made a mess of the house and intimated that Mia must not be interested in housekeeping.

Suddenly, it cooled. Frank was moody, but at times Mia was moodier. Everybody important seemed to have a guru including Mia's mother. They spent hours meditating. Mia had a good, deep mind, but Frank wasn't thrilled at hearing about Mia's guru. He wanted to get to Jilly's and be greeted by his friends and admirers. Mia, however, wanted to hear about gurus, and the discotheque Arthur was the perfect place to get all the guru news.

Frank wanted her to appear with him in a film, *The*

Detective. Agents and producers foresaw a husband-and-wife combination with great box office pull like Elizabeth Taylor and Richard Burton. But Mia's agent wanted her to do *Rosemary's Baby*. A clash, a misunderstanding, developed. Frank was insistent upon Mia's doing *The Detective*. He couldn't wait any longer.

They met in Miami Beach and talked it over—and quit speaking to each other. They parted, unofficially. Mia left for Bel Air and was incommunicado there,' surrounded by bodyguards'.

A couple of days before Thanksgiving, Sammy Davis called on Frank. Solemnly, he said, 'May and I have problems.' They were breaking up.

Frank laughed sadly. 'Mia and I have problems, too.' He confessed that they were breaking up in a dispute over their careers.

They had some drinks and compared their situations. Frank wanted a wife who would reduce her work, and Mia seemed to want to work more and more instead of less and less. There was a touch of irony here. Frank and Sammy had often quarrelled and made up, they'd formed a happy foursome with May and Mia. Now the foursome was breaking up and the husbands were commiserating with each other.

On Thanksgiving eve, Wednesday, 22 November 1967, press agent Jim Mahoney phoned me from Los Angeles that Frank and Mia had asked him to announce that they had 'mutually agreed to a trial separation'.

Friends tried to get them back together—the usual pattern. On 15 December 1967, Frank and Mia declared a Christmas truce; they would be together at Palm Springs over the holidays with about twenty other VIP couples.

The ever-optimistic Bennett Cerf was full of hope when he told me this. Frank had invited Mia; she had accepted, and this could be an end to the trial separation and a definite reconciliation.

It wasn't. It was more like a visit.

Mia decided to fly to India in January for a month of meditation with the mystic Maharishi Mahesh Yogi. He was the guru who had attracted such top-drawer celebrity disciples as the Beatles and the Rolling Stones. Mia's nineteen-year-old sister Prudence joined the yoga stampede when she opened a class in the heart of Brahmin Boston.

Maureen O'Sullivan was cheerfully philosophical about Mia. 'I'm having my regular swami session that I have every Thursday,' she said. 'We have such a wonderful swami on West End Avenue; there is no reason to go to India. I'm probably even more enthusiastic about it than Mia is.' Maureen was always in complete, enthusiastic approval of anything that Mia said or did.

The headline writers had fun. Mia was flying off to her guru and Frankie was home meditating. (What pretty woman he was meditating with was open to speculation.)

From New Delhi, via Reuters, came the flash that Mia was at the airport to meet Beatles John Lennon and George Harrison when they arrived for some mountain-top meditation with the Maharishi. With sixty others, they settled down in Western motel-style chalets built in a thick jungle high above the Ganges.

They wore austere Indian raiment when they wished; this was not necessary, nor did they have to forsake worldly pleasures.

They were, however, expected to disperse from morning lectures to concrete, underground, soundproof rooms or cells, and practise meditation by constant silent repetition of a *mantra*—a Hindu phrase describing some attributes of God—and also to indulge in some relaxation techniques similar to those encouraged for natural childbirth.

'I thought I could be a spokesman for my generation, for the millions of people under twenty-five who have no voice at all in the policies of this country or the progress of the world,' Mia said after her return.

She said meditation was 'not a religion but a science of the mind . . . a mind-expanding process . . . a thousand times better than using mind-expanding drugs like LSD. . . . I think LSD is invaluable . . . LSD opens up another 40 per cent of our minds. This can be quite dangerous for those who are not equipped emotionally to enter the huge abyss of a wide-open mind.'

Mia's meditation didn't bring her any closer to Frank.

They tried getting back together, but there were more outbursts. Mia went back to Arthur; Frank stayed on at Jilly's.

Frank 'took a walk', some people said. He wasn't able to control independent Mia. He felt she was involved in a commercial gimmick used by the Maharishi and had been victimized by giving publicity to the movement.

Frank's good friend Suzy, the society columnist, wrote that Mia had been supposed to get a divorce before the Great Meditation, but had wanted to meditate first. 'She should gain at least fifteen pounds and let her hair grow at least as long as the Maharishi's,' Suzy said. 'At nearly twenty-three, she should begin to look more like a woman and less like a sprite. Meanwhile, sprite or not, she has been deluged with movie offers with lots of lovely money attached.'

For months it dragged on—silence, avoiding each other, Frank with other girls, Mia around with Laurence Harvey, Mia rumoured with a new romance. The end was near.

And so, on 19 August 1968, after less than a year of trial separation, they divorced in Mexico, but in civilized fashion. Mia, unhappy about reports that she'd taken a $1 million settlement, authorized a statement that she'd asked and received nothing:

'It was offered, but Mia refused it because Mia did not want it or need it. Mia is also anxious to have it known that she didn't charge Sinatra with mental cruelty as reported. The only ground she gave was incompatibility. She says firmly that no cruelty was involved. She sincerely wanted the marriage to work and is unhappy that it didn't.'

Mia was still living in a house that Sinatra owned when she issued the statement. In 1975, nearly seven years later, as Mrs André Previn, she was invited by Sinatra to see his concert in London, and accepted. I was told that she attended and wept.

'I don't know what she would cry about,' her mother said. 'She's happily married to one of the best-known symphony conductors in the world with three children of her own and two Vietnamese she adopted.'

One friend of Mia's, looking back on it, says, a little

harshly, 'The thing that went wrong was that Mia wanted to go to discotheques and Frank wanted to go to Jilly's and let them kiss his ring.'

His marital problems aside, Frank had the world on a string. It was boom time, and he was the boom-time king. His golden throat and his 'One-Take Charlie' acting technique made his potential riches seem boundless. He was acquiring more homes than he could live in. With his million-dollars-and-a-percentage deal for films, he would be able to build a hacienda near Acapulco that would make neighbour Merle Oberon fretful about her famous ranch. He could add that to his New York brownstone, two Hollywood homes and his Palm Springs compound. It was just a passing thought of Sinatra's, and he acquired the land in Mexico for it.

It was yacht time and dress-up time in Miami Beach. The women got their real jewellery out of the vaults, and everybody seemed to tip fifty dollars for everything. Mia had fled, but Sinatra was there with Leo Durocher, socialite horsewoman Liz Whitney, Harold Gibbons of the Teamsters Union and James T. Aubrey, 'the smiling cobra' president of CBS who was as famous a swinger as Sinatra.

Sinatra and comedian Joe E. Lewis gave them laughs in their act at the Eden Roc.

'Listen, Joe,' Frank asked Lewis, 'ain't you ever been sober?'

'What'd you mean, ain't I ever been sober? I was sober four times yesterday,' chuckled Joe.

Several stags arrived at the Eden Roc one night. 'You couldn't get any dames, huh?' Sinatra greeted them. 'Welcome to the club.'

In the winter of 1968 and 1969, Sinatra began fearing for the condition of his father, Marty, the former fighter and fire department captain, who had suffered from a heart attack.

Sinatra had been a devoted son and, he hoped, a joy to his parents—except when he was battling with the press, and of course they usually sided with him. His father retired from the Hoboken fire department after twenty-four years, and Sinatra bought his parents a home on their fiftieth wedding anniversary in the New Jersey section that they loved. When the elder Sinatra became ill, Frank sent him to Dr. Michael Ellis DeBakey in Houston. It was in Houston in January that Anthony Martin Sinatra died at the age of seventy-four.

Sinatra was shaken by the death even though it was expected. He was tight-lipped, tearful and grief-stricken at the funeral at the Fort Lee, New Jersey, Madonna Church. It was a requiem mass for the man who had wanted his son to be an engineer or a prize fighter. The funeral was remarkable because it was attended by such celebrities as Sammy Davis, Jr., wearing a Nehru jacket, dark glasses and a flamboyant fur coat; and Bennett Cerf, Leo Durocher and Alan King.

'The hometown funeral rivalled one of the most spectacular and affluent ever seen in Hollywood,' wrote Barry Cunningham in the New York *Post*.

It was a cold day, and outside the chapel scores of women stamped their feet to keep warm while waiting to get a glimpse of Frank Sinatra. Twelve hearses were required to carry 150 lavish floral bouquets from Hollywood and Broadway friends. There were twenty-five limousines for the friends of the family, and others for Sinatra and the family, for the procession to the Holy Name cemetery in Jersey City. An honour guard of white-gloved firemen and 100 policemen ushered the mourners to the cars. Nancy, Jr., and Frank, Jr., followed as Frank, Sr., escorted the widowed Mrs. Natalie Sinatra from the church. Red roses from Frank draped the casket, and there was a red ribbon lettered 'Beloved Father'.

During the mass, the prayer reading was interrupted by women outside the church who were rapping on the window panes and shouting. Many were housewives who had never known Marty Sinatra, but saw this as a time to see their hero.

Sinatra did not seem disturbed by this. At the end, he said softly, 'Thank you, Father'.

Preparations for the funeral had been made over several days from Sinatra's suite at the Waldorf. A close friend,

Police Lt. Arthur Schultheiss, commander of the 14th Detective Squad, took charge of the traffic.

Sinatra wanted a speedy exodus from Newark airport in a California-bound plane belonging to Kirk Kerkorian, the motion picture producer and hotel owner. Chauffeurs of several limousines were carefully briefed so that Frank, Nancy, Sr., his mother and Nancy, Jr., and Frank, Jr., could board quickly without delays or interruptions by Sinatra fans. The exodus plan worked splendidly, according to one of the chauffeurs, Artie Kirchner, who was on duty for seven days.

'With all his problems,' Kirchner says, 'Frank worried about me. At the time of the funeral, he asked me, "Are you getting enough sleep?" '

SINATRA BARS WILSON!

With Mia now in his past, Frank had struck out as a husband for a third time. That unsettled him. He was destined to remain a swinging bachelor, a superstar superstud. That wasn't so bad. But people were always getting him into fights, taunting him about thinking he was a tough guy. Then one of his crowd, wanting to be a hero, would punch somebody and Frank, though innocent, would be the villain. One comedian suggested a song for Frank: 'Take Me out to the Brawl Game'.

The frustrations and anxieties resulting from his failing marriage, plus his manic-depressive make-up, caused him to explode; he couldn't help it and shouldn't be blamed. That was how Frank himself saw it.

Because of my reporting of his worst brawl, I, his staunchest defender in the press, was barred by him personally from attending one of his nightclub openings. I wasn't allowed in the room. This was historic in Show Business. I was crushed and humiliated by his treatment, which I considered totally undeserved. He never gave a specific reason. There was no appeal. He didn't have to tell why. The 'King' had spoken.

But I was only a minor annoyance. What a lot of strange wars Sinatra could get into! He had a private warfare with the Mexican government, which objected—unreasonably—to his depicting a quickie Mexican divorce in his picture, *Marriage on the Rocks*.

It did look like they were picking on the 'King'. Just when he was taking steps to build a home there, just when he was heading for an Acapulco vacation with a planeload of chums, the Mexican authorities decided he wasn't welcome. When they discovered he was not on the plane, they were disappointed that they couldn't inform him in person that they didn't want him around. The tourism people missed him; they knew he was 'commercial'. The photographers missed him; it had been so exciting on one of his previous trips when he told them, 'You miserable crumbs, you sons of bitches,' and shook his fist. A bodyguard had snarled at a photographer, 'I'll put a bullet in you' and grabbed a camera so Frank could rip the film out of it.

Attorney Louis Nizer and Jack Valenti, head of the Academy of Motion Picture Arts and Sciences, straightened out the quickie problem. Mexico 'forgave' him for something he hadn't really done—'insulted Mexico'—and let him know he could return any time he wanted to.

He returned and did a big benefit for needy Mexican children.

Around 1.30 on the morning of 8 June 1966, a month before Frank married Mia, Frank got into a brawl that was a preliminary to much bigger brawls, a sort of warm-up.

Some merry friends of Dean Martin were celebrating his forty-ninth birthday—actually, a week early—in the Polo Lounge of the Beverly Hills Hotel in Beverly Hills. Strange things happen there. Once, during the battling days of Elizabeth Taylor and Richard Burton, Elizabeth walked in, hit Burton in the mouth, then slid down and had a drink with him. Another time, Edy Williams, the sex symbol, took off her jacket and became the lounge's first topless customer.

Celebrating with Dean were Sinatra, Jilly Rizzo and some women of dubious identity. It got rowdy. At another table, Frederick R. Weisman, a fifty-four-year-old Beverly Hills executive, complained to the maître d' about the noise at the Martin–Sinatra table.

The details of the ensuing brawl will never be fully recorded, and one feels sorry for the reporters who tried to cover the story. The Associated Press said, 'Mr. Sinatra went to Mr. Weisman's table,' and 'Mr. Weisman cursed him,' whereupon Mr. Sinatra stated to Mr. Weisman, 'You shouldn't be talking that way while you're sitting down and wearing glasses.' Mr. Weisman arose from his seat, lunged at Mr. Sinatra, and struck Mr. Sinatra below the eye.

Somebody hit back. Weisman, former president of Hunt Foods and brother-in-law of financier Norton Simon, was taken in an ambulance, unconscious, to Mount Sinai Hospital, where he underwent cranial surgery for two and a half hours and was in critical condition.

Everybody played it down. New York *Times* correspondent Peter Bart wrote, 'It was not known how Mr. Weisman had been injured. Police Captain John Hawkins speculated that he might have lost his balance and fallen.' The police investigated, but filed no charges. Dean Martin was questioned. 'I never saw a thing,' Dino said. Jilly Rizzo hadn't seen anything either. That was about the end of it. Weisman recovered, and Jilly wasn't and isn't talking about it to this day.

The Big Brawl was yet to come.

It was around Labor Day 1967, a couple of months before Frank's break-up with Mia. Frank was drinking and gambling heavily at the Las Vegas Sands, where he was the star and part-owner. Friends blamed his marital troubles and said he was on a rampage and out of control.

I had already noticed his growing irascibility. In March, I had tried to do him a favour and got punished for it. Joan Albert, then press agent for the Miami Beach Fontainebleau, phoned requesting me to write something about how 'co-operative' Frank had been with the hotel help during his engagement there. 'He deserved a medal,' she said.

'It's pretty corny,' I said. But it was constructive, it would counteract rumours of his tantrums when he threw things at the help. I wrote: 'Frank Sinatra was so co-operative in Miami Beach, Fontainebleau employees wanted to give him a medal.'

A few days later, press agent Jim Mahoney phoned me: 'Frank wanted you to know he was very unhappy about the thing you wrote about him deserving a medal.'

'You're joking!' I said. 'That's one of the finest lines ever written about him.'

'Frank said, "What the hell did Earl think I was going to do—go down there and machine-gun everybody?" '

He was now becoming a censor. Why was he upset? Undoubtedly because he knew he had treated the help badly in the past.

On the weekend following Labor Day, Frank failed to make two scheduled appearances at the Sands, which blamed his absences on laryngitis. But I found he was having secret meetings with Caesar's Palace executives about switching to their hotel. They would take over what remnants he had left of Cal-Neva Lodge. This was a worthwhile story, and I pursued it from New York, learning that Frank had been seen around the casinos of both hotels and was 'being very ugly'.

Like somebody deranged, he was flinging away his chips, losing thousands. He was soon into the Sands for $200,000 markers. He blithely asked for more credit. Casino manager Carl Cohen refused. Frank exploded. His close friends had evidently smelled the approaching storm and taken cover. Frank realized that he had been turned down for credit at his own hotel. In anger, he made a hasty decision—he blew up, caused a scene, then rushed out of the Sands and told them to get a new boy.

Frank returned to his home in Bel Air late Sunday morning. Mia was still there. I phoned Sunday afternoon to check the story. Mia took my call.

She said Frank was asleep, but 'when he wakes up, I'll have him call you'. I was impressed. She spoke like the head of the house: 'I'll have him call you. . . .'

About two hours later, he did call me back. For one who'd been so rampageous a few hours before, he sounded good, he sounded sober.

He was defiant, he was wounded, he was letting off Sicilian steam. How ungrateful could those bastards be? He, Frank Sinatra, had made the Sands a world-famous hotel. He had brought tourism to an unbelievable peak in Las Vegas; it had become the gamblingest, swingingest city. A man got a little drunk and gambled carelessly, and they chopped off his credit with their goddamn computers. And for a trifling sum like $200,000, they stopped his chips and sneered at him from the cage. Screw them!

There would be plenty of hotels that, for $200,000, would be glad to have him dressing up their casinos.

I told him, 'They can't do that to you, Frank.' I meant it —$200,000 was the amount some plunger might lose in an hour. They needed Frank. But I didn't know the whole story.

'They did it to me, and I did it to them,' he snapped. He'd walked out, would never work for the Sands again, but would appear at competing Caesars Palace.

Frank was quoted later by others as saying that he had started with the Sands when it was a sand pile and he would turn it into a sand pile again. He did not say that to me.

I thanked him for returning the call and helping me verify the story of his split-up with the hotel. Many big names, when on the spot, will become unreachable. He had been frank. He might have invented another reason than the credit cut-off to have made himself look better, but he didn't. He had levelled with me.

Around sun-up in New York, Monday morning, I confirmed that Caesar's Palace had actually made a deal with Sinatra to star at that hotel. I wrote my story, phoned it to several papers and my syndicate, and went to bed with the realization that I had reported something rather historic, at least to Las Vegas.

Sinatra should have gone to bed, too.

He was boiling over again about the credit cut-off. After our phone conversation, he left Mia at home in Los Angeles and returned that night to Las Vegas. Still furious, and drinking, and beyond the control of friends, he went, 'like a bull', they said, back to the Sands, to which he had sworn he would never return.

To his way of thinking, he had been wronged, and the old Sicilian volcano re-exploded. Asking again for more credit and being refused, he swung into the luxurious Garden Room restaurant—where he usually sat like a potentate with the bosses—and started a quarrel with the mild-mannered casino boss, Carl Cohen, who had tried all his life to stay out of the newspapers.

'And the one incident I had in my life was with the guy who was always in the newspapers—Frank Sinatra!' lamented Carl Cohen later.

A dozen to fifteen hours had gone by since I'd talked to Frank in Bel Air. It was very quiet in the Sands that Monday morning, 11 September 1967, except for Sinatra.

When Cohen defended his action in denying further credit, Sinatra, in his anger, pushed a table towards Cohen and made a move to throw a chair. Cohen, a substantially-built man half a dozen years older than Frank, responded with a punch aimed at Sinatra's million-dollar vocal cords. Cohen's blow caught Sinatra in his mouth and dislodged the false caps of two teeth, leaving Sinatra with a very jagged look.

Sinatra got his teeth knocked loose during the hours when I was in bed, but the Las Vegas *Review-Journal* reported the battle in a page-one story that was a newspaper classic under the headline:

SINATRA HIT IN STRIP BATTLE.

It was written by Don Digilio, then the managing editor, now the editor:

> Singer Tony Bennett left his heart in San Francisco, but Frank Sinatra left his teeth—at least two of them—in Las Vegas.
>
> Sinatra parted company with both the Sands and his teeth Monday morning in the Garden Room of the Sands Hotel in a scene that was described by witnesses as a nightmare.
>
> It was Carl Cohen, vice president of the Sands, who finally halted Sinatra's wild weekend. The Sands executive bloodied the singer's nose and knocked his teeth out after Sinatra tipped a table over on him.
>
> Cohen will not talk about the incident, but a battery of witnesses, hailing Cohen as a hero, have come to the front to speak for the Sands exec and against Sinatra.

Said a waiter: 'Sinatra had been going wild at the hotel all morning. I am told that he even set fire to his room. The next thing I knew Sinatra jumped up and threw a table right on Carl. Cohen then jumped up and punched Sinatra. Obviously, I can't give my name, but boy, did he [Sinatra] have it coming.'

Said a security guard: 'Sinatra was yelling at Cohen because Carl had cut his credit off. The next thing I knew, a table was flying in the air and Cohen was pushing a table off his lap. He then hit Sinatra and Frank started yelling at Cohen for punching him. It was terrible, somehow a chair, tossed by Sinatra, split a security guard's head.'

Said a floorman at the Sands: 'You would have had to see Sinatra Monday morning to believe it. He went to the second floor of the hotel, went into the room where the switchboard is and yanked all the telephone jacks out. He was yelling at the top of his voice and everyone in the place was jittery. I came into the Garden Room right after the fight and Sinatra was still screaming about being punched. I don't have anything to say about it, but if I did, I would have got rid of Sinatra long ago.'

Said a bellman: 'Sinatra even took one of the baggage carts and drove it through a plate glass window.'

Sinatra had no defenders in Las Vegas that day. He had been on his rampage for two days and continued on it until, like a tornado, he wore himself out.

Among the questions asked afterwards was: where were Sinatra's so-called bodyguards? Also, where was Jilly Rizzo? Where was Jack Entratter, the hotel president and Sinatra's great friend, who had often smoothed over his injured feelings?

Sinatra seemed to be travelling alone that morning.

This story was splashed over California papers the next day. I have always wanted to report only facts that are mine exclusively. I had no wish to write a rehash of a story already fully told from Las Vegas. None the less, when one of my New York *Post* editors urged me to write a follow-up story, I succumbed.

The only fresh angle was that a New York dentist had flown to Los Angeles to repair Frank's smile. My story had to, however, include the details of the fight with Cohen—details that I didn't possess. The 'desk' picked up those details from the Los Angeles *Times* wire service, enclosing them in brackets with attribution to the *Times*. They were all quite frank about Sinatra. Anybody swiftly reading the story under my byline might have thought I was the authority for this damaging report about Sinatra. Anybody reading it slowly would note the difference.

Frank must have read it swiftly.

It must have been this reading of that story that inspired another Jim Mahoney remark, 'Frank didn't like the way you handled the story of the fight.'

Again I was amazed. 'Did he like the way *anybody* handled it?' I asked Mahoney. Could he have been pleased at anything written about such a display? Should I have defended his outrageous conduct?

Frank, his teeth fixed, moved his belongings out of the Sands. He was going to take Dean Martin and Sammy Davis, Jr., with him over to the opposition.

I saw Sinatra again in the late fall at Madison Square Garden, when he was leader of a meeting of the Italian-American Anti-Defamation League. Some newspapers criticized him for participating, claiming his image didn't help tolerance. One paper suggested that he 'just shut up'. He was surrounded by hangers-on and we merely said, 'Hi'.

I had no notion that he was angry at me. The following winter, Frank was in a penthouse at the Miami Beach Fontainebleau suffering from 'viral pneumonia'.

He rebelled at being ill and stubbornly maintained he wasn't. The idea that he could be laid up in bed like mere mortals made him mad.

One day a friend told me that Frank had had an altercation with Eddie Fisher when Eddie visited him and that he had 'rapped Eddie in the mouth'. That expression amused me and I wrote, 'There was a rumour that he'd rapped Eddie Fisher in the mouth' and 'also other people'.

'Probably all untrue,' I added. 'Frank's opening at the Fontainebleau was postponed from this Friday to next

Friday because Frank has been in bed with 102-degree flu.'

After getting a quick denial about the altercation from Eddie Fisher's representatives, I corrected the error in about twice the space of the original item.

'IT WASN'T TRUE AT ALL that Frank Sinatra rapped Eddie Fisher in the teeth in Miami Beach, as rumoured,' I wrote. 'Fact is, when Eddie had to drop out of his Fontainebleau show one night, sick, Frank, who was also sick, got Pat Henry to go on for him. And then Frank lent Eddie and Connie Stevens his jet to go off for a few days' rest. Eddie said he never had such great respect for Frank before.'

As a result of all the publicity about Frank's virus, flu or 'pneumonia', as it was coming to be called, the Floral Telegraph Delivery phoned and asked if it could send Frank a big heart-shaped carnation bouquet for Valentine's Day. They put my and my wife's names on the card. I didn't know, of course, that he was already mad and that this would enrage him.

Another thing that annoyed him was a rumour that his jet had crash-landed with Connie Stevens and Eddie Fisher aboard. Connie told about it lightly on the Merv Griffin TV show. The jet was not really Frank's, or it had been flown by a pilot not employed by Frank—in some manner, it was not actually a Frank Sinatra-owned jet at that moment.

By Tuesday, 27 February, Frank had recovered.

I wrote: 'The Jet Set rush to Miami Beach'll be on this weekend with Frank Sinatra definitely opening at the Fontainebleau Friday, although first he goes to Hollywood for the funeral of Claudette Colbert's husband, Dr. Joel Pressman.'

On Friday, my wife and I packed our bags for a fast weekend trip to Miami Beach to catch the long-delayed opening of our friend, Frank. Sinatra's loyal friend, Chuck Anderson, greeter at the 21 Club, asked me to take Frank a box of cigars that he knew Frank liked.

We left New York blissfully, anticipating a glamorous night. Our invitation had come from Harold Gardner, advertising and public relations head for the Fontainebleau. He had told us by phone that we would sit at his table.

Some good-time millionaires like Maurice Uchitel, big businessman from New York and Palm Springs, would take a table for twenty or thirty. His check would run into hundreds and, including tips, even a few thousand.

My wife and I arrived in Miami, a car picked us up, and we were soon in our suite at the Fontainebleau, which had a comfortable bar. I rang Harold Gardner in his office.

'Harold? Earl,' I said, 'What's the schedule?'

He didn't even cough. 'I'm glad you called,' he said immediately. 'I've got some bad news for you.'

'Yes?' I probably had a bad table, I figured.

'Frank says he won't go on if you're in the room.'

It was like being hit in the stomach. In my whole life, I had never suffered such shock.

'What's it all about?' I asked Harold Gardner. I suppose I stammered the question. 'What'd I do?'

'I don't know,' Gardner said. 'You know Sinatra. I just got the word you weren't to be let in.'

'But I flew down here just to see him!' I said.

'The security guys were told to keep you out.'

'My God, he makes me sound like a criminal or something.'

'He's been upset with this virus or pneumonia,' Gardner said. 'I talked to Ben Novack'—president of the hotel—'and he says there's nothing he can do.'

My wife had been overhearing my end of the conversation, and she was more indignant than I was.

'Of all the ungrateful rats!' I thought. I thought of my legal rights. Frank Sinatra probably could not keep me out of his show. I could call a cop or something. . . .

But suppose he meant it—that he would not perform if I was in the room? Several hundred people would be disappointed and would unanimously hate me. Also, some 'security' officer would probably break my head. Besides, I had been brought up to believe you shouldn't attempt to go where you're not wanted.

I surrendered to Sinatra's decree in what was one of the saddest moments of my career. I cannot describe the shame I felt, the dejection and the hurt of the rejection. After trying to be an honourable newspaperman with a reputation for getting along with big personalities, to get this slap in the face made me crumble spiritually.

The word *barred* is a degrading one in my business, and it had never been used against me before. A thicker-skinned columnist might have taken it as a compliment, but I could not be flippant about it; I was hurt.

'It's finally happened to me,' I said, 'the thing that's always happened to his other friends, and I never believed it did.'

'Let's call Joe E.,' my wife said. 'Maybe he knows something about it.'

Joe E. was amazed. He hadn't heard about it. We were all trying to be light-hearted about it, and Joe E. said that so it wouldn't be a total loss, he would take my wife to the show. They wouldn't be barring her.

My wife got the idea of calling Sinatra personally. She received the 'Who shall I say is calling?' reply from the operator and answered, 'Mrs. Earl Wilson'.

Frank wasn't in to her, either.

The Fontainebleau lobby was a crush of the VIPs of Saloon Society when my wife joined Joe E. to go to the opening. He had two other guests, columnist Jim Bishop and Mrs. Bishop. My spunky wife made them nervous because by this time she hated Sinatra. She wanted to heckle him.

When Frank paused to drink some tea, my wife said, 'Aw, put your teacup down and do what you can do.'

I sulked in my room and had a room-service dinner. I was thinking, 'Frank sure knows how to hurt somebody.' I felt very low.

Sinatra's show was acclaimed by both George Bourke in the Miami *Herald* and Herb Kelly in the Miami Daily *News* (each of whom made mention of me being barred).

SINATRA COMES ON WITH THE OLD GUSTO

the *Herald* said.

Bourke wrote in the *Herald*:

> Fourteen pounds and several shades of suntan lighter than normally, Sinatra belted out an hour and ten

minutes of song, most of which was as good as he ever did it, albeit with a throatiness not too distracting to the ear with decades-long tuning to his style.

Sinatra didn't stack the deck with easy numbers either. There were some songs that stood for no faking, and it seemed Sinatra undertook them defiantly, aware that a guy who'd had pneumonia shouldn't be expected to handle them and that there were some people who'd be making bets he couldn't.

Frank was wearing a formal white turtle-neck sweater with a pendant that resembled a fertility symbol such as the hippies wore. He introduced Mike Romanoff, Bennett Cerf, August Busch the brewer (one of his TV sponsors) and Jim Bishop—'but he didn't introduce entertainment columnist Hy Gardner, who was there, or Earl Wilson, who wasn't. Earl and Frank have PFFFT!, 'tis said.'

WILSON ON SINATRA 'GET-LOST LIST'

was a headline on Herb Kelly's story in the Miami *News*.

I cringed, I couldn't believe I had done anything that I shouldn't have done in being an honest newspaperman.

'Earl wasn't shut out from all clubs, though,' Herb Kelly wrote. 'He went next door to the Eden Roc, where Don Rickles insulted him. But they were friendly insults.'

I left the scene next day, returning to New York. Of course, there were many calls from friends who said things like, 'Welcome to the club!' 'Who does he think he is—de Gaulle?' 'He's gone from "King" to dictator.' 'Now you can run for Vice-President on the Carl Cohen presidential ticket!'

Variety's story from Miami Beach said, 'Anybody want a couple of boxes of good cigars cheap?' referring to the boxes of cigars I'd brought from Chuck Anderson to give to Frank.

One newspaperman, Dan Lewis, entertainment writer for the Bergen, New Jersey, *Record* and many other papers, thought I did wrong in accepting Sinatra's decree. 'Unfortunately,' he wrote, 'Wilson decided not to test the Sinatra edict, although as a nightclub editor, he had every right to attend, if he so chose. The pity is that we will never know if Sinatra meant to carry out his threat not to perform if Wilson came into the room.'

Seeing it as a freedom-of-the-press issue (I refused to take it so seriously), Lewis said, 'What is disconcerting is the precedent that has been dangerously established here. Frank Sinatra has decided which writers can come in and review his shows and Wilson, by accepting this dictum without giving it a proper test, may open the doors for other performers to attempt to emulate Sinatra.'

Danny Lewis' story brought out that there had been one more misunderstanding in all the misunderstandings between Frank and me. The Valentine's Day bouquet that was sent to him by the Floral Telegraph Delivery had reportedly been rejected by Sinatra, who thought it was some kind of an apology from me. I didn't know I was supposed to be apologizing for anything or had anything to apologize for.

By another twist, the day before I was barred, I wrote in my column: 'A woman patient in a N.Y. hospital who's never met Frank Sinatra, but has been his fan since he was with Tommy Dorsey, writes me of Frank's kindness since she wrote him about her illness. He wrote to her, sent her pictures and records and had his aide, Henri Gine, ask what Frank could do for her.'

I did a lot of deep thinking about how I should handle all this in my column. I was concerned about the awful possibility that I may have deserved to be barred. On my desk there is a prayer by the late Paul De Kruif that reads, 'Help me always to blame myself—and to give without thought of return.'

So I didn't write any blistering attack, as some had wanted me to do. I led off with reports on Woody Allen and Diahann Carroll starring at the Hilton Plaza, and Don Rickles and Lainie Kazan at the Eden Roc. Then, midway down in the column, I told of Sinatra barring me and of my bafflement.

'If I printed anything untrue,' I wrote, 'I will certainly correct it.' And I added, 'Gee, now I guess I'll be barred from Jilly's.'

There was one stinging remark that I would remember.

The Hollywood trade papers said, in reporting the barring, that Sinatra's office explained that Wilson was guilty of 'inaccurate reporting'.

Some of my friends have said—and still say—in blunt language, that I was a jellyfish and should have shown more anger and indignation at Sinatra's dictatorial order. I should have been righteously furious and forced him to bar me physically, and then brought a lawsuit, they say. I should have been damned mad at his arrogance and his petty sniping at me for doing a job that happened to displease him. Suppose he had actually refused to go on because I was there; wouldn't that have been a spiteful disregard for the hundreds of people who were waiting there to see him?

They wished to heaven I'd have made an issue of it. Maybe Sinatra would have been a better-behaved person today.

At first, of course, I was piqued and I resolved never to print his name again. After a time, I saw I wasn't being consistent. In the years of our friendship, I had been criticized by readers and sometimes by editors of being 'almost a press agent' for Frank. I had replied, 'But he's news.'

'Well, if he was news then, he hasn't quit being news just because he barred me,' I told myself. 'I'll print it if it's news.'

He gave several stories to his society columnist friend, Suzy, who was part of a new Beautiful People image he seemed to want.

Paramount president Frank Yablans tried to convince me during an interview that Frank was seriously going to film *The Little Prince* with music by the reunited Allan Jay Lerner and Frederick Loewe. Believing that I knew more about Sinatra's moods than Yablans did, I wrote the story, emphasizing, correctly, that it was in the discussion stage only. My story was accurate. The deal collapsed.

In other years, I was always running into Sinatra at parties and openings, but now it seemed rare that I even had a glimpse of him. One night at the Bistro in Hollywood, my wife and I sat at a table a few feet away from where Frank sat with Nancy, Sr., Nancy, Jr., and some others at a family dinner. Frank's back was to us. Nancy, Jr., and

Nancy, Sr., said hello to us; Frank didn't acknowledge us at all.

When Toots Shor opened his East Fifty-fourth Street restaurant and bar in 1972, Frank gave him a big stake—many thousands of dollars—as he had staked Toots before. One Saturday night in 1973, when Toots' place was about to fold (although we didn't know it), my wife and I planned to go in and say hello to Toots. I called in advance.

'Sinatt's here,' Toots said, employing his own special pronunciation of his name.

Years before, that would have been reason for us to rush right over. Now I hesitated. 'We're coming in anyway,' I said.

We found Barbara Marx there with one of Frank's intimates and Frank talking to Toots at another table. Frank and Toots finished their conversation. Frank then got up and left with Barbara, paying no attention to us.

The following Monday, I wrote that Frank was around town with Barbara Marx, Zeppo Marx's recently divorced wife. I was careful not to write that they were dating until I was sure she was divorced.

In the autumn of 1973, when it was announced that Frank would be appearing at Caesar's Palace, I wondered whether I would still—after five years—be barred from The Presence. I had seen him twice in those years. He had ignored me. If I received an invitation, should I accept?

All this speculation turned out to be quite needless. I wasn't invited.

'About the Sinatra opening,' publicist Lee Solters said one day, 'we don't know who he wants in. We submitted a list and we haven't got it back yet.'

'I won't be on it,' I assured him.

'Don't be sure. He's mellowed a lot.'

'Not that much,' I said. 'And don't do anything about it because it'll look like I've asked you to and I don't really care.'

And that was true, although over the five years I had often thought, 'How silly this is. I do have a strong admiration and affection for him, and the whole thing is some kind of misunderstanding anyway.'

A few days later, Solters called apologetically. 'Don't feel bad,' I said. 'I told you it would happen.'

'Sid Gathrid and I [Sid Gathrid was the Caesars Palace executive in charge of promotion, advertising, publicity and entertainment] want to make an issue of it,' he said. 'There are three people he doesn't want. You, Leonard Lyons and Rona Barrett.'

'Leonard Lyons!' I said. 'That's terrible!' My colleague on the New York *Post* had been very, very ill for a couple of years. 'Do nothing about it, nothing,' I told Solters. 'It'll look like I'm begging. Drop it!'

'No, we're going to speak to Mickey Rudin, Frank's lawyer.'

'Don't, you're going to embarrass yourself.'

It was all wasted conversation, for Solters advised me later that Rudin had said he wouldn't go into a matter that was strictly the province of Sinatra's press agent, Jim Mahoney.

There was a sort of 'enemies list' or 'shit list', because. the New York *Times*, the Washington *Post* and *Women's Wear Daily* were also barred by Sinatra from covering his opening.

The New York *Times* correspondent in Los Angeles, Leroy Aarons, had wished to cover the opening as a news story. Jim Mahoney told him, 'I'm sorry, you're not invited.' Mahoney allegedly added, 'You're in good company.'

It wasn't difficult for me to keep *au courant* with all of Frank's activities, despite the break-up of our relationship, because my sources, including some of his best friends, came hurrying to me to report his latest peccadilloes. They thought I would rush into print with new tales of his misbehaviour. But in my code of ethics, that would have been an act of vindictiveness.

Several friends tried to get us back together. I would never make a move to patch it up, because I was not guilty of any misdeed in my thinking. I was the aggrieved party.

'Oh, Earl's not a bad guy,' Frank said to a couple of the would-be peacemakers.

'Why don't you make it up then?'

Frank gave a negative grunt. That would be sort of a

confession of wrong on his part. He could never do that.

'Earl and I started out about the same time, and I gave him a lot of good stuff,' Sinatra told one of the publicists trying to effect a truce. 'But then he wrote something that disappointed me. . . .' What it was that disappointed him, he'd never say.

Still trying, one publicist made a bolder move. 'Why not invite Earl on one of your next projects or concerts?' he said.

'Yeah, why not invite him?' Frank said. He seemed to be serious.

'You're going to be invited to the next opening,' the publicist told me.

'It'll never happen,' I told him.

But on 10 January 1975, almost seven years after I was disgraced, I received a telegram from Ron Amos, public relations director of Las Vegas Caesar's Palace, saying, 'Frank Sinatra brings his special weave of musical magic to Caesar's Palace 16–22 January for a one-week engagement. Caesar's Palace is pleased to invite you to Mr. Sinatra's opening performance on Thursday, 16 January.'

I couldn't possibly attend. I was committed to act as emcee of a dinner in Palm Springs that night. So I declined 'with regrets'.

I was assured by the Caesar's Palace publicist that I would never have been sent the telegram without Sinatra's approval. One of the hotel publicists also told me later that Sinatra had asked him to 'give Earl an item' concerning the line-up of his next show. Sinatra said this 'just as though nothing had happened.'

Ironically, about this time, Jim Mahoney, the keeper and recorder of 'the list', found himself out. He was dropped —late in 1974—after fifteen years, and his associates said he never quite knew why. He had gone to a farewell party for Frank, as he was leaving on a trip; next thing, he was discharged. 'I didn't know it,' Mahoney said, 'but the farewell party was for me.'

I guess I mellowed, too. Sinatra took on a new publicist to replace Jim Mahoney. It was the same Lee Solters of New York, who had represented Caesars Palace and had vowed to reconcile us. He was doing a Kissinger and I wasn't a difficult subject any longer, nor was Frank.

Touring Europe and having his troubles with Germany, Sinatra was gloriously received in England. I wrote some items about how two ex-wives, Ava Gardner and Mia Farrow, attended, and reported other phases of the successful trip.

I then received a letter on Claridge's stationery, dated 1 June 1975.

> Dear Earl,
>
> Just a quick note to thank you for the assist and kind words in your column. I am having a great time on this tour despite some phony flak from German typewriters. I hope you can make Harrah's this summer where I will be with John Denver. I know it will be a ball.
>
> Love to Rosemary.
>
> Best wishes.
>
> Francis (Frank Sinatra).

The armistice was on! I glued a copy of the letter to the wall in my office and wrote to Sinatra that we hoped to attend his Harrah's opening and that I'd bring along the money clip inscribed 'Oil, youse is a Poil—Frankie' that he'd given me about 1942. I hoped my wife hadn't lost it, and she hadn't.

By now I had figured out why Frank had barred me.

He thought I had been disloyal. He had been helpful to me in phoning me back. He talked to no other newspaperman, only to me. To call back a reporter at that point in his life was almost unheard of in his code, but he had done it for me, his supposed friend. He somehow believed that in repayment I should have taken his side but, of course, I couldn't and didn't. I didn't take anybody's side, but tried to tell the story. Frank was convinced that, by his standards, I had betrayed him, and when I understood that, I could no longer be mad at him.

But about that trip to Harrah's to see Sinatra? Suppose he suddenly decided to bar me again?

I wanted some reassurances that I was welcome this time. I received them. My wife and I flew to Lake Tahoe on August 1, sat in choice seats at his opening, and were both surprised and pleased when he told a joke with my name in it during his act. Then we learned we were invited to his dressing room after his midnight show—by then around 2.30 a.m.

After handshakes, I produced the money clip, and Sinatra said, 'What are you drinking, Oil?' He called my wife 'Rosie'. He asked me, 'What's Toots Shor going to do?' He didn't mention 'the trouble', nor did I. We said we'd see each other the next day.

I saw him in the elevator next day. 'I got hung up today with a lot of people,' he said. 'I'll have somebody call you.' Attorney Mickey Rudin came to my room and for half an hour discussed plans for Sinatra's continuing career, some off the record.

And so it was back on again. I wasn't sure to what extent or with what warmth. When he did a Jerry Lewis Muscular Dystrophy Telethon at WNEW-TV in New York City on Labor Day, I thought it would be interesting to observe.

'Fine,' Frank said. But I'd have to stand or sit on a spare chair under the overhanging equipment in the back as there was no regular theatre audience. I found a place beside opera singer Robert Merrill, his wife and daughter, who seemed to be the only invitees. Sinatra kissed the Merrills before the show started and again waved me a greeting just as in the past.

Sinatra was in the happiest state I'd ever seen him. He danced, gestured, laughed with the orchestra, sang a little of the prologue to *Pagliacci* in one song as something extra for Robert Merrill, and took notice of two women in the orchestra, saying, 'Two of the guys are dressed up like chicks.' In his most casual manner, he said, 'This next number is by Jimmy Webb . . . oh it isn't? Whose is it? Oh, it's me! Yeah, I wrote a song once when I was with Tommy Dorsey. I was about nine.' It was his 'This Love of Mine'.

Robert Merrill commented, 'He's in marvellous voice.'

There followed considerable banter about Elvis Presley giving $5,000 to the telethon while ill in a Memphis hospital, and Sinatra said 'I'll send him a bottle of booze and he'll get well. Milk is bad for you. Ask Pat Boone.'

Jerry Lewis said from Las Vegas that he was in love with Sinatra, and Sinatra replied, 'If you were a girl, I'd give you a lot of trouble. I've never been out with a Jewish girl,' he reflected, 'but I'm game. . . .'

It was all nonsense and maybe not very intellectual or uplifting, but it was warm and friendly and Sinatra was likeable. He has more likeability than anybody I ever met. If there's such a word as unlikeability, he has that, too, but when he turns on his likeability, you think you must have been wrong about him ever being unpleasant.

HE DISAPPEARS—INTO A CRIME INVESTIGATION

Approaching the 1970s, Sinatra wasn't feeling well. He was showing symptoms of Republicanism.

His right hand was in pain, but he was afraid of an operation. His movies inspired critics to ask why he made such junk. He was worth $50 million; it seemed to everybody that it was just a case of 'Take the money and run'. When he was on TV, the reviewers grieved that his once fine voice was gone. He detested being bald. The hair transplants that he got to replace the toupees were painful and embarrassing.

One night when his ego was down, he said, 'I think I'm gonna retire.'

'You can't retire!' a camp follower exclaimed.

'I can't, huh?' he laughed. 'Watch me!'

The suddenly moralistic politicians were still harping on his 'racket connections'. They were constantly investigating him.

He was worried. He got to wondering whether he was a political kiss of death as comedian-satirist Mort Sahl had said: 'Once you get Sinatra on your side in politics, you're out of business.'

The spectacle of Sinatra, the fiery young liberal of the Franklin D. Roosevelt days, inching towards Republicanism revolted some friends. Because of his dislike of Bobby Kennedy, Frank just had to support Hubert H. Humphrey when Lyndon B. Johnson decided not to run for President. 'I don't think Bobby Kennedy is qualified to be President,' Frank said.

The Kennedy Democrats hooted at his audacity. 'How the hell would Frank Sinatra know who would be qualified to be President?' they said. 'Who'd tell him?'

The Humphrey camp passed it off with the explanation that Frank and Humphrey were old friends—an untruth. Some Sinatra intimates thought Frank was so anti-Bobby that he'd have voted Republican if Bobby'd been nominated for the presidency.

Of course, Bobby Kennedy was fatally shot in the Hotel Ambassador in Los Angeles on the night of 5 June 1968, while celebrating the California and South Dakota primary victories, and died the next day.

At the Democratic convention in Chicago, Nancy Sinatra, Jr., was more in evidence than her father. She was lunching with Jack Haley, Jr., and somebody wondered, in case they got married, wouldn't it be the first time Junior married Junior?

Frank went down the line with the personal appearances and the chequebook, but his Humphrey enthusiasm never became feverish. At one rally, Sinatra, his daughter Tina and Jerry Lewis asked Humphrey what work they could do, and received no answer.

Sinatra began to catch on: Humphrey was as scared of his support as Bobby Kennedy had been! The *Wall Street Journal* listed some of Sinatra's alleged racket friendships, including his closeness with the Fischettis of Chicago and Miami. It pointed out that Bobby Kennedy had considered Sinatra a liability. Now Humphrey's managers began to soft-pedal the Sinatra connection with his campaign.

Jilted again!

Richard Nixon beat Humphrey by 223,000 votes in California and that convinced Frank there must be something better than being a California Democrat. He remained for the time being a registered Democrat, but he was shopping around. He decided to become a political bedfellow of Republican Ronald Reagan. It didn't gall him as much as he had thought it would.

He was torn between depression and elation as always. In his down periods, he feared that he'd 'had it' professionally and physically, as well as politically. He had always kept in good physical condition so he could defend himself. Even a cold upset him mentally. He confided to one friend that his voice now got tired after three straight nights of singing. Were the pipes going? The pain in his right hand—the hand that held the microphone—actually scared him.

He kept the pain a secret until he withdrew from a Warner Brothers' film in 1970. Very quietly he underwent surgery for Dupuytren's contracture, a shortening or distortion of muscular tissue in the palm and fingers. The condition has been known since biblical times and was named for a Swiss surgeon who'd written about it in 1832.

'It hurts like hell' was Frank's non-medical description. His ring finger and little finger were pulled down by the shortening of the muscular tissue. The surgery involved excision of thickened tissue to allow the hands and fingers to open. After the operation, Sinatra was able to open his hand again, except for the middle joint of his little finger. The pain persisted for months, gradually lessening, but Sinatra often winced from the hurt.

Pacing—and smoking and drinking—Sinatra talked, sometimes to himself. Going from a mood of depression into one of elation, Frank could see himself as a man unique, one with absolutely nothing to worry about.

In London, he had just sung at two charity concerts so successfully that one paper said, 'Dinner-jacketed socialites offered the loudest welcome since Winston Churchill took his V-Day tribute.' Jokingly drinking some tea, he told the audience that Americans drank tea long before the English did, 'but we threw ours overboard.' He was fifty-four, he drove around London in a white Jaguar, he had a $96,000-ten-room bachelor apartment in Grosvenor Square, which he hadn't used in a year, and he'd had it redecorated in his favourite colour—orange.

Not only was he accepting no fee for the two 'Sinatra at Midnight' benefits, he was paying for the orchestra. Princess Margaret gave a dinner for him before the first concert and met him again after the concert, during which he sang twenty-two songs accompanied by Count Basie's musicians.

Walter Annenberg, Ambassador to the Court of Saint

James's, and Mrs. Annenberg, who were Palm Spring neighbours, gave Sinatra another dinner at their residence, Winfield House. Toasted by the Ambassador, Frank rose before the sixty guests and kidded them: 'Bless your distinguished little hearts.'

Society columnist Suzy wrote: 'There wasn't a woman in London who wasn't dying-dying-dying to be invited.'

Though in the heights when he thought of this remarkable triumph, he plunged into gloom when he remembered some failures. He had a king's castle in Palm Springs, more money than he could ever spend and so much power that it disturbed some people. But there were the movie critics tearing down his ego, claiming he went from one bad picture to another trying unsuccessfully to emulate Humphrey Bogart.

The loudest voice was Bosley Crowther's of the New York *Times*. 'It is provoking,' Crowther wrote, 'to see this acute and awesome figure turning up time and again in strangely tricky and trashy motion pictures that add nothing to the social edification and encouragement of man.'

He found *Von Ryan's Express* to be 'outrageous and totally disgusting', *Marriage on the Rocks* to be 'a tawdry and witless trifle about a bored married man', while Tony Rome, Sinatra's private eye character, always mingled with crooks, killers, lesbians, homosexuals and nightclub bandits.

Crowther wondered why Sinatra would allow his pictures 'to be sprinkled with many globs of sheer bad taste. What grieves a long-time moviegoer is to remember how bright and promising he used to be, beginning with his charming performance with Gene Kelly in the musical *Anchors Aweigh*.'

About a decade before, Crowther had written a complimentary article about Sinatra's performances. Sinatra wrote him a letter which concluded, 'Glad to have you on my team.' It wasn't the sort of thing a proud New York *Times* critic liked to have said to him.

Crowther said, 'I've had misgivings about Sinatra ever since.'

But Sinatra plunged right ahead with his Miami-based Tony Rome private-eye character, coming out with *Lady in*

Cement, with busty beauties Raquel Welch and Lainie Kazan among the hookers and heiresses. Vincent Canby, the new critic for the New York *Times*, found it a blend of 'vulgarity and sloppiness', and 'consistently crude'.

Sinatra quite obviously was interested in making money. The producers of *Tony Rome*, for example, were very proud of filming it in twenty-eight days when they had a forty-five-day shooting schedule.

'He's a restless actor,' producer Aaron Rosenberg said. 'We get everything lighted up before he arrives and do it immediately. We seldom have to take more than two takes, never more than four.'

That's why they were seventeen days ahead of their time limit.

The worst disaster, though, was *Dirty Dingus Magee*, with Sinatra, as a petty thief in tattered clothes, robbing his old buddy, George Kennedy, while the latter was relieving himself. Anne Jackson was both the mayor and the madam of the town, Yerkey's Hole, where she sold the services of her 'prostitootsies' to cavalrymen.

In one revolting scene, four stony-faced Indian women watched Sinatra make love to an Indian maiden in a tent. From the bushes, a girl with the fine-sounding name of Anna Hotwater said, 'What do we do now, make bim-bam?'

Dirty Magee replied, 'Bim now, bam later.'

Critic Archer Winsten of the New York *Post* sadly observed that Sinatra, 'a man of many talents, foremost of which is making money, seems to have decided that he can turn a better profit from inconsequential films, so he tosses off one after another'.

Why was Sinatra so fascinated with this disreputable, corrupt, sex-crazed, vulgar background for his movies? In real life he was polite, charming, handsomely dressed, notoriously immaculate. Why did he want to wallow around in this atmosphere, even though it was only cinematic and artificial?

It was all part of the Jekyll-and-Hyde personality. Besides, he had a 'success compulsion'—and he enjoyed being rich. He liked to have money so he could give it away.

*

As Sinatra started thinking about retirement, he was harassed by a persistent rumour that he had been having cancer tests. It wasn't true, but the story circulated strangely. The 'information' always came, supposedly, from a nurse or interne or security guard in a hospital. The hospitals were scattered from Boston to New Haven to New Jersey—and even to Italy. The rumour finally went away.

He got into another brawl over credit—at Caesar's Palace this time. He and business partner Danny Schwartz were on a gambling rampage. Sinatra's markers mounted to $450,000. The casino executives didn't want them to go to half a million. They put in a stop order, and the notice was posted at the cage.

Sinatra protested to Sanford Waterman, the casino manager, and there was a clash.

'Sinatra's fingermarks were on my throat,' Waterman said later.

'He pulled a gun,' Sinatra claimed.

'Sinatra never touched Waterman,' Sinatra's publicist said.

Sinatra walked out of Caesar's Palace, leaving the hotel without a star attraction, and went back to Beverly Hills. It was reminiscent of the brawls at the Sands two years before.

The District Attorney's office implied that if Sinatra ever came back to Las Vegas it wanted to ask him some questions. Sinatra retorted that he wasn't likely to be returning to Las Vegas—ever. (In fairness to Sinatra, another set of authorities said later that this outburst was badly handled by the local officials.)

The deaths of two close friends, Jack Entratter and producer Leland Hayward, influenced Sinatra to call it a career in March 1971.

'Life's too short in this rat race; I want to do some other things before they put me away,' he said. 'I want to get out while I'm ahead, not when I'm a has-been.' He'd been a has-been years ago; he couldn't face it again.

He was not at the best point in his career, and he knew it.

There had been 'little room or opportunity for reflection, reading, self-examination and that need which every thinking man has for a fallow period, a long phase in which to seek a better understanding of the vast transforming changes now taking place in the world', his announcement of retirement proclaimed. 'This seems a proper time to take that breather and I am fortunate enough to be able to do so. I look forward to enjoying more time with my family and dear friends, to writing a bit—perhaps even to teaching.'

It seemed proper, too, for him to be getting a Jean Hersholt Humanitarian Award at the Oscar party in April.

Frank wasn't getting out of Hollywood—far from it. He and Danny Schwartz had just realized a $5-million profit on their National General stock. Frank was going to be around in a business sense for a long time, even if he wasn't going to be singing.

Frank's actual stepping down from the throne, his abdication, took place in the Los Angeles Music Center 14 June 1971, after thirty-two years of being up at the very, very top. It was an epic evening of epic evenings.

Comedian Don Rickles endeavoured to inject a light note by yelling such things as, 'Hey, old man! What's a fifty-five-year-old guy doing here? Why don't you go home, take your teeth out and watch "Sesame Street"?'

Rosalind Russell, all fluffy and shiny in white, almost broke down.

It had begun weeks previously when Gregory Peck arranged a black-tie concert for the Motion Picture and Television Relief Fund. Sinatra had accepted—before he announced his retirement. When it became known that he'd sing for the last time at this sparkling benefit, the $250 tickets shot up in value.

Everybody was tense backstage, even Cary Grant. Frank vocalized and lubricated his throat with some vodka. Jack Benny was kidding about his violin. Bob Hope was asking Frank if he really, *really* meant it about retiring.

David Frost gave the mike to Roz Russell.

'This assignment is not a happy one for me,' she said, biting her lips. 'Our friend has made a decision. His decision is not one we particularly like, because we like him.

He's worked long and hard for us for thirty years with his head and his voice and especially his heart. But it's time to put back the Kleenex and stifle the sob, for we still have the man, we still have the blue eyes, those wonderful blue eyes, that smile, for one last time we have the man, the greatest entertainer of the twentieth century.'

Sinatra ran onstage, finger-pointing her and warning her, 'Don't you cry.'

They scrambled to their feet in the first of several standing ovations.

Frank sang about the old days, and he talked about them, too. He recounted memories: back to the thirties with Harry James, a song called 'All or Nothing at All' had sold about 8,000 copies; but when there was a musicians' strike in 1943, Columbia brought back Sinatra's 1939 record and it became that company's top tune.

'Nancy with the Laughing Face'—it still brought tears because everybody remembered it being about his daughter, who now was a top record seller herself.

On he went, talking about 'I've Got You Under My Skin', by Cole Porter, 'Ol' Man River', 'Fly Me to the Moon', and then he sang 'My Way'—whereupon the crowd leaped up and gave him another standing ovation.

But he wasn't finished.

There were several things he wanted to do, including 'meet some girls and build a house someplace'. His Paul Anka song, 'My Way', seemed to have more than ordinary meaning as he sang the words clearly: 'I've had my fill, my share of losing . . . and I may say, "Not in a shy way" . . . the record shows / I took the blows / and did it My Way.'

He gave them a dramatic ending. 'I've built my career on saloon songs,' he said, going easily into 'Angel Eyes'.

He asked for the stage to be darkened, just a pin-point spot on him. Midway through the song, he lit a cigarette. The smoke wrapped him within it. He was in silhouette. He came to the last line of the song: 'Excuse me while I disappear.'

And he did.

But back in the wings, Sinatra was misty-eyed as he embraced Roz Russell, for all the adulation made him feel like he'd been attending his own funeral. It was as though he was leaving life. He must be the most loved personality in Show Business, even more than Judy Garland, whom they loved for her weaknesses. Frank wondered whether he'd made a mistake in retiring.

Somewhere Don Rickles had been saying, 'Somebody help the old man on with his coat. Make way for the old-timer.' And Sammy Davis was yelling, 'He'll be doing a whole series of comebacks now after the retirement,' to which Frank replied, 'So how come I got tickets to South America?'

But Sammy Davis was right.

Sinatra was retired for about five minutes. The *sotto voce* rumours that he was buddying up to Governor Ronald Reagan to get back at the Democrats were confirmed when he issued a statement showing he was plunging into Republican politics.

To swinger Sinatra, Reagan was sort of a dullard. Jane Wyman, Reagan's first wife, once said, 'Ronnie's the kind of a guy you ask him what time it is, he tells you how they made the watch.'

In becoming co-chairman of Reagan's committee for re-election, 'Californians for Reagan', Sinatra pointed out that he and Reagan had been in the acting business for twenty years (you couldn't miss the point that they'd both gone beyond it and become bigger men) and now 'we share the same desires for the welfare of the people of the state of California and the nation'. Sinatra applauded Reagan's 'guts and fortitude' in putting down mutinies by Berkeley students.

'Now we must all work together to end the turmoil on the campuses and improve the communication between the students and what they refer to as the Establishment,' he said.

Sinatra was now in the Establishment!

He grinned when the students hissed at the mention of his name. One political writer said that most actors don't have as much political influence as a janitor at City Hall. Sinatra knew, though, that the Democrats would miss his financial contributions and his singing at the fund-raising rallies. Reagan's campaign didn't need money; that spoke revealingly of the kind of supporters he had. But the Democrats always needed money, and now he wouldn't be throwing it to them.

Frank's switch didn't astonish Jess Unruh, the liberal Democrat running against Reagan. He was realistic about Sinatra getting older and less rambunctious and less rebellious each year.

'I do miss those guys on the other side,' Sinatra said. The Republicans were a staid bunch of old bastards. It was a very dull campaign.

Reagan won—and Sinatra had a winner again. And that was nice because he hadn't had one for a while.

Ahead lay Agnew and Nixon.

But first, along came a congressional investigation of Frank's connections. It was another movie scenario: Frank against the Bad Guys; this time, the Bad Guys were the congressmen and he was the one who was wronged. So he claimed, anyway.

Sinatra collided with the House Select Committee on Crime in July 1972, in a remarkable confrontation that was a *coup de théâtre* for Frank. Digging into supposed mobster influence in big-time commercial sports, the committee, headed by Democratic Rep. Claude D. Pepper of Florida, wanted to ask him about being vice-president of Berkshire Downs racetrack in Hancock, Massachusetts.

The suspense was built up beautifully in the newspapers, with Sinatra giving the appearance of trying to avoid questioning.

The committee had US marshals waiting to hand him a subpoena when he arrived to sing at a gala for Vice-President Agnew in May.

But Senator John Tunney, the California Democrat for whom Sinatra had earlier raised $160,000 with a special show, didn't want to embarrass Sinatra and asked that he be allowed to testify in executive session. Pepper balked and said a celebrity should be treated like anybody else. Sinatra preferred to be 'invited', not subpoenaed, but the committee decided to subpoena him, and attorney Rudin said he'd accept it for Sinatra and produce him for the committee in about a week.

Then Sinatra left the country.

SINATRA DODGES HOUSE CRIME PROBE,

screamed the papers.

Sinatra was discovered having a night on the town in London. The Hotel Savoy said he'd left—destination unknown.

The committee became indignant and announced an ultimatum: 'If the retired entertainer does not come out of hiding within a week and agree to testify, we will seek a bench warrant in federal court compelling him to appear.' The committee would serve the bench warrant overseas, 'where Sinatra is believed to be.'

Sinatra had gone to London to discuss a film, but again he disappeared.

Attorney Rudin appeared in Washington to accept the subpoena, but then decided he couldn't accept it legally for his client.

SINATRA GAMBLING IN MONTE CARLO,

another headline said. (He was peripatetic.)

Attorney Rudin was nobody to be pushed around. He said the committee had allowed the news media to distribute unsolicited testimony without his client being given an opportunity to refute it. If all outstanding subpoenas against Sinatra were dropped, he would appear.

The committee chairman, Republican Pepper, now had a press agent, Michael Petit, who said 'Sinatra's appearance is voluntary'. He was not being subpoenaed. He was not being invited. He was inviting himself over!

The confrontation took place 18 July 1972, in the Cannon House office building. It has a marble rotunda. The ropes were up outside with a couple of hundred people surging against them for a look at the star witness. Inside the hearing room were about 500 spectators, mostly female, some squealy.

Joseph Barboza, the confessed murderer of twenty-seven persons, had told the committee that Sinatra had interests in two hotels as a front for Raymond Patriarca, a New England Mafia boss. And allegedly Sinatra was a vice-president and director in the defunct Berkshire Downs racetrack, which purportedly was financed by Cosa Nostra racketeers. Sinatra claimed he pulled out when he found out by reading the sports pages that they listed him as an officer.

The loquacious Barboza claimed that Patriarca—then serving a five-year term in the Atlanta penitentiary—had bragged that Sinatra was 'fronting points' for him at the Fontainebleau Hotel in Miami Beach and at the Las Vegas Sands. The Fontainebleau gave the committee an affidavit of denial.

The superstar made a superstar entrance.

He was surrounded by a flying wedge of stalwarts who just kept walking, opening a way for Frank, who wore a tan sports jacket, brown slacks, zippered boots—and a definitely belligerent look. The female fans were breathing hard as he was sworn in. The committee members had waited six weeks for this. They all had questions prepared.

Sinatra immediately began berating the committee, taking the offensive in an angry manner that caught the congressmen by surprise.

Sinatra shot a contemptuous glance at these men who had been, so he felt, harassing him. His attorney sat or stood at his side. Sinatra could have been at home or in a movie scene. He was not worried. He was merely mad.

To the delight of the crowd, he blasted the committee for permitting a 'convicted felon' to use it to indulge in 'character assassination' by claiming he was fronting for the Mafia.

His voice was not musically sweet and melodious now. It was raspy. It was cutting.

With his head held high and proud and his shoulders back, Sinatra spoke of his 'good name' and declared that it had been tarnished by the testimony of Barboza. Glaring fiercely, Sinatra snapped, 'This bum went running off at the mouth. I resent it. I won't have it. I'm not a second-class citizen, and let's get that clear right now.'

The committeemen, taken aback, swallowed hard or

gulped or coughed, hoping to get a word in. Sinatra brandished a newspaper clipping accusingly and read the headline:

WITNESS LINKS SINATRA TO REPUTED MAFIA FIGURE.

His voice full of sarcasm, Sinatra said, 'That's charming, isn't it? Isn't that charming?' He looked at the committee counsel. 'That's all hearsay evidence, isn't it?'

'Yes, it is,' admitted the counsel, Joseph Phillips.

The crowd, especially the girls and women, applauded the superstar witness, and Chairman Pepper threatened loudly that he would clear the room. Sinatra, enjoying his role, pointed a finger accusingly and said, 'It is indecent and irresponsible for a man to come in here and bandy my good name about and I would like the committee to do something about it.'

He had, he said, invested $55,000 for a 5 per cent interest in the track and then demanded, and succeeded in getting, his investment back.

'Everywhere he appears he gets ten or twelve propositions,' Rudin told the committee. That was the laugh line of the show. The women, and the men, gave it their own interpretation and howled.

'For example,' Rudin continued, 'a Joe Smith comes to us and wants to go into the drug business . . .'

Again there was loud laughter from the superstar's audience, and he and his teammate were figuratively chasing the committee around the ring.

'I'm talking about legitimate drugs,' Rudin said.

There were more howls, and Chairman Pepper pounded the gavel as Rudin continued.

'Mr. Sinatra only has to remember the songs and how to sing them, but I have difficulty remembering all the deals thrown at us in the last seventeen years,' he said.

Sinatra flared up when the committee counsel delved into his friendship or acquaintanceship with the late Tommy ('Three Finger') Brown Luchese, a celebrated Brooklyn and Manhattan rackets figure. 'Let's dispense with that kind of question,' snapped Sinatra, in the manner of a man taking over the investigation.

The committee had heard that Sinatra had met Salvatore Rizzo, the racetrack president, through Luchese.

Committee counsel Joseph Phillips said, 'I'm just trying to figure how Rizzo made such a favourable impression on you that you invested all that money.'

'Lots of people contact me,' Sinatra said. 'The gentlemen wanted me to invest in a racetrack.'

'But you had two meetings with him [Luchese]?'

'We shook hands. We said hello.'

'Would you remember me if I walked in and said hello?'

'If I wanted to.' (Another laugh for the superstar witness.)

But how did he get involved?

'That was ten years ago. I've met a half million people in that time,' Sinatra replied.

Rudin said that investing $55,000 in a track for Sinatra wasn't a huge transaction. 'That's the nature of a portfolio,' continued Rudin. 'You take some crap shoots, and you make some conservative investments. And besides, it was a little episode in that year. We were forming a record company as well.'

Sinatra interjected, 'I wasn't a child. I figured, if it works, it works. I've been in business ventures that failed.'

'Have you ever been to the track?'

'Not at all.'

Later he said, 'Would you believe I've only been to a racetrack four times in all my life, four times in all my adult life?'

Sinatra maintained he was constantly being exploited by people whom he hardly knew.

A West Coast promoter, he said, started a baseball team listing him as an officer. 'Listen to the gall of this man,' Sinatra said. 'A man I never met in my life named me president of a humpty-dumpty baseball team and then sent his bills to me.'

Sinatra was before the committee for a sparkling ninety-five minutes and was in charge all the way. His victory was so complete that two congressmen apologized. Rep. Charles Rangel, a Harlem Democrat, offered his hand and told Frank, 'You're still the Chairman of the Board.'

Conceding that Sinatra was right in charging that he'd

been wrongfully characterized as a pal of the New England Mafia, Rep. Morgan Murphy, Illinois Democrat, told him, 'We as congressmen and politicians aren't always presented as we'd like to see it. I resent it when we are taken advantage of, and I feel that in this instance, you were taken advantage of.'

And there were other complimentary and grateful things said about the superstar witness, who again got inside a flying wedge and made his way out of the hearing room and out of the marble rotunda while the crowd applauded him and the ladies squealed. He departed as a conquering hero instead of the villain they'd been picturing him for weeks.

'FRANKIE!' some of the young fans were screaming, but it was generally an older crowd that was satisfied just to applaud the retiree who had dared them to put up and they hadn't put up.

The next step by Sinatra was a clever one.

He had a byline in the New York *Times* on 24 July, with an article or letter on the Op-Ed page headlines:

WE MIGHT CALL THIS THE POLITICS OF FANTASY.

He wrote with a Washington dateline:

> At one minute after eleven on the morning of 18 July I walked into a large hearing room in the Cannon Office Building to testify before a group called the Select Committee on Crime.
>
> The halls were packed with visitors; the rows behind me were sold out. And every member of the Congressional Committee was present, an event which I'm told does not happen too often.
>
> It was apparent to most people that the whole matter could have been resolved in the privacy of a lawyer's office without all the attendant hoopla.
>
> . . . In practice, as we learned during the ugly era of Joe McCarthy, they [investigating committees] can become star chambers in which 'facts' are confused with rumour, gossip and innuendo, and where reputations and character can be demolished in front of the largest possible audiences.

In my case a convicted murderer was allowed to throw my name around with abandon, while the TV cameras rolled on. His vicious little fantasy was sent into millions of American homes, including my own. Sure, I was given a chance to refute it, but as we have all come to know, the accusation often remains longer in the public mind than the defence.

In any case, an American citizen, no matter how famous or how obscure, should not be placed in the position of defending himself before baseless charges, and no Congressional Committee should become a forum for gutter hearsay that would not be admissible in a court of law.

Sinatra's letter added that much gossip about him 'is complicated because my name ends in a vowel'. He continued:

Sitting at the table the other day, I wondered whether I had been called down to Washington during an election year, a year in which Congressmen have difficulty getting their names into the newspapers because of the concentration on the race for the Presidency.

And I wondered if the people out there in America knew how dangerous the whole proceeding was.

My privacy had been robbed from me, I had lost hours of my life, I was being forced to defend myself in a place that was not even a court of law. It wasn't just a question of getting them off my back; it was a question of them getting off everyone's back. If this sort of thing could happen to me, it could happen to anyone, including those who cannot defend themselves properly. I would hope that a lot of Americans would begin to ask their representatives, in the Government and in the media, to start separating fantasy from reality, and to bring this sort of nonsense to an end once and for all.

It was copyrighted by Sinatra.

A curious aftermath was an admission by Rep. Sam Steiger, Arizona Republican, that they shouldn't have been digging into the Salvatore Rizzo–Sinatra connections because Rizzo had already brought a civil suit against the Internal Revenue Service and didn't want to answer any questions in a way that might be different from what he'd said in court.

'I believe the committee is more at fault than Mr. Rizzo because we should have known about the civil action, and we didn't,' Steiger said. 'It was faulty research.'

Sinatra won hands down, anyway, and future committee probers would be more cautious.

It may have been Frank's greatest performance, better even than his Oscar-winning portrayal of Maggio.

Two years later, when successfully running for governor of New York, Congressman Hugh Carey paid tribute to Sinatra's handling of the Washington hearing: 'It was not one of Congress' finest hours. It turned out that there was no real question of Sinatra's implication in anything, except that he was a big personality. . . . Seldom did Congress look, frankly, more ludicrous.

'I watched the proceedings for a while and saw that he had the show well in hand. I almost waited for him to do a choreograph job on the committee and tell 'em how to dance out of the room.'

Sometimes it does seem that Sinatra and his lawyers can bend investigative bodies to their will as effortlessly as Frank bends musical notes. Performing one night in a club where the air-conditioning was disabled, he handkerchiefed away the perspiration and said, 'I haven't been this hot since I was before the New Jersey Grand Jury.'

Actually, he didn't sweat much before the New Jersey State Commission of Investigation's inquiry into organized crime. It had come two years before the House investigation in Washington. Rather, it was a defiant, laughing Sinatra who baited the investigators, leading them on, enticing them into quagmires.

His name had come up dramatically in an extortion trial in Newark in June 1969. He was mentioned frequently by Mafia boss Angelo ('Gyp') De Carlo in FBI-recorded conversations. Discussing a possible takeover of a Jamaica hotel via a $2 million mortgage, De Carlo was quoted as saying, 'I'll see Sinatra and have a talk with him.' Nothing more serious than that was suggested, and it was not established whether De Carlo was extremely familiar with Sinatra or was just boasting.

But the state commission leaped at that and other mentions of Sinatra and subpoenaed him.

'I'm not going to participate in any three-ring circus,' he said defiantly. His counsel challenged the constitutionality of the creation of the commission. Delay followed delay.

Eight months later, the state supreme court upheld the legality of the Sinatra subpoena.

By then, the entire dossier of hints and suspicions about Sinatra and 'his friends' had been raked over and built up anew.

The public was reminded that Lucky Luciano had carried a gold cigarette case inscribed 'To my dear pal Lucky from his friend Frank Sinatra.' Joseph (Rocco) Fischetti, a relative of Al Capone and another friend of Sinatra's, was supposedly one of the very few people allowed to see Sinatra without his toupee.

It was a little like a bad movie. The process-servers boarded Sinatra's yacht, the *Roma*, docked at Atlantic Highlands, New Jersey, and stumbled about, trying to find if there were any sinister mobsters in hiding. They never found any.

When Sinatra was served, he'd had eight months to prepare an answer. He resisted public grilling. He was willing to answer questions with depositions or in personal interviews, but not in open hearing.

'Notwithstanding the fact I am of Italian descent,' Sinatra said, pointedly, 'I do not have any knowledge of how crime functions in New Jersey or whether there is such a thing as organized crime.'

He was willing to fight against public interrogation all the way to the Supreme Court. The state commission didn't know whether it had the right to arrest him outside the state of New Jersey. If it couldn't grab him outside of New Jersey, he would simply stay out of his home state.

'Sounds like a damn good idea anyway,' Sinatra grinned.

He seemed to be enjoying the duel. Finally there was

a 'compromise'. He would return to the state and be questioned in private in a quickly-called closed session of the commission in Trenton.

On a below-freezing day in February, he flew in on a Grumman-4 at seven o'clock at night and was hustled, bareheaded and without overcoat, before two members of the commission. He submitted to questioning for an hour and fifteen minutes. The press didn't learn what Frank had said. But he didn't enlighten the commission much about organized crime. He maintained he didn't know what they were talking about.

The commission chairman, William F. Hyland, announced that Sinatra 'co-operated fully' and that a warrant for his arrest on civil contempt charges, which the commission had been fumbling like a hot potato, would be dropped next day.

It was. After all that effort, the commission blanked out.

Sinatra heckled the investigators in later years.

'Just a couple of clowns trying to get their names in the papers,' he said. 'And the papers blew it up. Don't believe the things they write. What else have they got to write about?'

In both the Washington and New Jersey investigations, Sinatra was given a clean bill. After considerable fulminating, the investigators backed down. They found nothing criminal or even illegal about his 'associations'.

Sinatra has been investigated by one investigator after another, and he was investigated by investigative reporters before that term was invented. He never has been linked to any criminality. It is the opinion of most of the investigators that he never will be.

'The mob guys use him,' is their conclusion. 'When they're allowed to be around him, they get some acceptance for this is a man who relaxes with presidents and ambassadors. Sinatra enjoys it because he's been in awe of them since boyhood.'

Frank lends some respectability to these characters. But he will never give them up, because that's Frank Sinatra, and if you don't like it, you know what you can do.

THAT MISHMASH WITH MAXINE CHESHIRE

It felt good winning with Ronald Reagan—even if he was a Republican—and Sinatra was snapping his fingers again and going through the motions of conducting an orchestra. He seized up an imaginary baton and led the musicians when he was in a good mood, just as Bob Hope was always taking swings with an imaginary golf club.

Full of enthusiasm, he plunged into the Nixon–Agnew campaign in the autumn of 1972. For the first time in his life, he was campaigning for the Republican national ticket.

Nancy, Jr., Frank, Jr., and Tina, whom he'd taught to be liberal Democrats, said, 'Our father must be out of his mind.'

Restless after more than a year of 'retirement', he was coming out of retirement right at that moment, although he didn't admit it. His original announcement of retirement had specified that it included political inactivity.

The press didn't care that much and didn't take notice of it.

Flying to Chicago to entertain a Young Voters-for-Nixon Rally, along with several rock groups, he swaggered in, and the 4,900 people rocked the hall. After all, it was Chicago and 'My Kind of Town' brought wails from the audience. His friends Vice-President and Mrs. Agnew sat in the front row, beaming as he sang a special lyric to the melody of 'The Lady Is a Tramp'.

'The Gentleman Is a Champ' was the new version, lyrics

written by Sammy Cahn, song sung by Sinatra, who'd sung the original in the movie *Pal Joey*. Probably no Vice-President had ever had a song sung to him by such an artist.

'I've come to know him intimately,/ and he's become like he's part family,/ and what I'm proud of is that he likes me/ I mean the gentleman is a champ./ He comes to Palm Springs a lot as you know,/ just to escape the political show./ He likes my hotel 'cause I charge no dough,/ but still the gentleman is a champ.'

That was Agnew all the way, but not to forget President Nixon, Sammy Cahn had added 'They're both unique,/ the Quaker, the Greek,/ they make this Italian want to whistle and stamp/ because each gentleman,/ I mean each gentleman, is a champ.'

Sammy Cahn was upbraided by Democrat friends later for writing those laudatory words, but he shrugged it off with, 'anything for Frank'.

Agnew returned the kind words to Sinatra a few nights before the 1972 election.

Sinatra and Ted—as intimates called Spiro Agnew—had become close through Bob Hope.

When he was installed as Vice-President, Agnew visited the Hopes in Palm Springs. The Hopes did not have an enormous showplace at that time; they had just a three-bedroom house of the kind that other people had in the simple unostentatious days.

The Hope place didn't seem quite large enough to handle the Vice-President and the entourage that he required now, and it wasn't long before Ted was visiting the Sinatra compound—'a million-dollar hideaway' near the Tamarisk Country Club—by helicopter. Frank named his guest annex in Palm Springs 'Agnew House' and put the Vice-President's name on its matches and notepaper. Agnew was Vice-President, but the local columnist Gloria Greer said, 'Agnew is not the king here; Sinatra is.'

Agnew played golf watched over by Secret Service men. After golf, he could get a sandwich, or almost anything else, from a kitchen said to have cost Sinatra $100,000 or watch a new movie that had been flown in from Hollywood that day, or he could simply lie down and take a nap in the completely refurbished guest house, which had special cables and phone lines for his official convenience. Who could blame Ted Agnew for finding this a cosy place to visit?

It was re-election time.

On Thursday night, six days before the national election, the Vice-President heaped eloquent accolades upon Sinatra for his generosities at a State of Israel Bonds dinner at the Los Angeles Century Plaza Hotel, at which Frank was given its Medallion of Valour. Agnew was then unblemished and was regarded as a possible President for 1976. The closeness of Frank and Ted was just becoming known, and Sinatra had been overheard saying, 'I'll make him President.'

Lucille Ball introduced Agnew ('I like him because he says a lot of things a lot of people would like to say, but haven't got the courage to say'), and then Agnew took over and extolled the Jews and Bonds for Israel so resoundingly that some people thought he was pulling for some Jewish votes the next Tuesday. Before the dinner, he and Sinatra posed for pictures of Sinatra getting the medallion, simulating the actual presentation. Baron Edmund de Rothschild put the medallion around Sinatra's neck and kissed him on both cheeks, although Frank thought that just a pat on the back would have been adequate. But Sinatra was co-operative with the photographers, and because it was a salute to Sinatra, the evening generated advance pledges totalling $6.5 million in purchases of bonds for Israel.

It was a tremendous success.

Burt Lancaster, the toastmaster, called Sinatra 'the world's greatest entertainer', and Agnew took it from there.

'A legend in his own time, not only in the world of entertainment, but in the world of philanthropy,' declared Agnew. 'A man who has unselfishly used his blessings, the blessings bestowed by a god-given talent and hard work, to benefit his fellow man.' He added that his friendship with Sinatra, while recent, 'is a very close one'.

'He has earned distinction as a humanitarian who avoids the spotlight,' the Vice-President continued. 'Frank is a very personal, as well as a very personable, man. He's genuinely interested in individuals and what is inside them. He never holds himself aloof from liking or disliking, and he's even been known to openly love and hate.'

Columnist Marvene Johes reported that Jilly Rizzo, who was circulating the room that night, told her, 'We hired a couple of sheriff's men to guard Frank, and I just wanted to make sure they're doing their job.'

'Jilly also revealed that he and Sinatra will fly to Washington, D.C., over the weekend to be with President Nixon and Vice-President Agnew when the Big Day is upon them Tuesday. "Then we'll just hang around there for a couple of days," revealed the non-jocular Jilly.'

The re-elected President Nixon and his Vice-President were happy men, and there were numerous celebrations in Washington. On the second night of the celebrations, Sinatra and his friend Barbara Marx went to a private party given by Louise Gore at the Washington Jockey Club. Sinatra was in a bad mood. Frank had been scheduled to act as master of ceremonies at a show, but the Secret Service had not been told he was bringing his comedian friend Pat Henry, and it had not given Henry a clearance. Sinatra was mad at the world.

Barbara Marx's hand was on Frank's arm as a *Woman's Wear Daily* reporter, Kandy Stroud, attempted to ask him a question. Miss Stroud later said that Sinatra was not in a question-answering mood and snapped, 'Who the hell do you think you are? If you want to see me, write me a letter.'

Up stepped Maxine Cheshire, respectable and respected syndicated columnist of the Washington *Post*, married and the mother of four. She had no suspicion that he was angry at her.

'He had always been so polite, such a gentleman, that I really admired him for his behaviour,' she said later. She had written of the close friendship of Sinatra and Agnew but her paper was anti-Nixon. She had been on dangerous ground once with Sinatra when one of her editors insisted that she ask him a tricky question: 'Mr. Sinatra, do you think that your alleged association with the Mafia will prove to be the same embarrassment to Vice-President Agnew as it was to the Kennedy Administration?'

A rough question to be asked when you're getting out of Gov. Ronald Reagan's limousine at a governors' meeting in Washington. But her editor had told Maxine Cheshire to ask it, and she did. 'I was afraid I'd get my head knocked off,' she said.

Sinatra had fielded the question nicely. He just shrugged and said, 'No, I don't worry about things like that.'

'No rudeness, no crudeness—and surely that kind of question might easily have made him mad,' she admitted.

Now in the Jockey Club, Maxine Cheshire was just introducing herself to Barbara Marx, to whom she'd spoken earlier on the phone, when the roof caved in.

Sinatra exploded.

'Get away from me, you scum! Go home and take a bath,' he shouted. 'I don't want to talk to you. I'm getting out of here, to get rid of the stench of Mrs. Cheshire. You know Mrs. Cheshire, don't you? That stench you smell is from her. You're nothing but a two dollar broad. Here's two dollars, Baby, that's what you're used to.'

With that he stuffed two one-dollar bills into Mrs. Cheshire's ginger-ale glass. Bystanders said he also applied a four-letter word starting with *c* to her and said, 'You know what that means, don't you? You've been laying down for two dollars all your life.'

Mrs. Cheshire's first reaction was total shock, and then she cried loudly and wetly into a paper napkin that her husband found for her. Reporter Sally Quinn of the Washington *Post* and Kandy Stroud quickly reported it all; Maxine Cheshire found herself the leading figure in a big controversy.

Sinatra had gone much, much too far, almost everybody agreed. After she had gotten over her numbness and tears, Mrs. Cheshire asked whether she deserved this.

Consoling herself that she was a friend of attorney Eugene Wyman, who headed the law firm that represented Sinatra, she was sure Wyman would get him to apologize.

She went to bed feeling it would soon blow over. She awoke to find European papers phoning for more details—

and to learn that Eugene Wyman had dropped dead that night.

Through other lawyers, Maxine Cheshire tried to get Sinatra to write a letter of apology. He refused. Mrs. Cheshire went to court. But she eventually withdrew the action when her lawyers told her that she couldn't write anything about Sinatra or Spiro Agnew while the case was in litigation. So Mrs. Cheshire had not had any apology when Sinatra had his explosion about woman journalists in Australia in July 1974, a year and a half later. Far from apologizing for the Washington incident, he reminded the world that he'd once given a woman in Washington two dollars—but had overpaid her!

Mrs. Cheshire's reaction was: 'The man is sick. He's schizophrenic. Sinatra is one of the greatest talents of ours in this country and yet he is sick.'

Yet everybody wasn't on her side. She said she got occasional letters from people saying, 'Sinatra was right about you.'

Some readers believed that she was hinting things about Agnew's private life in her columns, and this was what had outraged Sinatra. She denied this. She had ferreted out the Sinatra–Agnew friendship, had written about Frank Sinatra trying to help Mrs. James Hoffa get her husband out of jail, had reminded her readers that Sinatra had been an embarrassment to two Democratic administrations and was proving to be an embarrassment to Nixon.

'He must have had a very deep-seated animosity towards me,' she conceded in one of the year's greatest understatements. 'He started to count up how many he owed me. And suddenly there I was, and he let me have it. I understand it completely.' She felt that Sinatra would have hit a headwaiter, or somebody, or anybody, if she hadn't been there to receive his wrath.

Mrs. Cheshire said, 'I have received bushel baskets of mail almost unanimously on my side from lovely people such as GOP ladies across the country. They are outraged . . . also they don't know what that obscene four-letter word Sinatra used even means. My own mother didn't know either, and my poor husband had to explain it to her.'

In the end, Sinatra didn't suffer any physical or financial harm from his outburst of bad manners, and he kept on insulting Maxine Cheshire wherever he went. At first, immediately following the incident, his crowd didn't think the newspapers would report the tantrum because his language didn't seem to be printable. But the Washington *Post* and other papers found it all so outrageous that they either printed the word or hinted so strongly what it was that most readers eventually understood.

At the peak of the furore, Maxine Cheshire went on the NBC 'Today Show'. William Safire, then a speechwriter for President Nixon and later a columnist for the New York *Times*, criticized her sharply, saying that her act of 'injured innocence was deserving of Sarah Bernhardt'. He asked who had coached her in her lines and said she should be given prime time for her 'act'.

In the meantime, Sinatra wondered about Nixon's reaction to the controversy. He cared about this. Vice-President Agnew confided to him that the President was mad as hell. Nixon might have to back down on inviting him to the White House. Would Nixon give him the freeze as the Kennedys had done? Even though he'd given a reported $50,000? Even though he electioneered? Yes, it looked like Sinatra was again ripe for the guillotine.

One angle they forgot was that Nixon, too, hated the Washington *Post*. Agnew nudged the President's memory about that.

Therefore, on the night of 17 April 1973, three months after the cursing of Cheshire, Sinatra sang at a White House state dinner for Premier Andreotti of Italy, with the microphone being personally adjusted for him by the President of the United States.

Singing a programme he and Nelson Riddle had arranged, Sinatra captured the 200 guests in the East Room just as he has won nearly every room he ever worked in. He built up to a standing ovation—led by the President.

Sinatra was in tears at the evening's end, and one headline said:

SINATRA SINGS AND WEEPS AT A WHITE HOUSE GALA.

The President was twice moved to make a speech this remarkable evening.

Sinatra had been in retirement for a couple of years, but he was in strong, firm and warm voice as he sang 'The House I Live In', the thirty-year-old patriotic song with the theme, 'All races, all religions, that's America to me.' He swung from 'Moonlight in Vermont' to 'Fly Me to the Moon' and 'I've Got the World on a String'. He was self-assured as always and watched Mrs. Nixon in the front row keeping time by nodding her head. His own daughter Tina was keeping time, too, a few rows behind.

'Once in a while,' President Nixon said, 'there is a moment when there is magic in this room, when a singer is able to move us and capture us all, and Frank Sinatra has done that and we thank him.'

Nixon compared Sinatra to the Washington Monument —'The Top'—and said, 'This house is honoured to have a man whose parents were born in Italy, but yet from humble beginnings went to the very top in entertainment.'

'When I was a small boy in New Jersey,' Sinatra said in reply, 'I thought it was a great boot if I could get a glimpse of the mayor. It's quite a boot to be here. I'm honoured and I'm privileged.

'Today after the rehearsal I looked at the paintings of President and Mrs. Washington and thought about the modest dignity of the presidency up through the years. It makes me very proud of my country. Thank you, Mr. President, for inviting me here.'

Nixon stood up to lead applause at one point, though the programme wasn't finished, and Frank glowed and beamed and modestly said, 'You're very nice, very kind.'

Sinatra, who had been smiling throughout, suddenly looked very grave towards the end of the programme. He manoeuvred himself around to the side of the bandstand, where, some guests said, he was seen crying and dabbing at his eyes with a handkerchief.

Nobody could remember seeing Sinatra in tears in public before, and of course it wasn't very public even then. Sinatra was simply overcome with the emotion of having made it that far.

Press secretary Ronald L. Ziegler said it was Sinatra's first performance at the White House, which was itself remarkable considering the Democratic Presidents who could have invited him in the years before.

The Nixons escorted their guests to the North Portico, and the President invited Sinatra up to his private quarters. The Agnews had remained discreetly in the background, but now appeared and joined Sinatra. Continuing to be humble, and at his most charming, Sinatra said to the President, 'Lovely words, sir.'

Sinatra's final words to his host were, 'See you very soon.'

'July,' said Nixon. 'I haven't played for a year.' (Golf, of course.)

Sinatra had drinks later with Nelson Riddle, who hadn't seen a President lead a standing ovation before. 'You can't do much better than that,' Riddle said.

'What happened to those rumours I wasn't going to get invited?' chuckled Sinatra.

Actually, President Nixon had made it a much bigger Sinatra night than Sinatra had ever hoped for. In this corner: Sinatra, the winner and still champion! It made him think back to the Kennedy years when he was in the Georgetown Set. He was back on top again. It was good for a guy's ego. If actors are children and require gifts and pats on the head to keep them going, this was a real big lollipop for Frank.

THE SECOND COMING OF SINATRA

The rumours that Sinatra was coming out of retirement—that there would be a Second Coming of Sinatra—were heard in March 1973, coincidental with rumours that Spiro Agnew was going into forced retirement.

The seemingly undying friendship of Sinatra and Agnew is a remarkable story of Frank's loyalty to a friend in trouble. Frank often speaks of somebody as being 'a stand-up guy', and to him that's a high compliment. Sinatra was a stand-up guy for the slick, personable verbalizing former Maryland governor who became Richard Nixon's name-caller and mouthpiece.

During Sinatra's retirement, every day was a holiday at the Palm Springs compound, and Ted Agnew always seemed to be helicoptering in. Proud of his piano playing, Agnew had memorized scores of lyrics of popular songs, and would break into song without much coaxing. Cherry bombs would begin exploding. One visitor asked, 'How do you guys ever know when it's New Year's Eve? It seems like New Year's Eve here every night.'

'Oh, on New Year's Eve Frank puts on a funny hat,' one hanger-on said.

Sinatra found it easy to like Agnew, who seemed fated to be the Clown Prince. He was always hitting people with erratic golf drives or making speeches about the newspapers or being ridiculed by Johnny Carson on the 'Tonight' show. 'How are things, Mr. Vice-President?' Carson once asked him, and he replied, 'Great! But they'll get better.'

It was reported that Sinatra and Bob Hope paid for some of Agnew's tailoring, and also his travelling expenses, although he had a vice-presidential plane in which Jilly Rizzo occasionally travelled.

Sinatra was re-ascending his throne, and Agnew was being forced off his, as it turned out.

At no time did Sinatra hold back in his friendship for Agnew, although he tried to be discreet so as not to arouse further hostility.

It led to some curious manoeuvring. Sinatra and Agnew both got 'Splendid American Awards' from the Thomas A. Dooley Foundation at the Plaza Hotel in New York in March, but they were kept apart on the dais so as not to be noticeable together. (Sinatra was still a little 'hot' after the Maxine Cheshire incident and wouldn't be apprised for a couple of months that Nixon was going to make him a hero at the White House.)

Because they were kept apart on the dais, the newspapers called it a 'Strangers in the Night' meeting, a reference to Frank's then current hit song. Both the recipients were almost embarrassingly complimented by William Lederer, vice-president of the Dooley Foundation and author of *The Ugly American*.

'Sinatra—jeez, the things he's done, they're endless!' Lederer exclaimed. 'This is a man with a big heart.'

Thanking him, Sinatra said the award made him realize how little he'd done compared to what Dooley'd done, but he would be more helpful in the future—'I'll try, by God, I'll try.'

But Lederer was ecstatic about Agnew's model home life with his family. 'When they're home, the Agnews are merry, they're happy, and he plays the piano,' he said. A Secret Service man attached the vice-presidential seal to the front of the podium before Agnew spoke. Agnew's speech included praise of America's part in the Vietnam War. Sinatra kissed Mrs. Agnew, everybody applauded, and the vice-presidential party left the dais—Sinatra remained. This was deliberate so that they would not be photographed together; however, they met later.

Curiously, the concern in March was not what Sinatra

thought of the Vice-President, but what Agnew thought of Sinatra. Agnew's press secretary, Marsh Thompson, coolly said, 'That the Vice-President is here tonight suggests that he appreciates Mr. Sinatra.'

It was then that Sinatra, hungering for standing ovations and even headlines, needing that acclaim to get him over his insecurity, decided to unretire with the biggest unretirement in history. David Tebet, his good friend at NBC, vice-president in charge of talent, set up the 'retirement from retirement' for Sunday night, 18 November 1973—a one hour TV special with a black-tie on-camera audience. 'Ol' Blue Eyes Is Back' would be the theme.

As Sinatra resumed vocalizing to get back in shape for the show, his friend Agnew was getting deeper into trouble. Frank did not shirk in his loyalty or in his encouragement.

To suggestions that Agnew should quit, Sinatra shouted, 'Quit, shit! That would be an admission of guilt.'

Agnew told Sinatra of *sub-rosa* negotiations by which he could stave off criminal prosecution. Sinatra's friends say that Sinatra could not believe Agnew was guilty and gave the Vice-President a pep talk that inspired Agnew to go to a Republican women's convention and assure them that he would never resign.

'Sinatra really sold Ted the idea that he was innocent,' laughed one of Sinatra's admirers. 'He almost convinced him that he'd done nothing wrong. He almost got Agnew to blow the deal, and if he had, he'd have gone to the can. Frank was just too persuasive.'

Agnew's stunning resignation announcement that Wednesday afternoon, 10 October 1973, when the New York Mets, with Willie Mays in the line-up, were snatching the National League pennant from the Cincinnati Reds, didn't shock Sinatra. By then he knew it was coming.

Comedians leaped on it. 'Frank'll never make it to ambassador,' one of them said.

Mort Sahl was starring at the Shoreham in Washington. 'Sinatra and Agnew had a summit meeting out at Sinatra's house and decided on the proper policy,' Sahl said. 'They're all acting like Lincoln was just shot. It's not really that bad, you know. The deal for Agnew's light sentence was made in a motel room. That makes motel rooms have one more evil meaning. President Nixon is the captain of the *Titanic.*'

It was a sad time for Sinatra. He met Agnew in Chicago a few days later, along with W. Clement Stone, an insurance magnate and philanthropist, and discussed means of getting Agnew back on his feet. Frank mailed letters to many acquaintances asking them to donate $3,000 to Agnew.

One of the recipients, a liberal Democrat who showed me Sinatra's letter before throwing it away, said, 'That's a nice gesture—but he must be out of his mind!' He added, 'It looks to me like Sinatra went through his address file and sent one to everybody in it.'

Returning to his 'unretirement', Sinatra realized that he required assistance for his TV special from the press he claimed to hate. He needed publicity to assure an enormous audience and big ratings to delight the sponsors. But he couldn't resist blasting the papers.

In the *TV Guide* for 17–23 November 1973, which cover-storied his picture and his return, Frank suggested that it was the press that had hounded him into retirement.

> 'Being a public figure got to me,' he was quoted.
>
> People were always spiritually peeking in my windows. In retirement, it was worse than ever. Some of the picayune stuff would cease but there was always the press.
>
> I call them garbage collectors, the columnists without a conscience, the reporters who take longshots based on the idea that where there's smoke, there's fire. I'm blunt and honest. I could easily call them pimps and 'ho's'. [He presumably meant whores.] They'd sell their mother out. Most of them have no guts at all. Even if you get a retraction, it's always on page thirty-two.

Dwight Whitney, author of the article, wrote, 'There is no stopping him on the subject—I find myself wondering what would have happened if there were no press report to in a sense create the legend, no matter how imperfectly. Would there have been a "Washington Monument" of song? Frank obviously thinks so.

'He calls a lady columnist a dirty name, spits in the eye of the Press Establishment . . . and the more he does it, the more powerful he becomes.'

The TV special's publicity was more successful than the special itself from a ratings standpoint. There was a 'Second Coming' flavour to the show. Comedian Pat Henry wasn't quite joking when he asked the audience in the Burbank studio to greet Sinatra 'like he was the Pope'. Frank had added twenty violins to the orchestra to protect his voice, and he was in complete command. Pat Henry told some of his favourite Brooklyn jokes first. 'My Italian relatives invented acupuncture—but they did it with ice picks,' he said. 'I had an uncle who knew ahead of time the day he was going to die—the judge told him.'

Sinatra came from the wings, waved to friends in the black-tie audience, executed a couple of dance steps and began singing.

The show finished third in a three-horse race.

His 8.30–9.30 special collided with the movie *Hospital*, starring George C. Scott, on ABC. The movie walked away with a 44 share of the audience to Sinatra's 29, while Dinah Shore with her own special was attaining a 32 rating. To Sinatra worshippers, it was almost unbelievable that Sinatra would finish behind Dinah. Since a 30 share is the base they use to rate a show of success, his show, from a numbers standpoint, was a failure.

The show-business paper *Variety*, in totalling up the figures for the week, said that *Hospital* was fifth for the week, Dinah Shore twenty-third and Sinatra twenty-seventh. Curiously, NBC had delayed the Sinatra special a week to avoid competition of another movie, *Airport*, but was still submerged by the movie they thought they could beat. *Variety* said it was 'most unexpected, coming as it did against the highly ballyhooed return of Sinatra to the entertainment wars'.

However, the rest of the press, which he always claimed was unfair, almost unanimously rhapsodized over him personally.

TV columnist John J. O'Connor's headlined 1,000-word article took up a quarter of a page. 'Well, Ol' Blue Eyes did it. Frank Sinatra took an hour of television and turned it into the best popular-music special of the year,' he said.

> The arrogance, the contempt were gone. This was a mellower and more professionally mature Sinatra. A little older, a little heavier, he has let his youthful lankiness disappear completely; his neck seems on the verge of disappearing completely. . . .
>
> Sammy Davis, glimpsed for only a second or so, could be seen jumping up in his seat and clapping his hands.
>
> Sinatra was in control, and his instrument was music. The newspaper clippings became irrelevant. . . . The Sinatra special, expertly produced by Howard W. Koch and directed by Matty Passeta, was cleverly limited to two restrained production numbers. . . . The rest was music, undiluted and often startlingly moving. The big orchestra sounds were carefully managed by two conductors—Gordon Jenkins for the ballads, and Don Costa for the upbeat numbers. . . . The new material seems almost calculated to capture the new mellowness, the effective element of bitter-sweet maturity. . . . It's there, and it worked splendidly—for Sinatra, the songs and the audience. And in this case for television.

The New York *Daily News* critic Kay Gardella wrote, 'We thought we were through writing love letters to Frank Sinatra. Here we go again!'

He didn't wiggle or shake, he walked around the stage with the mike like he was born to be there, and once in a while he gave a hand instruction to the orchestra. He was heavier, and older, and looked tired and worn, and may have had bags under his eyes, but nobody really said anything very bad about him.

Though disappointed with the low ratings, Sinatra was pleased with the personal publicity and the excitement he had generated. He continued his 'unretirement' on a grand scale. He returned to Las Vegas to star at Caesar's Palace, the hotel that had been the scene of a pistol-waving incident. Las Vegas authorities had frankly told Sinatra he wasn't welcome in town. But now there was a different set of authorities and a different feeling. Las Vegas needed business, and Sinatra always brought in the big-rollers. He brought traffic into the casinos.

He cut the press list.

Leroy Aarons of the Washington *Post* wrote that he was ejected twice from the showroom at Caesars Palace on opening night. He said he was told 'Sinatra is upset with the *Post* for its articles on his friend Agnew and about Sinatra's alleged ties with the Mafia.'

Although there was an enormous celebrity turnout, hardly anybody mentioned in print that everybody was on the cuff—nobody paid. And that was about 1,100 people.

It had the flair of an old Hollywood première, with extravagantly dressed personalities striding past a gallery of about 300 onlookers in the casino and up the carpeted staircase to the showroom.

The celebrities were mostly in their fifties or older, some much older, like George Burns and Edgar Bergen. But there was also the younger set including Sally Struthers, Chad Everett and Leslie Uggams.

An old joke was repeated with new names: 'There are so many stars here tonight that if a bomb hit this place, the biggest names left in Show Business would be Alice Cooper and Pinky Lee.' Dolly Sinatra led the applause with her granddaughters Nancy and Tina, who was getting married the next day to Wes Farrell.

In the following weeks, Frank proved he was still the best and most tasteful song stylist, the biggest draw getting the biggest money—a thirty dollar minimum per person. In a few months that would go to forty dollars.

'You bet your ass Ol' Blue Eyes is back,' said a sign in the back.

Now Sinatra was in one of his elated moods and smiled tolerantly at the most pejorative remarks about him. Dean Martin opened the new MGM Grand Hotel in Las Vegas, coming onstage with a glass in his hand and a make-believe stumble in his step.

'Well, Ol' Red Eyes is back,' Dean grinned. He thanked Cary Grant for sending him a case of Fabergé men's perfume, adding, with a little skip, 'You know it ain't bad on the rocks.'

'I was talkin' the other day to the Dago,' Dean continued. 'We were sayin', "What's so great about a topless dancer? Once you've seen one, you've seen 'em both!" I said to Frank, "What's up?" and he said, "Oh nuthin'," and we just kept on like that. Ol' Frank's all right. All he ever wanted was a little house to lay his hat and a few close friends.' (A line borrowed from Dorothy Parker.)

'Frank was an unwanted child,' Dean said. 'Now he's wanted in about five states. But you have to give Frank credit. If you don't he'll bust up your joint. He had a black eye for a while, and they said it was accidental. Accidental, my ass. The fact is that I hit Frank in the eye myself. It's something I'd been wanting to do for twenty-five years. Hit him a pretty good shot, didn't I?'

Sinatra didn't even mind comedian Shecky Green saying 'Frank Sinatra saved my life one night. Five guys were beatin' me up in front of the Fontainebleau. After a while Frank said, "Okay, fellas, that's enough." '

Frank began manoeuvring to become more prestigious. He began courting some Big Names in other fields. He turned to the elite of the East Coast, where the blood was supposed to be bluer and the social nuances more subtle He wasn't astonished that they were happy to have him aboard.

He reaped reams of favourable publicity when he gave his Western friends, Rosalind Russell and Frederick Brisson, a twenty-fifth wedding anniversary—by plane from Los Angeles to New York and back—which cost him about $25,000. Everybody loved Roz . . . and what a generous gesture. Nobody accused Frank of having publicity in mind when he did it.

Frank believed he was growing now as a man and as a person; his character had begun to expand in the proper direction. He was no social leper, as some people in the Fourth Estate believed.

Frank wasn't a churchgoer, it was true. He wasn't evil, but he knew some evil people. He drank and ate with them, and he liked them. He'd never been convicted of anything shady or suspicious, he'd never been in jail. The worst you could say was that he hated the press and the cops.

Actually, he had good friends among the cops, one being veteran New York detective Arthur Schultheiss. He loved to reminisce about detective Johnny Broderick, who disposed of hoodlums by dumping them in garbage cans.

He was fond of a few journalists, among them Suzy, the society columnist, who incidentally was helpful to him in his aspirations to get a little higher in society.

The new Sinatra, the man with 'character', noted that Bennett Cerf was glad to bask in the brighter rays of Sinatra's spotlight. Cerf hoped to get Sinatra's autobiography in his own publishing shop some day, but his friendship was genuine.

Sinatra, in a big East River penthouse that he leased, became a gracious New York host. He was a connoisseur of wines, a man of parts; a slick, suave conversationalist who knew about Puccis, Guccis, yachts, stocks and bonds, the opera, Vietnam, Jaguars and how to get something at a considerably reduced price.

Roz Russell was impressed that he read history and Eric Hoffer. He had begun to collect French Impressionists and also got enthusiastic over Andrew Wyeth and Al Hirshfeld.

Sinatra became an absorber of information. He was an expert listener. He even got to understand algebra and smiled when one of his friends, discovering he was studying math, said, 'Say something in algebra'.

He never picked up any phony affectations. His talk was plain, frequently earthy, and filled with some slang that he himself created and popularized. Long ago he said, 'Hey, what's the scam?' using a word that referred to cheating at gambling. Then came 'It's a gas' or 'gasser'. He and Jackie Gleason made everybody understand, 'Get the broad with the big Charlies.' Along came 'bird', referring to the pelvic section, and 'ring-a-ding-ding'.

The Sinatra that had captured the Eastern elite suddenly found himself a force for good. Charity ladies and ambitious fund-raisers rushed to invite him to be the guest of honour at dinners and recipient of a new plaque. The speakers said he was one of the most generous men in the world.

Somebody was always remembering the time when Frank converted his plane into a hospital jet to fly non-stop to Barbados with a medical staff to treat Claudette Colbert's stricken husband, the late Dr. Joel Pressmen. People said that was class, and that was a term Frank liked. To have class was to have respect, as his father had told him.

In recognition of Sinatra being back and being Number 1, the American Film Institute picked him to be host at its March 1974 salute to Jimmy Cagney. The occasion was remarkable because there was a fight with photographers that he wasn't in.

The table seating list for that spectacular event at the Century Plaza Hotel was half an inch thick. 'There's not a rental limousine left in Beverly Hills tonight,' Irving Mansfield remarked to Howard Koch.

When the programme opened, nearly everybody was feeling the after-effects of the cocktail party and the wine. Frank came on a little breathily: 'Thank you, James Francis Cagney lovers everywhere.'

He said he had once walked up behind Cagney and snarled, 'You dirty rat.'

'He never turned around,' Frank said. 'He said, "Francis, that's the worst imitation anybody ever did." '

Frank said he'd been doing imitations of this 'feisty little Irishman' since 1938. He was singing in little roadside joints and he got a lot of tips from customers for impersonating Cagney.

'I drove my mother crazy doing my impression of him in *Public Enemy*. I would ring the doorbell and fall forward on my face. Come to think of it, I still do a lot of that today.'

Sinatra introduced Bob Hope who said, 'Blue Eyes came out of retirement. He found out that Caesars Palace paid better than social security.'

'Will everybody who believes in love clap hands for Mrs. James Cagney?' Sinatra asked, with an aside that, 'My own life hasn't worked out quite that way.'

He brought in the Italian angle good-humouredly when he introduced Cicely Tyson, the black star. 'Cicely?' he said. 'I didn't know she was Italian.'

Frank's conduct was impeccable, compared to the others. John Lennon was there, after a squabble at the Troubadour, where he had heckled the Smothers Brothers and been thrown out. Lennon was accused of striking a woman photographer in the eye when she tried to take his picture.

During the testimonial to Cagney, Jack Lemmon got very lengthy and rambling in his remarks. From the back, director Sam Peckinpah shouted out to him that the audience didn't want to hear him—but Cagney. The crowd booed Peckinpah. Sinatra was in the wings and took no part in this.

After the dinner, Peckinpah got into an argument with a bartender over a cheque and was hustled out by the hotel security guards, one of whom handcuffed a photographer who'd been taking pictures of Peckinpah in difficulty.

Here was an entire evening of stars and celebrities having trouble with photographers and Frank Sinatra wasn't even involved for a minute. He wasn't even nearby!

Surely he was on his best behaviour.

But back to work! Sinatra rediscovered concerts and became enormously successful touring the country, playing to crowds in the 40,000 neighbourhood. His worshippers had the same religious fervour of the Judy Garland cultists who had run up onstage at Carnegie Hall, thrown flowers at her feet and behaved as though they were at a revival meeting.

Hundreds of fans phoned for seats, stood in line at the box office for their tickets, then pushed, shoved and even fought to get a look at their hero when he strode by in person with his bodyguards.

Young entrepreneur Jerry Weintraub, who had had great success taking Elvis Presley on concerts, made it seem that Sinatra had risen from the tomb as he booked him for Carnegie Hall, 8 April 1974.

Sinatra had returned to the throne, and now he meant to hold it.

This phase of his second comeback was more successful than the 'Ol' Blue Eyes Is Back' TV show because there were no ratings, no competition.

Press-agented as a great fund-raising benefit for the Variety Clubs International, the concert was a sell-out with seats scaled at $125 downward, and reportedly scalped at $1,000.

'Frank Sinatra was a religious event,' wrote Jan Hodenfield in the New York *Post*. 'If you were a believer, he kept the faith as Chairman of the Board of romantic balladeers. If you were not, he was a somewhat portly 58-year-old who had trouble staying on key.'

'He forgot the lyrics a couple of times, even in his familiar "My Way", but he picked them up again with the comment, "You probably don't know them either," ' wrote Mary Campbell of the Associated Press.

Reading the reviews with Barbara Marx later in his Waldorf suite, Sinatra enjoyed the near hysteria of the people from the papers who obviously dug him.

A REFRESHED SINATRA WHAMS $100-TOP CARNEGIE HALL CONCERT

reported *Variety*'s Robert J. Landry. 'He did everything right . . . it was a phenomenon, a ritual, a mob ceremony. They shook, yelled, stomped, clapped together, stood up at least five times.'

Frank 'retched' at the name of columnist Rona Barrett, said she was 'almost as beautiful' as Barbara Walters, and added 'Yuck'. He also sneered at Eric Sevareid and Ed Newman—and his followers, not comprehending what that was all about, screamed more encouragement anyway. Sinatra looked trim, and rested, and sexier, one woman said, than when he was young, thin and so pimply that she closed her eyes when he sang.

Frank had told them, 'This is the second time I've sung since coming out of retirement. The first time was at the White House, and when I left, everybody sang.'

Only Pat Henry's warm-up stories—about Californians urinating in their swimming pools—got bad reviews in New York. Barbara Walters said she couldn't imagine why Frank was mad at her. She was the daughter of nightclub owner Lou Walters, who gave Frank work at the old Latin Quarter when he needed it.

The lean Sinatra face was now round and puffy, and he was heavyset. He at one point asked conductor Peter Duchin, 'Where the hell am I?' After holding one note all the way to the end, he groaned, 'I think I hurt myself.'

Working on his 'society' image, Sinatra gave a party at 21 after the show, which was attended by Mayor Beame and wife, Truman Capote, Arlene Francis and Martin Gabel—also Jilly Rizzo and Leo Durocher. *Women's Wear Daily* snidely called Sinatra's show his 'monthly comeback'. Cher wore a 'black Cleopatra wig and fire-engine red nails with baby blue decals'. Bette Midler found the concert 'nice', and Christina Ford cooed, 'He was fantastico'.

Women's Wear Daily suggested that the producers were guilty of a publicity stunt in presenting two surprised women behind the police blockade with $150 gift tickets. Bodyguards or security officers cleared a path for Frank, who was kind and patient, accepted compliments graciously and left the party about two in the morning.

People like Toots Shor were surprised that Frank remembered them and sent tickets.

Basking in that success, Frank went for three straight nights to the Nassau Coliseum at Uniondale, Long Island, playing to a less dressy crowd that totalled 40,000 . . . 'like cat's eyes peering down at the pudgy figure in the centre of the stage'.

Another triumph! 'The charm and magic never left. It was easy to forget the arrogance and the temper tantrums,' wrote Patricia O'Haire in the *Daily News*. He was singing to his people. 'They're much like him, getting heavier, smoking too much and drinking too much, but for a couple of hours they could remember when he was young. He brought it back.'

The thirteen-concert tour closing 27 April at Chicago Stadium played to a total of 197,757, according to entrepreneur Jerry Weintraub, and only the Atlanta date at the Omni Hall was a disappointment. The managers never mentioned it, but about 3,000 unsold seats there were masked over by black tape so as not to be noticed.

The reviewer for the Atlanta *Journal and Constitution*, Scott Cain, was enthralled: 'The star was in remarkably good voice. . . . Virtually every number was met with thunderous applause. . . . He declined to take credit for himself. "That's a beautiful song," he frequently remarked, invariably citing the composer and very often the arranger. He looks broader in the shoulders and has a larger chest than people generally suppose. He appears to radiate good health.'

However, two old pros in the reviewing profession turned in extremely sour notices. One was columnist George Frazier of Boston, by coincidence the first to call attention to Sinatra when Frank was starting his career and Frazier was entertainment editor of *Life*. Frazier's column in the *Boston Globe*, headlined

I STAND BY BABS WALTERS,

was hysterical.

Frazier started being mad at Sinatra for allowing Peter Duchin to lead his band. To Frazier, this was worse than 'converting a concert hall or a nightclub floor into a soap box from which he spewed indignities upon anyone who failed to kiss his ring'.

Frazier wrote,

> Hey, Frankie, whatsa matter—Barbara Walters got your goat? Hey Sinatra, you're a punk! I don't happen to be secretary-treasurer of a Barbara Walters fan club, but thank God, the reasons I dislike her aren't like yours, the product of a venomous mind.
>
> You wanna know something, Frankie, you tinhorn? Barbara Walters may have her faults, but she's something you've never been—she's a pro. Barbara Walters doesn't have to go around with bodyguards. The trouble with you, Frank, is you got no style. All your life you wanted to be a big man, but the wrong kind of big man. Look, Sinatra, Momo Giancana is just another version of Haldeman, and Agnew makes three. You're a sad case, Frankie, I think you're the best male vocalist who ever lived, but I also think you're a miserable failure as a human being.
>
> I'll go to hear you in Providence, because I'm crazy about the way you sing. But watch it, baby. Sing the song, Frankie, and for God's sake, sit down.

Frank got another blast from the late pro critic Ralph J. Gleason, in *Rolling Stone*, 6 June 1974. Gleason's article,

FRANK: THEN & NOW,

was savage, concerning what happened to his one-time hero.

Remember when he 'had the sound and the sliding grace of a good cellist and he phrased like a horn player', Gleason said:

> It is simply weird now to see him all glossed up like a wax dummy, with that rug on his head looking silly, and the onstage movement, which used to be panther-tense, now a self-conscious hoodlum bustle. It's even odder to see him with the bodyguards and hear all the gossip about his coterie of friends and their capers in this club or that hotel or that gambling joint . . . there are those of us who still dig his voice . . . but for whom Ol' Blue Eyes is a drag that Frankie never was.
>
> Today, he's swapped Charlie Lucky and the other mobsters for Spiro Agnew and Ronald Reagan and who is to measure the difference? All I know is that what seemed a youthful bravado 25 years ago seems like angry perversity now. You used to think of him as a guy who could be Robin Hood, who would help some poor cat who was in real need. Today the guys he helps are millionaires and he behaves, even if only half the print is true, like an arrogant despot with a court of sychophants Uncle Tomming their asses off.

Gleason contended that

> somewhere along the line he stopped believing in the art he had. . . . Now he can't spend his money in one lifetime even at his pace. His possible appearance on a TV show is the occasion for bodyguards and hush-hush phone calls and big security plans and a blanket of secrecy. Why? So the millions of Sinatra fans won't mob him and tear him to bits? So he won't be kidnapped and held for ransom?
>
> You know I swear to God I don't think anybody but he and those clowns on his payroll really think this panoply of power is necessary. For Frank Sinatra, whose voice made him the friend of millions of Americans, whose films made him even greater, to carry on like a

> Caribbean dictator holding back history with bodyguards and a secret police, is simply obscene.
>
> The voice is good today but I don't believe, any more, that he is one of us. He's one of *them* now, singing from the other side of the street, and I guess he doesn't have a whiff of how power-mad and totalitarian it all seems, those bodyguards and the Rat Pack and all that egocentric trivia that has nothing to do with music.
>
> And he was once a thorough musician, right down to his toes. But then he didn't wear a rug, and I have a feeling he wouldn't have. All that came later when, in truth, he had lost a lot more than his hair.

Paul Hendrickson of the same publication, who covered parts of the concert tour, evaluated it differently.

('Ol' Blue Eyes is Back', the album, had reached Number 13 at its best and been on *Billboard*'s list for twenty-two weeks. That was damned good or damned bad. It wasn't very high for the old Sinatra, but it was pretty high for the new old Sinatra.)

Hendrickson wrote:

> He is out there crooning to America once more, strutting around in crossbeams of light in an orange-sherbet cashmere sweater, stirring the ashes that nearly went dead. . . .
>
> Somehow it all begins to work on me, too. By the time the tour hits Chicago, the Voice is making me—yes—tingle. It is almost as if this haunting, beautiful voice coming at us from the stage has a life of its own. As if it doesn't depend at all on earthly concerns like time or change or even the greying thickened body it inhabits. Sinatra never sings a song quite the same way. And for that, he truly can be called the Chairman of the Board.

Hendrickson was impressed with the limousines and the private jet that got Sinatra back every night to the Waldorf before the late movie was over. He arrived for his concerts less than an hour before curtain time and was sitting in the plane waiting to take off while they were still yelling for more encores in the auditorium. He had a steak at two in the morning.

'The sense of raw power is frightening,' said Hendrickson.

His last two albums had sold only 63,500 copies and 35,000 copies compared with 160,000 he sold not so long ago. But the crowds, the crowds . . . Sinatra had the people, the fans; oldsters, maybe, but he had enough to fill nearly all those seats. *Nearly* all.

The tour could only be regarded as an enormous personal triumph.

One of Hollywood's stand-out achievers, Mike Frankovich, the producer and long-time studio executive, was eloquent on the subject. As head of Variety Clubs International, he had first proposed the tour as a fund-raiser for children to attorney Rudin.

'There's no reason for me to go out on a limb for Frank,' Frankovich said, 'but that was a great thing he did. For the first show at Carnegie Hall, Frank gave everything to the kids and paid all expenses. On six numbers he got standing ovations. He's anxious to do another tour next year. I'm going to put a Frank Sinatra wing on our hospital in Palm Springs. Listen,' Frankovich said, in confidential tones, 'nobody knows how many people Frank's taking care of, besides.'

Sinatra had been punctilious about making appearances. Close students of Sinatra would have been willing to bet that he would have cancelled an occasional concert. There are some who believe his occasional cancellations are planned to contribute to the image of Sinatra the unpredictable. But Frank seldom fails to make a prestigious appearance.

Coming up was the annual SHARE 'Boom Town' party in Los Angeles in May, a hard-drinking evening when the wives of picture stars try to dance like Rockettes. The party was to surpass all others. First Sammy Davis, Jr., pulled out after an argument with his wife Altovise. On Saturday afternoon, Sinatra rehearsed a dozen songs—then his throat started closing up. He phoned a doctor, who said he must not sing that night.

'Sinatra can't be here tonight, he's posing for a stamp,' Johnny Carson, the emcee, announced.

'Frank found out it was a national holiday—Luciano's birthday,' Steve Lawrence said.

Going back to Caesar's Palace in June 1974, Frank was a grandfather and was properly proud. Father Bob Perrella, 'the show business priest', broke the news to me ahead of the wire services because he was on the phone with Dolly Sinatra, who, after all, had been a midwife and was watching over Nancy, Jr. The priest phoned me that Nancy, Jr., and TV director Hugh Lambert had their first child and Frank's first grandchild late in May—Angela Jennifer, eight pounds, fourteen ounces. Father Bob got a call to fly out and christen the baby.

In one of his best moods, Sinatra toasted his granddaughter expansively on opening night. 'I wish her one hundred times the fun I've had and one hundred times as many guys as I've had broads,' he said. The crowd liked that, and he said, 'This audience is so good I may show up tomorrow night.' Tossing in another family touch, he said, 'My mother says to me when I leave on a trip, "Good-bye, Frankie"—she always calls me Frankie—"Have a nice trip, Frankie, and before you go, could you leave me a stack of twenties?" '

He got a rare bad review from *Variety*'s Bill Willard, who said his voice was gravelly and 'he was forced to bellow at times'. He said Sinatra told a tasteless joke that was 'very, very sickish'.—'The Polacks are deboning the coloured people and using them for wet suits.' Willard said some of the blacks with Sinatra, Ella Fitzgerald and Count Basie, 'heard it with frozen faces'. Willard added, 'He is one performer who seemingly can do no wrong, in voice or not.'

The opening was a letdown for anybody expecting many Big Name guests there as guests, 'on freebies'. Columnist Jim Bacon said, 'It was the most quiet opening he has ever had. No party, no chartered planeload of pals flown in. In fact, Frank didn't buy up his customary thirty ringside tables. And when the few pals he did invite went backstage, Frank was already gone. He walks off the stage in his tuxedo, jumps in his limousine and within an hour is back home in Palm Springs. This is Frank. If he were any different, he would be Rock Hudson.'

Sinatra was in his thinking mood. He was the Rodin of Show Biz. Agnew was out, Nixon was hanging on by his fingernails. If he had ever dreamed of being ambassador—and he probably had—that was out forever. There was no fun in going to Washington any more. Was he going to marry Barbara Marx? everybody was asking. Frank kept them guessing—they quarrelled . . . they got back together. He didn't need marriage. Somebody said she was like a mother to him at times. But he already had a mother. Frank Sinatra, the swingers' swinger, was growing moralistic as he became an ageing Casanova. He had even been observed shaking his head in disapproval about some of Sammy Davis, Jr.'s, rumoured social activities.

IT WAS A VERY BAD YEAR

In July 1974, Sinatra contributed to the culture of America by putting the words *hookers* and *pimps* on the front pages.

He has been called a chameleon—a lizard that changes colours. But he didn't change his colour; he performed strictly according to form when he flew to Australia in his jet with girlfriend Barbara Marx, lawyer Rudin and Jilly Rizzo in the most disastrous trip of his career.

He had high hopes for making a lot of money and new friends for 'Ol' Blue Eyes' when he arrived for a concert tour.

He remembered visiting Australia sixteen years before, in 1959, when he was thinner and hairier. The press at that time persisted in chasing him and quizzing him about a reconciliation with his ex-wife Ava Gardner, who was filming *On the Beach* there.

'You slobs,' he had snarled at them then, while protected by some 'tough-looking characters' the papers claimed were bodyguards. 'If I see you again, you'll never forget it. They'll find you in the gutter.'

Now on his return in 1974, there was sort of a replay of 1959, but bigger, better and more insane. It was his most damaging public relations misadventure since he punched columnist Lee Mortimer in 1947. Sinatra didn't escape without some scars.

His 'goon squad' triggered the trouble. Sinatra insisted it was a security patrol supplied by the local entrepreneurs.

Sinatra had never anticipated difficulty. He had even told publicist Jim Mahoney he wouldn't be needed on the trip. Things would be quiet Down Under. Jim was going to Scotland to vacation and play golf.

'See you when we both get back.'

It all began when a woman TV reporter tried to ask Sinatra, *en route* to a rehearsal in Melbourne, for an interview. In America it wouldn't have happened because it's known that he doesn't give interviews.

Suddenly there was a skirmish between guards, reporters and photographers. The Melbourne *Age*, that city's largest morning paper, reported that Sinatra's muscular protectors pushed photographers out of the way, then tied the cord of a television camera around a cameraman's neck.

The angry 'Show Biz King' left the rehearsal and stepped into a maroon Rolls-Royce. Later he strode from the car into a backdoor lift to get to his hotel suite, from which he ascended to new heights, or depths, in name-calling.

'Bums, parasites, hookers and pimps' were the words with which he lashed the Australian press people. He was especially violent about the women reporters.

'They are the hookers of the press,' he said. 'Need I explain to you? I might offer them a buck and a half. I once paid a broad in Washington two dollars. I overpaid her, I found out. She didn't even bathe. Most of them don't.'

The Australians are a proud and gutsy people who won't be treated like bushmen and primitives. They would not let their women be called whores or be insulted as Maxine Cheshire was.

'Who the hell does this man Sinatra think he is?' demanded Melville Wren, leader of the Labour Party in New South Wales. The whole country got mad at Sinatra, who issued new insulting remarks about the 'hookers'.

There was a half-page picture of one of the security guards scuffling with a TV cameraman in Melbourne. The guard's extended hand or fist was shooting out at the camera.

The Transport Workers' Union announced it would boycott Sinatra and would not service his private jet. It demanded that he apologize for his remarks.

'Apologize?' Sinatra in turn demanded that the Australian Journalists Association apologize to him 'within fifteen minutes', or he would leave the country. The president of the Labour Party, Bob Hawke, also head of the Australian Council of Trade Unions, laughed raucously at that threat, declaring that Sinatra 'will never get out of the country unless he apologizes' because no union would participate in fuelling his plane. Sinatra flew from Melbourne to Sydney where he had three concerts scheduled, but because of the row with the unions, he cancelled them.

'Mr. Sinatra will not only not apologize to the press, but he demands they apologize to him for the fifteen years of shit he has taken from the world press,' said a remarkable statement attributed to him, although attorney Rudin said it was never authorized and never actually said.

As is usual with Sinatra, the facts were distorted and exaggerated. It was reported, and printed, that room service was refused Sinatra and his entourage of twenty at the Southern Cross Hotel in Melbourne by the waiters' union.

Actually, the refusal of room service never took place. But the private Gulfstream Mark II jet was at the Sydney airport almost without fuel. The $650,000 tour had been scuttled. Something strategic had to be done and lawyer Rudin was trying to evolve a face-saving peace.

A four-hour peace conference was held to appease the angry Aussies and the frantic Frankie. Labour leader Bob Hawke flew from Melbourne to Sydney for the meeting in Sinatra's Presidential Suite in the new Boulevard Hotel.

'Mr. Sinatra regretted the incidents which have been blown out of proportion,' Rudin said. 'We believe he has nothing to apologize for. Mr. Sinatra was mistaken when he came, thinking Australia was a true, free country.'

The peace negotiations were not graced by the presence of 'Ol' Blue Eyes', who was asleep in an adjoining room. They issued a joint statement, a sort of apology, which said, 'Frank Sinatra did not intend any general reflection on the moral character of the working members of the Australian media.

'He, of course, reserves the right to comment on the quality of the professional performance of those working members of the media who he believes are subject to criticism on professional grounds, just as he acknowledges their right in this respect to his professional performance.'

But the show would go on! Sinatra would do a big free TV show that the whole country could see, in addition to completing the scheduled concerts that had been cancelled.

'Without Henry Kissinger's intervention,' one paper said, 'peace had been made.'

'This is an honourable settlement for both sides,' Rudin said.

'The unions recognize the unique international status of Frank Sinatra and his understandable desire to be protected from an uninhibited exposure to the media,' the statement said. 'It is the desire of all concerned that the Australian people can now enjoy . . . the remainder of Frank Sinatra's scheduled programme in this country.'

Sinatra regretted any physical injury 'suffered by patrons as a result of attempts to ensure his personal safety', Rudin said. The joint statement also said that what Sinatra 'might have regarded as an intrusion, was no more than a reflection of their [the unions'] desire to keep the Australian public informed about the presence and activities of this celebrity, and they express their regrets for any physical inconvenience that might have been caused by this enthusiasm.'

The papers played up the peace, and there were still more pictures—in fact, there were quite a lot of pictures, considering that the whole quarrel was about Frank not allowing any pictures.

One picture was of Frank in dark glasses. Another picture showed Barbara Marx in dark glasses.

Sinatra enjoys sitting on a stool and making a speech, and along about the middle of his concert in Melbourne, with a packed house listening attentively, he again attacked the press. Holding a cup of tea, he spoke out bitterly: 'We've been having a marvellous time being chased around the country,' he said. 'I think it's worth mentioning because it's been so idiotic and ridiculous what's been happening. We came all this way to Australia because I chose to come back here and because I haven't been here in a long time and I wanted to come back.

'I like coming here and I like the people. I love your attitude, I love the booze and the beer and everything else. I like the way the country's going and it's a swinging place.

'So we come here and what happens? Gotta run all day long because of the parasites who chased us, with automobiles. It's dangerous, it could cause an accident, they won't quit, they wonder why I won't talk to them. I won't drink their water, let alone not talk to them.

'If there are any of you press folks in the audience, please quote me properly. One idiot gave me a call and wanted to know what I had for breakfast. What the hell does he care what I had for breakfast. I was about to tell him what I did *after* breakfast.

'Boy, oh boy, they're murder. They've got a name in the States for their counterparts—they call them parasites because they take and take and take and never give, absolutely never give.

'I don't care what you think about anybody, of any press in the world. I say they're bums and they're always going to be bums. There are a few exceptions to the rule, some good editorial writers who don't go out in the street and chase people around.

'The press of the world never made a star who was untalented nor did they ever hurt any artist who was talented.

'So we who have god-given talent say the hell with them, it doesn't make any difference. What I see has happened since I was here, sixteen years ago, the type of news they print in this town has shocked me.

'It's old-fashioned. It was done in America and England twenty years ago, and they're catching up now with the scandal sheets. You use them to train your dog and your parrot. It's the best thing to do with it—or set fire to one of their cars.'

The audience didn't know what to make of this philippic and some of the members applauded doubtfully. But those under attack responded.

Columnist Roger Bush in his column in the Sydney *Sun* said.

STOP SINGING THE BLUES, FRANK!

Mr. S, how lonely you must be. How terrifying it is for you to go to bed each night surrounded by goons, afraid that somebody might possibly see you as you are. I am sorry for you, Mr. S.

The man who is afraid of others is invariably afraid of himself. The man who cannot like others obviously cannot like himself. The man who thinks he made it all by himself is nothing but a fool. So go home, my son, hide in your Hollywood palace. Trump up charges against those who looked for your coming.

Remember with humility that the greatest of all men came through a stable and rode not in a white Rolls-Royce but on an ass. . . .

Sinatra had some defenders. The Sydney *Morning Herald* editorialized that he should be free to express his opinion. 'All men—and that includes bad-tempered singers—have the right to speak their piece, even if their opinions are considered unreasonable, unpopular, stupid or offensive,' it said.

There were some press people who took the whole Australian fiasco as comedy. One was Lenore Nicklin, who wrote in the *Morning Herald* that 'Seventy of us parasites, bums and unwashed hookers brushed up as best we could for a press conference given by Mr. Frank Sinatra's lawyer, Mr. Milton A. Rudin.'

[Rudin] said he didn't want to lecture the press then proceeded to do so. . . . [Danny O'Donovan, one of the tour promoters] contributed a number of sentences which mostly began with 'At this point in time.'

Mr. Rudin gave the reporters a little lecture on their need for improvement and reminded us again that Mr. Sinatra had no obligation to speak to the press, and how both he and Mr. Sinatra had decided most of us were beyond redemption. 'I'd like to believe this is not Fascist Spain or Germany in Hitler's time,' Mr. Rudin said.

With an expression of considerable hurt, Mr. O'Donovan contributed the story of how during the fracas in Melbourne, 'cameras were being swung at people including myself'. Incidentally, Mr. Sinatra was kicked accidentally or otherwise on entering the Southern Cross and he took it like he takes everything else.

At Sinatra's next concert, he pictured himself as a defender of the freedom of expression. Everybody must fight censorship, he maintained.

'Whether I am right or wrong, or whether they were right or wrong, the fact remains that the main issue was that they tried to keep me from saying what I thought, and I think that's what we've got to fight all the time. I wouldn't consider censorship for all the tea in China.'

In the end, the two sold-out Melbourne concerts and three sold-out Sydney concerts comprised the biggest box office gross in history in Australia, and the television audience was the largest for a live concert in that country.

Sinatra could also enjoy the fact that when he made peace with the trade unions, the newspapers considered it equal in news value that day with the swearing in of Sir John Kerr as new Governor-General in Canberra, with a twenty-one-gun salute and 'God Save the Queen'. The two events filled the front pages—half and half.

One of Frank's final gestures was to pose for a photograph with Prime Minister Gough Whitlam. Frank insisted it not be taken by a commercial photographer. That was a bit much for some Australian papers, who refused to print it. None the less, the picture of the triumphant, but somewhat portly and puffy Sinatra smiling at the Prime Minister was printed around the world.

Both Sinatra and Rudin expounded upon the idea that Sinatra had the right to criticize reporters and critics just as they criticized him. This wasn't new, but was, curiously, a revival of Al Jolson's belief that he had a right to punch members of the press. Jolson, the Sinatra of his day, had once stood up at a fight night in Los Angeles and swung at Walter Winchell, who'd written something he didn't like.

Jolson missed, the only punch that landed in that famous battle was scored by Winchell's wife, June. She took off her shoe and hit Jolson on the head with it. Madcap actress Sylvia Miles objected to some criticism by John Simon in *New York* magazine, took a plate of food from a buffet table and poured it on his head.

Sinatra, of course, had been acting out the same dogma when he slugged Lee Mortimer, and now in Australia he had been restating 'Sinatra's Law' vocally instead of fistically.

Many American press people regretted that the Aussies didn't stand their ground more firmly against Sinatra's remarks about 'the hookers of the press'. The week-long battle was gag-fodder for the comedians.

Don Rickles told Bob Hope, 'Frank just called me—he's declared war on Australia.'

Hope said, 'You know why those Aussie labour leaders gave in? I think one of them found a kangaroo head on his pillow.' (This was a reference to the book and movie *The Godfather*, wherein a big movie producer, who won't give a film role to a Mafia-backed singer, finds the head of his favourite racehorse in his bed.)

Bob Hope also said, 'Frank spoke about "buck-and-a-half hookers". What a memory *he* has!'

It was almost eerie, or spooky, some of his friends said of Frank's constant hammering at the press. It was suicidal to his popularity; why did he continue it? Because he felt he was justified in his attacks, and as he put it, 'I'm not panderin' to a bunch of old bags just to get on the good side of them.' He felt he was being the man of principle, and it was the press people who were selling out. From a psychiatrist's viewpoint, it was deeper. Sinatra the masochist was driving himself on to a professional hara-kiri that would stop just short of applying the blade to rip out his bowels.

Sinatra the parent arranged for Nancy, Jr., and Frank, Jr., to appear with him at Harrah's Lake Tahoe in September 1974, and the thing wrong with that package was Sinatra the parent. *Variety* pointed this out succinctly. The show 'was marred by some hisses, catcalls and boos as Sinatra again lambasted the press, this time apologizing to hookers for comparing them to newswomen, and calling the press "a bunch of goddamn liars",' *Variety* reported.

Besides regretting that he'd insulted prostitutes by putting them in the same sentence with women reporters, he reduced the hooker value of reporters from two dollars to fifty cents.

'The whole press tirade was unfortunate because it substantially cooled an enthusiastic audience eager to see Sinatra perform,' *Variety* said. 'He remains a top male vocal stylist. Would that he also retained his professionalism and sense of smooth showmanship, but that was sacrificed this time around to demeaning, scathing and at times crude humour and tirade.

'Had Sinatra not chosen to unburden himself, he would have kept the crowd at his feet, because that's where they were when he walked on stage. But a good deal of them were not, and remained seated, when he ended the show.'

It was one of his worst reviews in years, and it made him seethe.

Mort Sahl made it worse when he said, 'Frank got mad because I was making jokes about his billing with Nancy, Jr., and Frank, Jr., at Caesar's Palace. All I said was "Coming Attractions: The Daughter, The Son, the Father and the Holy Ghost".'

It was not comical to Sinatra, who sued him for $10,000 he claimed Sahl still owed him on an old $20,000 loan. 'I had the money to pay back the rest, but his lawyer would never take my phone call,' said Sahl. 'I guess he thought I wanted to borrow some more.'

'What's happening?' Sahl asked. 'You can make jokes about the President, the Vice-President and the Supreme Court, but not Frank Sinatra?'

Some of the fights that Sinatra gets linked with are not of his doing, but because he's nearby, and famous, they become 'another Sinatra brawl'. Some of his followers are so worshipful that they actually want to beat up somebody to please him.

The big brawl that some people thought Sinatra would get smitten down for—one involving a battle in a Palm Springs men's room—finally came to trial in Los Angeles federal court, also in September 1974, and had a much different result than was generally expected.

In May 1973, assault and battery charges were filed

against Sinatra, Jilly Rizzo and two other Sinatra friends by Frank J. Weinstock, a thirty-six-year-old Salt Lake City insurance agent.

He brought a $2.5-million lawsuit, claiming that local authorities hadn't wanted to prosecute their probably most prominent citizen. The local authorities replied that they didn't have a prosecutable case because of the conflicting stories.

Weinstock claimed that Sinatra, Jilly Rizzo and another Sinatra friend, Jerry Armaniera, accosted him and beat him up in the men's room of the Trinidad Hotel in a row over some remarks purportedly made to Sinatra's girlfriend, Barbara Marx.

When the case came to trial, Sinatra didn't show up for it. He had, however, given depositions claiming to be innocent. He got off to a bad start by being late for the first date to give the deposition. His lawyer said he had trouble with his private plane. Opposing lawyers said he could have flown commercial planes like other people. (Sinatra hadn't been guilty of riding in a commercial plane for several years.)

Sinatra lawyers also asked that the press be barred from that proceeding. The court refused, but did agree to keep reporters out of the office of a San Francisco attorney, where the depositions were taken.

Weinstock took the stand to tell the story that had been long awaited by both friends and enemies of Sinatra. He declared that he and his wife Connie and two other couples had been sitting peacefully in the lounge when a Sinatra party of about a dozen came in.

A man from the Sinatra party came over and threatened him, Weinstock said, implying that the man was interested in his wife, and that he said, 'When the lady goes to the bathroom, you beat it or you're dead.'

Frank Rothman, Sinatra's attorney, contended, however, that Weinstock had approached Barbara Marx and said if she wished to go to the ladies' room he would be happy to accompany her.

When Weinstock's wife did go to the restroom, three or four men from the Sinatra table followed her, Weinstock said. He and his brother-in-law, Edward Fabian, went to the men's room, next door to the ladies' room, to watch out for Mrs. Weinstock and found themselves surrounded by three or four men, one of whom blocked the door so they couldn't leave.

'I was scared to death and wanted to get out,' Weinstock testified. He said that the man who'd threatened him hit him in the stomach and said, 'Have respect for the boss. If you don't want to get killed, shut up.' Sinatra by this time had come out of a toilet stall and, according to Weinstock, said 'There's the smart son of a bitch who was going to run off with my woman.' Weinstock denied making a play for Barbara Marx, but, he said, Sinatra hit him in the chest with the palm of his hand while the other men shoved him around saying, 'Respect the man, respect the man.'

Weinstock protested again that there was a mistake, he said, and then 'Sinatra took a step back, snapped his fingers and said, "Okay, boys, get him." ' Weinstock claimed that the men pummelled him about the chest, stomach and ribs and that when he was being assisted from the men's room by his brother-in-law, Jilly Rizzo hit him in the head three times.

Sinatra's deposition presented him as being rather remote from the whole vulgar incident. He insisted he did not hit Weinstock and claimed he never saw any fighting anywhere. 'I put my finger on his [Weinstock's] chest and told him to call me "Mr. Sinatra",' Sinatra said. One of the Sinatra witnesses testified that Weinstock had called Sinatra 'a Guinea bastard' and had said, 'You and your hoodlum friends think you own the whole world.'

The trial had some light moments. Weinstock's wife said her husband had become 'less lovable' and a worrisome insomniac since the altercation. The Sinatra camp said Weinstock hadn't acquired new medical bills and therefore hadn't been hurt. It produced a record of a divorce action started years before by Mrs. Weinstock, alleging that her husband beat her. Barbara Marx couldn't positively identify the man said to have insulted her. Weinstock's sister, Sally Fabian, said she was concerned over her brother getting mauled and had pleaded with Sinatra to stop the fight. She claimed she had said, 'Mr. Sinatra, you have made a terrible mistake,' and said that Sinatra had replied, 'Don't talk to me, Baby.'

The star witness at the trial, however, was the colourful Jilly Rizzo, the saloon-keeper and Sinatra intimate, who wore shaded pink glasses and spoke in double negatives.

He loudly and violently denied that he was Sinatra's bodyguard. He said he was just a long-time friend, and he was angry at alleged slurs on his Italian heritage.

'I don't protect no one,' the stocky, rough-talking witness said. 'He don't need no protection,' Jilly continued. 'He's man enough to stand up and defend himself in his own way like any man should.'

Rizzo did acknowledge that he slapped Weinstock, knocking him to the floor.

'He raised his hands at me and I've got glasses and one eye and no one is going to raise his hands to me and I slapped him,' Jilly said.

Jilly talked himself into trouble and talked Sinatra out of trouble. Weinstock failed to establish that Sinatra was responsible for the punching he got. Weinstock's brother-in-law, Fabian, testified that he could not substantiate that Sinatra said, 'Okay, boys, get him.' He said he'd been in the men's room and didn't hear such a remark.

The three-man, three-woman federal court jury deliberated six hours and on Friday, 13 September 1974, found both Sinatra and Jerry Armaniera not guilty of assault and battery. But it found Jilly Rizzo guilty.

It awarded Weinstock $1,000 in actual damages and $100,000 in punitive damages. It also declared that neither Armaniera nor Jilly was acting as an agent for Sinatra, which made Jilly solely responsible for payment of the damages.

The Sinatra camp, while jubilant that Frank had won, was stunned by the amount of the damages Jilly was ordered to pay. 'A hundred and one grand!' one of the crowd said. 'Jilly's punches are getting almost as valuable as Muhammad Ali's. For one slap—one hundred and one grand!'

Jilly's attorneys promptly filed for a new trial.

The Sinatra camp didn't really want a new trial, and Weinstock didn't either. They made a secret out-of-court settlement. One provision of the settlement was that neither side would discuss it.

I asked Weinstock's lawyer, Bruce Coke, in Salt Lake City if the settlement was for $5,000 as was reported.

'That is not correct,' he said. 'It is more than that. . . . I can't say for how much more.'

'Do you think there is any chance they will ever all get together and shake hands?' I asked.

'No,' he assured me. 'They never will.'

'Who paid the settlement? Sinatra or Jilly?'

'It was paid on a cheque from the lawyer. As far as we are concerned, Jilly paid it.'

Although Sinatra won that battle, the jibes from the press on other matters continued to pour in and hurt him.

One cartoonist who clearly didn't like him sketched him as a mass of wrinkles and lines under the eyes, smoking three cigarettes at a time, spilling ashes into a drink he held in front of him.

It was published that he had given up hair transplants and now had 300 toupees.

The Hollywood Women's Press Club went out of its way to give the Sour Apple Award ('for least co-operation') to Sinatra in December 1974. It hadn't bothered to give its denigration award to anybody since Jane Fonda had gotten out of line several years before. Sinatra was designated because, according to the ladies of the press, he 'called us fifty-cent hookers'.

The women tried to make light of it by having TV star Lily Tomlin appearing in a sketch as Santa Claus taking an imaginary phone call from a Mr. Sinatra.

'Will you speak to anyone?' she asked the purported Mr. Sinatra.

'He will speak to any two-bit hooker there,' was the reply.

'Mr. Sinatra,' Lily Tomlin said, 'they will not accept your call. Would you like to leave word?'

'Two words,' he answered.

'Sir,' she said back, 'what was that first word again?—*F* as in Frank? And a Merry Christmas to you.'

Sinatra declined to see anything funny about it and sent a letter to the president of the club, NEA columnist Joan Crosby, contending that the Sour Apple dishonour should have gone to film-makers who were purveying filth and un-Americanism on the screen.

Joan Crosby blasted back, claiming that 'every time he gets a hangnail it becomes news', and that Sinatra's trouble with the press was due 'to his inaccessibility and arrogance. Apparently because he's been hurt a couple of times, he's characterized all members of the press in one big lump. If they're gentlemen, they're bastards, and if they're ladies, they're hookers.'

Sinatra, she said, should discover that the trouble he was having with the press was in himself.

Frank was about as low in the public esteem now as he had been in the times when the press attacked him for leaving Nancy, Sr., for Ava Gardner. It distressed him to reach this depth again because, as 'King of Show Business' for years, he thought he was far above all this.

The downdraft news that was worse was the report that Sinatra 'bombed out in Las Vegas at Caesar's Palace'. While that was a slight exaggeration, the fact is that Sinatra, getting a forty-dollar-a-person minimum in January—a bad time of year for business—played to about 'a third of a house' on two nights. There were 400 customers in a 1,200-seat room.

He was suffering from the recession. And his price was too high. The same thing happened New Year's Eve. 'Frank Sinatra, at $100 a ticket, failed to completely sell out the Diplomat Hotel, Hollywood, Fla.', *Variety* reported. He was 'pricing himself out of the market'.

Sammy Davis also failed to sell out in a Las Vegas engagement. But then he wasn't the 'King'.

Frank continued to read bad news about the Sinatras.

TINA SINATRA FILES FOR DIVORCE—
BLAME FRANK.

After only a few months of marriage, Tina sued to divorce Wes Farrell, who was in the recording business. One of Tina's friends said she tried to remake Wes in her father's image and that he couldn't endure being constantly compared with Frank and always being found deficient. 'None of the women in the Sinatra clan can ever find a man to replace Frank.'

However, the couple reconciled happily and called off the divorce.

Sinatra acquaintances wondered about a chill that developed between Frank and his one-time business partner, Danny Schwartz. They had made a lot of money together, they had homes near each other on the golf course, but suddenly they weren't in and out of each other's houses. What had gone wrong? Nobody seemed to know. By autumn, 1975, all was evidently straightened out. 'Frank and I are super-friends,' Danny Schwartz said. 'When Frank retired, we sold our plane, and that led to a lot of rumours.'

There were rivers of booze to be drunk and a lot of lovin' to do, so Sinatra did not completely bog down in melancholia, even though things were worsening.

His passion for rather violent pranks was well known in Palm Springs and Las Vegas. He liked to toss ice cubes in the face of a pal. Some thought this was sadism; it was one of the games at Jilly's. He allowed his sense of humour to go its own way. The word got around again that Sinatra 'ought to change his image'.

He liked to send insulting telegrams. He feuded with Clark County (Nevada) District Attorney, and later City Commissioner, George Franklin. It went back to Sinatra's brawl at the Sands with Carl Cohen. Upon investigating the fight, Franklin as D.A. decided Sinatra was upset emotionally because he was breaking up with Mia Farrow, and took no action.

'They told me he would throw a drink down on a crap table just to amuse himself,' Franklin said. 'After ripping the jacks out of a switchboard, he would try to break down a door or set fire to his room. Nobody wished to sign a complaint. At the worst it would be malicious destruction.'

But Sinatra suspected Franklin of trying to keep him out of Las Vegas in that period and supported Roy Woofter, who beat Franklin. Franklin ran and lost again. Sinatra wired him: 'Good-bye,' and then on the second try: 'I am running out of money sending you good-bye wires. Suggest you settle down in a new business like maybe opening a penny-candy store. Good-bye.'

Sinatra could not quit while he was ahead. In this new troubled time, the autumn of 1974, he hopped on the Woofter bandwagon for re-election. He arranged an all-star show for Woofter. Las Vegans rejected Woofter. They seemed to resent Sinatra's intrusion and elected his opponent, George Holt. Now it was Franklin's turn to send a telegram. His wire to Sinatra said, 'For sale, one slightly used penny-candy store.'

The local political experts repeated, 'Sinatra's support is the kiss of death.'

Some of Frank's pranks were more cerebral. His close friend, 'Prince' Mike Romanoff, had died, and Frank could no longer mismail his shirts for special laundering in Beverly Hills. Mike would go into a fury if his shirts—and shorts—weren't laundered at a special laundry. Frank spoiled some of Mike's European trips by losing his laundry deliberately.

Sinatra admired the late actor Laurence Harvey, who would soon be dead of cancer but hadn't yet lost his sense of humour. A magazine writer doing an article on Harvey had assured him he could see it before publication.

'I'll shake him up,' Sinatra promised. He conspired with the writer to give Harvey a different version with startling 'revelations' about 'his father being a Communist' and other damaging statements. The author claimed he could not make any changes. Harvey was on the verge of seeing lawyers when he suddenly got suspicious that Sinatra had framed this as a trick.

Sinatra grinned and confessed.

One night in Palm Springs, Sinatra was the imperfect host. Seeming to be quite rude, he snapped at Roz Russell's husband, Freddie Brisson, who wanted a late snack. 'There'll be no night food. Lights out!'

Minutes later, there was Sinatra pushing a cart with cold cuts, cheese and drinks, serving them himself. Everybody had to eat—and tip the waiter. Another night he promised his guests a Mexican dinner. He flew them to the airport in a helicopter, boarded them on his jet and flew them to Acapulco. They returned next day full of tacos, tamales and tequila.

Away from the jokes and frivolity, Sinatra was deeply concerned about the change-your-image urgings and other discouragements as 1974 was swinging into 1975. He sank into one of his dark, vengeful moods. A lot of people didn't love him, or his work, any more. His records and albums didn't rate 'bullets' in the pop music magazines any more. He loved 'Send in the Clowns' (from *A Little Night Music*), which he had recorded, but many people told him they couldn't understand all the words. He told them, 'For Christ's sake, read the words, it's about a circus.'

The 'dirty sons of bitches' from the papers were picking on him. Besides being hurt by the slackening business in Las Vegas and Florida, he suffered and sizzled when he read a blast in the New York *Times* by Shaun Considine, saying that 'it may be time for both Sinatra and Peggy Lee to quit the bandstand'.

He'd been the 'Voice', the 'Crooner', the 'Has-Been'. He'd had it all—'the voice, the clarity, the phrasing. He also showed an impeccable choice in material and the sagacity to surround himself with the best arrangers-conductors. And equally important, Sinatra had the energy and the ego to survive the changes of the years.'

All that remains in his latest recordings is the ego, claimed Considine.

'On the up-tempo tunes he sings just for show, grunting and groaning in simulated passion, with a repertoire suited to his daughter Nancy. On the ballads, his voice is strained, his breathing labored. . . .'

Deeply sensitive about the smallest criticism, Sinatra was wounded by this barrage. While he tried to shrug it off with sulphuric language, he was mad. Some of his cronies became former cronies.

'Something serious has happened to Frank,' one of them said. 'He's got nothing in the world to be miffed at me about. I've only done him a thousand favours. And I can't get him on the phone. I hate to say it, but Rex Reed is right when he says something should be done about Frank Sinatra.

'Frank isn't as big as he used to be, you know. He's slipping bad. He's going to be making another comeback one of these days.'

The anvil chorus wouldn't let up on him. 'I believe he thinks he *is* the Pope,' one recently rejected friend said. They had been calling him the 'Pope', and he said, after one big standing ovation in Las Vegas, 'This audience doesn't fool me. You would have given the same ovation if Pope John or Pope Paul had walked onstage.'

He was cutting down—he laid off some people; he made some changes—did he need cash? Some critics were open, some spoke quietly. George Jessel said, 'I'm loyal, I love Sinatra. He lends me money.'

I asked him, 'Do you pay it back?'

Jessel said, 'Sometimes.' He added, 'He asks me to give him some lines for a speech or his act and then I get a note saying, "Forget that other thing," meaning the loan. Listen, the American people aren't crazy. Wherever he goes, they stand up for him. They don't do that for Tiny Tim.'

In beautiful Palm Springs, Sinatra is regarded as a kindly, benevolent neighbour, a force for good. They can't understand the brawls he gets into 'away from home'. A local family lost everything in a fire. Sinatra sent money for new furniture, with a warning, 'No publicity.' A playground was damaged. Told that $800 was needed, Sinatra said, 'Make it a thousand—no publicity.'

Lisle Shoemaker, executive editor of the *Desert Sun*, says, 'How many editors have a newsboy who throws three papers over Frank Sinatra's fence every day? When Sinatra has five guests, somebody calls and makes it eight papers. He wants everybody to have his own paper.'

Sinatra even has Chuck Scardina, the *Desert Sun* photographer, who's of Italian descent, as a friend. Sinatra helps him, at parties, to get right to the important people. As a promotion stunt, the *Desert Sun* asked Sinatra, who'd once photographed a Madison Square Garden fight for *Life* magazine, to take some pictures of Scardina. He agreed.

Sinatra greets Scardina, 'Hey, Paisan,' and beckons him to his side at nearly every function.

Despite this warm feeling for Sinatra in Palm Springs, some residents wish he'd 'calm down'. Some don't want to be near him, famous as he is, fearing trouble. 'If they see his car at a restaurant,' one person of prominence told me, 'they say "Let's go some place else". They don't want to face "getting involved".'

In his desire for privacy, Frank made another major decision of his life—to give up the compound. Although Frank Sinatra Drive was well hidden from the highway, everybody knew where it was. There were means of getting close to it from the Tamarisk Country Club grounds. He wanted even greater privacy and exclusivity.

First there were the rumours. 'He is going to move up to Idyllwild; he is going up higher, where it's cooler in the summer.' It became official with a for-sale ad in the *Wall Street Journal* in mid-December 1974:

FAMOUS STAR'S COMPOUND TAMARISK COUNTRY CLUB
RANCHO MIRAGE PALM SPRINGS

Situated on 2½ acres. Includes Main House Plus 5 Guest Houses. Completely Furnished. 12 Bedrooms in All! Separate Entertainment Area includes Projection Room and Theatre. Championship Tennis Ct. Jacuzzi Pools. Saunas! Servants Quarters. Heliport. Complete Security! Air Conditioned.

$1,750,000 . . . call Ed Kelley.
Mike Silverman and Associates.

Sinatra had been living behind the unpretentious-looking narrow white gate for six years. Gapers from all over the nation stared out of cars as they slowed down on Frank Sinatra Drive. But the gapers never got a glimpse of anything but the gate and the thicket of oleanders standing there like sentries.

His new place at Pinyon Crest was a surprising choice to some local residents because, in their opinion, it was less secluded than the compound.

Indeed, Will Thorne wrote in the Palm Springs *Press-Enterprise* that almost anybody could locate the new place:

It was eleven miles south of Palm Desert off State Highway 74, the address was 70-300 San Lorenzo, and the guest house and tennis courts sit near a road where normal traffic passes.

The new supposed hideaway was the former home of Bruce Odlum, the son of financier Floyd Odlum. The younger Odlum had shot himself over money problems. Sinatra immediately began making extensive and expensive improvements to bring it to the size of the compound with at least twelve bedrooms, twelve baths and a helicopter pad.

There was a suggestion of a medieval castle to the whole development—piles of grey rocks, twisted pine and live oak, and a beautiful view of the white desert down below. The grounds were about five acres, twice the size of the compound. Sinatra was not the only celebrity in the area. Red Skelton has not one, but three homes in nearby Spring Crest.

Suddenly work slowed down on the new hideaway; the compound was taken off the market. There was a recession. Hardly anybody had $1.7 million he didn't need.

The Sinatra compound remained Sinatra's. Offered $1 million, he loftily said, 'Were they kidding?' He would not yield his orange-oriented estate for a mere million. Frank surely was crazy about orange. He had special orange-coloured T-shirts for the guests. Roz Russell looked all right in orange, but Jilly?—and Leo Durocher?

Frank had several stand-up defenders and one was the remarkable Sammy Davis. Everywhere Sammy worked—whether it was at the Uris Theatre in New York, where he got $150,000 for two weeks, or at a benefit where he paid his own expenses—Sammy praised Sinatra.

'Let's sing some Sinatra songs,' he'd say. 'I do not genuflect when he walks into the room. Do I owe him a lot for the help he's given me? You bet your bird I do. He knocked on a lot of doors I couldn't get into. I would not be standing on this stage today if I hadn't had his help.'

Sammy laughed lightly and confessed during such a speech at the Uris that he had hoped that Sinatra, who was in New York at the time, would come in to see his show.

'I talked to him today,' Sammy said. 'I said, "Hey Frank, what's happenin'?" He said, "Sam, where you workin'?" I said, "Oh, I'm just doin' a little club date here at the Uris." Frank said, "I got to go to Chicago. See you back on the Coast." '

Frank knew Sammy was doing well and didn't need him. Sammy lifted his voice in 'I'll Never Smile Again', and the audience cheered.

'People say I idolize Frank,' Sammy said later. 'All right. I got a picture taken at the Capitol Theatre of Frank and my mother. He said to my mother, "I hope you know your son is going to be one of our biggest stars." Years later he walked over to my mother and said, "See, I told ya!" That makes up for all the other bullshit. When you need him, he's there.'

Sammy's loyalty to Sinatra inspired many jokes from comedians, like 'Sammy thinks he's the black Sinatra'. Milton Berle said, 'He is the Jewish Sinatra.'

THIRD COMEBACK OF A SUPERSTUD

Success compulsion seized Sinatra again and recharged his ego, giving him once more that old driven feeling. He hoped for new heights in personal popularity, for new acclaim for his singing, even for a new start in motion pictures. Approaching sixty, he attempted a third comeback.

The superstud of the superstars had a lot of work to do—and that interfered with his swinging. Appearance could be deceiving, but it surely looked like Sinatra had faded away, like an old soldier, into a one-woman Casanova, straying only rarely from the very patient Barbara Marx, whom her friends called the 'Sunshine Girl' because, as they said, she hadn't an enemy in the world—except herself. That's how nice she was. If Frank wanted to have a salami sandwich at 3.00 a.m., she wanted to have a salami sandwich at 3.00 a.m. If Frank wanted to go to Lake Tahoe alone, she wanted Frank to go to Lake Tahoe alone. If Frank didn't want to get married just yet . . . wait a minute! A woman could only go so far.

Love is vital to Sinatra—being loved by the world. He has to have it. He had it from the girls he had made happy. Scores of them remembered the occasion with a smile.

Somebody else had said it: 'There are just too many girls and so little time.'

He had seen them ready to scratch each other's eyes out to get into his bed, and he enjoyed seeing them manoeuvring for his body. Once he invited a slightly-known woman to a formal dinner party being given by a society lady. The woman didn't have a great wardrobe, but rounded up appropriate accessories from girlfriends, and as one said, 'was getting dressed for three weeks'.

Sinatra phoned her the day of the party.

'Bad news, Baby,' he said. 'I can't take you to the party. The hostess told me I can't bring anybody. I'm with her. She's my date tonight.'

The rejected woman wept, vowing her vengeance on the hostess, who had used the dinner as a device for getting a date with Sinatra.

Although he doesn't talk about his girlfriends, the list is impressive when totted up. I assigned myself to ask nearly every woman I interviewed if she'd dated Sinatra. Several spoke of him with a vague, dreamy smile. Lainie Kazan, who in her nightclub act recalled that she'd referred to herself as 'Lainie Levine, the walking sex machine', remembered meeting Frank in Miami Beach when he was filming *Lady in Cement* and starring at the Hotel Fontainebleau.

Finding that Lainie was singing next door at the Eden Roc, Sinatra invited her over, holding up his own show till she'd finished hers, then asked her, 'Why don't you come on the picture with me? We'll have some fun.' Raquel Welch was also in the cast and likewise received Sinatra's attention.

'He's a great talent and a great performer and a very delicious man,' asserted Lainie Kazan.

'And is that all you're going to tell me?' I asked Lainie.

'Listen, if anything happened, do you think I'd tell you?' Lainie replied.

The boudoir rating of Sinatra was Triple A—sensational. He was 'incredible in bed', ardent, gentle, yet strong—but not piggish. Infrequently there would be a complaint. One barracuda-type said he only wanted to 'ring-a-ding-ding' about three times a week, which to her was the same as being frigid.

He was, they said, irresistible once a woman turned him on. A blonde beauty named Joi Lansing, a health faddist who drank Tiger's Milk but died very young, found his ways peculiar. He truly helped her career, assisting her in getting movie and TV work.

'It took some explaining,' she said, 'when I told another man that I wanted to go over and see Mr. Sinatra for a couple of hours. He couldn't believe Mr. Sinatra's interest in me was purely platonic. As for Mr. Sinatra, he kept wanting to talk to me about his family.'

Shirley Van Dyke, a Hollywood actress whom he didn't know well, was found unconscious on her davenport after taking an overdose of sleeping pills and eventually explained she was 'sick and tired of being in love with Frank Sinatra'. Then thirty-two, she said she'd been in love with him since she met him while trying to sell an ad for *Billboard* magazine fourteen years before. She didn't boast of any contact with him, but said, 'Both my husbands got sick of my playing Sinatra records. He's the only one I ever really loved.' The shapely actress recovered.

Often the women talked, and of course some of them were bragging. He was generous with gifts, 'but he dumps girls, too, and when he dumps a girl, he gives her a nice cheque', one of them told me.

The bouncy little singer Jill Corey had a close friendship with Sinatra for about six years and willingly discussed it in 1975, some fifteen years later.

Sinatra's technique was simple and direct—and effective. Jill, then nineteen, was singing on Eddie Fisher's 'Coke Time' TV show and had a crush on Eddie.

'I literally walked on the street where Eddie lived, hoping he'd come out of the house so I could get another look at him,' she said, as though it were yesterday.

Sinatra, then starring at the Copacabana, saw her in his audience one night and kept looking at her. He then called, invited her to dinner, sent flowers and chauffeured limousine, and had her seated at his table, the 'Sinatra table'. He seemed to be playing the whole show to her, but she hadn't met him yet and didn't until she and her sister, who was chaperoning her, went to a party in his dressing room.

'I saw Frank on and off for a long time,' Jill Corey recalled. 'I think we thought of marriage. We had a little difference of opinion once when we were together in Las

Vegas. He left me alone while he went gambling. I thought that was not the way to treat a lady so I took the next plane home. But Frank was a wonderful man.'

It got to be a Sinatra Who's Who.

Before Angie Dickinson became Mrs. Burt Bacharach and subsequently a TV policewoman, she was a dear, dear friend of Sinatra's and dated him regularly. Angie told *People* magazine, 'He wasn't the sort of man I could ever live with, but we can still say "I love you" to each other.'

Jolie ('Mama') Gabor exclaimed to me that between husbands, her daughter Eva was having a mad fling with Frank: 'They loff each other, dolling, but eet's just a leetle flirtation.'

Kim Novak went from Sammy Davis, Jr., to Aly Khan—and to Sinatra. Frequently she was his guest in Las Vegas, leaning over the baccarat or blackjack table, wide-eyed, whispering breathily to him as he flung in his chips.

Sophia Loren, Frank's co-star in *The Pride and the Passion*, said, 'He is kindly, he is friendly, he is a tiger, he even helped my English. He is a gasser. I dig him.'

Bouncy blonde singer-dancer Dorothy Provine, who was nicknamed 'The Tiger' because of her energy, was another Sinatra enthusiast. Sinatra took beautiful Natalie Wood to Broadway shows and to Jilly's when both were free. He dated sultry-eyed Donna Reed back when she won an Oscar with him in *From Here to Eternity*, and Mona Freeman, and even took Grace Kelly to a private screening before she married Prince Rainier.

The girls weren't all famous. However, Princess Soraya interested him because of her personality. Model and fashion consultant Nancy Gunnerson, singer-actress June Tolley, and tempestuous actress Sylvia Miles were Sinatra friends. Sylvia Miles, who posed nude with several male friends for a magazine, *After Dark*, and has been seen nude in other publications, was discreet about their acquaintanceship.

'I found out,' she said, with a provocative smile, 'he reads *Nugget*.'

One beauty who treasured a friendship with Sinatra is Tiffany Bolling, a woman of fine family background, who played two important scenes with him in his film *Tony Rome*. She was overwhelmed by the opportunity. 'Mr. Sinatra,' she said, 'personally came and told me he thought I had a lot of talent for a girl who didn't have much experience.'

Sinatra, who was at the time escorting Jill St. John around Miami, invited Miss Bolling to lunch with him, Jill and some other friends, and later at a cast party gave her a large gold wristwatch with a gold band circled with diamonds. He told her it was a gift from him and the company as a compliment to her talent.

Marlene Dietrich fancied Sinatra. '*Mais oui*,' she said, her eyes lifted to the ceiling, 'he is the Mercedes-Benz of men!'

Over the years, Beverly Hills gossips have frequently been heard saying, 'Sinatra's seeing Hope Lange again.' Miss Lange is noted for her sense of humour. 'She is giving him some advice to the lovelorn,' said one acquaintance, 'that he isn't going to take.'

Eddie Fisher declared that Sinatra can also give advice to the lovelorn. 'I remember one time,' says Eddie, 'when he was counselling me to marry Connie Stevens while he was counselling himself to get out of his marriage to Mia Farrow.'

He has been a friend of the great beauties and sex symbols, starting with Lana Turner and Ava Gardner and going on to Marilyn Monroe. He admires classy ladies, and one was Lee Remick, to me just about the prettiest woman of her time. She played his nymphomaniac wife in *The Detective*.

The women who haven't been romanced by Sinatra have foolishly tried to figure out his ideal woman: one who doesn't use a lot of perfume, one who doesn't smoke heavily, one who's flat-chested (there was Mia—but there was also Lana Turner and Marilyn Maxwell!), one who is willing to be bossed, one who doesn't want a career of her own. That's how they've described the next Mrs. Sinatra, but they're probably all wrong. Sinatra just likes women—almost any woman sometimes.

The fortyish-plus Barbara Marx, a blonde former Las

Vegas showgirl with a college-age son, was good for him, they said. She coached Frank in tennis. Dinah Shore coached Barbara in her love game with Frank. They broke up and got together and broke up again and again.

But Barbara waits.

'She is the most patient woman in the world,' they say in Palm Springs.

'No,' says a small voice. 'The *most* patient woman is Nancy Sinatra, Sr.'

Having lived most of his adult life in Hollywood, Sinatra must be credited for never having been arrested for drunken driving nor been accused of home-wrecking.

'Frank,' one man told me, 'is the kind of a guy who could make it with your wife, tell you he did, and then tell you it was your fault because you'd neglected her.' The man who said it spoke in a manner that convinced me he'd been there.

Sinatra got slapped by 'Sexy Rexy' Harrison in February 1957 at a Hollywood party and didn't return the slap. The Hollywood set talked of nothing else for a while. Harrison, vacationing from his hit show *My Fair Lady*, was soon to marry British actress Kay Kendall. He went looking for his fair lady Kay at a party given by producer Charles Feldman and found her on the patio chatting with Sinatra. Both men had reputations as ladies' men, and Miss Kendall was flattered by the attention.

As Harrison joined them, Miss Kendall, who was standing near Sinatra said, 'Isn't this a beautiful shirt?'

Harrison conceded that it was and asked what colour it was.

'It's just an old shirt, an off-white, sort of yellow,' Sinatra said.

With that, Harrison slapped Sinatra, who bit his lips and clenched his fists, but didn't slap back. 'It's still yellow,' Sinatra said. Harrison slapped him again. (Bystanders didn't overhear any other remarks, and neither Sinatra nor Harrison would explain later the significance of Frank's seemingly innocent words.)

With excellent self-control and sense of propriety, Sinatra walked away as others were rushing over to see what had happened. Sinatra later said he didn't believe Harrison knew what he was doing and didn't want to take advantage of him.

Harrison laughs about it today. 'Oh, the *fracas*, the *fracas*!' he said recently, giving it the French pronunciation. 'They made so much of it at the time. It was so serious, we had dinner together the next night!' They are close friends now. Sinatra sent concert tickets to Harrison and his ex-wife Elizabeth and has flown them in his private plane. After all, the slapping was almost twenty years ago.

Any woman who dates Sinatra is likely to find herself in the newspapers. Pretty Nan Whitney, a former model and now a publicist, is still a friend after dating him in 1958 and getting into print briefly.

She was a popular young woman who'd been seen in Florida with Sinatra, and they were said to be closer than close. A New York paper assigned a photographer and reporter to get a story and photo of Sinatra the morning of 3–4 December. When Sinatra, Nan and some others left the Harwyn nightclub at 2.30 a.m. after having some drinks, the photographer took some pictures, but Sinatra's chauffeur closed the windows so he couldn't get any of the inside of the car.

Dissatisfied with what they'd obtained, the photographer and the reporter returned to the club, had drinks and food, and constructed their own story of what had happened: Sinatra had shouted to the chauffeur, 'Run over him . . . get him . . . kill the bastard'; the car had hit and injured the photographer in the leg and raced away with its siren roaring; the photographer entered a hospital to have his leg treated and would file a lawsuit. The story was headlined in this paper and picked up by other papers.

After talking to the doorman and the operators of the club, Ed Wynn and Tony Butrico, and hearing their denials, I was convinced that the story was untrue. Of course, there was a possibility that they were merely defending Sinatra.

I obtained a police report of the investigation of the photographer's complaint. It said that there was no siren on Sinatra's car. There was a siren, however, on another car, which had left about the same time, but had no connection with Sinatra. Tony Butrico said the photographer, on returning to the club, made no mention of having been struck by the Sinatra car. On being questioned by detectives, the photographer said that he 'presumed' that the siren sound came from Sinatra's car, but he was not sure. He also said that once Sinatra had gotten into the car he could not hear any of Sinatra's conversations because the car window was up.

The chauffeur told the investigators that Sinatra didn't mention the photographer. The photographer said he had his knee treated for bruises, and this was verified. He wore a bandage when he saw the detectives, but did not remove it. The detectives did not know whether there was any real injury.

It was getting to be a waste of newsprint and detectives' manpower. They told the photographer he could have the chauffeur arrested on a charge of third-degree assault.

'But,' said the police report, 'The photographer stated that "at the present time, I will not make a complaint and I want to give the matter more thought." '

It concluded that allegations contained in this paper that S. directed the driver to run down the photographer and that the car siren was blown had been thoroughly investigated but were without foundation.

I showed this report to Sinatra, who was then in Miami Beach, and he was overjoyed and slapped me on the back. My paper published my column correcting the story in the *Journal-American*. It developed that another newspaper columnist was in the Sinatra car. He could have written his version and defended Sinatra, but he did not. He was known to be an honest reporter and this raised a question about the accuracy of the police version. Regardless, Sinatra never liked the other columnist after that and declared that Wilson was 'a stand-up guy'.

Although it was really a small incident, Sinatra continued for years to be kidded and heckled about ordering his chauffeur to run over photographers.

About seventeen years passed. Nan Whitney became a publicist, with Sinatra's help. She went to work for Hollywood and New York press agent Jim Mahoney, who, as it happened, represented Sinatra. Later she went into publicity for herself.

In 1975, Nan Whitney visited the New York *Daily News* to leave some publicity copy for one of the columnists. There she chanced to meet the photographer who had caused Frank and her all that trouble in 1958.

'Why did you do that to us?' she asked him. 'Why did you say that Frank said those things? You know he never said that.'

'Truthfully,' he said, 'I have a picture showing that the window of Frank's car was closed and I couldn't have heard Frank say anything anyway. Besides, the paper blew the whole thing out of proportion.'

Sinatra has too often suffered because of exactly that sort of attitude.

Once *Playboy*'s Hugh Hefner was eager to entertain Sinatra at his famous Chicago Bunny-hutch, a sprawling converted town house called the 'Mansion'. A reputed great lover, Hefner was still starstruck. Sinatra was intrigued by the prospect of seeing him operate in his luxurious setting with an all-night kitchen, quick bar service, indoor pool, and Hefner's weakness: pinball machines. Sinatra went and found everything dull—except a beautiful, sexy-looking woman described as the private property of the host, 'Hef.'

After an hour or two, a bored Sinatra left the party and returned to the Ambassador East to retire.

There was a knock on Sinatra's door. A beautiful young woman stood there. 'Is Mr. Sinatra here?' she asked.

'Is he expecting you?'

'He asked me to meet him here and gave me this room number.'

'Won't you come in?'

She came in. She remained. Sinatra, for a while at least, had stolen Hefner's private lady because he was, as they used to say, 'a very fast worker'.

Sinatra's Third Comeback was quiet at first; then 'Fightin' Frank' took on two countries he hadn't been at war with before—Canada and Germany.

In the beginning, when he returned to Caesar's Palace in

March 1975, he seemed to have seen the light and cut down on his blasts at columnists.

He revealed his creativity in the new show by making use of moving platforms for his groups, an idea he himself conceived. He opened the show singing with his rhythm jazz group. Then it rode off on a moving platform. In the background, behind a scrim curtain, a backlight brought into view a string section playing for him as he went into his ballads. Presently another moving platform brought in the brass section. It was new and different. And except for one short slap at the press, Sinatra showed a quality he hadn't demonstrated recently. He was lovable.

'It's my new image,' he said.

He certainly didn't look like a has-been as he went to the Toronto Maple Leaf Garden in May. True, there were a couple of thousand tickets not sold for the second show at midnight, but 36,000 had been sold and he figured to grab about $400,000 for one day's work.

But there was bodyguard trouble again.

As he was swinging into the Royal York Hotel surrounded by his entourage of protectors and associates, a freelance photographer got pushed, and the Toronto *Star* front-paged that he'd been punched by a Sinatra bodyguard. It was printed a few hours before Sinatra's evening concert.

'It's a goddam lie, the usual bullshit, and this time I'm gonna make them prove it,' Sinatra said.

He was in a rage when he went onstage and lashed out at the newspapers saying that he would give the photographer $1 million if he could prove the charge.

Sinatra repeated the $1 million offer at the midnight show. The photographer never appeared to ask for the million. Sinatra and entourage got out of Montreal the same night, with Sinatra still mad, but believing he'd won that battle.

'Showed the bastards that time,' he said. 'Most of those stories aren't true.'

Sinatra's weakness is that he allows these niggling annoyances to disturb him. He is unable to dismiss them with a shrug because his sensitivity is as big as his ego. He cannot just let it go.

Understandably, he can't consider himself merely an average singer with average feelings. At that very time, as he and Barbara Marx and the rest were soon to be leaving for a concert tour of Europe, he sold $140,000 worth of tickets at the New Haven Veterans Memorial Coliseum and $180,000 worth at the Providence Civic Centre. Both were new records.

Cocky and buoyant for the most part, Sinatra was, however, concerned that tickets weren't selling well in Frankfurt, Berlin and Munich. He hadn't been in Germany in thirty years. It began to look like the Germans hadn't missed him.

In London, however, Prime Minister Harold Wilson invited him to 10 Downing Street almost immediately after his arrival. He and Barbara Marx stayed for twenty minutes, talking to Wilson and the Prime Minister of Fiji.

'How did you find the Prime Minister?' one of the on-duty bobbies asked Sinatra.

He said, 'I just walked to the door and there he was.'

From Claridge's where they were staying, Frank and Barbara also went to a tailor, where he got two mohair dinner jackets at about $600 each and two pairs of shoes at $250 each. Frank was chatty with the London cabbie and gave him an autograph.

In Germany, Frank got considerably rougher treatment than he'd received from the Australians.

The sensation-loving German press reheated the old stories about Mafia connections, the Leftists complained about the high price of concert tickets—from $75 to $125—and pictured Sinatra as a greedy capitalist, an old man trying to hold up the young people, who couldn't afford to see him even if they had wanted to.

'What is all this?' Sinatra asked as he heard the clamour. He was loved almost everywhere, especially in France, Monaco, England and Italy, but in Germany he was evidently a dirty name.

Word that he'd received a kidnap threat was published in one of the papers. A West German network announced it would run his Madison Square Garden TV tape during his concert tour—which would of course cut down on his paid audience.

It got worse. Hamburg, supposedly the sex centre of Germany and well known for its brothels, cancelled his show because the sales were slow. Munich and Frankfurt had about half a house, and then Sinatra cancelled Berlin. Only 1,500 seats had been sold in Deutschlandhalle although it could seat 12,000.

Sinatra had suspected he would get slaughtered in the papers, but it was worse than he had anticipated. His explanation for the cancellation was that he feared kidnapping but the papers said that was merely an alibi.

'Sinatra is afraid to face empty seats,' they said.

One reason for the interview-hungry German press' anger at Sinatra was his continuing refusal to give interviews.

'No interviews,' he kept saying. German reporters dogged his steps, hung about his hotels, tried to crash his rehearsals, pursued him to restaurants. They followed him to Paris and Monte Carlo, and their stories grew more intolerable to Frank.

In Munich, the press achieved a new low, according to the Sinatra camp. A German photographer took a picture of the empty concert hall well before the concert—and sent a copy to Sinatra at his hotel with a threat to publish it as a picture of his concert audience unless he gave an interview.

Still Sinatra refused. A few papers did publish the picture with the misleading caption.

Sinatra and attorney Rudin considered libel action against the papers, and the papers replied that Sinatra was a 'supergangster'. He was happy to be back in London a week later before a friendly audience at the Albert Hall that included two of his former wives, Ava Gardner and Mia Farrow, as well as Princess Margaret, Princess Anne and Princess Grace, of Monaco. It was his first London concert in five years, and he handed out roses, made some jokes about smoking, and gave all indications of having a happy time.

'This is one of the best nights of my career,' he said.

Replying to the German charges, Sinatra shouted, 'They

called me a supergangster. I could have retorted about the sins of their fathers. I could have mentioned a couple of places like Dachau. Don't call me a gangster, you bum! You are the gangster.'

It was almost midsummer 1975. In England as well as in America they had been believing that the Sinatra magic was gone and that he would soon retire. They had read it so often. They supposed it was true. This concert proved those reports wrong.

The reviews and the response were excellent. James Green, in the London *Evening News*, said, 'Somewhere inside the plumper figure and the fattened face, that skinny kid who hypnotized the swooners is trying to get out.'

In closing he sang 'My Way', with the words, 'And now the end is near . . .'

'Maybe, Frank,' James Green wrote, 'but not that near. Yet.'

Sinatra was happy that he'd gone to Europe during his Third Comeback, even if he hadn't gone to Berlin.

Sinatra was looking for a miracle to recoup from the German disaster, and in July and August, he achieved at least the very unusual. He and Harrah's Lake Tahoe Hotel got 672,412 telephone calls responding to a big advertising campaign for his back-to-back appearance there with young rock star John Denver.

'Impossible,' all the sceptics declared, but the Nevada telephone company claimed its computers authenticated the figures.

Pleased at the idea of working only one show a night, Sinatra was to appear in dinner jacket at supper, with Denver, open-throated and in denims, singing at dinner, for one week only, 1–8 August.

It was the idea of Sinatra's lawyer Mickey Rudin and Denver's manager Jerry Weintraub. The twenty-dollars-a-person minimum scared nobody, even though it meant that a couple wishing to see two shows would have to pay at least eighty dollars.

The ads and billboards invited the public to phone for reservations beginning at midnight 1 July. The hotel and Nevada Bell clocked 55,000 calls in one hour the first night;

85,000 in one hour the second night. Those calling were given recorded messages to stand by. Phone service in the Sacramento area was backed up hopelessly. There was an immediate sell-out for what Harrah's modestly called 'the entertainment coup of the decade'.

As I pushed through the casino on the gala opening night, Friday, 1 August, I felt the Sinatra magic. 'You can't even get space to have a drink at a bar,' grumbled a newspaperwoman friend there to cover it. 'There are lines at the restaurants. I'm going back to my room and wait for the show.'

After seeing and enjoying the Denver dinner show, I went into the casino to get bumped and pushed for an hour, then returned to the showroom at midnight to hear the Sinatra overture, 'My Way', and then . . . 'And now the comedy of Pat Henry.'

It was a replay of other nights. 'That wasn't an earthquake over at Oroville,' Henry said, 'that was Frank yelling for room service.' Sinatra was doing some weird things. 'He put candy all over me and tied me to a diabetic. Frank bought me a bullet-proof vest. I bent over and got shot right in the ass. I miss New York, I saw a cop fire three warning shots into a guy. You notice, all our Italian friends, how they don't have any necks, that's from standing in front of grand juries. I think now you're ready for the Boss.'

Pat Henry knelt, his knees touching the floor, as Sinatra walked forward through the orchestra of more than fifty musicians to the centre of the stage, smiling, shaking his shoulders to the music, obviously intending to have a happy night and recapture some good relationships.

Only a few press people had been invited, and in his opening show, Sinatra didn't mention his targets from the newspapers. Jokingly, he said that John Denver 'shouldn't talk like that about the press'. Of course Denver, a young innocent, hadn't said anything about the press. Sinatra said that Denver, who he thought looked like a 'butch Barbi doll', was a great talent as singer and writer.

'The young hiker,' Sinatra said, meaning Denver, 'tried to get me to go up into the mountains with him. I can't even get out of bed. I'd be afraid we'd find Smokey the Bear up there. . . . We might even find Hoffa.'

I saw the Sinatra show three nights, and he varied the act considerably, which is part of his theory that routines must be changed to be kept interesting. In one talk segment, he spoke of death. 'You got to love livin', Baby', 'Dyin' is a pain in the ass. I wouldn't wish it on anybody except . . .' His voice drifted away, then came back and he said that the subject's life story was shown in movie theatres and the shows were at 2.01, 2.03 and 2.05. He was after columnist Rona Barrett again.

He seemed to be controlling a burp. 'We had some ravioli tonight, and it repaid us a visit,' he said.

Although the early nightclub critics said Sinatra was better when he was *not* singing, he clearly didn't agree. As he went on talking, a woman called from the audience, 'You're over there; why don't you come over here?'

'My dear madame,' he addressed her, 'we got these marks laid out here.' He pointed to the floor, but later, pulling the mike cord behind him, he walked over to her side and spoke from there.

He kept it impromptu and informal, and warm. Stopping to take a drink at one point, he sipped from a glass he took from the piano, then commented, 'There's nothing worse than warm vodka. Can't this place afford an ice bucket?' The next night he drank something else. 'I had a hot vodka here last night and like to burn my bird off,' he said. He is still fond of the word *bird*, and in singing one of his favourites, 'I've Got You Under My Skin', he switched at one point to 'I've got you under my bird'.

Under the lights there was a glint of grey in his thin hair and deep smile creases around his mouth. He snapped his fingers, he swaggered, he did a little dance step, and again and again he rolled his shoulders. He was festive—and in good voice.

'Probably the greatest love song ever written,' he said, 'George Harrison's "Something"—"Something in the way she moves". You may hold hands and even grope if you wish.' A woman called out something from the audience.

'Aw, sheddep!' he called back to her, laughing.

A woman in a white gown suddenly tried to hoist herself on the stage. Some security officers grabbed her by the derrière and pulled her back down just as she was about to make it.

Loving the music, Sinatra lifted his hands in the gestures of a conductor as he went from song to song. He mentioned nearly every arranger by name and he brought out great guitarist Al Viola with elaborate praise.

Presenting the musicians, he said, 'They're the best I could find—I didn't look too hard. I found one of them in a keno game.' He concluded the introductions by turning to Bill Miller, his accompanist for a quarter of a century. 'Suntan Charlie,' Sinatra said. 'What a moon burn!' The legend is that Miller never is out in daylight.

Before singing 'Ol' Man River,' he told the audience, 'After tonight, I might never do this again. I haven't done it in a long time.' The audience, knowing how difficult it is to sing this song, alertly listened as he seemed to hit every note perfectly. As they applauded, Sinatra said, 'I drink a toast to you lovely people.'

They clearly loved him—almost unanimously—at that moment at least.

One new thing was a significant improvement. Sinatra had replaced his harangue at the press—most of it anyway—with the reading of some supposed fan letters. They were probably the work of gag writers; one was from a fellow who said Frank was probably too busy to gamble and that if Frank would bankroll him for $5,000, he'd gamble for him and give him half, if he won anything.

'Here's one,' Sinatra read from a card, 'from a fellow who says he saw in the newspapers that I had trouble with Germany. He says, "For my part, I say Screw the Germans —and I'd like to start with Elke Sommer." '

The 1,100-person crowd roared its applause all seven nights and gave him a standing ovation. (Denver got ovations, too.) One thing they liked was Sinatra's announcement, 'I'm a saloon singer and you can be served drinks during the show.' Harrah's, of course, liked that, too. Sinatra surely made himself some points with that date.

THE WANDERING GENIUS

A woman critic in New Jersey had the courage to write in the summer of 1975 that when Sinatra returned to his home state in the heart of Sinatraland, he didn't bring his voice with him.

The harsh critic, Gaye Bolte, women's editor of the Union City *Dispatch*, added that Sinatra was 'capitalizing on the sentimental tin ears of an audience . . . was doing a mediocre imitation of himself and should have remained retired'.

Others were kinder—sort of. 'His hair was silver', he had 'a noticeable paunch and a mean hawk's face', and he was decidedly 'an old Sinatra', one critic said, but the toughest professional listeners agreed that he had that beat, that beat-beat-beat. Sinatra is a singer who has never forgotten the beat, the beat-beat-beat.

He has great musicianship, the true pros say. I chanced to learn that opera star Robert Merrill was privately working with Frank to loosen, open up and relax his voice apparatus. Merrill, who had no time to coach or teach, volunteered out of friendship to work with Sinatra at the Waldorf-Astoria when he was staying there, helping him run the scales and vocalize. Merrill wears a watch from Sinatra as his thanks.

'He is so talented, he has such a phenomenal ear . . . he's very rare . . . and I think he's singing great!' said Merrill. So much for the lady from New Jersey.

The argument about whether he is great or again a has-been makes little difference to Sinatra, who is above it all.

He has become a wandering minstrel, an international troubadour, and he doesn't mind another critic saying, as Ava Gardner had once said, that he is arrogant. 'He sang about love and always he was mesmerizing in his careless arrogance,' read one review. 'And when he launched into "Nice and Easy", he was erotic as no other American singer, young or old, could be.'

Frank often wonders why the English hear something folks don't hear at home in the States. American-born London critic Henry Pleasants wrote that Sinatra was 'simply a musical genius who arrived at a moment pre-destined for that genius'. He rated him among the great singers of the century, with Richard Tauber and John McCormack, because of his personalized technique, of his speaking to the individuals in the audience. London critic Benny Green wrote that Sinatra is not only the best popular singer of the generation, 'but there is not even the remotest possibility he will have a successor'.

The idea that Sinatra might be a genius is intriguing. What is a genius, anyway? Does it have to be George Gershwin composing 'Rhapsody in Blue'? Could it just be a guy in a leisure suit in a Las Vegas gambling hotel smoking a cigarette and taking a drink and singing 'Send in the Clowns' to about a thousand people itching to get back into the casino?

After Sinatra did a concert at the Albert Hall in London, the Joshua Logans gave him a party. Frank sent 'coffins of flowers' and Logan, the director of Broadway and Hollywood musicals, spent the day 'finding vases for them'.

'To hear this man control those 6,000 people in such a masterful manner convinces you he is a genius,' Logan said. 'He doesn't just sing the lyrics, he plays the lyrics, and gets the emotion from them as though he were Shakespeare. He's the greatest performer of a song we've ever had. Furthermore, he is really a soft, sensitive man.'

Sinatra's response to the genius allegation was, 'Bullshit, I'm a workhorse and always have been.'

Frank spoke truly. Singing thirty to forty weeks a year, he is one of the hardest-working multimillionaires in the world, even though he makes it look easy. They write of

his magic and he knows it exists, but the explanation lies in the cliché: hard work. Corny, but accurate.

However, it pleased him when his fan, WNEW's disc jockey William B. Williams, said that he was 'the most imitated, most listened-to, most-recognized voice of the second half of the twentieth century' and added, interestingly, 'the Number 1 favourite of the other pop singers'.

Music has been his life. He was born to it without any hereditary justification, he has the gift, he is naturally musical. His life is a series of flashbacks pointing to his undeniable talent. He is worshipped for it by his followers, and he no longer finds it curious that they revere him.

He revels in comedian Pat Henry's references to Henry's subservience, suggesting a Sinatra megalomania. Allowed to go as far as he liked, Henry told 2,000 guests at a stag luncheon for Redd Foxx, 'It's not true that I kiss Frank's ass. I only know Jilly's ass. I haven't met Frank's ass yet.'

While this take of worship of the 'King' is exaggerated, it isn't far wrong. Once when Frank couldn't remember where he'd parked his car, half a dozen of his song-plugger friends divided Manhattan into sections and went searching until they found the car.

Sinatra tried to find practical jokes to top earlier practical jokes. Once he phoned Pat Henry at his home at North Belmore, Long Island, and asked him to join him at a New York restaurant. Kirk Kerkorian, a friend, was trying out a new plane. They needed some laughs. When they'd been airborne a short time, Sinatra informed Pat, 'I forgot to tell you, we're on our way to England and will be gone about five days.' Henry protested that he had promised his wife he'd bring her some cigarettes. 'Can't we stop in the Azores so I can tell her she'll have to get her own cigarettes?' They were in Europe for a week—Henry had to buy new clothes in London.

Another time, on his own plane, Sinatra handed Henry a script he'd been reading and said, 'You'll play the first detective. You'll get your feet wet.' Henry thus learned he was in motion pictures—cast in Sinatra's *Lady in Cement*.

Pat Henry (Pasquale Enrico Scarnato) likes Sinatra's self-confidence. He often rides in the Sinatra rented G-2 plane, which comfortably seats about a dozen, kidding with the valet, Eddie Fitzsimmons, who sometimes must pack clothes for Sinatra for a couple of months. Pat went with Sinatra to visit Frank's granddaughter. He has picked up some of Sinatra's egotism: he has an auto licence that reads 'Comic I'.

One of the accepted facts about Sinatra's personality is that he is 100 per cent loyal. This has extended to the belief that he is 100 per cent faithful to the lyrics of famous songs. That's not quite true. Sinatra has always been first to know how good he is, and he is quick to change the words when he feels the urge.

When the black song stylist Mabel Mercer celebrated her seventy-fifth birthday at the St. Regis Roof, she seemed quite flattered when I told her that Sinatra credited her with the success of his phrasing. Of course she remembered that he had come to her shows at the old Tony's club and the Byline Room on Fifty-second Street a quarter of a century before, when he was married to Ava Gardner.

'We would go to hear Mabel and then we would go home and Francis would listen to her records,' Ava recalled.

Mabel Mercer can sing a song 500 times and still be shattered emotionally by it as though she has just done it for the first time. But Frank can't do that with the same regularity because his audience knows his songs from his recorded hits. Besides, he forgets, or pretends to forget . . . and he kids around. He improvises.

He would be surprised to know the name of one singer who is indignant about him changing Cole Porter's 'lady' to 'chick' in 'The Lady Is a Tramp'.

'How dare he?' she asks, and adds, 'I can't stand him.' Devoted to comedy, and to change, Sinatra the showman believes that occasionally switching the lyrics makes him more human, more personal—and more controversial. If he didn't change the lyrics a little, who would be talking about how he sang 'The Lady Is a Tramp'? Nobody! Well, there's the showman's answer.

With his light comedic style, which some love and some purists detest, Sinatra is inclined to resort to scatting—using meaningless, improvised sounds that imitate musical instruments. Louis Armstrong substituted these sounds for words; Bing Crosby said 'buh-buh-buh' when he forgot the lyrics. Some lyric-lovers were disappointed when Sinatra ended 'Strangers in the Night' with a 'dooby dooby doo'. They thought he was making fun of the lyrics.

His friend, composer Alec Wilder, was horrified. 'Oh, Frank,' he pleaded, 'don't throw away the lyric.'

But Frank knew his audience. It was his first big hit in years and a gold album. Most people probably enjoyed the 'dooby dooby doo'. I still like it.

Sinatra the showman is not properly appreciated because he commits atrocities—which serve him well. He is charming you with 'All of Me' or 'Violets for Your Furs' or 'There Are Such Things'—and you are a captive of his enchantment—and then he playfully sticks his tongue out at some friend in the audience. He has broken the mood in a surprising violation of Show Business procedure.

But Sinatra knows he's magician enough to get you back with 'Come Fly with Me'—and then he does it again by launching a harangue against the hookers of the press and their pimps. Minutes later he shrugs that off, takes a drink, and sings 'My Kind of Town' and 'Bad, Bad LeRoy Brown'. It may be bad Show Business, but it's great Sinatra. He follows no rules but his own.

Despite the liberties that Sinatra takes with lyrics, composers and lyricists defer to him as the master and offer him the cream if he wants it.

In the 1950s, when he was still in his nosedive and hunting for songs, Carolyn Leigh wrote the words for 'Young at Heart'. His Oscar for *From Here to Eternity* was just around the corner, but he needed material. Miss Leigh wrote the pretty lyric, 'Fairytales can come true, it can happen to you', with Johnny Richards.

Nat ('King') Cole had turned it down. 'It's a song for old ladies,' he said.

Jimmy Van Heusen heard it and despite being a competitor of Carolyn Leigh, said, 'Frank, you got to do this one.'

It was a smash at the height of excitement over Sinatra's Academy Award, doubled his prestige, and started him off triumphantly at Capitol Records in a new association with Nelson Riddle. Carolyn Leigh became a big name herself in the music field when Sinatra introduced the song on a major TV show. 'When I walked into Al & Dick's, the other writers practically lifted me on their shoulders,' she remembers.

Four years later she and Cy Coleman wrote 'Witchcraft' and everybody, including Sinatra, was singing 'Those fingers in my hair—that sly come-hither stare.' Two more years passed. In Miami Beach, Carolyn Leigh was dancing with Cy Coleman in a nightclub. Columnist Walter Winchell introduced them to Sinatra.

'It lasted about twelve seconds,' she recalls. 'Sinatra said "Keep up the good work." I said, "I'll try." The reason for his success is that he is willing to subject himself to the role he's supposed to play in a song. If he's supposed to be hostile, he'll be hostile. He's willing to cut through the garbage and be himself, and that's credibility. And that's great!'

Miss Leigh's appraisal coincides with that of Joshua Logan who said that Sinatra *plays* a song rather than merely singing it. When he hurls his five-feet-ten, 165 pounds into 'You Make Me Feel So Young', when he throws back those shoulders and lets the music pour out, on one of his good nights, you are having a musical experience.

He keeps to the beat-beat-beat, and his musicians strain because they love him for his love of music. 'He is going to sing his song and he doesn't give a shit what anybody says; he's going to sing it His Way,' they tell you.

Sometimes he seems to some to be overdoing his individuality bit. In the very sexy 'Take It Nice and Easy', he changed the lyrics occasionally from 'the problem of course is / to hold your horses' to 'the problem of course is / to beat those friggin' horses', which gave a new meaning, and added a rather mild vulgarism, to the song.

But nobody objected, not even the authors, and the audience was amused. Sinatra has never sung any word worse than *friggin'* in forty years.

Sinatra has never been dirty, but he doesn't play down his sexuality. He may change 'I've got you under my skin' to 'I dig you under my skin'. One woman cried out from the audience 'Oh, Frankie,' and he called back, 'Does that grab you, Baby? I'll be right there.' Sinatra knows that his records have allegedly inspired millions of sexual experiences that would never have occurred without his help, and that he has been responsible for thousands of births by remote control. It has been more food for his ego.

The middle-agers who constitute the major portion of his audiences are not disturbed by his sexual references—in fact, they are hungry for more. And with his swaggering theatricality, he demonstrates that he knows they like it. He has suggested in some shows that he could solve the New York City financial crisis 'by charging the ladies of the evening a buck a piece. We could get them on their backs and the city on its feet', he said.

When he booked the Uris Theatre engagement, Sinatra said it would be the first time he played a legitimate house. 'I fooled around in a lot of illegitimate houses,' he said.

And joking about the name, the Uris, he said, 'The Uris! I'll send you some penicillin and clear it right up!'

One night a piece of feminine finery floated on stage landing at Frank's feet. It might have been a brassiere or a handkerchief. Sinatra turned towards the area it had come from.

'I'm sorry, lady,' he said. 'I don't do laundry any more.'

His command of any interruption is excellent. Other performers marvel at how he establishes himself immediately as the 'boss' in any situation on a stage. One trick is his masterful handling of the microphone. He thinks a microphone should be black and should not be noticeable or distracting. He makes it a part of his proud, kingly stride; he pretends it isn't there. He invented the trick of seeming to emerge from the orchestra at the beginning of his act. He is introduced, and suddenly there's a man up there in the orchestra with his back to us. He is slowly pivoting and coming towards us, and it is Sinatra with the mike in his right hand.

Just as people can't agree whether his voice is good or bad now, they can't agree whether his ego is pleasant or unpleasant.

In the *Village Voice*, Gary Giddins said, 'Sinatra never

stopped being a punk, Mr. Tough Guy with a tender soul. He presents himself less as an artist than as a shrine.' He seems to want the homage. He doesn't like professional photographers, but warms to the amateurs shooting from the audience in a sort of tribute.

He talks and talks, making jokes. When one woman gets weary of his patter and calls out, 'Why don't you just sing, Frankie?' he replies that she'd better shut up or he'll get Barbara Walters after her.

Choosing the right songs has accounted for Sinatra's success although he picked some wrongoes, too.

Sinatra got together two friends, composer Jimmy Van Heusen and lyricist Sammy Cahn, as a song-writing team in the 1950s. They collaborated beautifully and succeeded in selling their songs to him.

Sammy Cahn became known for his 'personal demonstrations' of their songs. He is a bald little man with a sort of Groucho Marx lope, an ordinary voice, the ability to play the piano only in the key of F, and tremendous bravery, persistence and enthusiasm for his own work. He puts on his own little show when trying to sell his songs to a singer. When he can't hit a high note, he leaps like a basketball centre and points to the ceiling.

Cahn and Van Heusen flew to Las Vegas to demonstrate a song in 1956. 'Mr. Sinatra will see you at breakfast,' they were told. And so—at 5.00 p.m.—they went to his suite at the Sands Hotel.

Sinatra, hung over, said, 'Oh, no, it's bad enough to see you before breakfast, but to have to hear you sing off-key, too.' Van Heusen played the piano, and Sammy Cahn scrambled about the room, pointing to the ceiling and screaming. After a few minutes, Sinatra opened his blue but red-rimmed eyes and said, 'Let's eat.'

Cahn said, 'From Sinatra, that was high praise indeed.'

The song was 'All the Way' for the movie *The Joker Is Wild*, and it won an Oscar.

Sinatra found himself so easily swayed by Sammy Cahn that he eventually banned personal demonstrations and insisted that songs be submitted on tape.

Cahn remained a Sinatra friend, always ready to write a special lyric for Frank to sing at a testimonial dinner. He didn't complain, although other writers grumbled, 'The bastard won't give me a break.'

With Sinatra, it is the song that is the right thing. The song has to be right.

When the enormously successful composer and producer Jule Styne was enjoying the popularity of his song 'People', which he and Bob Merrill wrote for *Funny Girl*, Sinatra frankly told Styne that it wasn't a legitimate hit. Although they were long-time friends, Sinatra said to Styne, 'You missed in the middle. After the first sixteen bars, it rambles.'

Styne retorted, 'But Frank—it's the Number 1 song! The whole world loves it except you.' Sinatra didn't dislike it. But as a singer he felt it didn't 'flow'. Nevertheless Barbra Streisand made it a big hit.

'I think Frank's the Number 1 singer and I still send him the first copies of my songs unless they're previously committed,' Styne says.

But just to salve his own ego, he listed some songs Sinatra had rejected as singles. 'He tore up "I Walk Alone" in front of me because he was mad at Sammy Cahn and me, but that only lasted ten minutes,' Styne said. Sinatra turned down 'Just in Time', 'Small World', 'Make Someone Happy', 'The Music That Makes Me Dance' and 'Rain on My Parade'. Styne said the last song of his that Sinatra recorded was 'Three Coins in the Fountain' about 1955.

'I believe he thinks I have talent,' says Styne. 'I think it's something personal and I wish I knew what it was.'

Sinatra has an affection for old-time songwriters that he frequently demonstrates. He and Jimmy Van Heusen remain close after thirty-five years; Van Heusen lives nearby; he often helps Sinatra rehearse.

When Frank was a cocky youngster hoping he could be another Crosby, he met composer Rube Bloom, who went to Madison Square Garden fights with him. Sinatra took Rube away from his Tin Pan Alley milieu (Lindy's, the Turf and, later, Jack Dempsey's) and was host to him at his various homes. Rube, Frank and Nancy, Sr., in a long white mink coat said to have cost $25,000, went to the opera in Los Angeles. A few years later, it was Rube, Frank and Ava Gardner, ravishing in red, going to the Diamond Horseshoe at the Metropolitan Opera in New York and to supper with Dorothy Kirsten at 21 afterwards. Frank became an opera buff and conjectured that he might have sung opera himself.

Rube's 'Fools Rush In' was one of Sinatra's favourite recordings, along with his 'Day In, Day Out', 'Take Me' and 'Maybe You'll be There'. Sinatra, in a rare example of kindness and thoughtfulness, suggested that Rube resurrect an old song 'Truckin' ' and convert it to 'Twistin' ' when the Twist became the popular dance. 'It got a modicum of play,' Rube reported.

Sinatra helped Paul Anka hit one of the greatest bonanzas of his prosperous career when he decided to record 'My Way'. Anka was already a big café star himself when he got to know Sinatra in 1968. 'The more I was exposed to Sinatra, the more I admired him,' he says. 'It was a turning-point in my life. I ran into him more and more, and I guess you could say we started to pal around.'

While vacationing in France, Anka heard a French pop song called 'As Usual' about a husband and wife who got up every morning and looked at each other and felt the same way about each other every day—'As Usual'. Anka liked the melody. The music was by J. Revaux and C. Francois, the lyrics were by Giles Thibault. Anka bought the publishing rights.

'In September 1968, about two o'clock in the morning, I got to work in my Park Avenue apartment at the piano,' Anka says. 'I had no idea what the song was going to be about. I must have been thinking about Sinatra because as I began to work on it, I realized this song was going to be for Frank and about him. I did the song in about forty-five minutes. It was Frank Sinatra's life story.

'I wanted to give it to Frank. It still needed polishing. The trouble was, I heard rumours he was retiring. He was at Caesars Palace and I was at the Sahara. Finally I cut a demo. I said, "Frank I'm sending you a demo." Then I waited to hear. I'd never sent him a song before. I was worried.

'He said he'd listen to it right away. I got a call back.

'He liked it!

'In his way, he was enthusiastic. You don't get a lot out of him, but you know where you stand with him. Three weeks later, he was in the studio recording.

'It was eventually "covered" by one hundred other singers. It was a big hit for Frank in England as well as the United States. It was on the charts in England for close to three years.'

Frank was so happy with the result that he sent Paul a note saying, 'You've got so much goddamned talent, you're a pain in the ass.' He signed it 'The old man.'

Paul sent Frank a tube of Preparation-H (a widely advertised haemorrhoid salve).

Sinatra has always been tolerant about some ribbing he's had to take from comedian Phil Silvers, who accidentally became one of his songwriters. Silvers claims that Pope Pius XII had never heard of Sinatra when Frank and Silvers got an audience while they were on a World War II USO tour. Sinatra had arranged the audience through influential Italian friends in Rome. The Pope, according to Silvers, said to young Frankie, 'Are you a tenor, my son?'

'No, your Holiness, I'm a baritone.'

'And what operas do you sing?'

'I don't sing operas, your Holiness.'

'Where did you study?'

'I never studied.'

As Phil told it, the Pope turned to Phil for more promising material and blessed some beads Phil had brought for Bing Crosby, whose fame the Pope already knew.

'And now they call Frank the "Pope"!' says Silvers.

Silvers became a Sinatra songwriter in an unusual way. Silvers, Jimmy Van Heusen and Jimmy's partner, Johnny Burke, were sitting around a pool in California. Silvers told a joke. Burke's wife, Bessie, laughed. 'Bessie, with the laughing face,' Phil said.

'Not a bad title for a song,' Van Heusen said.

'I'm tired, you guys do it,' Burke yawned.

Silvers wrote the lyric, Van Heusen wrote the melody. Later at a birthday party for Nancy, Jr., they changed the name to 'Nancy with the Laughing Face', and it became a favourite Sinatra song. Silvers still gets royalties. It took him twenty minutes to write it.

Sinatra could boast to Silvers that one song to which Frank had personally contributed, 'I'm a Fool to Want You', had done as well as 'Nancy'. (Sinatra does not follow Al Jolson's practice of accepting writer's credit on songs he introduced. In the 1930s and 1940s, Jolson would arrive from Hollywood to be greeted by New York songwriters who told him, 'Al, here's a song you just wrote'.)

Authors Jack Wolf and Joel Herron say that Sinatra honestly contributed to the lyrics of 'I'm a Fool to Want You', the song of anguish that he recorded during his heart-break romance with Ava Gardner. His name is on the music sheet: 'Words and music by Jack Wolf, Joel Herron, Frank Sinatra, copyrighted by Barton Music Co., 1951.'

When Columbia reissued the record in the mid-1970s, pop music critic George T. Simon found it Sinatra's most moving disc, and it had been voted among the ten Best Records of all time in England fifteen years before. Sinatra put the song back in his nightclub act. Dinah Washington, Tom Jones and Billie Holliday tried to outdo the original Sinatra recording, but none got into the song the pain that Sinatra put into it in just one take.

There are many close friends of the 'King's' who say that Vic Damone and Jack Jones sing better than he.

Sinatra has praise for both, although he says that 'my favourite singer is Tony Bennett'. But the original Sinatra sound is more compelling to women than the other voices. Sinatra is so aware of it that he has told cronies when they are worried about him not feeling well before an engagement, 'Don't worry about me because all I have to do is show up.'

He spoke a simple fact; it is not conceit. He knows that he can go onstage and sing very badly, and they will love him. He knows that his audiences are mostly presold on Sinatra and aren't going to dislike him even if he sings raggedly.

Living in a bibulous world and being very much a part of it, Sinatra has known all his life that drinking and lack of sleep are ruinous to singers. He has occasional periods of abstinence, which usually don't last long. He drank Jack Daniels sour mash whiskey or bourbon for years, then switched to a French wine, and lately has taken up vodka. He goes to bed when he remembers to, and has been known to get only two or three hours' sleep. His stamina is envied by members of his entourage who try to keep up with him. When he is going on a concert tour, he tries to get into condition, like a fighter, by swimming and exercising, and drinking less.

Although Sinatra is said to be Number 1 pop singer, he is far from the biggest record seller.

He did not have a gold record in the first half of 1975, but long-time big-seller Elvis Presley did and John Denver did, and so did more than eighty others, including Elton John, Olivia Newton-John, Charley Pride, Alice Cooper, David Bowie, Barry Manilow, Tony Orlando and Dawn and the Carpenters. Sinatra's fans are not by and large today's kids who rush to the record shops to make the rock stars richer, although Sinatra has cut through into that money vein.

Sinatra has had one gold single record. Just one. However, he has fourteen gold albums.

Elvis Presley has hanging on the wall in the big basement playroom of his sprawling home in Memphis eight gold single records—at the last count. The Beatles have twenty scattered around the world.

A gold record is awarded when a song has sold 1 million records. A gold album is awarded when an album has sold $1 million worth of albums or tapes. Sinatra's one gold record is 'Somethin' Stupid', and he had to divide that honour with daughter Nancy, Jr., who sang it with him in 1967. Daughter Nancy has two other gold records on her own—'Sugar Town' and 'These Boots Were Made for Walkin' '. That gives her a 3 to 1 advantage over her father in the gold record field.

It's the albums that Sinatra has always sold to the stay-up drinkers and the lovers.

Sinatra's gold albums came along like this:

1961 'Come Dance with Me' (Capitol)
1962 'This Is Sinatra' (Capitol); 'Frank Sinatra Sings for Only the Lonely' (Capitol); 'Songs for Swingin' Lovers' (Capitol); 'Nice'n' Easy' (Capitol)
1965 'Sinatra's Sinatra' (Reprise)
1966 'Sinatra: A Man and His Music' (Reprise); 'Strangers in the Night' (Reprise); 'September of My Years' (Reprise)
1967 'Sinatra at the Sands with Count Basie' (Reprise); 'That's Life' (Reprise)
1969 'Cycles' (Reprise)
1970 'Frank Sinatra's Greatest Hits' (Reprise); 'My Way' (Reprise)

Sinatra undoubtedly sold millions of single records and albums not accounted for in these statistics.

There was a ripple of excitement in July 1975, at the 'Sinatra office', an unpretentious bungalow on the Goldwyn lot at North Formosa Avenue in Hollywood, when the word spread that the 'Boss' ' new single, 'I Believe I'm Gonna Love You', was hitting the charts. The Sinatra addicts smiled and tried to remember the last time Sinatra had had a hit.

'It's been a long time,' they agreed. It had been a few years.

'Ol' Blue Eyes' and 'The Main Event' in 1974 hadn't been colossal. 'Let's Try Again', by Paul Anka and Sammy Cahn, got a little play. Sinatra helped get 'Send in the Clowns', the Stephen Sondheim song from *A Little Night Music*, off to a good start, but Judy Collins' recording of it was a bigger seller than Frank's.

'This one could make it,' Sinatra's booster, song promoter Juggy Gayles, tipped me about 'I Believe I'm Gonna Love You'. It was a departure for Sinatra. It wasn't actually country-and-western; it was played by the M-O-R disc jockeys (the Middle of the Roaders), but was produced by Snuff Garrett, well known for country-and-western records, and written by Gloria Sklerov and Harry Lloyd.

When it went from 82 to 52 on the *Record World* single charts, they got truly hopeful. *Billboard* called the reverse side, 'The Only Couple on the Floor,' written by John Durrill, a 'country ballad single', and gave it more attention.

How did Sinatra happen to make this record?

'I was talking to Nancy about tunes,' Sinatra explained to *Billboard*, 'and she said to me, "Daddy, why don't you do some country?" and I said, "I'd like to do some country, but we haven't found anything," and she said, "Why don't you get a hold of Snuffy?" '

A few days later Snuff Garrett and Sinatra, unaccompanied by entourage, began their first country recording—at Western Studios with twenty-five musicians instead of the usual fifty-five. Sinatra said he'd done country years before ('Cycles' in 1964) and he'd known Snuff for years. In fact, Snuff called him 'Mr. Sinatra', and he'd been talking for nine years about doing one song that 'Mr. Sinatra hadn't agreed to do yet'.

It was all a little risky. Sinatra usually polished his songs in the nightclubs before recording them, 'to get them down so I can find all the nuances I might not do if I do them in a hurry', he told *Billboard*.

'I should do that a lot more before going in to make it. This is an exception now with these two tunes. I've been working with one of them for three weeks.'

Sinatra gave 'I Believe I'm Gonna Love You' every chance. He sang it at concerts, he sang it before his biggest crowds, he sang it three times on one telethon. But when it got to about fifty on the charts, it stopped climbing and dropped out. His country tune didn't make it.

Frank's mirror told him he was getting older, and some reporter son-of-a-bitch even called him an 'ageing Lothario'. The frequent jokes about his declining virility weren't as hilarious as they used to be. On David Susskind's TV programme some guests speculated whether he was puffy-faced because of silicone or cortisone injections, or both. Susskind wired him an offer to appear. Sinatra's answer to the invitation was that his fee was $250,000 an hour.

Aroused by this brush-off, Susskind flippantly answered

in kind: 'Presume stipulated fee is for your traditional programme of intramural ring-a-ding-dinging with additional fillip of reading musical lyrics mounted on TelePrompter', Susskind wired. 'Please advise price for spontaneous discussion.'

Frank kept it going with a hot answer: 'The $250,000 fee is for my usual talent of song and dance. However, now that I understand the picture a little more clearly, I must change it to $750,000 for all parasitical programmes.'

Frank has a favourite word: *parasite*. All his enemies, photographers or columnists or TV interviewers, are parasites or parasitical.

Sinatra likes to think that he has complete crowd control and has never been heckled—except in the early days when jealous boyfriends threw eggs at him. In a talk-show conversation, he admitted to Bill Boggs, of WNEW 'Midday Live TV', that he is often scared before he goes on. 'Philadelphia and Chicago, any of the places where they have the enormous arenas that go straight up in the air, I look up and I can't believe there are people way up there.'

He likes the challenge of a serious or dramatic song that he can think of as a poem (such as those written by Rod McKuen). 'I try to transpose my thoughts about the song into a person who might at that moment be saying that to somebody else,' he told Boggs. (The personalized singing technique again!)

'Oftentimes I find myself thinking like a baseball pitcher,' Sinatra continued.

He would tell his conductor Bill Miller, 'I'm not getting the vibes I should, skip the next two tunes and go to the third one . . . it might grab them a little more. . . . You throw a knuckler, you throw a slider, you throw a fast ball. It mystifies them a little bit.'

Notwithstanding his overpowering self-confidence, Sinatra confessed to Boggs and the television audience that he can't stand hearing his own records played at some friend's house and that he tells them he'll leave if they insist.

'Oftentimes I was a little impatient in making a record and said, "That's it, press it, print it," and there is one little note in it, and I cringe and think, "Why didn't we do it one more time?" '

When he's hearing a clinker coming on a car radio, he turns it off.

Still thinking like a baseball pitcher, Sinatra said that sometimes as he is about to go onstage he is afraid that he hasn't warmed up enough, hasn't vocalized sufficiently. 'We've got ten minutes; am I ready to pitch? Should we run into the dressing room and get hold of Bill Miller and sing four or five minutes more of exercises? It gives me an extra added sense of security.'

When he retired in the early seventies out of weariness, Sinatra let everything go, including his conditioning with underwater swimming. When he undertook a comeback, he hadn't properly prepared his voice, he wasn't ready. That was when he got help from Robert Merrill.

In keeping with his getting older and inclined to reminisce, Sinatra embellished stories of his boyhood and his parents in the conversation with Bill Boggs. Part of Frank's stage patter had always been that his father, 'one of the greatest men I ever met', had guided his career. But now Frank revealed to Boggs, 'He told me, "Get out of the house and get a job." I got off his back.

'I was shocked,' Sinatra remembered. 'I didn't know where the hell to go. I remember the moment. We were having breakfast. I'd gotten up to go out and look for a job because I didn't want to go to college. He was a man who could never read or write his name and his big point was education, complete and full education.'

To satisfy his parents, Frank said, he'd planned to try to enter Stevens Institute in Hoboken to be a civil engineer, but his father 'got a little bit fed up with me because I wasn't looking for work, but was working with combinations, singing with bands for nothing'.

He was singing with a megaphone, in the Rudy Vallee manner, and listeners would throw pennies in it, trying to get him to swallow the pennies.

'This particular morning my father said to me, "Why don't you get out of the house and go out on your own?" What he really said was "Get out". And I think the egg was stuck in there about twenty minutes, and I couldn't swallow it or get rid of it, in any way. My mother, of course, was nearly in tears, but we agreed that it might be a good thing, and then I packed up a small case that I had and came to New York.'

His mother, now in her eighties, is 'a character' who can talk as rough as he can. He had built her a place of her own, but she kept coming back to his. She announced that 'that little S.O.B.' (her son) wasn't going to move her up to the new place.

Dolly Sinatra, even at eighty, always has referred to her son as 'Frank Sinatra'. Sitting in her son's presence, she will say to a visitor, 'Did you see Frank Sinatra on the show last night?' Frank laughs at this eccentricity. 'She wants to be sure that everybody knows who she's talking about.'

Looking at himself, Sinatra beholds an incurable optimist who knows that there will be trouble, but believes it will go away. When his cup is nearly empty, he says, 'Hey, look, there's still some left.'

Sinatra flippantly discusses his own personality on a Reprise album, 'Sinatra: A Man and His Music': 'Turning out a good record really lights my candle,' he says, 'it warms me all over with a pride and satisfaction of individual accomplishment. I feel like a little kid who makes his own mud pie with his very own mud and his very own fingers. I made a few muddy records in my day, too.'

His records are still selling in the thousands. Because of the petroleum shortage, record companies removed many songs from their catalogues. Sinatra did not suffer as many cut-outs as other singers. Many Bing Crosby records, for example, can only be found through collectors. 'At least a third of Sinatra's are still in,' an industry spokesman told me. 'That's because Sinatra still sells very well.' Columbia Records still offers four albums recorded in the early forties, when he was dismissed as a crooner whose popularity was believed to be ephemeral.

He is just a light baritone, with a two-octave range, and a way of singing with his heart. He confesses his own agony in his love songs, and the women in the audience want to take him right to bed with them and mother him under the sheets.

He has to sing for hours every day, he has to love the songs and never neglect one word or note, he has to give the lyrics a personal meaning to every listener. It's a big order and he has come close to achieving it. And he has survived crooning, Bebop, and other fads, and has stayed on through jazz, rock, acid-rock, soul and country-and-western.

During one of Sinatra's downdrifts, Eddie Fisher was selling more records than Frank. Years later, when it was Fisher who was trying a comeback, he said that Sinatra had succeeded because he worked with many arrangers, writers and conductors and other singers, getting strength from each.

It is a monumental list that includes many giants. Besides Nelson Riddle, Axel Stordahl, Gordon Jenkins and Billy May, there are Duke Ellington, Sy Oliver, Xavier Cugat, Mitchell Ayres, Phil Moore, Hugo Winterhalter, Ray Anthony, Bobby Hackett, Billy Butterfield, Pearl Bailey, Buddy Rich, Jeff Alexander, Johnny Mandel, Quincy Jones and about 100 others—including Irving Berlin.

Berlin, now in his late eighties, recently said to me: 'You be my song-plugger. Get Sinatra to record one of my songs!'

OL' GRANDDAD'S STILL PITCHIN'

Now as he has passed sixty, thirty-seven years after he got a job with Harry James and forty years since Rustic Cabin, Frankie Boy has become Grandpa Sinatra. The years have made him mellow, and he is a sweeter old Granddad than he had been, but he still has that burning fire to achieve. He has made a big mark on the world, but he wants to leave a bigger one.

He had once talked at cocktail parties of broads; he now burbles with excitement about his little granddaughter, Angela Jennifer Lambert. 'She's so bright!' He marvelled at one party. 'She calls me paw-paw!' He loves that part of his new image that shows him to be a doting grandfather.

The one-time skinny kid from Hoboken now holds his little granddaughter in his arms and puckers his lips in a kiss. He posed for pictures for *Ladies Home Journal*: 'Ol' Blue Eyes Meets Li'l Blue Eyes'. He said he was happy that little Angela would grow up in a family that loved each other. He mentioned her uncle Frank, Jr., her aunt Tina, and he spoke of his happiness that his own mother, Dolly, was still there big and strong, able to diaper her first great-grandchild.

'And,' he said, 'don't forget big Nancy'—Nancy, Sr.—'who is one of the warmest of women.

'All I ask is that little Nancy never lets the child grow up and see *The Kissing Bandit*, a picture I made some years ago. The picture was so bad that on leaving the theatre, I made a citizen's arrest of the cashier.'

While he's grown older, his schedule has grown speedier. He jets to Toronto for a concert and returns to New York before closing time at Jilly's. These bursts of activity give one a chance to see him in many scenes and help answer the question, what is Sinatra really like?

Despite his mellowing, there are still two Sinatras.

While roaming around the stage at a concert, Sinatra can talk of his granddaughter and the miracle of birth until you feel your lips quiver, but out in the alley, some security guards hired to preserve Sinatra's privacy might be yelling to photographers, 'How'd you like a camera up your ass?'

Nevertheless, Sinatra has become friendlier with photographers. 'Frank's all right now,' they say, 'as long as you ask permission. He says, "Since you have the courtesy to ask, okay." '

Sinatra actually tells them, 'Listen, you ask my permission! I have some civil rights, too.' In New York, at least, there is peace on the picture front.

Constantly trying to remember his own good luck, he works at 'being nice'. He nearly always says, 'Thank you', when asked for an autograph. He frequently thanks photographers.

Raquel Welch, after being around him for several weeks on a film, said, 'It's hard not to lose your equilibrium when everybody's chasing after you, and I was amazed at how well he kept his. I never saw him anything but a gentleman.'

Several people use Joshua Logan's words for him now: *gentle*. He walked along the Avenue of the Americas in New York one day with only Jilly Rizzo and another friend and was hardly noticed by passing pedestrians. One night he went into Jimmy Weston's club just as Hazel Scott was singing 'This Love of Mine', the song he wrote in 1941. When she finished singing, Sinatra gave her two forty-dollar tickets to a forthcoming concert.

He practises his loyalty as well as his generosity. He visited with former Vice-President Agnew while in Baltimore for a concert. Golfing with Agnew was more pleasant now than when Agnew'd been in office; there weren't those Secret Service men with their walkie-talkies protecting him. Sinatra took Agnew to dinner along with Barbara Marx at La Valaurisse restaurant in Palm Springs. He bought Barbara a platinum wristwatch and a Jaguar. One night, he and Barbara drove up to Walter Annenberg's estate in Sinatra's blue Rolls to the first party that former President Nixon attended since his departure from office.

That was sad for Sinatra—especially the attempt to be natural, as though nothing had happened, when talking to Nixon, who had, after all, been so gracious to him at the White House. Frank still addressed him as 'Sir'. It was always 'Sir'. Agnew, who was staying at Sinatra's house at the time, of course did not go to the Annenberg party.

Sinatra's trick of enjoying life is to be blithe about every crisis. At the outdoor concert in Baltimore, there was a moment when the orchestra pit before him was empty. Smiling down at it, he said, 'Fill it up with water and I'll walk across it.' Agnew, David Brinkley and others in the audience laughed. Agnew took Sinatra to Baltimore's Little Italy later and everybody had a jolly time.

Bob Hope is probably Show Business' greatest plaque-collector. Sinatra could never amass as many as Hope; he never was anxious to get them. But now that he is Grandpa Sinatra, people have begun thinking of giving him honours. One that amused him was an invitation to the site of the Rustic Cabin nightclub in Englewood Cliffs, New Jersey, where he'd started singing in 1936 for fifteen dollars a week. It is now a gas station. The original club burned down.

A bronze plaque, dedicated to Sinatra, was posted there by Andy Stellatos, the owner, in August 1975. The plaque says: 'It must truly be said that he did it his way and it all started right here.'

'The site is probably the only place in the United States that can boast it had Frank Sinatra as a singing waiter,' the press release said. The Sinatra publicist's office said that was wrong. It should have said he was a singing *head*waiter.

The affair brought out about 100 people. There were speeches by officials, special displays at the public library and a jukebox with 100 Sinatra records that played all day—without coins.

Some years before, the Hoboken City Council considered

naming a street for Sinatra, but didn't. One reason was it wasn't much of a street. One councilman said, 'I wouldn't consider it an honour to have that street named for me!' A headline writer asked in print,

IF WE CAN'T HAVE A SINATRA STREET,
WHY NOT A FRANKIE LANE?

A woman tried to twit Frank about his Hoboken days and said, 'They used to beat you up over there all the time.'

Sinatra retorted, 'I owned Hoboken when I was twelve and I still own it.'

Sinatra was unaffected by small jibes and was sceptical of honours offered, knowing that he was expected to sing or make a personal appearance without pay.

As an acknowledged great showman—one of the greatest, in the opinion of many contemporaries—Sinatra wonders what he can do now to top Frank Sinatra. What can he do for an encore, for a fitting finish to his career? A finish that he hopes will be several years distant.

He has discussed it with Mickey Rudin. When Sinatra retired in 1971, his friends gave the impression that he was perfection. He was not, but they pretended that he could not make mistakes. They spoke like eulogizers at a funeral. Now they knew from his later experiences in Australia, Germany, Canada and Washington that he made human errors. He wanted now to wash out all those errors and give new performances that would leave them wanting more.

'The Grand Old Man of Show Business', the grandpa, thought about it constantly, whether in his plane or while trying to sleep or having some drinks.

It had to be on a grand scale and enormously successful. There could be no nosedives or flops this time.

'I'd like to play New York again,' he said.

Of course, he'd had Carnegie Hall. Something nearer to Broadway. Something like the old Paramount Theatre, where he'd really started out.

There had to be a movie. A good movie—to take away the memory of those dogs he'd made before he retired. Not necessarily a star part, but a great part that would restore his acting prestige. Maybe he could knock off another Oscar. That would be a neat finish.

TV? 'No!'

Television hadn't done it for Sinatra lately. While he got praise from the Sinatra addicts, the ratings weren't good. Sinatra was still stinging from the opinion of John H. Corcoran in the *National Observer* listing 'Frank Sinatra, the Main Event', as 1974's 'most over-promoted low-rated special'.

To 'get back to Broadway, some place like the old Paramount', which was long gone, Rudin and Jerry Weintraub booked Sinatra, Count Basie and Ella Fitzgerald into the 1,900-seat Uris Theatre at Fifty-first and Broadway for two weeks starting 8 September 1975, at a forty dollar top price. It was a gamble because it was dead time—during the Jewish holidays. The price was the highest ever, there was still a recession, and Sinatra had already played the greater New York area several times.

Weintraub, riding a series of successes, predicted it would be another success.

'I'm not worried,' Sinatra said, cocky as always.

Sinatra was right not to worry. On his concerts in the year of 1975, he'd been making a fortune. In the booking agents' language, Sinatra was 'making Las Vegas money' on those personal appearances—often $50,000 to $60,000 a night just for his share. It was comparatively easy for a trouper like Sinatra: one show a night, about an hour of singing and talking, which he enjoyed. And he could do two, three or four a week. He could do a quarter of a million dollars in one week.

And the Uris! That pleased him and brought out the nostalgia. He rode over to Fifty-first and Broadway, which he had known so well while he was the young phenomenon. He noted that the proud Uris, fronted on Broadway by an attractive plaza and two new bank branches, was about ten blocks north of where he had scored his first big triumph at the Paramount Theatre in the 1940s.

This Uris is the epitome of the Broadway of today as the Paramount had been of yesterday. Looking about, Sinatra saw on the northwest corner the old Lindy's, where he had eaten cheesecake with Winchell and Runyon—yes, and Mark Hellinger, for whom they had named a theatre that is in this very block. Lindy's is now a Steak & Brew patronized by young people who buy rock-'n'-roll records.

He nodded his approval of the billing alongside the theatre.

THE URIS
JERRY WEINTRAUB PRESENTS
THE CONCERT
BASIE
FITZGERALD
AND
SINATRA

It was Frank's idea that he be named last rather than first.

But there were other recollections of this corner. This was where the plush Capitol Theatre once stood; Sinatra had starred there while wooing Lana Turner. Maj. Edward Bowes had lived in a penthouse in the Capitol Theatre, and it was practically on this spot that Sinatra and the Hoboken Four had won the Major Bowes Amateur Hour contest that was really the first rung on the ladder for him. Up the street was the Ed Sullivan Theatre, which was just CBS 52 when Sinatra was a national hysteria on radio.

There was mist in Frank's eyes as he thought of returning to the old scene.

And now he was expected to bring into the Uris Theatre about $1 million for two weeks, which would be a record for that house. 'A million-dollar gate!'

He was a buoyant, happy Sinatra, having a ball, just being a kid again, reliving some of his early lucky breaks. He was not high-hatting anybody. He surprised some people by disclosing things he knew about them. Meeting the agent and manager Sid Bernstein, he told him, 'You're a pizza freak like me. I heard about you going up to Patsy's.'

That was not Patsy's the Italian restaurant on West Fifty-sixth Street, where Sinatra went for spaghetti; that was Patsy's at First Avenue and One hundred seventeenth Street, which used a coal stove to make 'the original

Patsy's pizza'. Frankie the boy singer went there for pizza and now Grandpa Sinatra went there for pizza, and when Sinatra returned to Patsy's it was bigger than MacArthur returning to Manila.

A press agent, Joel Preston, saw Sinatra in a men's room, but hesitated to speak to him. Sinatra called out, 'Don't you ever say hello? I'm Frank Sinatra.'

Preston said, 'I thought it was very nice of him, considering that he was three urinals away.'

Broadway revitalized him. In Palm Springs, he'd probably be scrambling some eggs with olive oil at 3.00 a.m. or working crossword puzzles. In New York, he went to Jilly's for Chinese food and met Danny Thomas and talked about when they were both unknown. He impressed everybody with his manners; he was quick to pour drinks and light cigarettes, and several wives complained to their husbands that they were rude compared to him. If he was in a drinking mood, he might be pouring from mid-afternoon to 3.00 or 4.00 a.m.

'Since I've switched to vodka, they call me a Commy.'

Departing Jilly's at almost closing time, he said, 'I've got to get up early and rehearse.'

Old friends said he was in the best mood they'd seen him in years. 'How does he keep going like that?' they asked.

He got constant respectful attention from his staff and from Mickey Rudin. And from Jilly. Once he'd kept a penthouse on East Seventy-second Street and the East River. Jolie Gabor, then a neighbour, told me, 'All the vimmin vanted to go to bed with him. I vould have liked to, too.' But in recent years, he has made do with a suite with a piano at the Waldorf Towers, where he is regarded as a quiet, uncomplaining guest. Far past were the days when he used to throw cherry bombs out of the windows of some hotels on Central Park South.

In the grandfather's need to be young again, he rolled up two nights in a row to a New York night club and sang with Teddy Wilson, whom he'd known on Fifty-second Street, and his group. He enjoys the company of musicians, being one himself, and reminisced with Flip Phillips, tenor sax; Mousie Alexander, drums; and Milt Hinton, bass. As the group was playing 'All of Me', Sinatra arose without any fanfare and sang with them to the astonishment of the audience, which could hardly believe what it was hearing. Then he sang 'I Get a Kick Out of You' with the group. He talked to Teddy Wilson about the Tommy Dorsey era and then said, 'I'm coming back tomorrow night.'

The second night, Sinatra brought his accompanist, Bill Miller, and again he sang with the group.

'His voice was big and resonant,' Teddy Wilson said later. 'I hadn't heard him in years. In those days, his voice was small and thin. The people got up and cheered him. He loves to sing and he was just having fun. That's what makes him different from the others. He likes to sing and it's not a chore for him. It's a joy.'

Sinatra himself said to Wilson, 'Thanks, Teddy, for letting me on, I just felt like singin'.' Sinatra's humility cup was running over.

Sinatra's Uris Theatre engagement was not merely a triumph; it re-established him as the biggest attraction to play Broadway in modern times, with the gross for two weeks reaching a record-breaking $1,088,000. It was also a social success because on Wednesday night, 17 September, Jackie Onassis came to the theatre as Sinatra's date for the evening.

This *coup de théâtre* was Jackie Onassis' own idea. It was early in her widowhood, and she had not been seen around town. The night before, Frank had made a supper reservation for the seventeenth for himself, Jackie and the Peter Duchins. The word was spread via my column that Jackie would be coming to see his concert.

Jackie has the same kind of magic Sinatra has. Rumours flew. A Sinatra intimate had been saying, 'Frank and Jackie would be a perfect match.' Sinatra's friend Barbara Marx hadn't come to New York with him. He was a free man.

Jackie was coming without an escort; she was being picked up by Frank's plain-spoken pal Jilly Rizzo by car.

There was a mob scene, a carnival atmosphere, at the

Uris Theatre entrance, with photographers and fans rushing the front door, only to groan when they learned that Jackie had already entered by the stage door and was in Frank's dressing room.

During the show, Sinatra was bouncy and frolicsome, especially on the love songs, stamping and pointing more than usual. When he sang such lyrics as 'Let me try again', 'I wouldn't mind at all', and 'The problem of course is to hold your horses', there were sighs from the women who understood the suggestiveness of the words.

Wearing a simple black pants outfit, Jackie sat in the fourth row with the Duchins. She and the Duchins joined in the standing ovations and returned to the Sinatra dressing room after the concert. Then, with Sinatra's right hand encircling Jackie's left wrist, and Jilly Rizzo shoulder to shoulder with him on the other side, they went off to 21. Sinatra was looking cherubic but contented, with his chin down to his collar.

They made no effort to get the privacy of the second floor dining room; they had supper in the first floor bar area. A couple of columnists (I was one of them) had tables or bar positions overlooking Sinatra and Jackie, but saw nothing much to report.

It was clear, though, that sitting at this table with the Duchins was the most charismatic couple in the world.

Since it was Jackie's night out, they decided after midnight to proceed to the Rainbow Grill in the RCA Building, sixty-five floors up, to see a show starring comedian Pat Henry, who could hardly believe his friend Sinatra had really done this for him.

'But some of my jokes,' he confessed, 'I decided I'd better not tell.'

And that seemed to be the end of that saga. Barbara Marx joined Sinatra in New York a few days later. One magazine gossiper guessed that Jackie, in her new job as consulting editor for a New York publisher, was trying to obtain Sinatra's memoirs for her employer. Another calculated that Sinatra and Jackie had been together five times in the years they'd known each other. The most bizarre suggestion was that it was all a plot by New York

Governor Carey and Jackie to woo Sinatra back into the Democratic party. Maybe he'd run for office!

Sinatra wanted to create goodwill, and he achieved major gains in sympathy and public esteem in a simple way that he hadn't tried before—by singing three 'mini-specials' of twenty minutes or more—at midnight, 10.00 a.m. and 4.00 p.m.—on the Jerry Lewis Telethon for Muscular Dystrophy on Labor Day 1975.

He got people who normally sleep late Labor Day to get up at ten o'clock—or at least to turn on their TV sets—to hear him in his white open-throated leisure suit sing 'Chicago' and his new song, 'I Believe I'm Gonna Love You'—and talk again of being a happy grandfather.

He was undoubtedly the star of this telethon, and his part in it was not conceived by a publicist. It resulted from Jerry Lewis' simple phone call.

In a playful mood, and with more gesturing, pointing and shoulder-rolling than usual, Sinatra made it a lark all three shows. He reserved the right to change the lyrics.

'You are the sunshine of my life, you are the pizza of my eyes,' he sang once. 'That's Why the Lady Is a Tramp' became 'That's Why this Chick Is the Champ'. He prefaced 'They Can't Take That Away From Me' by saying, 'Here's a number originally done by Fred Astaire, whom I taught to dance, every step he knows.'

It was all in that light mood that the Sinatra addicts love. But he remembered he was there to get donations and brought from his pocket statistics of the millions raised.

'These figures absolutely knocked me out,' he said.

Jerry Lewis told him that the first year the telethon raised only 'a million-one'. 'I got that on me,' Sinatra replied.

Jerry Lewis, in Las Vegas, kept talking to Sinatra, in New York, on the split screen.

'If you get off the monitor,' Sinatra informed him, 'I got something to say to your people. I have here in my pocket a couple of pledges—the people pledging do not know it yet.' He grinned his devilish grin.

'Mickey Rudin, my lawyer, does not know it yet, but he's giving $5,000.

'I have a manager who books me in places [Jerry Weintraub]; he's going to give $5,000.

'We have a wonderful public relations firm, Solters and Roskin, and they're going to give $5,000. They're hooked!'

With another laugh, Sinatra said, 'I may come up with a few more—and they'll love it.'

Still keeping it light, still nodding as Jerry Lewis called him Francis Albert, Sinatra said to Lewis, 'I have a gift for you.'

Silence. Sinatra would do something dramatic.

'I have a marvellous granddaughter,' he said. Everybody already knew of his devotion to Angela Jennifer. 'I would like to give you a gift in her name of a cheque for $25,000.'

The applause from Jerry Lewis' audience in Las Vegas, and from the comparatively few in Sinatra's studio in New York, was enormous when Sinatra displayed the cheque. 'As soon as she begins talking,' Sinatra said, 'I would like her to know that she has given to this telethon.'

It was exactly the touch of sentiment needed. People liked it. Grandpa Sinatra again had done it His Way.

Besides giving the $25,000, Sinatra paid thirty musicians for the three sessions from his own pocket. It was an expensive telethon for him. And two months later, at a State of Israel Bonds dinner in Las Vegas, Sinatra stunned the crowd by pledging the purchase of $250,000 worth of bonds in memory 'of Mrs. Goldberg who was my parents' neighbour in Hoboken'.

A quarter of a million dollars! But it was okay. He was in one of his elated periods. Please God, don't let us be near when his mood changes, when plates and tables fly through the air, when strong men cower and cringe, and when everybody takes to the cyclone cellars. We like to have him around when he's warm, charitable and charming, which, it's only fair to say, he sometimes is but frequently isn't.

The author gratefully acknowledges permission to reproduce the following copyright materials:

"We Might Call This the Politics of Fantasy" (New York *Times*, July 24, 1972). Copyright 1972 by Frank Sinatra. Used by Permission of copyright proprietor.

"Frank: Then & Now" by Ralph Gleason: "He Did It His Way" by Paul Hendrickson, ROLLING STONE MAGAZINE, Issue 162, June 6, 1974. By Gleason/Hendrickson. From Rolling Stone, © 1975 by Rolling Stone. All Rights Reserved. Reprinted by Permission.

ANGEL EYES

Earl K. Brent and Matt Dennis.
© Copyright 1946 (Renewed 1973) Dorsey Brothers Music, New York.
All Rights Reserved. Used by Permission.

MY WAY

Music by J. REVAUX and C. FRANCOIS
Words by PAUL ANKA
Original French Lyric by GILLES THIBAULT
© Copyright 1967 by Société des nouvelles éditions Eddie Barclay, Paris, France
© Copyright 1969 for U.S. and Canada by Spanka Music Corporation, 445 Park Avenue, New York, N.Y. 10022
USED BY PERMISSION. ALL RIGHTS RESERVED

STRANGERS IN THE NIGHT

Words by CHARLES SINGLETON and EDDIE SNYDER.
Music by BERT KAEMPFERT.
© Copyright 1966 by Champion Music Corporation and Screen Gems-Columbia Music, Inc.
USED BY PERMISSION. ALL RIGHTS RESERVED.

I'LL NEVER SMILE AGAIN

Words and Music by Ruth Lowe

OL' MAN RIVER

Jerome Kern and Oscar Hammerstein II.

ALL OF YOU

ALL OF ME

Gerald Marks and Seymour Simons

ALMOST LIKE BEING IN LOVE

All special lyrics written by Sammy Cahn are used by permission of
Mr. Cahn.

THE HOUSE I LIVE IN

SOMETHING

George Harrison

YOUNG AT HEART

Carolyn Leigh and Johnny Richards

WITCHCRAFT

Carolyn Leigh and Cy Coleman
Copyright 1957 by Morley Music Co.

NICE 'N' EASY

Keith-Bergman-Spence
© Copyright E. Shaw Music Corp. 1960

I'VE GOT YOU UNDER MY SKIN

Copyright © by Chappell & Co., Inc.
Copyright Renewed.
Used by Permission of Chappell & Co., Inc.

YOU ARE THE SUNSHINE OF MY LIFE

Stevie Wonder
© 1972, 1973 Jobete Music Co., Inc., and Black Bull Music, Inc.

LET ME TRY AGAIN

French Lyric by MICHELLE JOURDAN
English Lyric by PAUL ANKA and SAMMY CAHN
Music by CARAVELLI
© Copyright 1973 by Editions Musicales
Vendanges and Nouvelles Editions Eddie-Barclay, France

SPANKA MUSIC CORPORATION AND FLANKA MUSIC CORPORATION,

445 Park Avenue, New York, N.Y. 10022, Sole Selling Agent for USA and CANADA